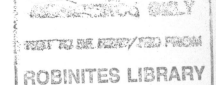
THE
CHINESE

THE
CHINESE

JASPER BECKER

JOHN MURRAY
Albemarle Street, London

A catalogue record for this book is available from
the British Library

ISBN 0-7195-5439 X

Typeset in 12/14pt Garamond by
Servis Filmsetting Ltd, Manchester
Printed and bound in Great Britain by
The University Press, Cambridge

To Toni and Michael

Contents

Contents

Illustrations

Illustrations

The author and publisher wish to thank the following for permission to reproduce photographs: Plates, 1, 13, 17, 18, 19 and 21, South China Morning Post Photo Library; 2, 3, 4, 5, 6, 7, 8, 9, 10, 12, 14, 20, 22 and 23, Adrian Bradshaw. Plates 11, 15 and 16 were taken by the author.

Acknowledgements

WRITING THIS BOOK would not have been possible without the support of the *South China Morning Post* and the expertise of its staff. I would like especially to acknowledge my debt to the editors, Jonathan Fenby and Robert Keatley, who gave me the freedom to write; the paper's China experts, Willy Wo-lap Lam, Daniel Kwan and Vivien Pik-kwan Chan; and the librarian Gracia Wong.

In Beijing I owe much to the reporting of my colleague Mark O'Neill who also read the manuscript, and to the research of Ma Jun and Madhusudan Chaubey. Mark Hopkins, Susan Whitfield and Frances Wood were also kind enough to read a draft and offer their comments.

Gail Pirkis, my editor at John Murray, deserves the most credit. This book is her concept and she played a decisive role in developing the style in which it is written. Without her knowledge of China, it might never have appeared.

Many fellow journalists in Beijing have also provided invaluable insights as have diplomats, Chinese friends and strangers, not forgetting the innumerable taxi-drivers who have spoken their minds so freely over the years. Though space does not permit me to list them all, I offer my thanks to them and also to the many academics on whose ideas and research all journalists rely so heavily.

Life in Beijing may not be glamorous but each of us enjoys the feeling of belonging to the ancient and select club of China-watchers. We all seek to add our penny's worth to a common fund of knowledge but in the end our real debt is to those Chinese who have had the courage to speak out.

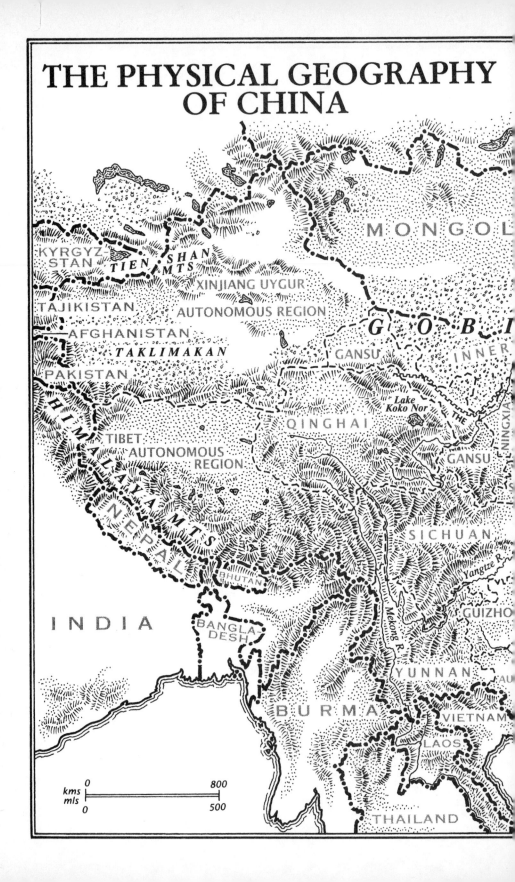

THE PHYSICAL GEOGRAPHY OF CHINA

MONGOL

KYRGYZ-
STAN
TIEN SHAN
MTS
XINJIANG UYGUR
AUTONOMOUS REGION

TAJIKISTAN

AFGHANISTAN
TAKLIMAKAN

PAKISTAN

G O B I

GANSU

INNER

Lake
Koko Nor

THE

NINGXIA

QINGHAI

GANSU

HIMALAYA MTS

TIBET
AUTONOMOUS
REGION

NEPAL

BHUTAN

SICHUAN

Yangtze R.

BANGLA-
DESH

INDIA

GUIZHO

Mekong R.

YUNNAN

BURMA

VIETNAM

LAOS

kms 0   800
mls 0   500

THAILAND

RUSSIAN FEDERATION

HEILONGJIANG

Amur R.

Songhua R.

JILIN

MONGOLIAN AUTONOMOUS REGION

A

LIAONING

NORTH KOREA

JAPAN

Yellow R.

DOS

WALL

Beijing

HEBEI

Gulf of Bohai

SHANXI

SHANDONG

SOUTH KOREA

Yellow R.

GRAND CANAL

Yellow Sea

XI

HENAN

JIANGSU

ANHUI

Tai Hu

Shanghai

East China Sea

HUBEI

Yangtze R.

N

W   E

S

Poyang Hu

ZHEJIANG

Dongting Hu

JIANGXI

HUNAN

FUJIAN

XI
G
MOUS
N

GUANGDONG

Taiwan Strait

TAIWAN

Land over 3,000ft

West R.

Pearl R.

HONG KONG

MACAO

Desert

Mountains

HAINAN

South China Sea

PHILIPPINES

MC

THE POLITICAL GEOGRAPHY OF CHINA

MONGOL

KYRGYZSTAN

Urumqi

XINJIANG UYGUR
AUTONOMOUS REGION

• Kashi

TAJIKISTAN

AFGHANISTAN

PAKISTAN

GANSU

INNER

KASHMIR

QINGHAI

Yinchu

NINGXIA

Lanzhou

TIBET
AUTONOMOUS
REGION

GANSU

NEPAL

SICHUAN

Chengdu

Lhasa

Chongqing

BHUTAN

GUIZHO

INDIA

BANGLA-
DESH

Guiya

Kunming

YUNNAN

BURMA

VIETNAM

LAOS

kms
mls

0

0

800

500

THAILAND

INTRODUCTION

Through the Open Door

THE CHINESE STATE is probably the oldest functioning organization in the world, dating back more than 2,000 years. It is also possibly the most successful in history, controlling more people and more territory, and for longer periods, and exercising a tighter grip over its subjects than any other comparable government in the last two millennia.

At the beginning of the twenty-first century the People's Republic of China governs the destiny of close to 1.3 billion people, or 21.6 per cent of the world's population, making it the most populous country on earth. In describing the different groups who comprise this vast population, this book aims to provide a broad overview of the current state of China.

At the base of the social pyramid are the peasantry who constitute around a billion people, more than the combined populations of the United States of America and the European Union. The book starts with them, probably the largest single identifiable group ever to have existed at any point in recorded history. But they are not uniform and the first chapter describes the very poorest of them, the 100 million who struggle to farm patches of stony soil in remote uplands.

The final chapter describes the apex of the pyramid, the tiny group of self-selecting rulers who live in the pavilions scattered among the gardens and lakes of what was once the imperial palace in the Forbidden City in Beijing. In between, the book looks at other groups, some defined by geography, some by economic or political status.

Many chapters draw on my own travels around China during ten years as a resident reporter. Yet much of China remains hidden. For one thing it is too big to be knowable. I have been to Shandong province a number of times but it has a population of 90 million, bigger than any European country. And China is secretive. Few foreigners, if any, have ever attended – or at least reported on – a meeting of a Chinese Communist Party (CCP) cell, let alone a session of the ruling Politburo. It is equally rare to be able to interview an officer in the People's Liberation Army (PLA) although it has a membership greater than the population of dozens of UN member states.

Intense secrecy and manipulation of information have long been regarded as an essential part of successful government and diplomacy, and though, as Marxists, China's Communist rulers have embraced concepts of modern 'scientific' government and so gather huge quantities of data, this has not made it any easier to understand the country.

The information travels up through the bureaucracy, and every layer revises it to conform to the targets set by its superiors. The central government constantly complains about the false statistics it receives but it is equally guilty of putting out false or deliberately distorted information. And not only is the present unclear but the past often changes too. The central state controls the archives and strives to ensure a monopoly over the reporting and recording of history. Although its verdicts on past events change frequently, this is never a cause of much shame or embarrassment.

Foreign scholars and outside agencies such as the United Nations or the World Bank are put under enormous pressure not to challenge Chinese statistical claims and rarely do. Many experts prefer co-operation to conflict, but anyone who spends time working in China eventually comes to doubt even basic facts.

How many people are there in China? One American ambassador, Admiral Joseph Prueher, remarked that he could not even find this out but he was told it was anywhere between 1,250 million and 1,300 million. Therefore, a population almost the size of Britain's may or may not exist. How much arable land is there to feed them? Official statistics say 95 million hectares (234 million acres), but satellite surveys suggest 140 million hectares (345 million acres).[1]

Some experts, particularly economists, tend to argue that even if the reported facts, such as economic growth rates, are overstated they do at least represent a reliable trend. I doubt that. I suspect – but can rarely demonstrate – that many figures are simply made up to suit the propaganda needs of the day. It is this cloud of uncertainty surrounding so much in China that explains why so many books are written about the country.

Yet compared to most periods in its history, China may now be said to be more open and less mysterious than it has ever been. Even so, greater access has done nothing to clarify Western perceptions of China, which have ranged from wonder to disgust, from hope to fear – one book on my shelves, written by another journalist in the 1930s, is entitled *China: The Pity of It*.[2] In the past century and a half, since the restrictions on foreigners roaming around China were first lifted, Western visitors have been both fascinated and saddened by the romantic ruins of old Cathay, a dead but once glorious civilization like that of Greece, Rome or Egypt. Yet within the same period, the modernization of China has also led to a hysterical fear of China as a nuclear-armed global power bent on spreading Communist revolution. Even within the last twenty-five years writers have sincerely and convincingly portrayed China as either an oriental Utopia or a Communist hell. Between these extremes, visitors have dreamed of the vast profits to be won from selling to 'John Chinaman', a dream that still provides the dynamic for the West's relations with China.

By contrast, the Chinese state continues to feel threatened by outsiders seeking to win the loyalty of its subjects, just as it did over a century ago. Buddhism, Islam and Christianity have won many converts in China and continue to do so, but rarely with the support of the state.

China is big enough to permit many views. Precisely because the country eludes generalization, some observers have tended to grasp at straws, too willing to convert a trend into a prophecy – many people are buying cars, so eventually half a billion will own cars; some groups want democracy, soon everyone will. And, perhaps frustrated by the sheer scale of the country and its apparently cyclical rather than linear history, many reporters tend to finish their tours saddened and disappointed. When Deng Xiaoping came to power in

1979 and spread the word that 'to get rich is glorious', the Chinese were presented as striving to learn how to become a capitalist democracy. Two decades later, it is clear that China is still far from becoming more like America or Europe.

This desire for change, and a belief that change for the better is possible, also exists within China – the name 'New China' is given to innumerable buildings, roads and institutions – and it dates from the latter half of the nineteenth century when repeated military defeats at the hands of more technologically advanced Western countries convinced reformers that China had lost its way and was in decline.

The same belief in the need for change fuelled the Chinese Communists' attempt under Mao Zedong to transform the country through a planned programme of social engineering on an unprecedented scale. Society would be altered, culture renewed and Chinese man remodelled to function in a new scientific, rational, model world. The state ran everything and the Party was 'always correct, great and glorious'. The attempt failed. China did not advance very far, and Mao's vision cost the lives of perhaps 75 million Chinese. It is therefore not surprising that a sense of failure also permeates the way in which the Chinese perceive themselves.

A new 'new' China has emerged since 1979 and in some areas the state has disengaged itself from its citizens' lives so that the new China seems to be functioning much like the old, pre-Communist China. Still, through all the upheavals and revolutions of the past century, China has held together, and the state and its bureaucrats continue to issue regulations and levy taxes.

Recent books have portrayed China as the next superpower, the new evil empire or as descending into chaos and civil war. As I was writing this book, a letter from a reader appeared in the *South China Morning Post*, declaring that: 'History shows that no country as large as China can hold together for long. Different political, ethnic and religious elements split such countries apart before long: look what happened to the Roman Empire or the USSR.'[3]

Yet the immutability of the Chinese state is perhaps its most remarkable characteristic. The Roman Empire is no more but the Chinese state goes on much as before. In recent years the leading stories on China in Western newspapers have carried headlines such

4

as these: 'Bureaucracy cut by half to save central government expenditure'; 'Honest officials praised in propaganda campaign'; 'Anti-corruption campaign nets top official'; 'Tough campaign launched to stop piracy and smuggling in southern coastal waters'; 'Beijing orders crackdown on subversive sect'; 'Government critics arrested and anti-government books burned'; 'New taxes levied to expand education'; 'Army generals rotated to ensure loyalty to centre'; 'Army suppresses rebellion by minority peoples in far west'. Exact parallels could be drawn from the reigns of any one of the 157 Chinese emperors. Only in China can one interview an official charged with civil service reforms who, in describing those reforms, recalls how officials of the Han dynasty (206 BC–AD 220) dealt with the problem of nepotism.

To understand the role of history in contemporary China, it is necessary first to look briefly at that history.

The Chinese bureaucratic state traces its origins directly back to the first Emperor of China, known as Qinshi Huangdi. Born in 259 BC, and therefore a contemporary of Hannibal, he became king of the state of Qin at the age of 13. Thirty-eight years later, Qinshi Huangdi had conquered all neighbouring states and had created what became known as the 'Middle Kingdom'. The word China stems from Qin, which was originally a small, impoverished state on the fringes of the Chinese world.

The Qin state lay in western China in what is now the province of Shaanxi, centred in the valley of the Wei River, a tributary of the Yellow River (Huang He) which is held to be the original birthplace of Chinese culture and the homeland of the Han people, as the Chinese now refer to themselves. The First Emperor established his capital in Xi'an, now the provincial capital of Shaanxi, and it is not far from there that his huge necropolis guarded by an army of terracotta warriors can be found. The Yellow River region, especially its upper reaches, is now regarded as denuded and backward, and the loess plateau through which the river winds is one of the poorest regions in China. Yet as well as Xi'an, the capitals of several later Chinese dynasties were established along its banks, at Luoyang and Kaifeng.

The success of the Qin state is attributed to the Legalist political system established in the time of Qinshi Huangdi's grandfather by his chancellor Lord Shang. Together they created an austere totalitarian society in which everyone informed on each other. As in Sparta, a centralized military bureaucracy enforced a harsh legal code, and the entire population was mobilized into 'productive occupations', either military service, farming or manufacturing – this state had little use for merchants or intellectuals. Above all, however, in contrast to its neighbours, the Qin state destroyed the privileges of the feudal land-owning aristocracy. Everything was owned by the state and administered by a bureaucracy according to laws issued by the Emperor who enforced obedience through fear and terror. The laws and regulations were written down, and to enter the bureaucracy candidates had to pass written exams. Although the state encouraged education it also banned all books other than those it approved and forbade free discussion, public meetings and indeed any organization that was independent of the state.

During Qinshi Huangdi's reign, his prime minister Li Si took further steps to create an efficient totalitarian state by nationalizing land and ensuring a grain surplus. A key responsibility of the civilian bureaucracy was, and still is, to guard against floods by building dykes, to levy a grain tax on the harvest, and to store and distribute the surplus to feed the urban population and, above all, the army.

Under Qinshi Huangdi this efficient and highly organized state conquered its larger and more sophisticated rivals and succeeded in 'unifying' China. The boundaries of the state were smaller than those of today's China but included the heartlands where the vast majority of China's population still lives. These comprise the two biggest river valley systems in eastern Asia, that of the Yellow River and the Yangtze, including the Sichuan plain upstream, the vast North China plain that stretches south from Beijing and, richest of all, the land of rivers, canals and lakes between the two great rivers.

In the conquered lands all traces of the inhabitants' original culture, language and ethnicity were expunged. The territory was divided into thirty-four administrative units, just as today China is divided into thirty-four units, each ruled by appointed plenipotentiaries. Weights and measures were standardized as was the width of axles on vehicles so that carts and chariots could follow the same ruts on the imperial roads. In his eleven years in power, the First Emperor also established a single currency and a single script with 3,000 characters, the basis of today's writing system. Equally important, he 'unified' people's thoughts, as the current government might put it, by famously burning all books apart from Legalist works. Recalcitrant scholars were branded and sent to build the Great Wall and the most influential, some 460, were buried alive.

Prior to the Qin conquests, there had been a period in China when 'a hundred schools of thought contended' including that of Confucius (551–479 BC). He favoured the old rural aristocracy and a style of government that exuded a sense of benevolence and mutual respect between classes. A gentleman, a superior man, had to act according to a code of conduct, to observe a sense of *noblesse oblige* towards the lower orders. In the Qin state, however, power was everything, and while everyone had duties few had rights. Religion played its part, for the Emperor was regarded as the Son of Heaven who interceded on behalf of the people, but there was no organized church in the sense that there was in medieval Europe. The explicit goal of any treatise on government was, and still remains, how to establish 'a rich and powerful country'.

The Qin empire ended in a rebellion by Liu Bang, a minor official who in 208 BC led a revolt by former aristocrats who wished to re-establish the former kingdoms. The founder of the Han dynasty, which was to endure for 400 years, Liu Bang retained the unified state with its centralized bureaucracy, the Qin penal code and the Legalist political system. However, the worst excesses of the Qin system were modified and its harsh morality softened by the adoption of Confucianism. The Han dynasty made a knowledge of Confucian texts the cornerstone of government recruitment but beneath this veneer, Legalism remained the basis of Chinese government right up until the twentieth century. Even the Mongols and Manchus, who at one time or another conquered China and ruled its people, retained the same political system.

Today Chinese society is still not unlike that of the Han dynasty. Then, out of every hundred people, eighty or ninety were peasants in the countryside. That is still the case today. Then a peasant was obliged to give a month of his labour free for work on state projects such as building dykes or roads and to be ready for military conscription. Today, China's peasants must fulfil the same obligations, and, like their ancestors, they farm the land but do not own it and cannot leave it without permission. In Han times in each county absolute power was concentrated in the hands of the magistrate, who dispensed justice and issued orders on all aspects of administration, just as a Party secretary does today. The magistrate's work was subject to inspection tours by his superiors and after a fixed number of years he was rotated to another position. He lived in a 'yamen' where all civil offices responsible for taxes, education, the army, the police, justice and civil engineering were based. The same is true today.

In contemporary China, just as in the Han dynasty, out of every hundred people, ten might live in an urban area, usually a county town. The number of large cities, as then, is limited by the problem of obtaining and transporting regular supplies of surplus food. In 1999, out of a population of 1,300 million, some 300 million were classified as having urban residency permits but only about 60 million lived in big cities.

As in the Han dynasty too, only a small part of the population has access to higher education and goes on to form the core of the bureaucracy. In the Han dynasty, the imperial academy in the capital at Xi'an trained about 30,000 students a year, although of course many more people were literate. About half a million men held degrees in imperial times out of a population of between 50 and 100 million. These days perhaps 2 per cent of the population has a university degree although literacy rates are supposed to be very high.

The ratio of bureaucrats to the population has not changed much either. Although around 36 million people are employed directly in the government administration and some 58 million are CCP members, only a few of these are not clerks, teachers or pen-pushers of some kind. The real size of the ruling élite, from county magistrates upwards, is thought to be no more than 4 million. Officials are now termed *ganbu*, or in English, cadres, from the Communist term taken from the French *cadre* or official. As in imperial times, bureaucrats are ranked in over twenty grades.

The First Emperor's imperial system, with its civil service and ideological examinations, was only formally dissolved in 1911 when the Manchu empire collapsed. Before then the power, wealth and durability of the imperial state over so many centuries inspired neighbouring peoples in Japan, Korea, Vietnam and other parts of south-east Asia to copy it. These countries functioned as tightly run bureaucratic states for many centuries before they came into close contact with the Western world, and it is perhaps this characteristic, this willingness of the population to submit itself to the orders of an authoritarian bureaucracy, that has enabled them to adapt and modernize in recent years and to emerge as industrial powers while the rest of the developing world has lagged behind. Most countries in Africa, the Middle East and South America lack such a legacy.

The legitimacy of the Chinese state has survived invasions, civil wars, natural catastrophes and many periods in which China was not united or when its rulers were weak or favoured some creed such as Buddhism, Daoism or, more recently, Marxism-Leninism. Indeed, some argue that the Communist state, despite its claims to be modern and scientific, was embraced precisely because it corresponded to ancient notions of how a successful state should be run. Even the catastrophic mistakes of Chairman Mao have not been enough to destroy its foundations and result in either the break-up of the state or the adoption of another form of government.

If the Chinese are far more tolerant of the exigencies of the state and its servants than Westerners, they are also far more comfortable with the idea of living within an empire. Although the last Chinese dynasty, the Qing, is now generally held in low esteem, the expansionist policies of its Manchu rulers are still much applauded. The current territorial demands of the Chinese government are based on what the Qing armies, who conquered China in 1644, achieved, when China reached its greatest territorial limits and when the Chinese state was at its apogee.

This history of expansion can be traced back to the Han dynasty's attempt to expand the territory of the First Emperor's state southwards. The southern coastal states of what are still called Zhejiang and Fujian were occupied by the Emperor Wudi (141–87 BC) who moved their populations inland. Then in 111 BC, he defeated and absorbed the independent kingdom of Nanyue, what is now the provinces of Guangdong and Guangxi and part of northern Vietnam. His successors continued to shift the state's centre of gravity southwards until by about AD 600, the Yangtze rather than the Yellow River is thought to have constituted the economic and political heartland of the state. When nomads such as the Jurchens or Mongols invaded and established states in the north, part of the population, and particularly the élite, fled southwards, accentuating this trend.

In the mountainous provinces of Fujian, Guangdong, Guangxi, Guizhou and Yunnan, Han Chinese now dominate the towns in the valleys and the delta regions, while what are called ethnic minorities – races such as the Miao (Hmong), the Dai (Thai) and the Zhuang – tend to live in the mountains and are still considered poor and backward. Some emigrants from northern China, known as Hakka or guest people, still retain a separate identity, culture and language in the south.

Current research into the genetic make-up of the population of China has concluded that the populations of northern and southern China are quite distinct and that, genetically, northern Chinese are closer to Caucasians than they are to southern Chinese.[4] The difference also emerges in language. Dialects such as Cantonese might equally well be classified as separate languages for they are incomprehensible to northern Chinese. Modern standard Chinese is based on the Chinese spoken in Beijing, supposedly that used by imperial court officials or Mandarins.

The imperial tradition held that the peoples of conquered territories voluntarily submitted to absorption within the empire and to the adoption of the culture and language of their rulers. Whatever language or dialect was spoken, all were required to write using the same standard Chinese characters. This sinification policy continues today: great efforts are made to ensure that schoolchildren, whatever their race, are taught in standard Chinese.

More distant regions of south-east Asia, despite being repeatedly invaded by Chinese armies, including those of the Mongols and the Manchus, remained outside the empire. Countries such as Vietnam, Laos, Burma, Cambodia and Thailand retained their separate identities but operated within China's sphere of influence, submitting tribute and copying some Chinese institutions. In more recent years, these countries have also been settled by Han Chinese migrants trying to escape the restrictions of first imperial and then Communist China. In the north, Korea too was repeatedly annexed, most recently by the Manchus, but retained its independence and monarchy.

The principal danger to China has always come from the north and the north-west, and to stabilize these regions successive dynasties either attempted forced settlement to colonize them or built walls to keep out their indigenous inhabitants. The First Emperor built the Great Wall to keep his subjects in and keep the nomads of the steppes out. However, the biggest period of wall building took place during the Ming dynasty (1368–1644) whose rulers largely rejected any notions of 'peaceful coexistence' with the barbarian tribes in the northern grasslands. In other periods attempts were made to colonize the Gansu corridor, through which successive waves of invaders entered China, and the provinces of what are now Qinghai and Xinjiang.

In 1644, Manchu nomads crossed the Great Wall from Manchuria and established the Qing dynasty, a highly authoritarian, neo-Confucian regime. Although they expelled all Chinese from Manchuria, their legacy is the addition of territories that are now the three northernmost provinces of China – Liaoning, Jilin and Heilongjiang. However, large-scale exploitation and settlement of these regions only took place in the final decades of the Qing dynasty with the advent of the railway.

Various Mongol tribes were junior partners in the conquest of China, and Mongolian lands fell under the domination of the Manchu court. Although, as with Manchuria, Chinese settlement of Mongolia was forbidden until the end of the nineteenth century, Mongol chieftains regarded themselves as vassals of the Manchu emperor. The dispatch of Manchu armies to Xinjiang also ensured the loyalty of the western Mongols, and Tibet fell under the sway of the Emperor when Manchu forces crossed the vast Tibetan plateau in the late eighteenth century.

In the reign of the Manchu emperor Qianlong (1736–95), when China reached its furthest limits, its wealth and stability triggered a huge increase in the population which rose from 143 million in 1741 to 432 million in 1851. But in Qianlong's reign, the seeds of the Qing dynasty's downfall were also sown. Western powers began to make their presence felt. In 1793 Qianlong received and rejected the embassy of Lord Macartney who proposed state-to-state diplomatic relations and free trade between Britain and China. Foreign traders remained confined to a small strip of land outside Canton (now Guangzhou). However, increasing pressure by British merchants to open up China to foreign trade eventually resulted in the First Opium War (1840–2) and the humiliation of China by a foreign power.

Thereafter China was steadily forced to grant further concessions to foreigners and to open its doors to the West. Peace treaties, now known by the Chinese as 'unequal treaties', at the conclusion of the First Opium War and a second war that broke out in 1858, ceded the island of Hong Kong and the peninsula of Kowloon to Britain, provided for the establishment of treaty ports within China, and permitted the opening of foreign embassies in Beijing.

In 1850, China was shaken by the outbreak of the Taiping Rebellion, led by Hong Xiuchuan who proclaimed himself the brother of Jesus Christ. In the protracted war that followed, 20 million Chinese lost their lives. Uprisings in many other parts of the empire by Muslims and tribes in Yunnan and Guizhou in the south further sapped the strength of the empire, and corruption became rife. Still, the empire held together, despite the shortage of tax revenues and the growing inferiority of its armies. However, in 1894, the Japanese inflicted a crushing defeat on the Chinese army and navy over Korea and at last the Emperor Guangxu asked a group of scholars to modernize the country by following the Japanese and Russian models. The so-called Hundred Days Reform movement of 1898 ended when the Empress Dowager Cixi imprisoned the Emperor and had some of the reformers executed. Thereafter, reformers fled abroad and sought support among the overseas Chinese and the growing number of students studying abroad who formed 'Revive China' groups. Among those fleeing was Sun Yat-sen, the father of the Republican movement in China.

An attempt by the Empress Dowager Cixi in 1900 to use another rebellion, that of the Boxers, to expel foreigners from China failed, and in retaliation Western powers and Japan imposed heavy reparations on China. Tentative reforms, including the abolition of the civil service exams in 1905, were then made but by now the Qing dynasty had, in the eyes of many, lost its mandate to rule. In 1911, following an uprising that began in Wuhan, the young emperor was forced to abdicate and a republic was declared.

After the fall of the last imperial dynasty the debate about how to create a modern Western state intensified and the merits of Westernization, science, technology, democracy, and the rule of law were hotly debated, a debate that culminated in the May Fourth movement of 1919. The date refers to student protests in Beijing over a decision at Versailles at the end of the First World War to give Germany's concessions in China to Japan, but the term is more widely used to describe a movement to modernize Chinese culture. This included writing in the vernacular and abandoning the use of ancient Chinese which was as hard for the majority of people to understand as Latin would be today in the West. The two slogans of the movement – democracy and science – are still high on the agenda eighty years later.

At the end of the nineteenth century China had been in grave danger of being dismembered by the colonial powers including Japan, and after the collapse of the imperial system Mongolia, Tibet, Yunnan and other vassal states broke away, declaring themselves no longer bound to China. In the rest of the country, in the absence of control at the centre, warlords now held sway. In imperial China loyalty to the ruling dynasty had bound the multiracial empire together. However under the Manchu Qing dynasty Han Chinese were treated as a subject people and forced to wear a pigtail or queue. When Sun Yat-sen returned to China in 1911 and was elected as the first President of the Republic of China he articulated a new nationalism intended to revive the Chinese race. A race which had once been the most advanced had degenerated. Sun believed that it must be revived or face extinction in what he regarded as a global struggle for racial superiority. This belief in the need to regenerate China in the face of a foreign threat to the Chinese race still has many adherents both on the mainland and in Taiwan. At the same time, however, many Chinese were being educated at foreign-run schools within China or had been sent abroad to learn Western methods. The new nationalism and the desire to learn from abroad coexisted uneasily.

The biggest split among Chinese modernizers of the period emerged over what political institutions were best suited to this newly regenerated state. Chiang Kai-shek, who succeeded Sun Yat-sen as the head of the Nationalist Party (the Kuomintang, or KMT), though he became increasingly dictatorial, nevertheless attempted to adopt many of the elements of a modern liberal Western state. These reforms, although derided by many for their often considerable shortcomings, were astonishing in the context of Chinese history. The crushing hand of the central state was lifted. For the first time in thousands of years there came into being in China independent schools and universities, a free media, an independent judiciary, independent trade unions, competing political parties and a capitalist system of competitive enterprise, and for the first time the Chinese enjoyed freedom of movement within the country and the freedom of assembly.

While these new institutions were often corrupt or inadequate, the credibility of the whole endeavour, which some called 'complete Westernization', was undermined by the encroachments of the Japanese. In 1931 the Japanese army occupied Manchuria and created the state of Manchukuo with Pu Yi, the last Qing emperor, as its puppet head. In 1937 it then invaded the rest of China. By the end of the 1930s, the Japanese had occupied Beijing, taken control of Shanghai and massacred the inhabitants of Nanjing, the KMT capital, and the KMT was forced to set up a temporary capital in Chongqing, on the upper reaches of the Yangtze.

While Chiang Kai-shek had chosen to adopt one model from the West, other Chinese were inspired by the collapse of imperial Russia and by the new Communist government that had seized power there. The Chinese Communist Party was founded in 1921 in Shanghai by a small group of intellectuals. At first it existed as an offshoot of the Kuomintang but in 1927 it split away after trying to foment uprisings among Shanghai's working class.

The Communist movement, supported by Moscow, offered an alternative vision. China was weak not because of the shortcomings of the Chinese race but because of the existence of class conflict between the rich and the poor. The ruling classes, capitalists, landlords and even the wealthy peasantry had to be destroyed before an egalitarian Utopia could be built. After Chiang Kai-shek crushed the Party in urban areas in a sudden campaign in 1927, it took refuge in rural China.

As Chiang Kai-shek sought to re-establish control, the Communists set up a number of soviets or mini-states in mountainous areas, often straddling the borders of different provinces. In 1934 Chiang's forces encircled the largest, on the borders of Jiangxi and Fujian provinces, forcing the Communists to break out and embark on what became known as the Long March. Traversing some of China's poorest and most remote regions, and harried by the armies of Chiang and local warlords, the Communists finally found safety in Yan'an, a poverty-stricken area in the heartland of the old Qin kingdom on the loess plateau. From there, now led by Mao Zedong, they succeeded in capturing Chiang and, holding him hostage in Xi'an, forced him to agree to a united effort to fight the Japanese. Thanks to the Japanese threat, therefore, the Communists now received aid and survived.

In Yan'an Mao established his control over the CCP and developed his political philosophy. In many public statements, it appeared to be liberal, advocating the right of minorities to secede, endorsing free elections and democracy, supporting trade unions and labour rights, promoting the freedom of intellectuals and so on. In reality, Mao's kingdom in Yan'an was closely modelled on that of Stalin's Soviet Union. Mao created a personality cult around himself and wielded absolute power through a series of persecution campaigns.

With the defeat of Japan at the end of the Second World War, the civil war in China between the Kuomintang and the Communists intensified. The KMT was defeated and fled to Taiwan, and in October 1949, Mao announced the founding of the People's Republic of China.

In the light of what followed, many Chinese intellectuals believe that Mao and his followers had always despised the liberties of Republican China and intended to establish a totalitarian state, copying the Soviet model down to the smallest detail but also attempting to recreate the system of Qinshi Huangdi, the First Emperor. Mao openly admired him and reportedly spent as much time studying imperial tracts on government as those on Marxist dogma. Separating the strands of twentieth-century totalitarianism from China's own totalitarian legacy is not easy. Some Chinese, even now, prefer to draw some sort of comfort from the fact that at least Mao was a homegrown tyrant.

After 1949 Mao set about creating a minutely organized and centralized bureaucratic state in which officials commanded all resources and could intervene in every aspect of life. At the same time a determined effort was made to destroy the 'four olds', that is everything linked to the past.

The history of the Mao era can, at one level, be depicted as a series of political campaigns by Mao to assert and maintain absolute power. In 1956 the Hundred Flowers campaign was launched to encourage free speech under the 2,000-year-old slogan, 'Let a hundred flowers blossom and a hundred schools of thought contend'. Those unwise enough to do so fell victim to the Anti-Rightist campaign the following year, when over half a million intellectuals were punished. In 1958, in an attempt to create a socialist Utopia, Mao instituted the Great Leap Forward, in which the peasantry were stripped of their possessions and amalgamated into giant communes. The famine that resulted led to the death through starvation of over 30 million people. In the wake of the Great Leap Forward, which ended in 1961, the Party split into two factions, one of which advocated limited concessions to the peasants that helped end the famine. Deng Xiaoping was among that faction's adherents.

In order to restore his prestige, in 1966 Mao embarked on the Cultural Revolution, attacking his critics among the leadership, dismantling the bureaucracy, persecuting intellectuals and encouraging young Red Guards to roam free. After his death in 1976, an attempt by the Gang of Four, who included Mao's widow Jiang Qing, to seize power was thwarted and Deng Xiaoping, disgraced during the Cultural Revolution, was rehabilitated. In 1979 he established full control of the Party at the Third Plenum of the Eleventh Party Congress and embarked on a programme of reform.

Mao had ruled as a semi-divine being beyond any law. Much like Qinshi Huangdi, he moved from villa to villa in secret, rarely meeting his subjects or administering the bureaucracy which served him. Most of the institutions first established in the 1950s, including the organs of the CCP, were subsequently ignored or partially disbanded during the Cultural Revolution. This ten-year period is often referred to in China as 'the ten years of chaos' but a faction of the Party remained in control throughout and the People's Liberation Army ran most of the country's institutions. China in the 1970s was a heavily militarized state, and returning the country to civilian rule has been a lengthy process.

Deng Xiaoping's reforms revived many of the issues debated in the first half of the century. Mao had done his utmost to destroy China's traditional culture, the glue which had bound the imperial state together. In place of a shared culture, China now defines itself in strident nationalist and racist terms but the search for wealth, modernity and national strength goes on. There has been a renewed effort to create durable political and legal institutions that will enable the Chinese to absorb modern technology and the elements of a capitalist market economy. Political reform, however, has been slow.

In 1989, the split within the Party between those who wished to modernize the political system and those who feared this would result in the downfall of the Communist totalitarian state emerged into the open. For over two months, students calling for democracy led street protests in almost every city in China. The spark was the unexpected death of the Communist Party General Secretary, Hu Yaobang, a liberal who had been dismissed by the Party's revolutionary gerontocracy. The students who occupied Tiananmen Square in Beijing backed his successor, Zhao Ziyang, who was also pushing forward a programme of political reform. Though these were the biggest political protests in Chinese history, the Communist Party decisively crushed the movement by sending an army to occupy Beijing. Troops backed by hundreds of tanks and armoured vehicles invaded the capital on the night of 3/4 June and fought the demonstrators for control. Since then the Party has remained in power, operating a totalitarian police state, while its sister parties in eastern Europe were swept from power when the Iron Curtain fell later that year. The essence of Chineseness is now often presented by the current rulers as the imperial, totalitarian state, and once again foreigners are accused of plotting to break up China by advocating democracy.

The pages that follow, however, do not concentrate on politics or ideology, or the prospects for radical change. Instead they look at how each section of society has fared during the twenty years of reform, from the poorest to the mightiest in the land. The wealthiest live, as they always have, in the big cities and along the coast and rivers. The poorest are to be found in the mountains that drop like a series of steps from the Himalayas in the west to the eastern seaboard. We start, though, in the beautiful limestone mountains of south-west China.

I

Eating Bitterness

IN CHINA, THE poorest of the poor go hungry surrounded by some of the most beautiful scenery on earth. The domed limestone hills of the south-west float like giant sugar-loafs beneath a wide blue sky. Streams run with clear water that from a distance looks the colour of blue jade, and the thick, semi-tropical vegetation is fragrant with the blossom of wild mulberry and apricot.

In the Guangxi Zhuang Autonomous Region, which borders Vietnam and Guangdong province, a party of officials walk up a dirt track to inspect a village that is benefiting from an international poverty-relief project. The local officials are out in front dressed, despite the heat, in grey trousers and white nylon shirts, while the World Bank experts follow behind, stopping occasionally to admire the scenery that has inspired so many ink-brush paintings.[1]

Getting here has required a day and half's driving from the provincial capital of Guiyang and now there is a two-hour hike into the hills before we reach a tiny village, a hamlet of stone houses called Biao Liao. The village lies at a point where the valley forks in two. Here the first comers found ground just flat enough and wide enough to plant a field of maize, though it had first to be laboriously cleared of rocks which now lie in piles around the edges. Since then the peasants have cleared more fields, even along the foot of the hillsides where the gradient is barely manageable. But these fields are almost the size of tablecloths, too small and irregular even for a bullock to plough. Still, on every available patch of ground, something is being made to grow.

Unlike in northern China, rainfall here is plentiful and reliable, but the water quickly drains off, disappearing into limestone caverns and subterranean rivers. Outside this village, the peasants have built themselves water cisterns lined with cement to hoard the rainwater needed for their fields and animals.

'Welcome to the World Bank Delegation' and 'End Poverty by the Year 2000' declare the red banners strung up across the houses as we enter the village, watched by a gaggle of silent children. The tentacles of China's state bureaucracy penetrate everywhere, no matter how remote. Even here on a surprise visit to a village we thought we had selected at random, we are expected and the villagers have been assembled, ready to answer questions.[2]

'How long have we lived here?' repeated one villager sitting on his porch. He looked around, bemused by my opening question. No one could remember when this place had first been settled.

'Why do we live here?' he asked, stopping to pull at his pipe, a long tube of bamboo. 'We are poor,' he replied at last. 'That's why we live here.'

'Some villages are even poorer,' added a woman helpfully. Mrs Qin had invited us into the cool interior of her house to escape the sun. 'Back there, two or three days' walk away, the Yao people don't even know how to use stone for their houses,' she said as she waved her hand at the track behind her house which disappeared over a saddle between two humped hills.

Where you live in China is a good guide to wealth and social status. So is race. Mrs Qin, who wore an embroidered tunic, belonged to the Zhuang people, as did everyone else in the village. They are one of the largest of the fifty-five ethnic groups identified in China as minority peoples. The Yao are another. Altogether the non-Han Chinese number 108 million, or 9 per cent of China's population.[3]

The lands where they have traditionally formed the majority of the population are officially designated as minority autonomous regions – Tibet, Xinjiang, Inner Mongolia, Ningxia and Guangxi, each the size of a province. Elsewhere individual prefectures (groups of counties in a province) or individual counties may be designated as minority autonomous areas. Together these areas are so extensive that they cover 64 per cent of the country, but much of the land is either steppe or mountain and therefore invariably poor – it is easy to forget that 40 per cent of China's territory is grassland and 57 per cent lies at over 3,000 feet above sea level.[4]

Ethnic minorities, mountains and poverty generally tend to go hand in hand in China. Geography is often destiny. The sort of poor land which the Zhuang have to farm will never bring in a surplus. Indeed most years the few dozen families living here run short of food for several months of the year after the harvest has been eaten.

Inside her house, Mrs Qin sits us down on stools in front of the ancestral altar and brings tea. She barely looks at us foreigners but keeps glancing at the official who has accompanied us. She is 30 but looks 45. Her husband is away, working as a contract labourer. On the altar are grimy black-and-white photographs of him and other members of what is obviously a large family. Alongside the photographs there are coloured posters of Chairman Mao and other Communist leaders. Like others in the village, Mrs Qin has four children. When the one-child policy was introduced after 1979, minorities like the Zhuang were exempted from it as a way of regaining their loyalty after the Mao era, and were allowed three or more children.

The house is large and attractive compared to many peasant homes in China and has home-made bamboo furniture, but it contains few manufactured goods. After all, there is no electricity here nor a telephone. There is no piped water either.

Mrs Qin does not speak Chinese and so a local official translates. Her household, like most in the village, has a yearly income of less than US$50, or 400 yuan.* Like much of peasant China, the villagers live in a largely cashless subsistence economy. Mrs Qin says their income has risen by only a few dollars a year and some years the maize harvest does not stretch to the next harvest.

'Sometimes we are hungry and have nothing to buy food with,' she admits. Most families survive on a diet of maize, sweet potatoes and beans, eaten twice a day, often in the form of gruel. In an emergency, the state provides handouts of rice.

---

* Yuan is the name of the basic currency unit. *Renminbi*, or people's currency, is the official name for the currency of the People's Republic of China. At the current exchange rate US$1 equals RMB8.3.

The World Bank reckons that in this area and others like it, at least half the children are malnourished and 90 per cent suffer from chronic worm infections. The villagers have no access to medical services or drugs and the infant mortality rate is high. One in ten children born does not survive infancy. In general, the poor in China, especially minorities living in remote uplands, are also prone to diseases caused by mineral deficiencies. Goitres are common, so are diseases affecting bone and skin, and there are high rates of mental retardation.

In this village, perhaps in its way a model village, the inhabitants look healthy and strong. They are not too far from the road or from the booming coastal regions – a ripple from the global economy has spread even here. The men can climb the steep slopes of the karst hills to cut down wild bamboo for sale. We passed some on the way up, carrying large bundles on their backs to the road where they can sell them to a pulp mill. Even more important, Mrs Qin's husband has been able to leave the village in the last few years and join a work gang hired out by the local government to builders in coastal towns. He earns just 4 yuan a day, or half a dollar, after bed and board. Better-paid work is hard to find because outside his village he is helpless, unable even to understand what people say to him, for like his wife Mr Qin cannot speak Chinese and is illiterate. The Zhuang have no script and no recorded history.

As part of the World Bank poverty-relief programme, this village now has a tiny school which we are shown. It is actually just two stone rooms with a few benches inside. The schoolmaster, a young Zhuang, stands grinning shyly at the visitors. His salary is pitifully low too, just US$20 a month, but he says he is still better off than the villagers. The school was built in 1994 and is a rarity. In much of south-west China only about a fifth of the boys and only one in twenty girls ever finish primary school. Schooling is not free – the villagers have to pay fees which are quite high, US$14 (120 yuan) a year. This school has two classes and the children are taught in Chinese, learning by rote and copying Chinese characters written up on the blackboard. If they stay long enough, they will absorb Chinese history and culture, memorizing Tang dynasty poems, the aphorisms of Chairman Mao and the latest Party slogans. The lessons reflect a policy of assimilation and the schoolteacher, unlike the other villagers, has discarded his Zhuang clothes in favour of a modern shirt and trousers to show that he no longer relishes his minority identity.

The World Bank poverty-relief project supported the setting up of the school and the provision of basic medical care but it is also aimed at enabling the peasants to find ways of earning their own money to pay for these services. Mrs Qin benefits from a micro-lending scheme, a new type of programme in China. She has borrowed money to invest in breeding animals, and on the front porch she keeps a pig which is busy suckling a new litter. Close by is an empty goat pen. One of the World Bank experts energetically climbs up the steep hillside behind the house to see how her goat is faring and to look at the bamboo, sugar-cane and mulberry trees in which other villagers have chosen to invest. The Bank expects the loan for the goat to be repaid one day.

Making Mrs Qin and her fellow villagers self-sufficient and lifting them out of poverty will take a long time. The World Bank pilot project helps 1.5 million people but altogether there are about 25 million of the very poor in south-west China, mostly minority peoples living in these limestone karst mountains. In neighbouring Yunnan province, which has a population of 40 million, 9 million out of the 11 million poor belong to ethnic minorities. Together they constitute the largest concentration of severe poverty in China, but two other regions are similarly affected – the north-west and the loess plateau of northern China.

The north-west comprises the Tibetan plateau which accounts for nearly a third of China's land area and which is now divided up among different provinces – the eastern parts of Yunnan and Sichuan, Qinghai, the Tibet Autonomous Region (TAR) and the Xinjiang Uygur Autonomous Region. This land of stony mountains, steep-sided and forested valleys, and open grassland lies at between 7,000 and 20,000 feet above sea level. The inhabitants are Tibetans, Mongols and others who practise nomadic pastoralism and sedentary farmers such as the Turkic Muslims, known as Uygurs, and the Hui Muslims, Han Chinese who converted to Islam. Until 1949,

Chinese migrants in this region were always a minority, but since then the Party has built large-scale prison camps and military bases, and has resettled demobilized soldiers in paramilitary colonies.

The third concentration of extreme poverty is in the loess plateau, a vast network of heavily eroded gullies carved out of the land around the upper reaches of the Yellow River. Here the loose friable soil is fertile enough, but the region has little rain, a mere 4 to 16 inches a year that falls almost entirely in violent downpours in the summer months, causing flash floods across the treeless terraced fields. In a mountainous area of 240,000 square miles, home to 80 million people, that stretches over the provinces of Gansu, Ningxia, Shaanxi, Shanxi and Inner Mongolia, perhaps half the population earn less than US$20 a year. And even that figure can fluctuate – incomes depend so much on the amount of rain that falls in a year and whether or not there is a harvest.

Poverty can be found everywhere in China but if geography is one determinant, remoteness is another. As a rule of thumb, the further a village is from a good road the poorer it is likely to be. When Deng Xiaoping launched his economic reforms in 1978, it was reckoned that 40 per cent of the population lived in villages far from any road or telephone. Now, after twenty years of reform, nearly all county towns are linked by good roads but China still has a much lower density of roads to land area than most of the rest of Asia. The majority of people rarely leave the county in which they were born. And the more rugged the landscape, the more expensive it is to construct roads and the slower change will come.

When, in 1979, the Communist Party revealed that 250 million people, or about one in three peasants, were living on the verge of starvation, the news came as a shock.* Many had thought that Chairman Mao's egalitarian communes had at least ensured that everyone had enough to eat and was adequately clothed. At the same time China released population data that revealed a death toll of at least 30 million as a result of the famine which followed the establishment of the communes in 1958 during the Great Leap Forward. In

---

* Some Chinese reports speak of a lower figure of 200 million, or one in four peasants.

the 1970s there were recurrent localized famines and since then the official media has hinted at other famines.

Chinese leaders now claim credit for pushing through agricultural reforms which boosted grain production from 286 million tonnes in 1976, the year Mao died, to 407 million tonnes in 1984, when China became a net food exporter for the first time in a generation. Private farming, referred to as the household contract responsibility system and perhaps the most significant of the agricultural reforms, allowed a great mass of peasants, perhaps 200 million people, to escape from dire poverty. These were usually Han Chinese peasants living in areas where agricultural conditions were adequate and where, with the right approach, grain yields could quickly be raised. In addition, peasants were allowed to specialize in whatever crops were most suitable for the land they farmed. Under Mao, everyone had had to grow grain irrespective of whether the land was better suited to grazing sheep, planting fruit trees or growing tea bushes.

By the late 1980s, Beijing believed there were just 100 million people left trapped in dire poverty and when, in 1993, a new seven-year programme (called the 8–7) to eradicate poverty was launched, it targeted just 80 million people unable to feed or clothe themselves for at least six months of the year. Of these 58 million lived in mountainous areas. By 1999, however, the government had admitted that its commitment to eradicate poverty by the year 2000 could not be met, leaving between 20 million and 50 million in hardship, hardship being defined as living below a certain average rural county income.[5] In fact, there must be people everywhere whose incomes fall below the average no matter how prosperous the county or town in which they live. Indeed, in the late 1990s, the government began to acknowledge the existence of another 20 million urban poor, some living in the richest coastal cities.

The use of shifting definitions of poverty makes for confusing comparisons. In the mid-1990s, China's poverty line was set at an average daily income of US$0.60, or US$216 a year. However, when in 1996 the World Bank set about estimating the scale of poverty according to international standards, it used an average daily income of less than US$1 a day and came to the conclusion that China had 350 million out of 1.22 billion living below the poverty line.[6] Viewed in this way, China's record is comparable to that of India. According to its own definitions, India has a third of its population living under the poverty line, that is about 250 million. If the World Bank definition of a dollar a day is used, however, then over 300 million live below the poverty line.[7] Nevertheless, it is true that India certainly *looks* poorer, especially in its crowded cities. However, in China the police keep the rural poor out of the cities. No one can enter a Chinese city without permission, and those that do so are soon caught and expelled.

Most observers praise both China's record in poverty relief and the organization of its emergency relief system for victims of drought, floods and other natural catastrophes. However, amidst the praise, blame must also be laid at the door of the Communist Party, for under Mao it pursued policies which deepened the plight of many people, especially the minorities who farmed marginal land that was easily damaged.

In southern China, over the centuries, waves of migration and conquest pushed the indigenous inhabitants into the poorer mountain areas, the better land being taken by Han Chinese. (Even today, in the valleys of poorer areas, Han Chinese are to be found living in the towns, working in factories and farming the best land.) Historical accounts also suggest that some minorities such as the Miao emigrated from Laos and Thailand (where they are known as Hmong or Meo) which is why, as latecomers, they ended up with poorer land. The historical record is murky, but many minority groups are certainly found on both sides of the frontier, a factor which made them mistrusted during periods of xenophobia such as occurred under Mao.

Ironically, it was the very poverty and remoteness of these areas, and their inhabitants' hatred of Han Chinese officialdom that encouraged the first Communist rebels to establish bases there. In the 1920s, Deng Xiaoping himself led a rebellion among the Zhuang in Guangxi province, in a region not far from Mrs Qin's village. The revolt was suppressed but other Communist rebels established bases among the Miao and Li peoples in the mountains of Hainan, the tropical island off China's southern coast.

In 1934, after the Kuomintang's military campaigns had forced the main Communist forces to leave their base in the Jingangshan mountains in Jiangxi province, and embark on the Long March, they traversed the poor and remote mountains of Guizhou and Yunnan and then turned north through the Tibetan lands of what is now Sichuan. There were no roads in these mountains, only tracks, and even the Communist troops were astonished at the poverty they encountered, it being said that they came across whole families so poor that their members were forced to share a pair of trousers. Here, amidst the mountains of Guizhou, Yunnan and Sichuan, the Red Army was almost wiped out when it was surrounded and disarmed by the fierce and warlike Yi tribes, a Tibetan race whose lands straddle the mountains. By promising the Yi chieftains better treatment if the Communists won power, the Red Army was allowed to continue on its way to the loess plateau, the Communist General Liu Bocheng cementing the alliance with the Yi chieftain Xiao Yedan by drinking chicken blood in a ceremony that made them blood brothers.

During this period too, desperate for support, the Party promised the minorities on whom they then depended the right to self-determination, Mao declaring that 'The Mongol, Hui, Tibetan, Miao, Li and Gao Li peoples can voluntarily decide whether to break away from the Chinese Soviet Federation to set up independent regions.'[8]

By contrast, the KMT's founder Sun Yat-sen had believed that the Chinese race was under threat in the struggle for the survival of the fittest. 'If we want to save China and to preserve the Chinese race, we must certainly promote nationalism,' he argued in the early 1920s. 'Our position is extremely perilous: if we do not earnestly promote nationalism and weld together our four hundred millions into a strong nation, we face a tragedy – the loss of our country and the destruction of our race.' Amongst these 400 million, he went on, there were only 'a few million Mongolians, a million or so Manchus, a few million Tibetans, and over a million Mohammedan Turks. These alien races do not number altogether more than ten million, so that for the most part, the Chinese people are of the Han or Chinese race with common blood, common language, common religion, and common customs – a single pure race.'[9]

Under Chiang Kai-shek, the KMT increasingly opposed self-determination for the minorities and encouraged assimilation, spurred on by signs that China was fragmenting. A movement for self-determination was particularly strong among the Inner Mongolian tribes who, though few in number, controlled vast territories. They had before them the example of Outer Mongolia which had broken away from China after 1911 when the Manchu empire collapsed and which the Soviet Union had turned into a puppet state in the early 1920s. Chiang Kai-shek refused to recognize the new state. (Successive Chinese leaders have continued to consider it part of China's unfairly lost territories.) In Xinjiang pan-Turkish movements flourished among the Uygurs, and a Hui Muslim warlord controlled a powerful and largely autonomous army. In Lhasa, the Tibetan government ruled Tibet as an independent state. Yunnan, where the majority are non-Han Chinese, also declared independence after 1911. Even Cantonese in Guangdong agitated for independence. The KMT suspected foreign governments of fostering separatist movements as Moscow had in Mongolia and as the French were doing in Yunnan and Guangxi, across the frontier from their colony in Vietnam. Finally, in the 1930s, the Japanese created the state of Manchukuo in Manchuria, with a titular emperor, Aisin Goro Pu Yi, the deposed heir to the Manchu dynasty.

When the Communists seized power in 1949 they were no more sympathetic to these various movements towards autonomy than the KMT had been. Earlier promises of self-determination were quickly forgotten. Within a few years, those who looked for self-government or even defended minority languages and cultural identity were imprisoned.[10]

Some nationalist political leaders were arrested immediately. Other leading figures – writers, musicians, scholars – who considered themselves the guardians of their cultures were swept away during the Anti-Rightist movement of 1957. Advocating 'bourgeois nationalism' was now a counter-revolutionary crime.

With the launch of the Great Leap Forward a year later, the Party set about destroying temples, churches and mosques, and arresting religious leaders. All religious, folk and tribal festivities were banned as part of a wider assault on rural traditions. Tibetan and Mongol nomads, for example, were forced to hand over all their possessions, including their livestock and jewellery, and were dragooned into highly regimented people's communes. At the same time, traditional agricultural practices were abandoned and Tibetan farmers were forced to concentrate on growing grains other than barley, often at altitudes where failure was guaranteed. As a result of collectivization many of their animals died. This combined assault on their traditional livelihood reduced many Tibetans to a state of semi-starvation for the next twenty years. In 1959 the Tibetans in eastern Tibet rebelled and gathered in Lhasa, looking to the Dalai Lama for leadership. The rebellion was crushed and the Dalai Lama fled to India.

The drive towards assimilation reached its climax during the Cultural Revolution. Boundaries drawn up after 1949 had created ethnic autonomous areas, although they were allocated in such a way as to ensure that minority peoples rarely formed a majority. Thus most of the six million Tibetans in the People's Republic of China found themselves outside the boundaries of the Tibet Autonomous Region. Now, however, even the appearance of special treatment for minorities was dropped. The boundaries were withdrawn and it became deliberate policy to settle large numbers of Han Chinese, including prisoners, demobilized soldiers, Red Guards and educated youths, in border areas where minorities predominated. Inner Mongolia was split up, its boundaries only being restored in 1979. And everywhere, the wearing of traditional dress and teaching in minority languages was forbidden.

The cumulative effect of these various policies has been to make the minorities still poorer and even less able to adapt to the modern world. The Tibetans are a case in point. When Tibet was a theocracy, one in four males became a monk at one of hundreds of monasteries, so literacy was common. Now, Tibetans suffer from what is probably the lowest literacy rate in the world. In rural areas as many as 70 per cent cannot read. The 1990 national census found that only 20 per cent of Tibetans finished primary school, less than 3 per cent received junior secondary school education and only 0.09 per cent reached university. Education receives a lower percentage of government expenditure in the TAR than in China as a whole and the percentage declined further in the 1990s. Most of the spending is concentrated on schools for Han Chinese children.[11]

In 1980, the Communist Party leader Hu Yaobang acknowledged the mistakes made in the Mao era and ordered a revival in Tibetan teaching. Even Han Chinese officials had to learn to speak the language. However, after independence protests in the late 1980s, these policies were shelved. According to United Nations Development Programme statistics for education, life expectancy and income, the Tibetans now rank among the poorest people not only in China but in the world.

The Tibetans are not alone in being worse off as a result of what has happened since 1949. Another poignant but less publicized example are the Flowery Miao whom I came across in Guizhou. In the early 1900s, in Zhaotong, a largely Chinese city in the plains, representatives of the Flowery Miao came and knocked on the door of a Cornish missionary named Samuel Pollard, begging for his help. Pollard answered their call and soon established a school and a hospice among them and began to preach. By the time the mission closed in 1950, 800,000 Miao had been converted to Christianity. Pollard also invented a special alphabet for them by adapting a mixture of Braille, Pitman's shorthand and Roman characters, for like the Zhuang, they had no form of writing. He even translated the New Testament into Miao and had the first Miao bibles printed in Japan and shipped to Guizhou.

Pollard died in 1915 and was buried in the mountains above the mission station at Shimenkan in what is now Weining county. The mission flourished until 1950 when the Communists ordered the English missionaries to return home, but then in 1995 a curt dispatch by the New China News Agency (Xinhua) appeared recording that Pollard's tomb had been restored and declared a national monument.[12]

In the interim, Weining county had been closed to foreigners, and when I arrived, it seemed as poor and remote as it must have been when Pollard first came. There were still no paved roads, and in the desperately poor villages each minority tribe could be distinguished by its own brightly coloured and intricately embroidered clothing. The Miao wore the same striped and flounced skirts as they had in Pollard's day. When he arrived they were still practising cannibalism, and in the mountains he found wolves, wild boar and tigers. Now the hills have been stripped of their forests and the animals have gone.

With me came two men, now in their seventies, who had been educated at the school that Pollard had founded.

'He taught us everything. I cannot find the words for my feelings,' said Tao Yumi. 'I've not been here for fifty years.'

Tao was short with a neat moustache. He and his companion Wang Dechen had dressed in jackets and ties for the journey. As they gazed around the remains of the mission scattered over a hillside where the pines and rhododendron gave out a fresh alpine smell, they both fell silent. Pollard's brick house was now a ruin but from its windows he would have gazed at the same panorama of endless mountain ridges.

Tao recalled how he had come here as an orphan and been adopted by the missionaries. We walked across the brow of a hill to where Pollard's newly restored tomb looked out across the valleys and peaks. Tao translated the tombstone's inscription, carved in Pollard script, and that of another missionary, Heber Galsworthy, who was murdered by bandits in 1938.

Galsworthy's house, designed like a comfortable villa in a London suburb, was still in use but little else remained of the hospital, the gardens or the school itself. Here was where the chapel once stood, murmured Tao. He remembered how its bell rang for each lesson. Recently, a new school has been built – we found a few ragged children outside a run-down concrete hut. Tao spoke to them hopefully but none of them understood much Miao. The teaching is all in Han Chinese, he said wistfully.

Wang explained that while the older generation of practising Christians can read the Pollard alphabet, no new books have been printed in the script for forty years. The younger generation are not familiar with it and, unless it is reintroduced into the schools, it may die out.

Haltingly, the two men recalled what had happened to them since leaving the school. They had both worked as teachers but in the late

1950s they were labelled as hostile elements because of their association with the foreign missionaries. Eventually, they were barred from teaching, and during the Cultural Revolution they were beaten up and forced into manual labour.

As we walked around, some local officials emerged from Galsworthy's old house – now used as an office – spotted us and became suspicious. A large fat man with the air of a local Party chief ordered the two elderly Miao to be brought into a room and interrogated. From outside, I could hear them being threatened and asked to sign a confession. I went to the Party chief to explain.

'We have our own power here, we do what we like,' he sneered.

The interrogators had no phone with which to contact any superiors and seemed barely able to write. They kept asking the old men for help in forming many characters. Eventually they finished their report and let the two go with a warning.

'We are used to it. Besides, what can they do to us old men?' said Tao, quite unruffled. He laughed and for a second the two grinned at each other like naughty schoolboys.

Tao then directed our car to the county town of Weining, where the missionaries had built a larger school and hospital. Some handsome red-brick buildings still remain and we visited the nearby house of a retired teacher, another product of the English missionaries' education. At first he and his wife looked too nervous to say anything and everyone froze when a curious neighbour came in. But then their grown-up son, seemingly desperate to explain what had happened to the Miao in recent times, began to speak. The Miao are now poor again and illiterate. Up to 80 per cent of the Miao population do not earn enough to feed and clothe themselves, let alone pay for schooling. Only 7 per cent of those attending the Weining school are Miao and they have difficulty in passing exams which are in Chinese and which depend on being able to write Chinese characters.

'It was better before the Revolution. Now the Miao cannot afford the fees. It costs 2,000 yuan [US$250] a year,' he said. 'Many believe there is no point in sending their children to school if they just have to go back to farm afterwards.'

The missionaries had managed to get sixty of their converts into universities, and the generally high levels of education among the

Miao that had resulted from their teaching had raised the minority's social status. Now almost all the children at the secondary school are from the local Chinese population.

The son explained that in Weining's administrative centre, almost everyone is Han Chinese. Many were relocated here when the authorities drained a large lake and surrounding marshland to plant grain during the Great Leap Forward. What remains of the lake is now protected as a nature reserve and some of the farmland has been abandoned.[13] The result has been that 30,000 Han Chinese peasants are now unemployed. I had glimpsed some of them in Weining's muddy streets, squatting on their haunches, killing time and smoking.

The son complains that Miao who escape the grinding poverty of their villages and find work in towns are obliged to assimilate. Integration means speaking Chinese even at home, wearing the same clothing as everyone else and abandoning their faith and customs. However, before he can elaborate, a neighbour slips out and summons the state security police who enter the house without a word to the elderly couple and sit down.

'You have no permission to be here or to talk to anyone,' says one of the officials brusquely. He is too poor even to afford shoelaces but everyone cringes and falls silent. We have to leave, and a police car – an expensive Japanese luxury Pajero jeep – follows us out of the county to make sure we speak to no one else. The authorities are still frightened of what people might say.

Minorities like the Miao, the Zhuang or the Tibetans are gradually recovering from the effects of Chairman Mao's policies but the pace of change is slow. Guizhou is only just beginning to take the first steps towards rehabilitating Pollard and his script. Maoist agricultural mistakes, such as the draining of the local lake, are only slowly being reversed. Replanting the forests and restoring the area's ecological balance is starting but will take at least a generation.

However, it is not just the minorities who are still suffering the consequences of Mao's policies and the environmental damage wrought by his agricultural communes. The ecology of many poor areas of

China bears witness to his mistakes, even areas like the loess plateau where in the years between 1964 and 1976 the Communist Party committed huge resources under the slogan 'In agriculture, learn from Dazhai'.

Dazhai is an obscure village in Shanxi province, a few hundred miles west of Beijing, which in 1964 was singled out as a model commune for having wrestled with nature and won. The villagers had, the state media trumpeted, levelled terraces, raised dams to prevent soil erosion and dug reservoirs to guarantee water supplies. And in doing so they had boosted food production to unprecedented levels.

The Dazhai method, which relied on mobilizing the population to carry out enormous amounts of back-breaking labour, was adopted throughout the country, even in regions like Tibet where it was wholly inappropriate. Then, after 1979, the Party admitted that much of Dazhai's acclaimed success was pure fiction. Dazhai's grain harvests had never been as big as had been stated, and the army had contributed much of the labour employed in all that earth-moving.

Twenty years have passed since these revelations but poverty still exists on the loess plateau. Infant and child mortality rates remain extremely high, 50 to 100 per cent above national averages. In Shanxi province, about 9 million people inhabit the poor uplands and of these a third live in dire poverty. About 80 per cent of the women are illiterate and even in the late 1990s, half the boys and nearly all the girls failed to attend school. Shanxi has also recorded the highest rate of birth defects in the world, partly attributed to the absence of Vitamin B in the diet. Mental retardation is prevalent too, with whole villages afflicted by the lack of trace elements such as iodine.[14]

For all its poverty, the loess plateau has a stark grandeur about it. From the air one sees the vast badlands of treeless gullies and water-less rivers branching out in an endless intricate pattern. Through it all the Yellow River carves its way with slow and lazy strength, like a giant serpent. On the ground, a drive to northern Shanxi, where the silt-laden river forms the border with Inner Mongolia, takes one through a landscape which might be on Mars. The riverbeds are dry. The hills are barren. The villages are silent. Some homes consist of nothing more than a door and window facing a tunnel carved into the hillside.

Elsewhere people live in villages closed in behind tall fortress-like walls of thick mud, part of a network of fortified settlements built to resist recurrent invasions by horsemen from Mongolia.

We stop at Zijinshan, a collection of villages built in the shadow of 30-foot-high Ming dynasty watchtowers, part of a massive early warning defence system. From here the ground drops away down steep gullies to the Yellow River which lies hidden a thousand feet below. Across the river is Mongol territory.[15]

A gaggle of grinning urchins stare at me and my companions – a gloomy local official dressed in a bulky grey suit and an enthusiastic environmental expert from Taiyuan, the provincial capital, who wears thick glasses and an open-neck striped golfing shirt, and who smokes Marlboro.

'They should only have two children, but they have at least three or four,' scowled Zhang Fengxiang, the local man. 'The population has increased so quickly that this land has to support four times as many as in the past.'

Zhang has lived here all his life and says that a century ago this place had few inhabitants, and that the land and the ravines were covered by forests. When these were cut down to make way for ter-raced fields, the climate changed and the periods of drought increased. Tree-cutting was especially reckless during the Great Leap Forward when the wood was used to fuel backyard furnaces.

Now water is so scarce that the peasants dig holes in the ground to use as cisterns. People rarely wash and in winter the dryness sucks the moisture out of one's skin. Zhang stops us in front of an old woman crouching by the side of a cistern. She lowers a bucket down and then throws the water over a small patch of cabbages. She does not look up.

'If there is no rain, life here is hopeless,' says Zhang, his lips tight-ening in bitterness.

In contrast, our environmental companion Dr Xu Maojie, an enthusiastic defender of the Dazhai model, is now just as unreserv-edly optimistic about the new methods being tried in this district. He argues that the model of Dazhai enabled people on the loess plateau to grow enough food to keep abreast of population growth and insists they have now learned from past mistakes. Later in the day, he takes me to see one of the newly constructed earth dams, built across a gully to trap the soil flushed down in the rains. Standing on top of this earth and concrete barrier, he says that this dam has been designed by an engineering expert but admits that most of the dams built in the Mao era collapsed, especially during savage storms in 1973 and 1977.

'But that's only because they were crudely designed and built by the peasants without proper experience,' he says brightly.

A 1992 World Bank study is less enthusiastic about the benefits of the Dazhai model: 'Agricultural productivity and incomes were diminished during the 1960s and 1970s when, as part of the national policy of achieving self-sufficiency in grain production, upland farmers were encouraged to switch from pastoralism to extensive cultivation of grain.'[16]

The early dams gave way and so did the terraces carved out of hillsides in the process of making more land available to plant grain. Digging up steep slopes also exacerbated soil erosion and the degradation of this marginal land. 'Many of the existing terraces built in the 1970s under large-scale campaigns have been abandoned and left unused,' notes a later World Bank report.[17]

Now, terraced fields are still being built but they are wider and more stable, and it is forbidden to use slopes with a gradient of more than 25 degrees. Less land is sown with grain and output has fallen, but instead a new effort is being made to plant grass, bushes and trees that will help stabilize the soil. Giant white characters at least a mile long painted across an entire hillside proclaim the Party's unrepentant ambition to 'Control the mountain, govern the water, and change the heavens.'

In the Mao era efforts to limit erosion were made – the air force even tried seeding from the air – but the survival rate of the plants was only about 20 per cent. The seedlings quickly died, as often from neglect as from drought. Now, private ownership is being promoted as the answer. In the late 1990s peasants were being offered leases as long as a hundred years if they were willing to plant trees in the steepest gullies. On gentler slopes, the government often uses international aid to plant tough drought-resistant vegetation.

Today, all over this county, the hills are dotted with flecks of whitewash marking little stone terraces where tens of thousands of trees have been laboriously planted by hand. Peasants can now contract out this land as it is returned to forestry and use the new pasture for their sheep and goats.

Zhang wants to go back to the county town of Pianguang for lunch and says there is no time to talk to the villagers here. Along the way we pass a river whose waters have turned literally coal-black. 'Coal-washing plant. Cement plant,' he says curtly, barely glancing out of the window at the smoke belching from factories built on the river bank.

Over lunch in the small dining-room of the Party headquarters, as dish after steaming dish appears, the other cadres who have joined us respond to questions about the environment with a brevity bordering on rudeness. They care about money. Nobody has been paid for six months and the factories, some of which we passed, are not making profits any more. Owned by the county as collectives, they used to generate enough money to finance local government expenditure. Now not only are profits down but the provincial government wants to shut the factories and clean up the river. How will they all live if the factories are shut down?

There is not enough money to pay for cleaning up the river, let alone the billions and billions needed to restore the loess plateau. Nevertheless, Beijing has announced, as it does from time to time, another new thirty-year plan to build tens of thousands of earth dams and plant millions of trees.

'Just a generation or two, what's that in China?' Dr Xu smiled complacently, blinking behind his thick glasses. So far, just a few small-scale projects are under way, covering 5,700 square miles out of a total of 240,000 square miles, an area bigger than France.

In the meantime, some of the poorest are being moved out of the mountains. In Ningxia, further upstream on the Yellow River, a fifth of the population, a million people, are being transferred out of the most hopeless areas. Hundreds of thousands from Gansu, Shaanxi and Qinghai are also to be moved. In south-west China, the government plans to relocate millions from the karst mountains, including 300,000 in Guizhou, 200,000 in Guangxi and 100,000 from poor mountainous areas in Guangdong.[18] If the government does not help them, they will leave anyway if there is a drought. In winter when there is nothing to do, many local peasants already drift to the cities, looking for work. Their children come too and survive by begging or stealing food.

Major resettlement programmes like that in Ningxia depend on the construction of a series of huge dams along the Yellow River to pump water to irrigate new farmland. For decades, much the greatest percentage of foreign loans and central government grants has gone towards building giant hydro-electric power schemes along the Yellow River, starting with the Sanmenxia dam, completed in the late 1950s. The Xiaolangdi dam, under construction in the late 1990s, cost over US$1 billion and is the largest foreign aid project ever undertaken in China, an expensive temporary solution to loess soil erosion. The dam will trap silt to prevent it being deposited on the riverbed downstream. There it would otherwise build up, raising the riverbed and water levels above the dykes and flooding the densely populated farmland that borders the river.

At Wanjiazhai, near Pianguang, I saw another of these giant projects, a dam built to pump water through a hundred miles of tunnels and canals to Taiyuan, the provincial capital, and to the important coalmines at Datong. Without it, Taiyuan and all its industrial plant would have to be relocated, and Datong, one of the country's biggest energy sources, would have to be shut down.[19]

There may yet be a water crisis no matter how many dams are built. There is less and less water both in the Yellow River and under it. Every year since 1985, more of the river has ran dry and for longer and longer periods. In 1997, it ran out of water 600 miles short of the sea for nine months. The Fen River, a major tributary of the Yellow River which runs through Taiyuan, is dry for all but a few weeks each year at the height of the summer storms. Locals still remember how it was once deep enough for shipping and how in winter people enjoyed skating on it.

Over-extraction from underground aquifers has also caused the water-table around Taiyuan to drop 300 feet, leading to severe subsidence. Taiyuan is not the only city in crisis. The whole Yellow River valley is home to 130 million people and along its course the underground water level is dropping by over 4 feet a year. More than half of China's 600 cities face water shortages and the danger is particularly acute in northern China.

Experts disagree about the causes behind this looming ecological catastrophe. Some have examined historical meteorological data and have detected a temporary trough in a fifty-year cycle of rainfall. Others blame a century of man-made environmental damage, especially in the Mao era, for altering the climate and creating a desert.[20] Whatever the case, each year provinces along the Yellow River must fight a fierce political battle over the allocation of water quotas. Provinces upstream can withhold water at will because the 3,380 reservoirs that have been built can hold the equivalent of 90 per cent of its water at any one moment. More are being built. By the year 2030, there will be a total of 27 major dams along the river.[21]

Making room for the dams creates further problems. The Sanmenxia dam displaced 300,000 peasants from their land. Thirty years later many of them are still living in poverty. The Xiaolangdi dam is displacing another 200,000 who must be found new land or provided with some other form of employment. All over China at least 10 million people were displaced by dams and hydro-electric power schemes during the Mao era, creating a huge class of landless and impoverished peasants. The largest and most ambitious dam project, the Three Gorges dam across the Yangtze, will mean relocating upwards of 1.5 million people.[22]

In the long term, the water crisis poses a still graver threat for China. Currently, water taken from the Yellow River is distributed virtually free, but eventually water-usage fees will have to be introduced. Those farming poor land in the upper reaches of the river require twice as much water to grow the same amount of food as those downstream in the fertile plains. Water will be sold to the highest bidder. Farming marginal land on the plateau may no longer provide a living if peasants have to pay for their water.[23]

An even more frightening prospect for China is emerging from evidence that the fate of the Yellow River is being repeated in the larger Yangtze River valley. Illegal tree-felling, soil erosion, silting and dam-building were among the causes listed for recurrent record flooding in the 1990s. As a solution some proposed diverting water from the Yangtze to the Yellow River. Others have advocated measures to safeguard the environment of the mountains through which the waters of the Yangtze drain. So far, the Tibetans and the other minorities who predominate in these mountains and plateaux have been powerless to prevent the tree-felling, mining and other ventures run by migrants from the rest of China that cause soil erosion and in turn flooding.

Inevitably, the more money the Chinese government throws at assisting its very poor, the more people emerge who claim to need it. Under the seven-year poverty alleviation plan started in 1993, the government increased spending to an annual figure of 17 billion yuan (US$2 billion) which was supposed to be channelled to the poor in the mountains. The effect has been the opposite. By 1999, the number of designated poor counties had doubled to 592, with a combined population of 199 million. At the same time counties in rich coastal areas fought to have themselves designated as poor in order to qualify for special loans and handouts. This meant that although the pot was larger, the money was spread more thinly over a far larger population. The genuinely needy received less aid than before and those living in poor areas saw no increase in their incomes.

A study carried out in the late 1990s found that even within designated poor counties, the poor rarely benefited.[24] Regulations ensured that the majority of subsidized loans went to those who already owned something – a factory, a business or an orchard. The average loan of 10,000 yuan was only given to those who had collateral worth 12,000 yuan. Consequently, the families of officials living in county towns cornered most of the loans and more often than not spent at least part of the money on new vehicles – a particular favourite is the Pajero jeep which can be seen everywhere in poor districts. The repayment rate on the loans averaged just 54 per cent.

Often, the more remote the county, the more eagerly its local officials sought to invest in commercial ventures – a brewery, a tannery, a dried-fruit packaging factory, anything that could bring in more money than mere agriculture. Unfortunately, poor counties far from the marketplace were often the last to invest in a commodity or product and did so just as supply exceeded demand and prices started to fall.

A more successful form of aid might have been the food-for-work programmes by which peasants are paid to build new roads or water reservoirs. However, in practice, the same study found that local government officials often pocketed the funds because peasants can in any case be ordered to perform a month's corvée labour for nothing; or the officials paid the workers in kind with unsaleable goods made in their bankrupt factories. 'We find no significant effect of poverty alleviation funds, except for a slight negative effect for subsidised loans,' the authors concluded.[25]

Experts now push for micro-credit lending schemes where loans are given directly to those who need them such as Mrs Qin and her fellow Zhuang villagers. The idea is that this allows them to produce something which can be sold in the market, and it bypasses potentially corrupt local officials. Perhaps that in turn explains why such schemes are slow to be adopted.

However, the perpetual battle between officials and peasants is not at its most acute in these almost forgotten villages. It is in the villages of the densely inhabited plains that the struggle to resist taxes by predatory officials flares into violence, as the next chapter explores.

2

Local Despots and Peasant Rebels

H ARSH TAXES, LOCAL despots, hopeless revolts and a peasantry powerless to fight for its interests – in a century of change, not much seems to have changed in the Hunan countryside where Mao Zedong and so many other Communist leaders grew up.

'It started when a peasant couldn't pay his taxes. Yan Youcai killed himself by drinking a bottle of pesticide. When people heard what had happened, they got together and marched on the centre,' said the elderly woman whom I interviewed in 1999. She squinted up at the afternoon sun, her tanned face a mass of wrinkles.[1]

'Every year there are more taxes. Every year they get richer and buy more cars,' she went on in a low querulous voice which wavered between indignation and resignation. Her husband, dressed like her in faded blue cotton and black felt shoes, smoked his thin-stemmed pipe impassively and said nothing. However, one of their sons who sat with us was clearly uncomfortable at the turn the conversation had taken and got up.

'You don't need to talk about this,' he said abruptly, and with that he left the room.

Even six months after the event it was still dangerous to talk of such things. 'They', the local Party officials, could take revenge on anyone informing outsiders about unrest in a district where both Mao Zedong and Liu Shaoqi, Mao's one-time successor, had been born.

The conversation faltered for a while. Mrs Liu, as she was called, shared the same name as everyone else in Huaminglou, the ancestral home of Liu Shaoqi. He had once been second only to Mao in the Party and his house was now a museum. It lay just opposite, on the far side of a pond. A large comfortable home with walls of yellow-brown mud, thatched roofs and black beams of cypress wood, it was big enough to house twenty people. Inside were a series of court-yards and stalls for oxen and pigs. Hunan is famous for breeding the latter – indeed, the Chinese character for 'home' shows a pig under a roof.

Mrs Liu's house was not quite as big but it had electricity, a television, brick walls and a tiled roof. She too kept pigs and she was also drying maize on the concrete floor of the courtyard. Most of the food the family grew, they kept for themselves to eat. An old stone mill standing in the courtyard was no longer used, replaced by an electric polishing and grinding machine. Still, if one did not look too closely, the scene was much the same as it might have been a century ago when Liu Shaoqi was born. The villages in Hunan nestle among low wooded hills, a picture of rural tranquillity. In the terraced paddy fields, newly planted rice, bright green in colour, exudes a moist fragrance. In village ponds, fish rise to snap at insects, disturbing the placid waters and sending out slow ripples to the banks.

The small uprising had started in January that year, just before the Spring Festival when each family normally slaughters a pig to eat during the three-week holiday, the biggest in the agricultural calendar. The local Party boss had decided to levy a new pig slaughter tax just before the festival and everyone had to pay whether they slaughtered one or not. At the time local people had enough to eat but little cash because in 1998 pork prices had collapsed, dropping by half. China rears 40 per cent of the world's pigs and Hunan is a big exporter but demand from Hong Kong had dwindled because of the Asian financial crisis. In such market conditions no commercial breeder with any sense would slaughter a pig unless he had to.

The revolt started in Ba Tang village, about ten miles away, when the suicide's body was found. Fellow villagers set out in protest for the county headquarters of the Party, a modern edifice of glass and concrete, and they carried the body with them. As they marched, thousands of other peasants joined them. There was safety in numbers. Nervous officials summoned the police to block the road but more peasants, some estimate as many as 10,000, gathered and began to overturn cars and set fire to government buildings. A unit of the People's Armed Police arrived in trucks and opened fire.[2]

Nine peasants described as the ringleaders subsequently confessed to crimes of 'looting and beating'. Some reports said that two were sentenced to death but another report recorded that all nine received prison terms of up to six years. The police statement on the event, as is customary in China, was punctilious in specifying the damage to state property – 496,896 yuan.[3]

By the time of my visit four months later, peace had temporarily been restored. Even so, nervous Party officials kept a close watch on the peasants, and I was dogged by plainclothes police who followed my car and eavesdropped when I set out on foot, loitering behind trees.

Mrs Liu recalled that local taxes first began to be levied in the mid-1980s, soon after the people's communes were dissolved and the peasants began to prosper. The first local protests here at the village of Huaminglou took place in 1988.

'First it was an education tax. The officials told us Beijing had passed a law on compulsory education and now we had to pay a tax for the schools,' she said. How many children did she have, I asked. Five, she answered with a touch of pride, and now with nine grandchildren such a tax was something that mattered.

Within a few years, local officials all over the Chinese countryside were levying hundreds of different kinds of taxes and fees – for getting married or buried, for being sterilized or for having a baby. They charged peasants for the delivery of telegrams or letters, for the militia, in the name of roads, electricity and water conservancy. Sometimes the purpose of a particular tax was left vague, it being described simply as a land fee or a poll tax.

'If we are unable to pay them, they just take something else – a television set, a bicycle, a pig or sacks of grain,' grumbled Mrs Liu. 'We call them *tufei* or *tumu* – country bandits or local despots.'

Even in Mao's own village of Shaoshan, about 20 miles down the road from Huaminglou, peasants seethed with a repressed anger.

'We know now about the law. It says we should not pay more than 5 per cent of our income in taxes,' observed a local, who had stopped his ox and wooden plough to talk. 'These days we have television so we hear the news.'

Just beyond his fields lay a huge imperial-style park dedicated to Mao's memory in which the local government had invested millions. In design it resembles the New Summer Palace in Beijing or the hunting park at Chengde which the Qing emperors built for themselves, but its purpose is quite different. People come here to venerate Mao. A massive white sculpture of the Great Helmsman, depicting him in his winter coat, one hand raised aloft, stands in a marble hall. Nearby, a vast stage is set with mock-up models depicting every famous episode in his life – from the missionary-style brick house in Shunyi, Guizhou, where he first won control of the Party on the Long March, to the house where he planned his triumphal entry into Beijing in 1949. And as one walks around, choral music blares from loudspeakers.

At the height of the Cultural Revolution (1966–76), millions of believers would descend on this village each year to express their devotion in front of the humble house where Mao was born. Just a trifle smaller than that of Liu Shaoqi, it lies in a small nondescript valley, more of a gully really, with rice terraces and a pond. The house has clearly been rebuilt a number of times and inside there is not much to see except a few sticks of furniture.

Within a few years of Mao's death in 1976, the number of visitors had dwindled to next to nothing. After the 1989 Tiananmen pro-democracy protests, the state decided to revive the cult of Mao and make it a base for patriotism. Party members began to travel there in organized groups to deepen their ideological fervour. The local Party committee built the park to make money from them. It costs 20 yuan to enter and nearly every visitor buys a plaster bust, a recording of Mao panegyrics or some other souvenir.

'You can't make any money from agriculture,' explained the ploughman. 'Look at me, I am just growing this rice for my family and to fulfil my quota for the state. To make cash I go to town and work as an electrician.'

On my visit to Shaoshan, the state-run guesthouse had plenty of rooms available, for these days there are not many visitors. Policemen lounged in the lobby beneath an enormous revolutionary painting of a beaming Mao standing in a huge field of wheat surrounded by smiling peasants. Just beyond the lobby there was a beauty parlour where a group of heavily made-up girls sat waiting. Within a few minutes of my checking in, the phone rang. 'Do you want a massage?'

Adjoining the hotel was a 'social club' where, that evening, I ran into a middle-aged but still handsome woman called Mao.

'The girls all work for me. I contracted out this place,' she said with pride. On the dance floor a couple smooched under disco lights and a portly man in suit and tie crooned a karaoke song. Other officials in suits sat together on the fringes of the dance floor, clutching their peasant girls and drinking steadily.

'They come here on tours,' explained Mrs Mao. 'It's all paid for out of expenses.'

'What about the police?'

'Oh,' she said, 'they invested in this place and take a cut.'

The local Party committee was deep in debt and salaries were being paid late. The Mao Memorial Park was not making as much money as they had thought it would and several other commercial ventures had failed. In desperation the committee had decided the year before to branch out into prostitution and now it ran three or four brothels.

'I used to be a teacher here but the salary was never paid,' said Mrs Mao. 'Anyway, do you want a girl? You can have one by the hour or for the whole night.'

Next to one group of men, a seat was free. 'Young, isn't she?' said a neighbour of his companion as he belched. His girl giggled coquettishly and pretended to slap her admirer. He and his friends were from a town in Anhui, another agricultural province, and had taken advantage of a recent campaign to 'talk more about politics' to come here. No, he said, he wasn't shocked to see this sort of thing, even in Mao's home village. The same happened in Anhui, and probably everywhere else.

'Take my county. You can't get rich from farming. It's business or industry that counts, but our textile factory went bust. Then the Party secretary's son ran off with a loan that was meant to be used to build a tannery and we couldn't pay the peasants for their cotton harvest, so we had to get another bank loan. Debts can pile up,' he said. 'If that is how things are and there is no money for wages, you have to go in for any kind of business.'

It was difficult to make out his features clearly in the dim lighting but he had a round, determined face and thick, short hair that stood up like bristles. Around his ample waist, he sported a bunch of keys, a mobile phone and a beeper. He leaned over, exuding a mixture of garlic and beer, and with a confidential air explained his position: 'It is hard. These peasants can be of low quality, some of them don't understand anything. They are like children and we are like their father and mother. If we don't tax them how can we do anything to help them? The Centre says do this, do that, but they never give us any money. We have to find it ourselves.'

History's wheel has now come full circle in Hunan. In the late 1920s, as a young Marxist, Mao returned to his father's thatched house to study the grievances of the peasants. In his *Report of an Investigation of the Peasant Movement in Hunan* (1927), he predicted that millions of oppressed peasants would soon rise up like a hurricane in a movement that would shake China to its roots. The peasants were hungry, poor and oppressed by local despots who extorted taxes or who in times of shortage lent them grain or cash at punitive interest rates. Though Marxist theory talked of an urban proletariat creating revolution, Mao believed that disaffected peasants might form the basis of a political movement, and he put forward his ideas just after the KMT had crushed the Communist Party organization in China's major cities, forcing the surviving Party leaders to seek refuge in the remote countryside.

In 1998 and 1999, peasant riots occurred all over Hunan. In Qiyang county in the south-west, police opened fire on 10,000 people who had gathered outside the Party headquarters. A group calling itself the 'Society for Reducing Taxes and Saving the Nation' fought with police in Daolin county where a peasant was killed by an exploding tear-gas canister.[4] There were also riots in Qidong, Wenfushi, Dazhongqiao, Luodi, Xingxi, Xupu and Yizhang as well as in Ningxiang. Bombs exploded in many places, including one which went off on a bus as it passed the provincial Party offices in Changsha. Other peasants blocked railway lines.[5]

Ironically, however, Hunan might well be called the crucible of the Chinese Communist Party. Many prominent leaders were born here, not only Mao and Liu Shaoqi but also Marshal Peng Dehuai, General Secretary Hu Yaobang and Prime Minister Zhu Rongji. Hunan's red peppers are supposed to nurture a fiery, rebellious temperament, and perhaps this is so, yet it is interesting how many of these leaders were born into rural families who understood the peasantry and the power wielded over them by the local élite.

Liu Shaoqi left the Hunan countryside to study revolution in Moscow where he was taught the Marxist-Leninist theory that cast the proletariat as the vanguard of the revolution. When he returned to China in 1922 he organized miners' strikes in Hunan and then went on to playing a leading role in the Shanghai trade union movement. Yet it was Mao, not Liu, who in 1935 emerged in command of an army enlisted from amongst the peasants and based in the poorest rural regions. Liu was to remain in Mao's shadow for the rest of his life, always serving as number two in the Party. Though he became head of state, Mao remained Chairman.

In the 1980s, the Party belatedly erected a 70-foot-high statue of Liu, covered in gold paint, which now towers over the surrounding paddy fields. Yet during the Cultural Revolution Mao had targeted Liu as 'the number one capitalist roader'. His house in Huaminglou was daubed with slogans and cartoons, and his relatives were beaten and paraded through the village. Liu himself died in 1969 in an obscure vault of a former bank in the city of Zhengzhou, on the Yellow River, where he had been left, half naked, after severe beatings. In Liu's memorial hall, there is a photocopy of his death certificate made out in a different name. The entry for 'occupation' has been filled in as 'unemployed' although Liu was still nominally President of China.

Mao felt that Liu had betrayed him during the Great Leap Forward (1958–61). That attempt by Mao to create a socialist rural Utopia had collapsed in a massive famine that killed over 30 million peasants, and it was only because of Liu's efforts that many more did not die. In April 1961, in the depths of the famine, Liu returned to his village and that of Mao to see for himself how bad the famine was. Local

48

officials did their best to conceal the truth – at the museum, a care-taker recounted that they had even plastered the trees with mud and painted them so that Liu would not realize that starving peasants had stripped them of all their bark. Liu was not deceived, however, and on his return to Beijing, he took responsibility for authorizing mea-sures that relaxed the state's grip over the peasants, giving them the opportunity to grow more food for themselves.

Behind Mao and Liu's personal and political differences lay ancient traditions defining the role of the state and the duties of the peas-antry which still underlie politics today. In ancient China, the state sought complete control over the peasants' production of a surplus of grain. The bureaucracy collected, stored and distributed the grain, much as happens in a modern planned economy. For without grain reserves a ruler could not wage war or ensure domestic stability.

In the fifth century BC, the first Legalist political philosopher, Li Kui, advised rulers to profit from this monopoly: 'They should buy and sell grain to inhibit price fluctuations, since high prices harm con-sumers and low ones harm producers.' In 338 BC, his student, Lord Shang, chief minister of the Qin kingdom, instructed that 'The mer-chants shall be prohibited from buying grain and the peasants pro-hibited from selling grain.' After the unification of China under the Qin, the control of agriculture became the single most important responsibility of the Emperor. Edicts have been discovered in which the Emperor Wudi (born in 157 BC) of the Han dynasty laid out in great detail which crops should be planted and when, and what yields were to be expected, and gave instructions that the surplus should be stored in state granaries. Even in this century, in the last years of the imperial system, it was the duty of the Emperor to conduct a cere-mony at the Temple of Heaven in Beijing where he symbolically ploughed the first furrow and marked the start of the agricultural year.

In addition to collecting a grain tax and delivering grain to feed the army, the bureaucracy and the court, officials could also, on the Emperor's behalf, demand a month's corvée labour from the peas-ants to build and maintain roads and river dykes.

When the Republic was established in 1911, rural China began to move away from this system of state control towards a market system in which middlemen bought and sold grain as a commodity.

The new railways and river steamers could move it from one part of the country to another, from surplus areas to those in deficit. Food could also be imported from North America into big ports such as Shanghai. In addition, the introduction from the West of chemical fertilizers, better seeds and new crops began to encourage the growth of small-scale private commercial farming. In the 1930s per capita food production reached record levels.

Even so, the commercial distribution system never worked well in much of rural China. Too many people lived far from roads or ports along the big rivers or the coast. When there were shortages, no one transported food, at least not at affordable prices, so people fled instead. And when there was a good local harvest, local prices fell and peasants lost money although a hundred miles away there might be plenty of demand.

During the 1920s and 1930s, despite record levels in food production, China was racked by local famines which killed millions. At the same time, in the absence of control at the centre, the countryside was subjected to the depredations of the armies of warlords who requisitioned food from the peasants, paying them only with IOUs or worthless paper money, and press-ganged many into working as unpaid labourers or recruits.

When the Communists came to power in 1949, Mao restored the imperial system of control. The KMT was portrayed as being unworthy because it had not fulfilled its responsibilities: guaranteeing the collection and distribution of grain in times of famine and maintaining the dykes along the Yellow and Yangtze Rivers. The Communist Party quickly abolished all private grain trading and a veteran revolutionary, Chen Yun, was put in charge of re-establishing the state monopoly over grain. Peasants were forced to pay a grain tax and middlemen, charged with being 'capitalists', were arrested. By 1955, the state had sole responsibility for buying, storing and distributing surplus grain. That year, citizens were issued with residence cards and grain ration coupons. Only state grain shops could distribute grain.

The peasants also became the victims of what was called the

'scissors effect'. In order for the state to raise capital for industrialization, the peasants had to buy industrial manufactures at relatively
high prices but they in turn were paid relatively low prices for the
food they grew. This vast transfer of wealth from the peasantry to
the cities in the 1950s went hand in hand with other changes. Farmers
were ordered to pool their land, tools and livestock in co-operatives.
Many resisted, preferring to consume or destroy their property
rather than hand it over. Agricultural output fell but Mao insisted on
pressing ahead with collectivization in the face of advice to the contrary from within the Party. In 1958, he launched the Great Leap
Forward, his attempt to drag the country into a Communist Utopia
where there would be no money, no private property and no want.
The state would feed and clothe everyone. Every peasant would also
become both a soldier marching to work behind a red flag, gun in
hand, and a worker making steel.

In the new giant people's communes into which the peasants were
dragooned, science was to replace traditional farming methods. Mao
wanted huge fields and industrial economies of scale. As in the Han
dynasty, the state would plan and supervise agriculture down to the
last detail, even specifying when peasants should sow or reap. Mao
also claimed to embrace modern science and ordered the peasants to
employ new agricultural techniques pioneered in the Soviet Union.
These were taken to extremes. Furrows were ploughed twelve feet
deep. Densely spaced rice seedlings were planted in fields which the
People's Daily proclaimed produced double, then triple, then ten times
the food they had before. Propaganda photos showed wheat stems
growing so close together that children could sit on top of them,
pumpkins the size of cars, and miracle rice plants that produced
three ears rather than one. In a frenzy of hysterical adulation Party
officials throughout the country outbid each other in reporting the
size of the harvest. Those who dared to raise doubts found themselves at best detained or at worst beaten to death in a 'struggle
session'. In consequence, peasants were forced to hand over almost
the entire harvest in the autumn of 1958, 1959 and 1960, leaving
them with nothing to eat.

Even so, the quotas were not met. Mao, apparently believing the
wildly exaggerated production figures, concluded that the selfish

peasants were hoarding their grain. Squads of officials were dispatched to find the peasants' hidden caches. If they did not find grain, they took something else instead, clothes, jewellery, livestock, wood, furniture, anything they could seize.

In imperial times, the state had always required peasants to hand over part of their harvest – perhaps 15 or 20 per cent. In return the local magistrate was obliged to maintain granaries so that the population could be fed in times of natural disaster. Now, under Mao, the state took everything but gave nothing in return.

'We believed the state would give us grain when we were hungry. We knew the granaries were full,' explained one peasant to me who had survived the famine in Xinyang prefecture, in Henan province. This was one of the worst-hit areas where even official reports say one in eight died but others claim half the population perished. In his memoirs, the deputy Party secretary of Xinyang, Zhang Shufan, recalled that the peasants had preferred to die rather than rob the granaries: 'It proves how obedient our people are, how much they observe the law, how much trust they gave to the Party, and how great is the guilt which some of our leading cadres should bear toward such people!'[6]

By the time the peasants realized that they would not be helped, it was too late. Most, already weak from hunger, possessed nothing at all, neither food nor money, and often not even their own work tools. Militia guards manned the streets, making flight impossible. Letters from those seeking help were opened by the authorities and the writers arrested. The famine that followed was the greatest China had ever experienced.

In 1961, after his visit to his home village, Liu Shaoqi authorized peasants to grow food in private plots. At the same time he reduced the quotas that had to be delivered to the state and allowed a certain amount of private trade. In many places peasants tried out what was called 'the household contract responsibility system' which allowed a household to contract out a field for a given period, deliver some of the harvest to the state and keep the rest for themselves. More commonly, a contract was jointly signed by a group of householders who formed a work team. In the words of a fellow reformer, Deng Xiaoping, 'It does not matter whether the cat is black or white as long as it catches mice.' In other words, in addressing the famine, ideology was not the highest priority. (Deng was to revive the aphorism memorably after Mao's death.)

At the same time, the reformist wing of the Party also tried to put those responsible for the famine on trial and to make amends to the peasants. In some communes what remained of their property was restored to them. Even so, there was precious little left. A third of all livestock had died, and pots and pans had been melted down to make 'steel' in backyard furnaces. Even the wood used for roofs and doorposts had been seized.

For several years after the famine, Mao retreated from public view. But then, in 1966, in a bid to regain power, he launched a counter-campaign targeting those involved in 'capitalism', whom he termed 'capitalist roaders'. In what became known as the Cultural Revolution, all private enterprise was again outlawed. Not until the 1980s would peasants be able to start rebuilding their lives. One Henan peasant told me it was twenty years before he ate a proper meal and not just gruel and sweet potatoes.

The peasants suffered in other ways too. Throughout the Mao era, the imperial tradition – which still continues today – requiring peasants to contribute a month's corvée labour each year, was taken to extremes. The peasants were forced to spend months working on giant public projects. Dams, river dykes and water reservoirs were erected in every county. Huge efforts were made to terrace land for cultivation, in imitation of the model village of Dazhai. And public health campaigns required the participation of all. The peasants were given no respite.

Mao's failure in the Great Leap Forward did not lead to any slackening in the drive to make out of the Chinese peasant a new 'socialist man' who would fit into the 'new China', a society supposedly organized on scientific principles. During the Cultural Revolution all forms of religious worship were banned and churches, mosques, temples, shrines and many monuments were destroyed. The basic rituals that punctuated the peasants' lives, marking birth, marriage, death and the seasons, were forbidden. Along with 'feudal superstitions', the Party banned even simple entertainments such as card-playing.

The peasants might obey but Mao could not compel them to deliver the surplus of grain needed to underpin the industrial and military expansion of which he dreamed. By the 1970s, tens of millions of 'educated youths' had been sent off 'to learn from the peasants' because per capita food production was reaching levels perilously close to famine.

Then, in 1976, Mao died. Almost immediately, and perhaps spontaneously, the peasants began to divide up the land themselves and grow food as they thought fit instead of following state directives. According to the Party's history, the first to do so were a group of peasants in Fengyang county in Anhui who signed a secret compact in 1977.

In 1978, Deng Xiaoping, rehabilitated after his fall from grace during the Cultural Revolution, established himself in power at the Third Plenum of the Eleventh Party Congress, in what is now hailed as a turning-point in recent Chinese history. He officially endorsed the Anhui experiments and began to dissolve the communes, authorizing the adoption of the household contract responsibility system that had been experimented with in 1961, encouraging 'free markets' where agricultural goods and handicrafts could be sold, and even allowing peasants to hire outside labour. At the same time, the *People's Daily* reassured everyone that 'to get rich is glorious'.

In each subsequent year, and especially up until 1985, the first and most important edict the Party issued concerned agriculture. Just as under Mao, the state anxiously watched to see whether the peasants would grow enough grain if given a certain degree of freedom. In the past, the communes had been ordered to 'take grain as the key link' so they had ploughed under orchards, drained lakes and terraced steep hillsides to maximize grain production to the exclusion of every other crop. Even the tombs of the Qing emperors in Hebei province had been planted with corn which was grown in the marble-lined lakes and canals and amongst the stone spirit guardians.

Now, in the first years of the 'reform period', as the Party has come to call it, everyone was nervous. Were the new policies just a temporary measure to boost food production, like Lenin's New

Economic Policy in the early 1920s and the post-Great Leap Forward relaxation? Many suspected the Party would suddenly reverse its decisions, take away the household plots and punish those who had taken advantage of the reforms. Some senior leaders around Deng disliked the reforms, especially Chen Yun, who had established the state grain monopoly in the 1950s and who was a likely successor if Deng lost power or died.

The reformers were anxious too because if grain production did not rise, their policies were in danger. As it happened, and as has already been noted, grain production rose steadily, reaching a record 400 million tonnes in 1984 when China became a net exporter of food for the first time in recent history.

That same year, the state freed peasants from the obligation to grow a fixed minimum amount of grain and allowed them to run businesses or work in non-agricultural enterprises. They could even leave their villages to look for work in urban areas. Yet after peaking in 1984 grain production (which in China includes potatoes and soybean) fell in the second half of the decade, the area sown to grain declined and Chen Yun took to warning that a grain shortage was leading to disaster. But what was now the best way to rekindle the 'enthusiasm' (as it was often phrased) of the peasants to grow grain? Should the state rely on market incentives or return to compulsion? The Party split between those wanting to liberate the peasants entirely and trust to market forces, and diehard conservatives who insisted that when the state did not keep the peasants under strict control, it could not guarantee grain production and so risked social anarchy.

In fact, Deng's reforms, bold though they were at the time, were half-measures. Under the household contract responsibility system the peasants had not been given ownership of the land and were not free to do what they wanted. They had signed fifteen-year leases but remained tenants of the state. This was a step up from being a serf on a commune, but the cadres still had the final say on how the land should be used, and they could at any time take away a peasant's plot or assign it to another use. A peasant could not (and still cannot) pass his plot on to his son or sell it and retire on the proceeds. As a result, rather than risk ploughing money into land that might soon be taken away, peasants preferred to spend their money on building new and better homes of brick and tile. A house, at least, was unlikely to be taken away. At the same time, the fewer specific orders the central government issued, the more autonomy local officials had. If a peasant had a grievance, under China's rudimentary legal system he could not realistically appeal to a court or other higher authority for redress. Even if he did succeed in doing so, local officials had many ways of exacting revenge. The local Party chief controlled birth quotas, sterilization, the registration of births, schooling, the licensing of small businesses, entry into cities, the issue of bank loans, the sale of seeds, fertilizer and diesel fuel for tractors, and access to farm machinery. And he determined whether a peasant had fulfilled his contract to deliver grain to the state.

The debate at the top of the Party went back and forth throughout the 1980s. Reformers argued that the drop in grain output was not as serious as it was made to sound. The Chinese were simply eating less grain because they were enjoying more of everything else. Land that had been turned over to grain between 1956 and 1976 was now being restored to its original use, as orchards or fish ponds for example. The state had also lifted price controls on hundreds of items although it continued to control the cost of 'essential' commodities such as grain, rubber, sugar, chemical fertilizers and cotton.

In consequence, in the cities 'free' markets and private restaurants flourished. Though teams of inspectors patrolled the stalls, checking that prices were not excessive, finally, after thirty years, there was a choice of what to eat. Early each morning, the police allowed local peasants to cycle through the road blocks on the outskirts of each city, ingeniously carrying on their panniers fresh eggs, chickens, all kinds of vegetables and fruit, live fish and even pigs. Anyone could buy this produce with cash. There was no need to queue up at a state shop with ration tickets. By the mid-1980s, astonishingly, fat people began to be seen again on the streets of Beijing.

Nevertheless, conservatives continued to voice their fear that the state was tempting disaster. If it paid the peasants more money for their grain in an attempt to rekindle enthusiasm, then it stood to lose money unless it raised retail prices. However, if urban dwellers felt threatened by rising prices they in turn might start food riots. The state would then have to raise wages and that would lead to inflation. In fact the conservatives' fears proved justified.

In 1986 the state began to slash subsidies on some goods. Waves of panic buying and hoarding of products such as salt and matches followed, and inflation soon reached double digits. The real value of urban incomes began to decline. In 1988, China was forced to reintroduce rationing of pork, sugar and eggs, and it began to import ever-larger amounts of grain. A record 16 million tonnes was imported in 1989.

The late 1980s saw the debate over the future of the peasants reach its peak. The reformers, then still in power, urged the full commercialization of farming. 'If the countryside is not rich, then China will not get rich,' the *People's Daily* warned. Liberals wanted the peasants to be allowed to buy and sell land, or at least to have 'land-use rights'. This, they argued, would allow some peasants to develop into specialized grain farmers who could acquire enough small parcels of land to make modern farming possible. At the time China's 180 million peasant households worked an average of one and a half acres of farmland, holdings too small to justify investing in high quality seeds, irrigation equipment or mechanized farming. Before they were toppled from power in 1989 in the wake of the Tiananmen protests, the reformers raised grain procurement prices and opened China's first wholesale grain market since 1949, in Henan province's Zhengzhou. A futures market was also planned.

By 1989, grain output had recovered sufficiently to match the 1984 record but the conservatives, led by Chen Yun, pointed out that the area sown to grain had fallen by 4 per cent. With 15 million new mouths to feed each year, per capita grain production was dropping and China was becoming too dependent on imports, making it vulnerable to an embargo. The press complained that investment in public works such as irrigation had fallen by half, the river dykes were not being repaired, and public health and education programmes were losing ground. There was also a near famine in parts of south-west China and it proved impossible to ship surplus grain from the north-east to alleviate it.

Worst of all, corruption in the countryside was diluting Communist power. It was all too easy for cadres to make money by buying what the state sold, cheaply, at fixed prices and then reselling it at higher, free-market prices. This was true of essential commodities in short supply such as chemical fertilizers but it was also true of grain, since consumers were prepared to pay a high price for good-quality rice.

As some cadres exploited the dual pricing system, many farmers became openly rebellious. The state struggled to pay them in cash for their deliveries and instead they were given worthless IOUs. When peasants refused to grow grain or hand it over if they did grow it, many rural cadres resorted to force to meet state delivery quotas. Ugly riots ensued.[7]

To address the issue, in 1988 the reformers promulgated a law on village democracy that in theory allowed the peasants to exercise some measure of supervision over local cadres. In practice, however, the law only enabled villagers to choose their headman, a figure who ranked below the lowest level of the Chinese bureaucracy in authority.

After the conservatives won power in 1990, they ushered in policies to boost the role of the state and restore order in the countryside. Private grain trading was forbidden and the state concentrated on raising grain production. The ten-year decline in the area of irrigated land was reversed. A series of huge water conservancy projects involving the moving of over 5 billion cubic yards of earth were initiated. At the same time the Prime Minister, Li Peng, supported calls for 'recollectivization' in order to create large and modern farms.

Yet by then it was clear that market forces, once set in motion, could not be so easily stopped. The Party was forced to make a second and then a third attempt at freeing grain prices. The state, it appeared, was simply unable to fund and manage the grain monopoly any more. It lacked the fiscal resources to pay the peasants a market price for their crops while at the same time sheltering urban consumers. In 1988, it was short of US$19 billion to pay the peasants. By 1992, that figure had risen to US$22 billion. It was all very well raising procurement prices but the bigger the harvests, the deeper grew the hole in the central government's coffers. Soon agricultural subsidies were absorbing as much as a sixth of all state spending.

State grain companies ran up huge losses and increasingly large debts. Even in a good harvest, about 15 per cent was lost through wastage. At the same time the state also ended up buying the worst rice which nobody wanted to eat since the peasants delivered as their quota a hybrid rice which tasted bad and kept the rest to eat themselves or to sell on the free market. The hybrid had been created in the late 1970s by a peasant scientist, Yuan Longping. It produced high yields and so was used for the first crop each year. (In southern China farmers average two and sometimes manage three crops a year.) However, as urban dwellers prospered they could afford better quality and often imported rice. Wily peasants therefore bought their unused rice coupons from them and returned the rice acquired with the coupons to the state as their grain tax while they themselves concentrated on non-agricultural enterprises.

By 1992 the state grain companies had run up a debt of 43 billion yuan and the peasants meanwhile were owed a further 33 billion yuan in IOUs. The result was frequent riots, prompting one Party leader, Tian Jiyun, to warn his colleagues that 'if there are problems in the villages, no one in the present regime can hold on to power'.[8]

A revival of reforms by Deng in 1992 resulted in a second push towards full commercialization. The city of Zhengzhou bought computers and tried to set up a futures market modelled on the Chicago Board of Trade, and the first contract for 10,000 tonnes of wheat to be delivered in the autumn at a fixed price was signed between Hunan's Lengshuitan Flour Mill and the Henan Huaxian County Grain and Oil Company. Agricultural commodity markets also sprang up everywhere.

The government, which had not dared increase the price of grain delivered to the urban population, fixed twenty-five years earlier, now suddenly raised retail prices by over 60 per cent. Inflation soared to an annual rate of 20–30 per cent and once again the government panicked. Beijing reintroduced price controls on twenty-seven food items, and grain coupons were reissued in twenty-nine cities. All grain exports were banned and the expensive computerized trading systems for everything except green beans were mothballed. Finally, the state designated a hundred grain production bases where peasants had to grow grain, and provincial governors were set targets to ensure that their cities were also supplied with cheaper vegetables.

In 1995 conservatives seized on a report by an American expert, Lester Brown, who warned that within twenty years China would have to buy up all the grain sold in world markets if it was to feed its population.[9] In response the central government jacked up grain procurement prices again until the state was buying corn at twice the market price in the United States. In 1997, for the first time, it bought the entire summer crop, over 110 million tonnes – double the state procurement seen a decade earlier.

The expiry of the fifteen-year land leases signed after Deng launched the first reforms in 1978 stimulated another round in the fundamental debate. The Party remained split. Some, like the veteran rural reformer Du Runsheng, said the peasants must be given title to their land while others argued the opposite. Song Ping, a Party elder, stated, 'We must go down the road of collective prosperity. We must ceaselessly develop and strengthen the collective economy.'[10]

In a compromise, the state authorized thirty-year leases but in practice many peasants were given contracts for just ten or even five years.[11] Leaders in Beijing might issue directives, but it soon became clear that they could neither raise taxes nor distribute revenue in the countryside. Local officials were free to do as they pleased, and when the state tried to pump money into the rural economy, it was simply embezzled. In 1997, state auditors reported that some 80 billion yuan which was supposed to have been used to buy grain had gone into the building of hotels and luxury houses, the purchase of cars and mobile phones, and speculation in stocks and shares.[12]

The state grain system, which employs four million people, had in 1998 managed to lose US$26 billion in six years and run up debts of US$12 billion, partly because of four years of record harvests. The losses for the state tobacco and cotton monopolies were equally large.[13] In addition, China's 50,000 rural credit bank branches, which were supposed to channel peasant savings into improving farming, had been ransacked. 'Many are in a state of de facto bankruptcy as the losses they have accumulated over a long time far exceed their total deposits,' the *China Economic Times* reported.[14]

Local cadres also continued to act with impunity, raising and spending taxes as they pleased. It has been estimated that in 1996 alone, local governments collected 116 billion yuan in illegal fees.

Not surprisingly, agricultural incomes stagnated and there were repeated riots by furious peasants protesting against the depredations of 'local despots'.[15]

In 1999, China braced itself for a third attempt at ending the grain monopoly. After a series of record harvests, economists were more concerned about deflation than inflation. The Zhengzhou Grain Futures Market reopened, as did a Cotton Exchange, thereby ending a monopoly that had endured for nearly half a century. At the same time, the Prime Minister Zhu Rongji announced plans to halve the numbers employed by the state grain and cotton bureaux. The state now wanted procurement prices to fall to market prices and domestic prices to align with international prices.[16]

There seemed to be no other choice. A third of the grain traded in China was now handled by middlemen, disparagingly called 'grain rats'. Increasingly, all those services once provided exclusively by the state – banking, milling, storage, the use of mechanized farm machinery and the distribution of oil, seeds and fertilizer – were being dominated by the private sector.[17]

The gradual privatization of the Chinese countryside could bring about a historic change in the status of Chinese peasants. Yet much depends on whether the ideas of Adam Smith or the warnings of another British philosopher, Thomas Malthus, will triumph.

In his gloomy *Essay on the Principle of Population* (1798), Thomas Malthus warned of the propensity of population growth to outstrip any increase in food production. By the year 2025, when China's population might peak at 1.5 or 1.6 billion people, its peasants must raise grain output to 650–700 million tonnes from nearly 500 million tonnes in 1999.[18] Otherwise, China must import more grain than is currently traded in the whole world. Even now, the yearly success or failure of Chinese peasants in growing wheat or cotton is often the 'swing' factor in setting world prices.

Most observers think that Chinese agriculture is sufficiently backward to allow plenty of scope for improvement. Satellite analysis shows that China has 50 per cent more arable land than official statistics report.[19] To avoid taxes, peasants and officials often misrepresent the true state of affairs. Some argue that on this basis corn yields are a quarter of those obtained in the United States and that overall grain yields amount to only 60 per cent of those in Europe.[20]

After 1978, the switch to household farming spurred technical improvements which lifted yields. Chemical fertilizers became popular as did small tractors for ploughing and haulage, and plastic sheeting became available. The latter enabled peasants to extend the growing season quite considerably. These developments together helped lift close to 200 million peasants out of dire hardship to what the Chinese call *xiao kang*, or small prosperity.

Yet those early gains have run their course and agricultural techniques in China remain by and large fairly primitive and inefficient. Nearly 90 per cent of harvesting is carried out by hand, as is over 80 per cent of sowing. Growing grain is regarded as an unremunerative activity and it therefore tends to be left to women. Since the mid-1980s men have sought other kinds of better-paid work. However, literacy rates among rural women are low and few are trained in applying pesticides or fertilizers correctly.[21] In consequence such substances have been misapplied to such an extent that chemical runoffs are blamed for raising pollution in lakes to dangerous levels.

As little as 10 per cent of Chinese grain is actually sold commercially and even this is not usually packaged or transported outside its province of origin. By contrast, some 70 per cent of the food grown in China is eaten at home by peasants or stored as surplus, traditionally under the floor. The remaining 20 per cent is contracted to the state which generally cares about quantity not quality. That proportion often ends up as animal feed.[22]

Compared to neighbouring countries such as Japan, Taiwan and South Korea, China actually has much more arable land per head of population. It also has the scope to expand its total area of quality farmland.[23] However, the latter would require investment in irrigation and better seeds, investment that an individual peasant might not be prepared to make unless he was assured ownership.

If China were to move towards high-yield, commercial grain farming, it might have to embrace enormous social change. Some 400 million to 700 million people are now involved in planting crops but a commercial farming sector might need to employ no more than 200 million people. What would the rest do? Even in the late 1990s, rural unemployment was put at 160 million out of a total rural labour force of 400 million.

The great strength of the current system is that at least each household has the security of a plot of land on which to grow its own food. No one knows what might happen if some peasants were encouraged to sell their plots to professional grain farmers intent on setting up bigger and more efficient farms, but some fear that a sudden increase in the number of unemployed and landless peasants might be a consequence. Another fear is that if the state really withdrew, China would have to depend on Adam Smith's 'invisible hand' to distribute grain around the country. China's storage and transportation systems are still not adequate for the workings of a market, and Smith himself warned of the tendency of merchants to conspire to rig prices to their own advantage.[24]

At present the state still controls two-thirds of the grain market but the state system is now so hopelessly corrupt that China seems to be heading towards a largely commercial system whether it likes it or not. Yet in the absence of any real civil or political rights, individual peasants could soon find themselves at the mercy of a few monopolists.

The 600 million Chinese peasants who live in that vast monotonous archipelago of villages across the North China plain and the provinces of Shandong, Henan, Jiangsu, Anhui, Jiangxi, Sichuan and Hunan probably constitute the largest unenfranchised group in the world. Forbidden openly to organize themselves to defend their interests against either the central state or local despots, they form secret underground armies, cults and millenarian sects as they have done throughout history. The state seems involved in a continual battle to crush them, and from time to time faint reports of this repression, as in the events that took place in Ningxiang and Xiangtan, reach the outside world. So unconstrained by ethical considerations is the power wielded by some local officials that no economic system can function effectively. Given the chance, peasants would quickly organize themselves into associations or even political parties but at present that seems a remote prospect.

Change, when it comes, may start first in the most prosperous rural areas, such as the Yangtze and Pearl River deltas, where rapid industrialization has created an energetic, educated and self-assured society with knowledge of the outside world. The next chapter looks at dynamic villagers there who have prospered by starting up rural enterprises.

3

Getting Rich is Glorious

WHEN THE BUS pulled up outside one of the villages in the coastal province of Zhejiang, the party of foreign journalists tumbled out and fell momentarily silent before an avenue of tiled villas complete with balconies and fountains. It was 1986, and the Party wanted everyone to see just what getting rich in China meant.

Mr Zhou, a tall and assertive man from the Foreign Ministry in Beijing, bustled about, dividing us up into groups to go and look at one of the houses. In front of the nearest one two men waited, a small, pinched-looking local official who was sweating nervously under a white nylon shirt and Wang, the owner of the house, a man with a sly and lazy air whose belly tumbled out over the top of his shorts.

'Come in, come in,' Wang urged us, as we passed through a large wrought-iron gate and across a courtyard covered in shiny marble paving stones. The courtyard was dominated by a fountain, as pretentious as any Roman fountain, in the centre of which a fish made of grey concrete was spouting water. In a corner stood a bright red motorcycle, and in another a new white washing-machine.

The house, still not quite finished, had three storeys but many of the rooms were empty, their concrete floors and walls bare. It was almost as if their owners had not yet decided what to do with them. In their backyard, the Wangs still kept pigs, but every floor of their house had a bathroom and the biggest boasted gold taps and a jacuzzi. By the time we had finished the tour and sat in the front parlour sipping tea out of gold-rimmed cups, Mr Zhou from the Foreign Ministry was looking a little shaken.

'Wang is a rich peasant,' he explained unnecessarily. 'You see, since the Third Plenum of the Eleventh Party Congress some peasants have been allowed to get rich before others.'

This phrase, repeated like a mantra throughout the 1980s, referred to the Communist Party's convocation held at the end of 1978 which consolidated Deng Xiaoping's hold on power and adopted new policies. It gave the signal to abandon Mao Zedong's egalitarian crusade, dissolve the people's communes, reopen markets and allow the peasants to lease land and start their own businesses. Party newspapers soon began boasting about the number of '10,000 yuan households' which were emerging.

Wang slouched back in his chair with a smirk on his face, saying little but clearly enjoying Mr Zhou's discomfort. He knew, as we did, that Mr Zhou almost certainly lived in a cramped one-bedroom flat in a Beijing apartment block that smelt of cabbage and cinders.

Mr Zhou kept glancing around, taking in the big imported Japanese colour television, the large stereo and speakers, the new plastic telephone, the plump sofas in red imitation leather and the see-through plastic and steel coffee tables, still not quite sure whether this was for real or some contrived Potemkin village. Mao's China had been full of model communes to which visitors were taken on visits which, as Mr Zhou knew only too well, were plotted as thoroughly as any play.

On the walls, there were calendar posters in which slim Chinese beauties posed in bikinis but the Wangs had also hung up reproduction posters of classical European paintings showing half-naked gods and goddesses, very plump and full-breasted.

In the doorway watching us stood a number of women, an old crone dressed in faded blue cotton tunic and trousers guarding a couple of children and several younger women. Mr Zhou's gaze switched to their nails, painted bright pink, and their piled-up and lacquered hair, clearly wondering which was Wang's wife and what his relationship with the other women might be. Then, apparently deciding that all this was too far from Communist austerity to be contrived, he changed the subject. Addressing Wang in a hearty, patronizing tone, he asked: 'And what about your son, eh? Education is very important.'

After Wang had replied unintelligibly in the local Zhejiang dialect, Mr Zhou turned to us with an air of triumph. 'You see, even though Mr Wang is a rich peasant, he knows education is very necessary. He wants his son to be an educated man, a scientist or an engineer.'

Here was one area where Mr Zhou, as a scholar and official, enjoyed a sense of superiority over a mere peasant who spat watermelon seeds on the floor. He felt, much as any Confucian gentleman might have done, that money could not be used to buy status. But which of the children was Wang's son? Who was destined for scholastic honours?

At this moment, the local official, who had said little until now, broke in and began to warn us that we must go or we would be late for a banquet with the governor. Herding the now suspicious journalists out of the parlour, he tried to avoid questions about the one-child policy.

'We have to be very strict,' he insisted, as the waiting bus gunned its engine, 'only one child except in exceptional circumstances. Of course, those who break the rules must pay heavy fines,' he added.

'And Wang, how many children does he have?'

'Yes, yes, he paid the fines,' the local official said hastily, correctly guessing that the bus would leave before he could be pressured into saying any more.

Even in the early 1930s, when Mao Zedong's guerrilla forces controlled only remote rural areas, it was Communist Party policy to destroy the class of *fu nong*, or rich peasants, in these so-called soviets. The notion came directly from Stalin's assault on the kulaks in the Soviet Union, and in China, too, the rich peasants were executed and stripped of all their possessions.

It therefore came as a shock to revolutionary veterans to see in the 1980s how swiftly the *fu nong* class became rich again and how quickly they trampled over Party edicts and reverted to old 'feudal' ways. Zhejiang officials naturally preferred not to draw the attention of these Maoists to what was clearly not so much reform as restoration.

When peasants could afford it, they acquired concubines and paid off local officials to breach the one-child laws. They buried their parents in grand style, and in some places they dug up their ancestors to reinter them in marble tombs, ignoring pleas to avoid extravagance and conserve scarce arable land. Whole hillsides in parts of coastal China soon became sprinkled with white horseshoe-shaped graves.

The speed and direction of change were doubly striking because even the authors of the policies that had prompted change, Deng Xiaoping and his lieutenants Hu Yaobang and Zhao Ziyang, had not predicted such immediate success. Lifelong believers in Communism, they had hoped their first cautious steps might lift food production. Instead they found they had set in motion a form of industrialization.

'Generally speaking, our rural reforms have proceeded very fast, and farmers have been enthusiastic. What took us completely by surprise was the development of township and rural industries,' Deng Xiaoping told some Yugoslavian visitors in June 1987. 'All sorts of small enterprises boomed in the countryside, as if a strange army had appeared suddenly from nowhere. This is not the achievement of our central government. Every year, township and village enterprises achieve 20 per cent growth. This was not something I had thought about. Nor had the other comrades. It surprised us.'[1]

The township and village enterprises to which he referred, generally known as TVEs, were actually old market towns that in the 1950s had become the administrative headquarters of communes. Such urban centres boasted small enterprises that distributed, stored and processed agricultural products and produced manufactured goods such as garments, shoes, umbrellas, pots and pans, ploughs and other agricultural tools. In the richer parts of China, these centres might also maintain and restore trucks and tractors.

Some were private enterprises that had been nationalized. Others were factories that had been built during the industrialization drive that culminated in the Great Leap Forward of 1958. In the wake of the subsequent economic collapse and during the Cultural Revolution when anti-urban policies predominated, these townships were neglected. And since there was neither surplus food nor cash crops to trade in markets, they lost their *raison d'être*.

Now they had taken off again, and local officials were able to plough money into repairing buildings, buying new machinery and expanding production. These enterprises were on a different scale to the sort of businesses set up by peasant households after 1979. The latter specialized in breeding rabbits, pigs or fish, or ran restaurants, or tailoring or carpentry businesses, but many of the TVEs were enterprises that employed hundreds, sometimes thousands of peasant workers.

By the mid-1990s, over half of China's industrial output came from rural enterprises that operated outside the planned economy. They were owned and managed by local Party committees but they did not come under the direction of national ministries. As will be seen, the furious explosion of growth eventually peaked and by the end of the 1990s many of the TVEs had collapsed under a mountain of debt.

From the outset in the 1980s, peasants in every part of China wanted to get rich in the same way. In particular, they sought to emulate three regions centred on river deltas. The first, referred to as Su Nan (an abbreviation of the Chinese for southern Jiangsu), includes the rich Yangtze delta region, Shanghai and Hangzhou, and also the northern part of Zhejiang province. Before the revolution, this was the wealthiest part of China, famous for its three crops of rice each year, its fish, pearls, silk, tea and fruit. Linked by a dense network of canals, lakes and rivers, this was where the first industrial textile mills were set up in the early twentieth century, and many of China's leading capitalist families came from towns in the region such as Wuxi, Shaoxing, Ningbo, Suzhou, Wuhu and Yangzhou, the birthplace of Jiang Zemin, the current leader of China. The country's twelve richest counties are also to be found in this area, among them China's richest village, Huaxi, which became so wealthy from its factories that in 1993 its revenues amounted to 500 million yuan and it was able to buy each of its 300 families a new Audi saloon car.

A second model was Wenzhou, a coastal enclave further south in Zhejiang province that had once been a treaty port but which had none of the communication advantages of the Yangtze delta towns. Mountains cut off the port from the rest of China, and in the 1980s it had no railway or good roads linking it with the interior. Yet Wenzhou flourished because the locals started up their own little factories producing all kinds of small haberdashery articles that they somehow manage to sell everywhere.

The third centre of rural prosperity lay in the Pearl River delta which benefited not only from its proximity to Hong Kong but also from favourable central government policies. In 1979 the province of Guangdong was designated as a laboratory of reform and Deng Xiaoping staked his reputation on the success of the newly established Shenzhen Special Economic Zone (SEZ), the export processing zone he established adjacent to Hong Kong, and two others in the province, Shantou, from where many had emigrated before 1949, and Zhuhai, adjacent to Macao.*

All three regions were part of a strategy of providing special policies and resources for the seaboard regions, and cities like Shenzhen were built from scratch according to a blueprint. However, it was not such designated planned development that necessarily created the new wealth, but rather the unplanned rural enterprises that operated on the margins of what was officially permitted.

In Su Nan, people like the Wangs more or less ignored the Party's directives or at least its ideology. Wang worked at one of thirteen textile factories in what was formerly a brigade, or subdivision, of the Red Mountain Commune and was now a township. Despite being dubbed 'farmers', the Wangs employed poor peasants from the interior to farm their land or do the dirtiest jobs in the factory. Many others subcontracted work from state enterprises in Shanghai and were helped by engineers or technicians sent from China's great industrial centre.

In another county in Zhejiang, Party officials introduced us to Lu Guanqiu, a model 'farm entrepreneur' who took a tiny toolshed with seven workers and turned it into a collective employing 1,000 workers producing auto parts. By 1990, it employed 2,000 workers, was exporting abroad and had also branched out into industrial-scale breeding of pigs, poultry, eels and snakes. Such men with real entrepreneurial drive and vision often came to dominate the whole economy of their township even though political power rested with the local Party.[2]

---

* For more on the Special Economic Zones, see Chapter 5.

Then there was Bu Xinsheng, the diminutive but caustic manager who took the Haiyan General Shirt Factory in hand and turned its products into a national brand. Once a faltering and run-down collective factory with 100 employees, within seven years it was employing 800 people and turning out 1.7 million shirts a year. Bu imported Japanese machinery and methods, including the singing of a factory song that he had written himself, the refrain of which was: 'Try Harder, Try Harder.' As a result, he became a national model fêted by the media, was appointed as a delegate to the National People's Congress and was visited by thousands, including senior Party leaders. Yet his willingness to fire lazy workers made him hated.

'I was attacked on the street. They even came to my house so I had to hire bodyguards to protect myself,' he told visiting journalists. To transform the factory, he had doubled salaries, introduced piecework and punished workers who indulged in reading newspapers, eating, sleeping and whistling on the job. In other words he had put an end to all those practices which the Chinese media liked to call 'eating out of the same big pot'.

While Bu openly scoffed at the officials who interfered in everything he tried to do and eventually fell out with local Party leaders, Lu Guanqiu was more cautious. 'This is a socialist country, and this factory is a socialist cell,' he said, explaining why he had turned down an annual bonus tied to profits that would have amounted to US$80,000, a far cry from the annual earnings of his workers, which averaged US$240.

In 1987 Zhejiang's brash Shirt King fell victim to an ideological chill. Bu was ousted from his position, vaguely accused of 'arrogance, high-handedness and imperiousness, and ignorance of state policies'. The *Zhejiang Workers' Daily* went further, condemning him as a 'dictator'. Even so, a decade later Bu was to be found running his own shirt company in the northern port of Qinhuangdao where he had hung up a giant portrait of himself outside his headquarters.[3]

Although they functioned outside the state plan, the rural enterprises of Su Nan belonged to the former communes and much was made of the fact that these were not private family concerns but collectively owned units which were therefore socialist. As such these collective factories tended to adhere to the same restrictions and work practices as the state factories managed by the central government. Even so they had an advantage over real state enterprises because they operated under fewer layers of bureaucracy and therefore could respond more quickly to changing market demand.

By contrast, in Wenzhou nearly all the factories were run by real private entrepreneurs. In fact Wenzhou cared less about model workers and economic theories and showed less evidence of state interference than anywhere else in China. Perhaps this was because the region lacked a tradition of state involvement. Long regarded as vulnerable to a possible invasion of the mainland by Taiwan, Wenzhou had never possessed any commune enterprises.

There were other reasons behind Wenzhou's astonishing entrepreneurial flair. The area has a population of nearly 8 million people but little agricultural land. Traditionally, locals travelled about China as pedlars or itinerant tailors. Indeed Beijing had its own Wenzhou enclave where tailors were ready to copy any garment that was brought to them. Many also emigrated, and Wenzhou communities can be found even in such unlikely spots as Holland and Italy.

In the Mao era, hundreds of thousands of Wenzhou inhabitants were punished for resisting collectivization, but in the 1980s the place began to boom, despite the fact that it was a bumpy twelve-hour drive from the nearest railway or big city. Locals fanned out across China, chiefly selling buttons, combs and other trinkets ignored by the state planners in Beijing. In little villages all around the port, small workshops sprang up with a few pieces of machinery where teenage girls sat endlessly punching out buttons, and Wenzhou soon boasted of being the world's button capital.[4]

Everyone in Wenzhou cheerfully ignored regulations on working hours, health and safety, insurance and pollution, and most of all the limitations on the number of workers a businessman could hire (in the 1980s, this amounted to just six). They could do so because they did not rely on state banks for credit or on the state bureaucracy for contacts to market their goods abroad. Wenzhou is full of private banks, operating seven days a week, and many locals have relatives living abroad. Just to be on the safe side, however, many enterprises registered themselves as 'collective enterprises', a practice known as 'wearing a red hat'.

Even the local government did not bother much with applying for central government aid because it could finance its own investment in roads and bridges from local taxes. Where bigger sums were needed to build ports or power stations, wealthy tycoons from Hong Kong, Taiwan, Thailand or Indonesia stepped in to help their ancestral home.

An entirely lawless distribution system quickly grew up along the whole of the southern coast of China. Ports such as Wenzhou, Shishi or Shantou became smugglers' havens that imported whatever was wanted, duty-free. Contraband cigarettes, music, metals, oil and petroleum products, and manufactured consumer goods such as cars and television sets were brought in. Pirated CDs and video tapes, fake designer jeans, shoes and leather goods went out.

Dozens of commercial markets sprang up in once obscure towns such as Yiwu where, each day, several hundred thousand people congregated at over 25,000 stalls selling textiles, shoes, haberdashery and other household goods. Hangzhou had its sweater market, Haining a leather market. Altogether there were over 4,000 such markets in Zhejiang with an annual turnover of 254.5 billion yuan.[5]

As elsewhere, the wealth created from all these rural enterprises fuelled a housing boom as everyone quickly moved out of their mud and straw huts and into two- or three-storey houses. Wenzhou even began running out of land to house the dead because so many new and extravagant tombs were being built. On top of a hill outside the port, the local government was forced to build a public cemetery in which, to save space, the coffins of the deceased were stacked on shelves like cans of beans in a supermarket. The shelves, however, remained empty. Even in death, Wenzhou's people preferred to be buried in private.

In the neo-Maoist backlash that followed the Tiananmen massacre of 1989, Wenzhou came under pressure to rein in its capitalists and some were even arrested. Leftist ideologues complained bitterly that the bourgeoisie were taking over and that 80 per cent of the enterprises registered as 'collectives' in Fujian and Guangdong were actually private businesses. Five years later, with the tide running the other way, Zhejiang officials felt it safe to boast that many of its township enterprises had 'thrown off their red hats' and were now the country's biggest taxpayers.[6]

From the beginning the Pearl River delta in Guangdong province enjoyed the blessing of Deng Xiaoping. That fact alone made it a model that the rest of rural China wanted to copy. Yet it too thrived in the murky region where benign tolerance of private enterprise drifts into corruption, and capitalism becomes barely distinguishable from piracy. 'If something is not explicitly prohibited, then move ahead,' said Ren Zhongyu, Guangdong's Party Secretary, in 1980. 'If something is allowed, use it to the hilt.'

From 1979 onwards, Deng permitted 'special policies' in Guangdong. The province's peasants were exempted from the one-child policy and allowed to have two children, and the provincial government was exempted from having to contribute tax revenues to the central government coffers. There were also other factors that favoured development. Three of the country's four SEZs were in the province, and Guangdong was, and still is, the ancestral home of the largest group of overseas Chinese. And it was served by Hong Kong, China's most important port, its biggest source of capital and its 'window on the world'.

Guangdong benefited too from its special political ties. It lay within the military command of Marshal Ye Jianying, the kingmaker after the death of Mao who led the coup against Mao's wife and engineered first the protection and then the elevation of Deng to supreme leader. For nearly a decade, Ye's son, Ye Xuanping, served as provincial governor, and a former senior official in Guangdong, Zhao Ziyang, became in the 1980s first Prime Minister and then Party General Secretary.

This kind of political protection, so lacking in Wenzhou, allowed the Cantonese to remain one step ahead. The province abandoned Communist dogma long before the centre did so, and after the backlash following Tiananmen, it was to Guangdong that Deng chose to go in order to restart his reforms. In 1992, he began his southern tour, taking in Shenzhen and Zhuhai, which set in motion a new wave of investment.*

The Pearl River delta, with a population of 14 million people crammed into 4,000 square miles, is much smaller than the Yangtze delta, where 70 million live in 38,000 square miles, and is also amongst the world's most densely populated areas. Places such as Nanhai, with nearly 2,000 people per square mile, have the same population density as New York. However, like the Yangtze delta, the region benefits from a network of waterways linking 200 small ports and 20 larger ones. The hinterland, by contrast, is poor and mountainous. In the 1980s so many counties within it were designated as poverty areas that half of all Cantonese were said to live in them.

Unlike the Yangtze delta, where Shanghai's huge concentration of industry and know-how spread its influence throughout the Mao era, the explosion of economic growth in Guangdong followed years of neglect. Until 1978, state investment on a per capita basis was the lowest in the country. As the Party and the army relaxed their iron grip, Guangdong resumed a pattern of growth that had been interrupted for thirty years. Places such as Humen, a county in the Pearl River estuary, that had once prospered during the nineteenth century, moved effortlessly from smuggling opium to pirating Reebok trainers. Now the area is just a couple of hours' drive from Hong Kong. Along the motorway that links Hong Kong with Guangzhou (formerly Canton), one passes through several border fences and checkpoints that, like a set of airlocks, still isolate the former British colony from Shenzhen, and Shenzhen from the rest of China. At night the journey offers an oriental vision of the Industrial Revolution. The sour air is thick with pollution and, as one passes factory after factory, through the illuminated windows one can glimpse endless rows of peasant girls seated patiently in front of their machines.

Humen (literally Tiger's Gate) lies in the prefecture of Dongguan, one of the prosperous areas called the 'four tigers' bordering both sides of the estuary. Early European traders also called this the Bocca Tigris, the Jaws of the Tiger, with rather different implications. The

---

* Deng's southern tour was strongly reminiscent of those undertaken by the Manchu Emperor Qianlong between 1684 and 1707.

Portuguese, Dutch, French, British and American traders who sailed up the Pearl River from Macao on their annual visits to the port of Guangzhou where they were permitted to trade, had to pass by strong fortifications.

Eventually, the Qing dynasty permitted the traders to live on an island outside the walled city of Guangzhou where they set up their 'factories' for selling opium and buying Chinese porcelain, silk and tea. It was here that the First Opium War started in 1839 when the Qing Emperor Dao Guang ordered an end to the trade in opium and sent a high mandarin, Lin Zexu, to confiscate the traders' stores without compensation.

At the centre of Humen's county town, the local authorities have now built a pair of gigantic hands which reach out of the ground to snap in half a huge opium pipe. Behind them, a giant frieze shows how boxes of opium were smuggled ashore in Humen. Nearby, at Sandy Point, the Qing navy constructed one of a series of gun forts which commanded the entrance to Guangzhou. A pontoon and chain were stretched across the waterway in an effort to stop the Royal Navy from approaching and bombarding the city. Such defences proved fruitless.

At Sandy Point Fortress, where the British fired the opening shots of the First Opium War, there are now statues erected to the memory of its commander, Chen Liangsheng, his son and even the commander's horse, which patriotically died of hunger in Hong Kong where it kicked every Englishman who came near. Visitors are invited to enter a chamber of horrors and take part in 'search-and-destroy drug smuggler missions'. This involves blasting laser guns at grinning automatons with red hair who glide along on rails rasping 'Bastard! I'll chop you.' Further along the coast is the Lin Zexu Memorial Hall where the confiscated opium was actually destroyed in pits and where visitors can fire rubber balls from cannons at Royal Navy men-of-war painted on a wall.

Humen now owes its prosperity to Hong Kong, the island ceded to the British at the end of the First Opium War. Locals boast that its 1,500 Hong Kong-run factories have made the county so rich that it pays more taxes to Beijing than anywhere else. Its 100,000 citizens are now outnumbered by its population of 200,000 migrant workers, and the prefecture of Dongguan as a whole has become the industrial backyard of Hong Kong, drawing 1.5 million migrant workers from all over China.

There are so many factories, warehouses and dormitories where once there were only poor villages, fish ponds and paddy fields that even the local officials in Humen lose their way.

'Ten years ago, there were no roads here, not even telephones,' Li Chi-chung, the Hong Kong manager of the Kin Hang Electronics firm, told me on a visit in 1997. He preferred to dress casually in jeans and a polo shirt but the local officials wore business suits with belts strung with beepers and mobile phones.

We passed from the factory floor to a canteen where girls who worked twelve-hour shifts assembling headphones were eating lunch out of enamel bowls.

'And it was so easy to employ people,' Li added. 'If you wanted fifty workers, there would be five hundred waiting outside the next day, many of them high-school graduates. Now if you want fifty only five apply.'

Wang Kangquan, a paunchy Humen official in charge of propaganda, laughed at this. 'Nobody likes to work here much now. Locals won't work in factories,' he said, scratching his shock of thick grey hair. Peasants now lived off the rent from their built-over farmland and were able to send their children to be educated at private boarding schools.

Over dinner that evening Wang fell to reminiscing about the past. We sat in the private room of a restaurant whose portico was supported by a pair of naked Greek caryatids and surmounted by a giant bust of Caesar in a helmet. Nearby, turtles, pigeons, pheasant, rabbits and other wild creatures were held in mesh cages waiting to be eaten. Dish after dish arrived, and a bottle of Hennessy XO brandy appeared as Wang recalled the hard times of the past. 'I was the Party secretary of a production brigade in Bai Sha with 4,000 peasants and it was my job to stop people escaping. We all knew life was much better in Hong Kong. Every year about a hundred people would try to escape and about forty would succeed.'

Young people would pretend to go out bird-hunting, throw away their guns and then walk at night across the hills to Shenzhen. From there they could paddle across the river. Others would try to flee by boat or bicycle to a colony which, by the 1970s, was running short of labour.

'You should have a Chinese heart. Britain invaded Hong Kong so you should stay here and think of our national dignity,' he would tell those who were caught before they were sent off to be punished with a three-month stint of hard labour. 'Of course, in those days we local people envied those who had succeeded in getting to Hong Kong. We knew there was plenty to eat and buy there.'

Then, after 1979, it was his turn to go to Hong Kong, initially to try to distribute local farm products – fruit, fish and preserved ducks. Later, touting for investors, Wang often came across the very people he had once caught and punished. 'When I met such people, we would say nothing. We never mentioned the past, only business,' he said. The former brigade of Bai Sha, with a population of 5,600, now has 85 factories employing 15,000 migrant workers.

'I wouldn't want to live in Hong Kong now. Look how expensive housing is there and how small. Here we all have three-storey houses,' he said, and he paused to fill my glass. 'Besides, everyone works so hard in Hong Kong.'[7]

Smuggling contraband goods from Hong Kong to small ports such as Humen is still the real way to get rich, much as it was when Hong Kong was first founded. In 1998 and 1999, anti-smuggling campaigns in the province often netted the entire bureaucracy of a port, and hundreds of local officials running the harbour, the customs, the police and the Party organization were imprisoned. But hard work, at least by the 7 or 8 million migrant workers packed into the rich Pearl River delta, has done much to change the fortunes of the province and has inspired many inland provinces. The trickle-down effect has been immediate. The Pearl River delta imports pigs and rice from Hunan and Sichuan while migrant labourers from those provinces send home their wages, thereby injecting cash directly into the local economy.

Yet it is not only wealth that has trickled down. In the 1980s and 1990s the envy excited by the overnight wealth of peasants like those in Humen, reckoned to be no more industrious or educated than those anywhere else, created a feverish desire throughout China to embark on a similar industrialization. The formula for success seemed so simple that cadres in townships in the most neglected corners of the country felt able to plunge into the production of leather goods, shoes, shirts, suits and household appliances.

Attracted by low wages and low taxes, small and large manufacturers from Taiwan, South Korea, Italy, the United States and elsewhere eagerly co-operated in providing the necessary equipment, capital, brands and marketing. In 1979, Chinese garment factories produced just 744 million pieces of clothing, or less than one per person. Between 1991 and 1996, China imported textile manufacturing plant worth US$5 billion, enabling it to become the world's largest garment-maker. In 1996, it exported garments worth US$38 billion, or 16.7 per cent of global clothing exports. In the shirt sector alone, China had 4,000 factories, some with an annual capacity of a million units, and another 500 coming on stream each year. National output peaked in 1997 at 1.55 billion units.

The figures in other sectors of the textile market were no less astonishing. In 1989, China had 3,000 leather factories. Seven years later there were 20,000 employing 1.5 million workers. In the same period Guangdong's exports of shoes quadrupled. By 1998, it was producing 20 per cent of the world's leather shoes, some 2 billion pairs a year, and the whole of China was producing 6.3 billion pairs. China had become the world's biggest producer of leather products, and leather shoes were its second largest export item.

The country also became the world's biggest manufacturer of sports shoes, a billion pairs a year from 5,000 manufacturers. For while the world's top brands manufactured and assembled their products in China, they also spawned a host of counterfeiters. In southern Jiangsu, home to some of the biggest rural shoe-making factories, it is said that nine out of ten pairs of sneakers on sale are fakes.

The explosion of investment in new manufacturing capacity which spread across China helped absorb a vast surplus of rural labour, estimated at 130 million people, mostly under the age of 30. In their heyday, between 1985 to 1995, rural enterprises were creating up to 12 million new jobs a year, and in the 1980s they absorbed 80 million surplus rural labourers.[8]

By 1998, however, domestic and international demand had been satiated and rural enterprises stopped growing. Amidst a vast and growing inventory of surplus goods, the number of registered rural enterprises fell by 2 million to 20 million. In just two years, 1997 and 1998, some 20 million peasant workers lost their jobs. Many returned to their villages, and the remittances from those working in townships and cities began to shrink. Since this income represented about a quarter of the spending money available to peasant households, unsurprisingly rural consumer demand fell. At the same time, unemployment loomed ever larger as a political challenge. Each year a further 13 million new labourers join the job market and some officials believe that net rural unemployment is rising by 9 million a year.[9]

The turning-point coincided with the Asian financial crisis that began in 1997: in fact the two events may well have been intimately connected. China was after all competing with its neighbours to export the same products. Even before demand slumped in the Asia Pacific region, Chinese manufacturers housed staggering amounts of unsold goods: 1.5 billion men's shirts, 300 million pairs of leather shoes, 20 million bicycles, 10 million watches and 700,000 motorcycles. As the stocks piled up, factories in most manufacturing sectors began running at 50 per cent, and often less, of their capacity.[10]

With demand never achieving the potential suggested by China's population, many rural enterprises began to collapse under their debts and go bankrupt. Changes to the tax system exacerbated the crisis. In 1994, Beijing had introduced new tax laws requiring rural enterprises to pay taxes directly to the central government instead of to local governments. The latter consequently no longer had a vested interest in offering their support. The corporate tax rate also rose from 14 per cent to 33 per cent, the same rate as paid by state-owned factories.

It was often areas in the interior that had jumped into the market last that collapsed first. In Hunan province, the rural enterprises set up by local governments ran up cumulative debts of 6 billion yuan. As described in Chapter 2, townships all across Hunan, no longer able to pay their staff, began to raise taxes from the peasants who responded in anger because their own incomes were declining.[11]

As the rural enterprises went under, the rural banking system crumbled with them. The 50,000 agricultural co-operative banks that take peasant savings and had loaned them out to these ventures ended up with liabilities that exceeded their assets. The major source of fresh credit in the countryside therefore dried up, leaving places like Wenzhou with its private banks or the Pearl River delta where Cantonese could raise money in Hong Kong in an advantageous position.

The shake-out among rural enterprises coincided with an ideological shift. The opening of stock markets after 1992 had prompted a greater tolerance towards raw capitalism, at least in some parts of the country. Indeed, spontaneous privatization began to take place even before the Communist Party officially endorsed the idea at its 1997 Congress. In the Pearl River delta, the Cantonese were quick to grasp opportunities, or as the Chinese saying has it, they were the first to dare to eat a crab.

Shunde prefecture, another of the four 'tigers' of the Peal River estuary and situated just across from Humen, is home to some of the biggest and most profitable collective enterprises in China, especially those making household electrical appliances. Here they began turning the collectively owned enterprises into joint-stock companies before anyone else.

'We just did it without consulting anyone. We sold them all, several hundred in total, because even in 1992 we could see this was inevitable,' said Shunde's Deputy Party Secretary, Zhao Guanya, as he sat at the vast teak boardroom table of the Wanjiale Group, the largest manufacturer of gas-fired water-heaters in Asia. 'Everyone agreed to keep quiet about it. We were worried that if some left-wing ideologues in Beijing heard about it, they might stop us,' he said with refreshing candour.[12]

Often, just what this very private privatization amounted to was hard to discern. In Wenzhou, where 90 per cent of industrial output was the work of family businesses, it was easy to see. By casting off their 'red hats', they simply stopped pretending to be collectives. But up in the Yangtze delta, where the Su Nan model had won much praise, a survey by Professor Qin Hui of Qinghua University revealed a very different pattern. There Party officials were often intent on acquiring the profitable factories for themselves and leaving the debts of bankrupt ones to be shouldered by the banks or local government. And factories which had begun to lose money after 1995 and were subsequently sold off mysteriously started to make money after a buyout. In many cases, the Party secretary of an enterprise sold it to himself, naturally at a very reasonable price and sometimes without even telling the workers.

'In some cases, I found that there was no evaluation of assets, no open bidding or auction. The guardian of the collectively owned assets simply seized possession of them,' Professor Qin said. 'However, these things only came to light if there was an open fight between different Party officials.'

In one case he investigated, villagers tried to sue the Party secretary for misappropriating collectively owned assets and were surprised to find that, unknown to them, he had signed a contract selling them to himself two years earlier. In another case, a factory with an annual output worth 8 million yuan was sold for 700,000 yuan, and that price included valuable urban land. Even if an outside body such as a state asset office was involved, a Party secretary could easily direct a county audit department to obey his orders and provide a favourable valuation. Or he could set up a fake bidding process which he or his cronies would be sure to win.

Professor Qin also found cases where 'the temple is poor but the abbot is rich'. Factory managers who had enriched themselves by pocketing the profits and who had paid taxes by taking out loans from state banks were naturally able to afford to buy the indebted factory when the local government wished to rid itself of its burden. Or a manager might leave a struggling enterprise and set up his own factory, taking with him the capital, customers, staff and technology that he needed.

Other peculiar forms of privatization took place in Shandong province. There I visited Zhucheng, a county town of a million people which pioneered experiments in turning its 280 TVEs into joint-stock companies. Zhucheng's managers ran collective factories where the majority of shares were issued to themselves and a minority to the workforce. As was often the case, such shares could not be traded outside the factory, so they were of doubtful value. Sometimes the workers had to find the cash to buy shares in an indebted factory or they would lose their jobs. Sometimes they lost both their jobs and the money they had invested.[13]

At Zhucheng I met Duo Baorong, chairman of the board, Party secretary, general manager and majority shareholder of the Sida Insulating Material Company which made electrical insulating material. A front-page article in the *People's Daily*, of which he had a blown-up copy in his office, praised him for transforming an ugly duckling into a swan. When Duo took charge, he turned a small, loss-making TVE into a profitable giant. He was now determined to take over the 200 smaller and often struggling domestic competitors. Private ownership was, he said, a 'magic wand' which transformed the attitude of both workers and managers. By jumping the gun on privatization, his company now had a head start: 'Everyone knows that the first to make reforms always has a competitive advantage.'

The lack of transparency and of proper accounting standards not only made the affairs of collective enterprises impenetrable but also confused the true ownership of other ventures. Some factories registered as foreign joint ventures turned out on closer examination to be local companies run by a local Party boss but registered in Hong Kong to benefit from tax exemptions and the right to import goods tax-free. On the other hand, genuine foreign investors might find that their joint-venture partner had set up a rival company in order to acquire the know-how and technology cheaply after he had driven the joint venture into failure.

For the peasant, the Party's power to appropriate his valuable and scarce arable land for industrial purposes was often the most significant and bitterly disputed part of this process. Whether or not a factory was built or flourished, the land underneath could often be resold to developers by Party officials at ten times the sum offered to the peasant. The peasant usually received some compensation but nothing like the amount earned by members of the peasant *rentier* class of Humen such as Mr Wang. In protest some peasants resorted to sit-ins and demonstrations or appeals to higher authorities or they tried to take their local government to court. More often than not such attempts were in vain.

By the end of the 1990s, the glow around the rural enterprises, or TVEs, had begun to fade and they were no longer being routinely hailed as 'China's economic miracle'. Instead many were being blamed for causing rampant pollution and in 1997 the central government took action, ordering the closure of tens of thousands of TVEs engaged in mining and washing coal, tanning leather, making paper and dyeing textiles.

A report by the Institute of Rural Development of the Chinese Academy of Social Sciences claimed that losses attributable to pollution by rural enterprises were equal to 3.27 per cent of China's gross domestic product. 'Although this sounds an enormous figure, experts point out that this only covers the losses which can be calculated. The real losses caused by pollution are much higher,' commented the *Beijing Morning Post*.[14]

Rural enterprises were blamed for spewing out 4.3 billion tonnes of waste water a year and the central government launched a series of military-style campaigns called Zero Hour Operations to enforce regulations along major rivers, the Huai He, Hai He and Liao He, and three key lakes, Tai Hu, Dianchi and Chao Hu. The first Zero Hour Operation required local governments to shut down all the factories along the Huai He that failed to meet discharge standards at midnight on 1 January 1998. They included 500 paper mills. Dubbed the 'biggest sewage ditch in central China', the action was preceded by a propaganda campaign. The *China Youth Daily* published a photograph of a desperate 60-year-old peasant kneeling in front of Xie Zhenhua, director of the National Environmental Protection Agency, pleading for him to save the livelihood of fishermen. Discharges from thousands of small factories in Henan and Anhui provinces were poisoning the Huai He's water, killing fish, ruining crops and harming people.

Many of the factories closed, among them 21,000 small and medium-sized paper mills that had sprung up in the 1990s and that had created over a million jobs. Hebei province alone closed 10,000 plants, including the United Paper Mill in Wuji county, about 130 miles south of Beijing, which I subsequently visited.

'We've been shut down for five months. It's the same everywhere,' said a labourer, waving his arm at the brown countryside. The red-brick chimney behind him was smokeless as were others on the flat, treeless horizon. 'Of course, we lost a pile of money and laid off twenty workers but what can you do?'

A year earlier, he and a group of local farmers had invested about a million yuan in buying new production machinery with the capacity to make a million tonnes of paper a year. Further down the road, dozens of smaller tanneries had also closed down.

'Most of them were not making any money anyway. The quality was too bad,' he said. For the moment he was going back to growing vegetables. 'These campaigns always blow over in a while. Then we will get back to work or sell the machinery to another part of the country.'

Though such campaigns generate much publicity, local government officials rarely enforce punitive fines on the polluters, many of which are factories operated by the very same group of cadres.

In 1999, the press highlighted the first case of police offering a reward and then tracking down and arresting two peasants who had dumped six tonnes of dangerous chemicals near reservoirs that supplied two counties in Zhejiang province. Zhejiang is home to 3,000 chemical plants as well as a concentration of thousands of township textile and dyeing plants, all anxious to get rid of their waste cheaply. The black glutinous mixture of benzene, naphthalene, indolene and pyride dumped by the two peasants was corrosive enough to kill all the fish in nearby streams and burn the latex gloves of the investigators. If the drums of waste buried in a roadside pit had contaminated the reservoirs, up to a million people could have been poisoned.[15]

The central government was also only partially successful in its goal of forcing local governments to close 20,000 out of 80,000 small rural coalmines. Often local officials depended heavily on the profits they generated. The coalmines illustrate another cost of rural industry, the loss of lives as a result of poor health and safety standards. Every year, about 5,000 miners are reported to die in accidents at these small mines.[16]

Yet whatever the defects of the TVEs, their importance is bound to grow in the future. Before the slowdown, Chinese experts had hoped to keep rural unemployment down to around 100 million by 2005, but some experts now fear there will be an army of between 150 million and 200 million.[17]

The employment problem goes deeper than finding sufficient demand for products in a country where, though there are 900 million peasants, the average annual income is only about US$230. It may also be a consequence of new manufacturing technology which requires less labour. Even in traditionally labour-intensive industries such as textiles many machines are now so automated that they no longer require untrained operatives. And thanks to earlier policies which destroyed traditions of craftsmanship and neglected industrial training, few Chinese peasants have the skills in woodwork or metalwork that might support a different kind of industry.

The Chinese government has even tried to issue instructions to local governments not to use heavy earth-moving machinery in construction projects in order to create more pick-and-shovel jobs, but to no avail. Too many county governments have bought or leased tractors and bulldozers operated by a government TVE to want to leave them idle. Besides, not even China's rural labourers are so lowly paid that machines cannot, in many cases, do the work more quickly and more cheaply.[18]

As China changes, the task of preventing this army of the rural unemployed from migrating to the booming cities will become politically and economically impossible. As the next chapter describes, China needs to urbanize quickly and on a massive scale.

4

Behind the Walls

Mrs guo yenfen still lives in the sprawling courtyard house that her rich banker husband bequeathed her nearly fifty years ago, in one of the last walled cities left in China. Hobbling about on her bound feet, she poked at the briquette stove to heat up some tea in the dank single room which is all she has left.

'My husband had a heart attack quarrelling with officials about the house,' she recalled. 'They wanted to move in a lot of other families.'

Six families now share the house which lies behind a big red door off one of the alleyways in Pingyao, Shanxi province, about 300 miles south-west of Beijing. Just as in the capital, the old houses have ash-grey brick walls, green-tiled roofs and carved wooden lattice windows. In the late 1950s, when Mao had Beijing's vast city ramparts torn down, the walls protecting many of China's towns and villages were also demolished. Yet by some quirk of fate, Pingyao, with its seventy-two towers and moat, survived unscathed.

Mrs Guo, a country girl married off as her husband's second wife, witnessed the decline of Pingyao as a major domestic banking centre, the Japanese occupation and then the civil war between Communist and Nationalist forces.

'Everything was lost. All the furniture disappeared when the Japanese devils came,' she said, 'apart from these things.' And from a cupboard beside her mattress, she pulled out her late husband's abacus and a pair of brass scales.[1]

Pingyao survived even the rampages of the Red Guards during the Cultural Revolution and it remains a complete model of fourteenth-century Ming dynasty urban planning frozen in time. Through it all, the city has retained a robust medieval air of cheerfulness in its cramped streets and alleys. Cyclists ring their bells as they push patiently through streets lined with squatting peasants smoking long pipes. On either side are stalls piled with fresh vegetables and fruit or meat hung from hooks. Some vendors display magazines with half-naked women on the covers. Behind shuttered openings, shopkeepers slouch in grubby vests, slurping tea or exchanging banter with passers-by who dodge the stray dogs rooting in the rubbish.

Ever since UNESCO declared it a World Heritage site, the city has woken up to its potential as a tourist attraction. When I visited it in 1998 the streets were full of workmen busily hammering and sawing to restore the houses of the wealthy to their former glory. For once all private property had been divided up at the start of the Great Leap Forward, no one in Pingyao had wasted so much as a pot of paint on them.

In the past, cities in China were for the rich who lived in them in privacy and splendour. The Communists had no interest in preserving this memory. Yet the entrance to Mrs Guo's house is still protected by a spirit wall, two stone lions and a blessing etched over the lintel. Out on the street stand twin carved marble posts where a nobleman would tie up his horse.

Indeed, all around Pingyao, the landmarks of an archetypal Chinese city can be found. Designed according to the principles of geomancy, in shape it is almost rectangular, with four narrow gates which used to be shut at night. A Daoist temple that became a granary after 1949 is identifiable by the fallen statues of Laozi's disciples that still lie exactly where they were once cast down. A Buddhist temple that now houses a junior school stands opposite the green-tiled roofs of a temple dedicated to Confucius. In another corner of the town, a red-brick Catholic church built by missionaries is the only place of worship still serving its original purpose.

From Pingyao's centre rises a bell-tower that used to sound the hours and another tower with floating eaves that once housed the city's god. Behind a big gate at the southern end stands the *yamen* of the magistrate together with the offices of his officials and a parade-ground for the troops. Now it is the Pingyao Party committee's head-quarters and where the People's Police, judges of the people's court and the state prosecutor all have their offices. Their titles may be different but their functions are the same.

All that the Communists added was modern industry. Near the west gate stands a huge chemical factory, a utilitarian concrete box with chimneys, and there are others scattered around the city. The Communists believed in building belching factories, even in the centre of Beijing, as a mark of progress. Most are now either bankrupt or are being moved out in the interests of tourism.

In pre-Communist China, cities like Pingyao prospered as service centres. This now forgotten Shanxi town was once the country's foremost finance centre with forty-one banks or *piao hao* – literally ticket offices – as they were known.

'Capitalists? Capitalists?' puzzled Pingyao's head of tourism whom I encountered showing visitors round the restored courtyard house of the first and biggest *piao hao*, the Ri Sheng Chang Bank. 'Oh, you mean private entrepreneurs. We don't call them capitalists any more.' Between 1823 and 1932, the Ri Sheng Chang grew into a network with fifty-one branches around the country that allowed China's capitalists to offer merchants bearer bonds, promissory notes, bills of trade and even an early form of credit card. Pingyao became so rich that when foreign armies occupied Beijing after the Boxer Rebellion, the Empress Dowager fled her capital and came here. From Pingyao's banks she was able to raise 200,000 taels of silver from one house alone to help pay the enormous indemnity imposed on China by the foreign powers.

'She came and tasted my family's yellow rice wine,' boasted Guo Huairen, the sixth-generation descendant of an artisan who founded a shop on Pingyao's main street. The shop has now, like the Ri Sheng Chang, been restored to its former glory and Guo hopes it will attract tourists. As with most old cities, the locals are being moved out of the centre – Pingyao is relocating 25,000 of its 45,000 inhabitants.

In pre-1949 China, commerce was in the hands of firms, and around Pingyao are the vast rambling mansions that testify to the wealth of some of them. The House of Cao, for example, was protected by a private army of 500 martial arts warriors and resembled a fortress rather than a palace. Only a handful of the buildings that once covered over 700 acres remain. The rest were destroyed during the violent land reform of the late 1940s and early 1950s.

'All the descendants of the Cao family were persecuted and many were beaten to death,' recalled an old man who now wheels tourists around in a bicycle rickshaw. A few survived by fleeing to Hong Kong or America.

At the Qiao family mansion nearby, a guide explains how its founder, Qiao Guifa, started by peddling beancurd and yams. In five generations, the House of Qiao grew into a commercial empire that included 18 businesses trading in oil and vegetables, 200 shops, several coalmines and a bank with 20 branches across China. At the peak of its glory, 70 members of the clan lived here and were waited on by 170 servants. For generations, members had to observe the founder's 50 guidelines on how to employ people and 97 rules of behaviour, now listed in a display. Frugality was the order of the day, and concubines, gambling, drinking and the smoking of opium were all forbidden.

The Communists, who wished to destroy the 'feudal' family as the basis of Chinese society, broke up these estates. Yet in Pingyao's case, its fortunes were declining well before 1949. The rise of Shanghai with its modern factories and financial institutions brought ruinous competition.

Even so, when the Communists won the civil war, Shanghai, as a foreign-dominated city, fared no better than Pingyao. 'Shanghai is a non-productive city,' a Communist newspaper famously declared in 1949. 'It is a parasitic city. It is a criminal city. It is a refugee city. It is a paradise for adventurers.'[2]

In the first half of the twentieth century Shanghai's population had quadrupled as it drew in the workers who manned its factories and the refugees who sought an escape from invasion and famine. Visitors were both horrified and enthralled by the city with its crowded and insanitary housing, its child labour in the silk factories, its beggars who died in the streets, its prostitutes, its gangsters and the vast and ostentatious wealth of its grand families.

After the Communists entered Shanghai, Mao's government set about implementing the programme of the Communist manifesto in earnest. Bourgeois property was to be abolished; that of emigrants and rebels confiscated. Credit was to be centralized in the hands of the state by means of a national bank with state capital. Agriculture and the manufacturing industries were to be combined, with the gradual abolition of the distinction between town and country and a more equitable distribution of the population across the country.[3]

Rao Shushi, the first Communist chief of the Shanghai Municipal Committee, proposed that Shanghai's population be dispersed into the interior, along with its schools and factories. In addition its industries were to produce entirely for domestic consumption instead of the 'imperialist economy'.[4]

The Communist Party soon set about closing down Shanghai's service industries. Banks, the stock exchange, bookshops, publishing houses, tailors and beauty parlours, restaurants, tea shops and food markets were either all shut down or placed under state control. Shanghai's prostitutes were rounded up and sent for re-education as were many more respectable people including the professors at Shanghai's prestigious colleges and universities.

To establish its control over urban China as a whole, the Party resorted to several measures which closely resembled the practices of imperial China. Among them was the grain monopoly. Within a few years, urban dwellers could only obtain grain with ration tickets and these were issued through their work units. Ration tickets eventually became the sole means of obtaining over forty different kinds of goods and services including haircuts and hot water. In addition independent travel became difficult because transport was now a state monopoly and train and bus tickets were also rationed.

Hand in hand with these measures came the household registration system. The police issued residence permits, or *hukou*, to every approved urban resident. Each person also came under the control of a street committee which had responsibility for public security and which kept files on each citizen. The arrangement was not unlike the imperial *baojia* mutual security system by which the population of a city was grouped into 1,000 households, consisting of 10 *jia*, each of which contained 100 households. Under the *baojia* system each household was registered and supervised by a headman, and within a group of households all were held equally liable for the illegal acts of any individual member.

The collapse of the *baojia* system after 1911 gave Chinese intellectuals the freedom to travel as they pleased. Thus Mao was able to visit Hunan to organize the peasants, and other future leaders were free to assemble in Shanghai where the Chinese Communist Party was founded in the early 1920s. A decade later, Chiang Kai-shek's government tried to reintroduce the *baojia* system but it never attained the absolute authority over most of the country that the Communists achieved after 1949.

From the mid-1950s individuals were unable to enter or leave cities without written permission, and control posts were set up on every road. Those who managed to evade the controls and stay with relatives then found they could no longer freely obtain food or clothing.

The population was divided into two major categories, urban and rural, and then subdivided according to class and political loyalty. With a rural *hukou,* it was impossible to move to a city, although many peasants wanted the benefits which then became available with an urban *hukou*: access to a generous state welfare system including kindergartens, good hospitals, guaranteed supplies of food and clothing, and pensions. A *hukou* was hereditary and passed down through the maternal side. When urban people were 'sent down to the countryside' during the Cultural Revolution, they often retained some privileges linked to the possession of an urban *hukou.*

Peasants were also categorized according to race and class. Those from 'poor peasant' backgrounds were favoured and those from 'landlord' or 'rich peasant' households were liable to be victimized in each ideological campaign. Urban Chinese were stratified in a similar way and such labels, once given, were hard to change.

The Great Leap Forward attempted but failed to bring the peasantry into 'socialism' and provide them with the same cradle-to-grave welfare benefits as urban Chinese. At the same time a crash industrialization drive led to the first of the massive population transfers which have marked the last fifty years. From early 1958, over 19 million peasants were brought into the cities, often with their families, adding an extra 31 million to an existing urban population of nearly 100 million. At this time, it was estimated that 15.4 per cent of China's population was registered as urban, probably the maximum extent it reached under Mao, for although the urban population subsequently grew in absolute terms, it declined as a proportion of China's total population. Even in 1996, only just over 17 per cent of the Chinese were regarded as urban.

Between 1953 and 1979 the number of urban centres in China was recorded as dropping from 5,402 to 3,600.[5] However, it is difficult to know how accurate these figures are. Tracking the changing size of China's population is not easy because different criteria were used in the censuses taken in 1953, 1964 and 1982. In addition, Chinese often kept their urban *hukou* even after years spent in a village or labour camp.

The second great transfer of population took place after 1960 when the Party sent wave after wave of city-dwellers into the countryside in a deliberate policy of de-urbanization. Estimates vary but it is thought that between 70 million and 90 million were relocated in the two decades up to 1979. Among them were at least 11 million of the rural peasants brought to the cities in 1958 and another 17 million of the so-called 'educated youth'. Most Chinese intellectuals and cadres also spent lengthy periods in the countryside during this period 'learning from the peasants'. Then, during the late 1960s and 1970s when Mao believed a nuclear war with the Soviet Union was likely, many engineers and technicians, along with their machinery, were moved out of the cities and sent to build factories in remote parts of the interior, to become what was dubbed the Third Line. Their efforts would enable China to fight on if its cities were destroyed in a nuclear war. At its peak, the Third Line employed some 20 million people.

To what extent these population transfers were driven by ideology or necessity is unclear. Judith Banister, an American demographer, has noted 'a profound, sometimes irrational anti-urban bias in Maoist thought, which sees city people as leeches, corrupted by material comforts, and peasants as hardworking, productive, rugged virtuous people'.[6] A shortage of grain may have been one reason. China's demoralized peasants, still in their communes despite the failure of the Great Leap Forward, could not or would not produce the grain surpluses that would feed a growing urban population. Nor did China seem to have the means to transport and distribute foodstuffs. Instead the system of economic planning emphasized self-sufficiency. Each part of the country was supposed to be able to feed and clothe itself. Even Shanghai, whose boundaries were enlarged to include substantial rural areas, had to be autarkic.

The Soviet Union coped with its own food shortages by encouraging urban families to grow vegetables in allotments outside the cities, but in China private plots were discouraged. Instead many urban work units set up farms to which staff went on a rotational basis. Some, like the May 7th Cadre Schools established during the Cultural Revolution, also mixed punishment with ideological remoulding. At the same time, life in the cities came to resemble that in the countryside. Even in Beijing, people kept chickens or raised pigs in their courtyards, and there were none of the specialized services such as restaurants that one would normally expect to find in a city.

The result of all these policies was that China developed quite differently to most other developing countries. There, peasants generally flooded into the cities, increasing the urban population by an average of 5 per cent a year. In China, the rate was perhaps half that.[7] As Judith Banister has commented, 'If no attempts had been made to affect rural-to-urban migration during the last three decades, China's urban population could be at least twice its current size.'[8]

While other countries in Asia were busy modernizing and enlarging their cities, China's remained frozen in time from 1959 onwards. Beijing saw the completion of a number of grand construction works, including the Great Hall of the People, during the frenzy of the Great Leap Forward but after that very little else was built there, with one exception. While Seoul or Hong Kong built brand-new underground transport systems, Beijing's citizens were busy digging a huge network of tunnels and underground nuclear fall-out shelters. Little new residential housing was built. Instead people were forced to occupy temporary quarters such as former temples or opera houses or to live in a large building that had, like Mrs Guo's house in Pingyao, been divided up into small rooms.

Although China's population expanded in the thirty years to 1979 from 500 million to 900 million, not a single new city was built. In 1986, when I visited the giant mining and steel complex at Panzhihua, a Third Line project in the remote mountains straddling Sichuan and Yunnan, the consequences of this lack of building became clear.

'We lived here in tents for nearly twenty years,' said Mr Lang, a Shanghai-born and educated engineer, who had been sent here after graduation along with tens of thousands of others. In the first ten years he was only allowed to return to Shanghai twice, a journey of two weeks. 'My children were born in tents,' he added with a touch of pride, showing me the photographs on a table in his new high-rise apartment. After 1979 a furious round of building was set in motion to house those who had sacrificed everything. Now he was free to leave. 'But it is too late to move back to Shanghai. Our life is here,' he said, though both his son and his daughter had returned to the city where Lang could still claim an urban *hukou* for them.

Deng Xiaoping's post-1978 reversal of Maoist rustification policies allowed tens of millions to try and make their way back to the cities. Some had lost their urban residency for good, for example 'educated youths' who had married peasants in the countryside, but many others did return to take up university places or to face unemployment. At the same time, the relaxation of the administration of the *hukou* system allowed peasants living around the big cities to transfer their residency with a timely bribe.

The swelling urban population sparked a new debate about whether it was wise for China to abandon its Maoist anti-urban policies or whether the country should embark on a process of rapid urbanization. A national conference of urban planners held in 1980 concluded by calling for strict control of the growth of population in big cities and urging the building of more small towns.[9]

Delegates agreed that three categories of small towns should be developed, each limited to 200,000 people, with a balance of the sexes and a mixed industrial base. Existing towns that already possessed some industries should be developed into local economic, political and cultural centres. It was reckoned that there were over

3,200 of these, about half of which had populations of over 10,000. Secondly, towns should be built where mines, power stations, resource projects, railways, harbours, tourist attractions and the like had already provided a focal point. Finally, it was proposed that satellite towns, such as had already been built around Beijing, Shanghai, Tianjin, Wuhan and Shenyang, be created to accommodate factories that were to be moved from nearby cities. In conclusion, the conference called for the development of the main towns in China's 53,000 communes, many of which already possessed a flourishing industrial and commercial life.[10]

One of the most powerful advocates of small towns was the anthropologist Fei Xiaotong who in the 1930s had studied small towns in southern Jiangsu province. In the early 1980s, he returned to carry out fresh studies. In the interim these small market towns had fallen into a state of ruin, with many inhabitants sent to the countryside, but under the new policies they were beginning to regain their prosperity as people moved back. In Su Nan, new factories set up in the 1970s, when the Cultural Revolution disrupted industrial production in Shanghai, began to flourish. Based on these impressions, Fei convinced Chinese leaders that Su Nan should be adopted as a national model.

Fei also put forward a second proposition. In accordance with Marx's idea of achieving 'a more equitable distribution of the population over the country', he endorsed the further colonization of the wide open spaces of minority regions such as Inner Mongolia, Xinjiang and Tibet.[11] This had already begun under Mao, with the dispatch of political prisoners and demobilized soldiers to these regions in production and construction brigades. Now, Fei suggested, 'The labour corps, whose members do not register their residence in the places to which they go, are welcomed by people in the minority nationality regions. At present they undertake only construction work, but it is likely that they will take up other occupations in the years ahead. At present they stay away from home for only short periods, but in the future they will stay away for longer periods. When their ranks have grown, they will help in bringing about a more even distribution of population.'

This is essentially what has happened. Throughout the 1980s and

1990s, official policy has been to avoid expanding the population of the few big cities and to encourage a gradual migration to western China, thus continuing a process that had started in the final decades of the Qing dynasty. Then, to reduce the pressure of population, the Manchus allowed Han Chinese to settle on the other side of the Great Wall. Hitherto, they had ensured that their ancestral steppes and forests were reserved for their own people. With the advent of railways linking eastern China to Inner Mongolia and Manchuria, these taboos were broken and the migration of tens of millions of land-hungry peasants was facilitated.

While only a few voices outside China, such as that of the Dalai Lama, have opposed the settlement of minority lands, the small towns strategy has been a contentious issue within China and critics have warned that small cities are costly to build and waste eastern China's precious and diminishing reserves of arable land.

In 1984, some former commune headquarters were relabelled as townships, thereby creating an extra 3,430 new towns and bringing the total to 6,211. At the same time, the population of existing cities appeared to grow because of a change in the definition of urban residency. All the peasants living in suburban and rural areas were now considered urban so that at a stroke, for example, the population of Beijing jumped from 6 to 9 million. Such changes have also allowed farmland to be zoned as urban and appropriated for construction.

The small towns strategy was again challenged at a conference in 1987 when critics argued that large urban and industrial conurbations were the key to modernization. Yet in the end, the Ministry of Urban and Rural Construction decided to double the urban population by the year 2000 only by expanding the number of small cities. It also adopted a new definition of a 'city'. This time it included small towns with a population of at least 60,000 or more engaged in non-agricultural activities and an annual GDP of more than 200 million yuan. Between 1986 and 1990, the number of such cities rose from 295 to 446. By 1996 there were 666 although 400 of these had populations of less than 200,000.

In *China on the Edge*, the environmentalist He Bochuan has criticized this policy of allowing townships to absorb 140 million people as disastrous: 'Based on the present patterns of development in the new townships, the price we are paying in terms of the destruction of arable land involved in building new cities is eleven times higher than would be the case if we simply allowed this population to be absorbed into existing large cities.'[12] In addition, the explosive growth of rural industries has, he continues, involved a chaotic and wasteful use of land: 'For example, between 1979 and 1984, about 55 million people left the villages and went into township enterprises. There was no concept of systematic town planning in these county towns. People built all over the place with no thought to providing the necessary education, hygiene and cultural facilities. Almost 34 million acres of farmland were lost in the process.'[13]

An alternative vision has been outlined in a report by Wang Jian, a researcher in the State Development Planning Commission, who proposes creating nine 'mega-cities' to absorb the hundreds of millions of peasants expected to leave the countryside: 'The money must go to the east to attract the population from the west. Continuing to do the opposite would be a waste. Cultivable land risks being swallowed by a human tide. It will then be as difficult to pursue industrialization as to feed the population.'[14]

For much of the 1990s the debate on urbanization rumbled on, and in the meantime, as the townships with their TVEs expanded at an even greater rate, eastern China began to resemble a vast and messy construction site. Take, for instance, Xinji, a small market town in Hebei province and a centre for the leather and tannery industry. In 1990 the town occupied less than 3 square miles. Since then urban planners have organized efforts to pave roads, lay power cables and install sewage pipes for a town which is expected to cover nearly 10 square miles by 2010, and contain over a million inhabitants. Already Xinji has features typical of such towns: roundabouts set with stainless steel sculptures dedicated to the soaring future, steel and glass towers for state banks and Party headquarters, and five-storey blocks of housing scattered across the ricefields.[15] One American visitor, horrified by what she had seen on visits to some of these towns, described them as 'high-tech bathrooms, built in endless variations of shiny white tile and blue glass. Others are exercises in Orwellian architecture: in Yonglian, a village in Jiangsu, inhabitants live in rows of identical houses, stroll in a grey maze of concrete walkways and work at a community steel plant that dwarfs the land-scape.'[16]

The small towns policy is aimed at conserving precious farming land by moving peasants into large units where they are supposed to live like factory workers in high-rise apartment blocks. Planners seek to stop peasants building their traditional houses with their court-yards, vegetable gardens and sheds where a family can independently store its own reserves of food, livestock, tools and other necessities.

Propaganda routinely hails the results of this form of forced urbanization. Jiangsu province claims to have reclaimed 500,000 acres of farmland by consolidating 280,000 villages into 50,000 townships.[17] In a description of Zhejiang, where 14 million, a third of the province's population, now live in 965 small towns, the New China News Agency (Xinhua) has painted this glowing picture: 'These small towns have all constructed industrial zones consisting of factories, residential quarters built in a planned way and many stores of general merchandise, banks, post and telecommunications offices, hotels, farmers' markets, cinemas, karaoke dance halls and teahouses.'[18] Indeed the only thing that worried one Xinhua corre-spondent about Zhejiang was that increased urbanization had resulted in 'behavioural problems of adjusting to city life such as spit-ting, littering, vulgar language and traffic violations'.[19]

The national model for the urbanization of the peasantry in a socialist Utopia is Zhangjiagang, a county in southern Jiangsu that I visited in 1996. Here, everyone must memorize and apply the detailed rules and advice laid out in a 'Civilized Citizen Study Book'. It lists 'six musts' and ten 'must nots' which proscribe bad language, lewd behaviour, noisy quarrelling, the jumping of red lights, the erec-tion of illegal stalls and much more. But it is also a guide to good manners for peasants, telling the *nouveaux riches* of the Jiangsu delta how to speak properly, how to apologize and how to address their neighbours, relatives and others by their proper names. The peasants are told not to gape at foreigners or crowd around in amazement. They are instructed to wash their hands before eating and after going to the toilet, to bathe frequently, to cut their nails and not to spit because doing so spreads germs.

Inside every house, a framed list of rules hangs on the wall. Every household is regularly inspected to see if it passes muster, and neighbours are obliged to report on families whose members have raised their voices in anger, on husbands who curse or beat their wives and on mothers who smack their children.

'If they fail, the family is ostracized so that if the son goes out, then people will point at him and some privileges will be taken away,' an official explained to me.

The authorities have also targeted many traditional practices such as building tombs and ancestral shrines. Now everyone has to be cremated, and in private homes no one is allowed to set up a shrine to the kitchen god or to visit fortune-tellers or traditional healers.

In Yanshe, the county's administrative centre, which has 120,000 inhabitants, visitors are taken to the gleaming new indoor food market where peasants must scrub the mud off their vegetables before bringing them inside. A special pedestrian shopping street, broad and wide, is lined with rubbish bins labelled in English. Public latrines sparkle with cleanliness. Pedestrians keep to the pavements, cyclists to the cycle lanes. Motorists stop at red lights. No one honks their horn, and noisy motorbikes and dirty tractors have been banned. A special detachment of seventy police patrols the streets day and night to stop people spitting or smoking.

'We are very tough,' admits the local police chief Zheng Guoqing. 'Anyone caught smoking on the street is fined and has to stand there wearing a yellow garment until he catches someone else violating the regulations.'

'The model we want to follow is Singapore not Hong Kong. Singapore is very orderly and clean but Hong Kong has too much crime, gambling and prostitution,' explains another official, Li Lingjun.

The police chief claims that dancing girls, prostitution, gambling and begging no longer exist in Yanshe, and that the crime rate has dropped dramatically, with only 200 arrests and 4 executions in the previous year.

On one of the main streets the New China Bookshop is crowded with customers browsing for educational works beneath banners urging citizens to expand their scientific knowledge. Shop assistants are regularly inspected and customers are requested to fill in questionnaires rating their performance. Visitors are also taken to see a model infants' school which has its own swimming-pool in the basement and classrooms where children learn English on computers.[20]

The county of Zhangjiagang has been turned into a centre of pilgrimage by President Jiang Zemin. By 1996 some 650,000 had come to see this embodiment of 'spiritual civilization', the goal Jiang has set the country, where houses and offices carry 'double civilization' metal plaques above their entrances, testifying to the fact that the residents have reached an official level of material and spiritual civilization.

Zhangjiagang is lucky because a fresh start could be made here. Towns like Yanshe were built from scratch on reclaimed land and sandbanks close to the Yangtze River. Here collective TVEs and many plants which have attracted foreign investment employ over 100,000 migrant workers and have created the sort of wealth that enables the county to engage the country's best town planners. At another township, Nansha, Yang Guiqing, a planning expert from Shanghai's Tongji University who studied in Liverpool, is helping to create a Milton Keynes on the Yangtze.

Nansha, which lies off a new motorway, does indeed resemble a modern garden city. It has pleasant two- and three-storey town houses and shops, green spaces and a pedestrian precinct. With its pleasing uniformity of architectural style and high-quality building standards, it is a far cry from the slovenly friendliness of old Pingyao, though some might regard its quietness as unnatural, even sinister.

Nevertheless, despite the Party's strenuous efforts to control and plan China's urbanization process, it has been unable to stop peasants from spontaneously moving into the big cities. In the 1980s, about 10 million migrated to the dozen or so large cities with a population of over 2 million. A further large-scale migration occurred after Deng's 1992 southern tour, when major cities such as Beijing and Shanghai experienced an astonishing burst of economic growth. Vast sums of money, on a scale not seen for forty years, were thrown at their development and construction which in turn sucked in huge numbers of rural construction workers.

Journals such as the *Economic Reference News* worried about the 'blind influx of job-hunting peasants' but acknowledged that they were needed, at least temporarily. Rather than forbidding them entry to the cities, it proposed forcing them to register and pay special taxes for the privilege of working there.[21] Other experts warned that a 'floating population' of 60 million or even 100 million was poised to invade the cities. The Minister for Labour, Ruan Chongwu, foresaw paralysis of the transport system and general anarchy in the cities. The *People's Daily* concurred: 'The movement of this labour is to a large extent without any control, seriously affecting public order, family planning and other sectors.'[22]

By 1995, when the authorities prepared a series of counter-measures, Beijing claimed it had 3 million migrants, few of whom possessed residency or work permits. Most had settled in twenty-five 'villages' of migrants from certain areas who specialized in particular trades. Tailors tended to come from Wenzhou, maids from the province of Anhui.

To counter this influx Beijing prepared a plan for the 'comprehensive management of the rural population'. In November that year, Beijing's police moved in to bulldoze the Zhejiang 'village', a settlement that had thrived by turning out 200,000 overcoats and 100,000 padded jackets a day, and to evict its 100,000 residents. In the same period cities all over the country enforced new regulations to stop rural migrants from renting accommodation and to restrict the availability of temporary residence permits. Beijing alone set up 365 committees to monitor compliance and issued approved migrants with special identity cards or blue cards bearing a hologram that made them more difficult to forge. Women over the age of 18 had to produce a certificate showing their marital status and listing any children to ensure they did not evade the one-child policy. The province of Fujian, with a 'floating population' of 3 million, became the first to pass a law making it compulsory for migrant workers to be sterilized if they already had one child.[23] Attempts were also made to attract certain types of people. Shanghai began by issuing laws that barred migrant workers from twenty-three occupations, among them work in finance and insurance, and various types of management jobs. Then it followed Beijing by asking companies to pay a 100,000 yuan tax for each migrant they hired while individuals with 50,000 yuan to spare could purchase a *hukou*.

In the spring of 1996, the Ministry of Public Security launched a massive 'Strike Hard' anti-crime campaign in which its officers swept through residential areas, checking identity papers and expelling migrants. The media claimed that the migrants were responsible for nearly half of all crimes committed in the cities. According to figures released, in the first nine months of 1997 police in 15 cities sent home 190,000 migrants and picked up 100,000 waifs from the streets. By 1998, curbs on migrant workers had cut Beijing's floating population to 2.86 million, a fall of 436,000 from 1994, and in 1999 another 300,000 were expelled.

At the same time new identity documents issued in 1996 abolished the difference between the agricultural and non-agricultural categories in the household registration of urban dwellers, a change that blurred the distinction between urban and rural residents of Beijing and other major cities. In the case of Chongqing in Sichuan, the change had a dramatic statistical effect. Hitherto, Chongqing, perched on a hill overlooking the Yangtze, had been a small city, with a population of only 3 million, though it had as many peasants again living in its environs. When in 1997 it became a municipality like Beijing or Shanghai, an area around the Three Gorges dam reservoir inhabited by low-income peasants was added to its jurisdiction. Chongqing now has a population of 30 million, leading some to claim that it is the world's largest city.[24]

In recent years the Ministry of Labour has set up a computerized system to try and track the movement of labourers and create a nationwide labour market data system. At the same time 15,000 rural employment agencies have worked to channel migrants to the cities in an orderly fashion. In 1996, in Guangdong province, Shenzhen's migrant labour force declined for the first time. By 1999 Shanghai's migrant population had dropped to 2 million, far below the 5 million projected by trends in 1992. As has been noted, a similar decline in Beijing's floating population occurred at the same time.[25]

In the meantime, the pace of urbanization has slowed remarkably, the rate of rural migration dropping from 6 or 7 per cent a year to less than 3 per cent by 1998. In some places it has even gone into reverse as state-owned enterprises have shed surplus labour. Some 15 million were laid off by these enterprises between 1990 and 1995, and it was thought that between 15 and 20 million more had been made redundant between 1996 and 2000.[26]

To provide new jobs for these people, many cities have begun to urge those laid off to take over the jobs being done by migrants. In Shenyang, the capital of Liaoning in China's rust-belt, the deputy Party secretary of Shenyang, Wen Shizhen, told his city's 800,000 unemployed to reclaim the 1.1 million urban jobs held by its 700,000 peasants and 400,000 outsiders.[27] At a national level the *People's Daily* in 1997 likewise urged redundant state workers to emulate rural migrants and take difficult, dirty and dangerous jobs at low wages, pointing out that 36 million peasant workers had found work in the cities in the previous two years, equal to the number of state workers expected to lose their jobs in the near future. City dwellers ought, the newspaper concluded, to learn to fend for themselves at a time when the country was restructuring its economy.[28]

Some cities, including Beijing but especially those in the hard-hit north-east, have begun to encourage redundant workers and coalminers to go back to farming, offering incentives such as interest-free loans, three-year tax exemptions and free farm equipment to those who switch to full-time farming. Some have even been offered posts as village officials, as well as membership of the Communist Party and full retention of the benefits that they used to hold as urban workers.[29]

Shanghai, which had become a byword for China's teeming cities, now finds itself in the remarkable position of grappling with a declining population. Since 1993, the city has actually recorded negative population growth each year. Eighteen years ago, there were 180,000 children born every year in Shanghai. Now the annual figure is well under 70,000.

In 1998 I visited Mao Peiyan, headmistress of a Shanghai primary school, one of the last left in a city where for several years a hundred primary schools were closed down annually.

'There used to be a hundred schools in the Huangpu district. Now there are just twelve,' said Mrs Mao without much regret.

Mao Fang, a researcher for the municipality's Education Committee, believes the trend will continue: 'The closures are bound to accelerate because the numbers are dropping by a big margin. There are now 700,000 primary school students in Shanghai but by 2003, the number could drop to 400,000.'

The cause of the decline, according to Professor Peng Xizhe, director of the Institute of Population Research at Fudan University, has been the fall in Shanghai's fertility rate. In the 1950s, Shanghainese had an average of six children, more than in the countryside, but in the 1970s the city took the lead in enforcing the one-child policy. By 1979, 90 per cent of urban couples had voluntarily pledged to have just one child and Shanghai, even including its rural areas where 5 million of its 14 million live, had a fertility rate of just 1.6. Similar rates are recorded only in western European countries such as Italy.

Ironically, this decline in the city's population has become a cause for concern. According to Professor Zuo Yuejin, Vice President of the Shanghai Academy of Social Sciences, 'There are now 90,000 deaths a year and about 60,000 births. We need more people, otherwise there is going to be a lot of empty housing here.' He worries that if fertility does not pick up then in less than a generation Shanghai's population will fall by half. Unless substantial immigration occurs, the city will soon be smaller than it was before 1949. 'Now some Shanghainese don't even want to have one child and they are remaining childless voluntarily. The government may even have to encourage people to have children.'

Shen Weibin, a history professor at Fudan University, has since 1996 argued that migrants of all kinds should be allowed into Shanghai. 'The world's great cities are all immigrant cities. It was immigrants who made Shanghai a great city before the Second World War. After 1949, the city started to die because it cut off the flow of immigrants. Now it is the immigrants who have rebuilt the city and are bringing it back to life. These people do jobs that local people do not want. Even Shanghai people who have been laid off do not envy them. They would not work in such conditions. The less skilled will go home once they have finished their jobs. Those with skills and ability will stay and become Shanghai people.'[30]

His advice has been heeded. In 1999, with half the property built in the post-1992 construction boom left standing empty, Shanghai announced it would give *hukou* to students who graduated from its universities even if they had been born elsewhere, provided they could find a job. Peasants could buy a Shanghai *hukou* by purchasing property costing 1 million yuan (subsequently reduced to just 400,000 yuan). Rural migrants were also allowed to send their children to Shanghai schools, making it easier for them to bring their families with them. In fact, there are now so many empty schools in the city that Shanghai has even begun to bus in peasant children from its rural areas to offer them a better education.

China's leaders have also been forced to recognize that He Bochuan's warnings were justified. The small towns policy came under attack when, at a Politburo meeting in February 1997, members saw NASA satellite photographs of seventeen Chinese cities. They provided damning evidence that agricultural land was being paved over at two and half times the rate reported by official statistics.[31]

The State Land Administration Bureau has calculated that China is losing 0.5 per cent of its cultivated land each year and that if China's per capita arable land currently stands at 0.25 of an acre, then there will be only 0.17 of an acre per capita left when China's population levels off at 1.6 billion.[32] However, the American ecologist Lester Brown believes that even this figure is wildly optimistic. Judging from the experience of other countries, the ratio of grain-producing land to population could fall even more dramatically. 'If the nation continues on essentially the same industrial path as that followed by Japan, South Korea and Taiwan, and this reduction continues, China will have lost roughly half its grain land by 2030.'[33]

Brown goes on to stress how Japan, despite all its efforts to subsidize rice growers, saw its area sown to grain shrink by half between 1955 and 1994. Likewise Taiwan lost 42 per cent of its grain farmland and South Korea 46 per cent during industrialization.

Much of the land being sacrificed in China lies within a narrow thousand-mile coastal belt and its fertile deltas. Most of China's farmland is in mountainous areas that are vulnerable to soil erosion, and only these delta plains can yield multiple crops. Reclaiming land from other more arid terrain which produces only one annual crop is costly and unprofitable. Still worse, the State Land Administration Bureau has discovered that 40 per cent of the lost farmland is in fact lying idle. 'Around many villages, the areas of idle land adjacent to the villages are much larger than the villages themselves, resulting in "hollow villages",' reported Xinhua in 1997. And the *People's Daily* waxed indignant on the subject: 'This kind of disregard for the future of our country, for the life and death of poor people, and for the well-being of our children and grandchildren cannot be tolerated!'[34]

China's shocked leaders reacted at once by ordering a one-year freeze, later extended, on authorized land transfers and declared that the country needed the world's toughest agricultural land protection regulations. Subsequently, violation of the Land Management Law was made a criminal offence carrying a five-year prison term.

Detailed regulations on the use of collective land by township and village enterprises followed. The conversion of farmland into even fish ponds or woodlands was forbidden, and if land did have to be used for non-agricultural purposes, a plot of the same area and quality had to be returned to agriculture. In Guangdong province alone forty proposed new golf courses were cancelled and many projects to build amusement parks, luxury villa parks, science parks and industrial development zones were suspended.

The seizure of land by real-estate developers has in fact sparked numerous rural protests of which reports occasionally surface. In Sichuan's capital, Chengdu, in January 1999 over 400 villagers staged a protest after their farmland had been appropriated for a science and technology park that was never built, unfurling banners in front of the provincial government offices that read: 'Give back our land' and 'We want to survive'.[35]

Panic over the loss of farmland and the evident waste of resources when apartment buildings in big cities were being left empty has led to a re-examination of the urbanization policy. In late 1999, the State Development Planning Commission came out in favour of developing super-large and large cities and expanding medium-sized cities in the tenth five-year plan (2001–5).[36]

Chinese statistics list 207 million people as currently living in cities, or approximately 17 per cent of the total population. If illegal migrants to the cities and the 150 million people who are treated as urban because they live in small rural townships or in areas under the jurisdiction of cities are included, then around 30 per cent of the population live in the cities.[37]

The Planning Commission has also released a report proposing that urbanization be speeded up so that by the year 2015, half the population will be classified as urban, which is the international norm. To achieve this, the urbanization rate will have to accelerate by 1 per cent per year until 2015. In the first five years of the new century 85 million will have to become urban dwellers and over fifteen years altogether 300 million peasants will have to leave their villages. The biggest city in China is now Shanghai with 9 million people but with such a shift of population towards the cities China may soon have mega-cities like Mexico City with 17 million or Seoul with 14 million. Even more significantly, if China were to reach the same urbanization rate as most developed countries – 70 per cent – when its population peaks at 1.6 billion towards the middle of the next century, over a billion people will have been moved in the course of a single lifetime.

The first new cities built after 1979 were those like Shenzhen, the earliest of the so-called special economic zones, described in the next chapter.

5

Inside the Zones

IT BECAME A familiar experience in the early 1980s when visiting a Chinese city, however small or remote. A column of cars would be driven along a bumpy dirt road in a cloud of dust, passing gangs of labourers and ramshackle huts, until it reached some dried-out paddy fields. Then everyone would get out and stand on the edge of the fields looking a little bewildered.

'This is the so-and-so special economic zone,' a local government official would say proudly. Everyone would look around, trying hard to visualize a new Hong Kong, and nod in an embarrassed silence.

'Foreigners are warmly welcome to invest,' the official would then say, beaming a generous and forgiving smile at the visitors as they tried to imagine glass skyscrapers and humming factories churning out computers.

At a nearby office, there would be a model town with Lego blocks of the tall new buildings still to be erected arranged in squares and lines. Around the briefing room would hang blown-up photographs of senior politicians from Beijing, showing them visiting the zone and conferring their blessing. Copies of their calligraphy would be prominently displayed as incontrovertible proof.

Finally, as the visitors were seated in front of mugs of tea, an official would laboriously read out a document detailing everything, from the exact longitude and latitude in which the zone lay to the millions of dollars already invested.

Tens of millions of Chinese now live and work in these development zones which are responsible for half of China's exports and the bulk of government tax revenues. When the first special economic zone (SEZ) was set up in August 1980, it represented the most daring of all the reforms that Deng Xiaoping had launched within months of consolidating his power.

That August troops of the People's Liberation Army Construction Corps occupied a tongue of land around the village of Shenzhen, in the province of Guangdong, and erected a barbed-wire fence to separate the zone from the rest of the country. To the south lay a small river, the border with the New Territories of Hong Kong and another line of fences and watchtowers.

Shenzhen's motto — 'Time is money, efficiency is life' — was blazoned on billboards and an army of construction workers began to create a new city in the ricefields, the first that China had built in a generation. Everything had to be provided from scratch — a port, power stations, roads, water supplies, housing, schools.

The explanation of its purpose varied over the years. Sometimes it was described as a laboratory for internal reforms, sometimes as a symbol of China's new open-door policy. In 1984 Deng himself called it 'a medium for introducing technology, management and knowledge . . . a window for our foreign policy . . . and to import foreign technology, obtain knowledge and learn management'.[1]

When the idea of special economic zones was first mooted in July 1979, the coastal provinces of Guangdong and Fujian were singled out for special treatment because they were close to Hong Kong, Macao and Taiwan, and the original homeland of most overseas Chinese. At the same time, Deng Xiaoping appealed to the patriotism of all the 'children of the Yellow Emperor' in inviting them to come home and invest in the motherland.

Delegations were sent around the world to investigate other export processing zones, including one led by the future president Jiang Zemin, which in 1980 visited Sri Lanka, Singapore and Mexico.[2] Yet it was the Chinese nearer home — the Taiwanese who had set up three successful export processing zones in the 1960s — and those in Hong Kong and Macao who were regarded as the key to the zones' success, not least because economic integration was also envisaged as a means towards political reunification.

At first, there were four special economic zones: Shenzhen itself;

Zhuhai, next to Portuguese Macao; Shantou (formerly Swatow), home to the Chaozhou diaspora who had emigrated in large numbers to Hong Kong, Thailand, Singapore, Malaysia and cities in Europe and America; and, in Fujian province, Xiamen (formerly Amoy), opposite Taiwan. Then, in 1984, explaining that 'egalitarianism will not work' and that 'some areas will become rich first', Deng extended special privileges to fourteen open coastal cities, all former treaty ports.[3] Four years later, he went further, declaring that 'we should create several more Hong Kongs', which encouraged cities all along the 'gold coast', as the southern coast of China became known, to create their own zones. Indeed, the whole of Hainan, the tropical island off the southern tip of Guangdong province, was declared one huge SEZ.

In the wake of the Tiananmen Square massacre in 1989, the reassertion of Maoist policies for a while prevented further development, but then in late 1991 Deng went south to restart the reforms. His visit was dubbed the *nan xun*, or the emperor's southern tour. Although conservative politicians tried at first to keep news of the visit secret it soon became known that Deng had praised Shenzhen and Zhuhai, and had called for a faster 'opening up'. Within months every province, city, county and township seemed to be announcing a new zone. At least 2,000 were opened in 1992 and within a couple of years there were a further 10,000 covering a total area of over 6,000 square miles.[4]

Most significantly, at about the same time Deng finally gave the green light to the opening up of Shanghai and the creation of the biggest SEZ of them all, Pudong, a neglected area the size of Singapore that lies across the Huangpu River, opposite Shanghai's famous Bund. The reopening of Shanghai has completed the cycle that first began over a century and a half ago. Shanghai, established as a treaty port in 1843, became by far the most successful treaty port in East Asia, indeed the greatest city in the East, until the late 1930s. Now, nearly half a century after its apparent demise under Communism, it was being restored to its rightful place in China's destiny.

Initially, the political symbolism of Deng's decision meant more than anything else. Shanghai, as the heartland of state industry, had been a bastion of ultra-leftism during the Cultural Revolution, noted for its proletarian revolutionary fervour. Now the capitalists over whom the Party had triumphed in 1949 were being invited back, just as Deng's opponents had feared when he came to power in 1979.

The entire open-door policy, as it was termed, was a reversal of Maoism which had sought self-reliance and development of the interior, and had neglected the coast. In fact many of the zones were designed to help relocate factories that Mao had moved inland. Even the phrase itself was redolent of colonialism and the period when, at the end of the nineteenth century, in the face of the scramble for trading concessions in China by European powers, the United States had called for an 'open-door' policy to guarantee all countries equal access to Chinese markets. Leftists gathered evidence to show that the SEZs were simply replicas of the old 'foreign concessions' and said they amounted to 'selling out the country'. Chen Yun, the conservative leader and adherent of central planning, warned that 'foreign capitalists will come on the scene and corruption will rage' while the Marxist ideologue Hu Qiaomu described the zones as 'foreign colonies' and the whole open-door policy as 'colonialism without foreign masters'.[5]

Deng remained unmoved. As far as he was concerned, the most valuable element of the SEZs consisted in what was euphemistically termed 'mind emancipation'. He wanted Chinese bureaucrats to 'liberate their thoughts' and discard habits entrenched by the planned economy. Shocking things were suggested. Xiang Nan, Party Secretary of Fujian, asked why the whole province could not become an SEZ run by Taiwan's KMT, and there was even a suggestion that the Dalai Lama might come back and run Tibet.[6]

In 1992, a senior Party leader and reformer, Tian Jiyun, spoke at the Central Party School, the Party's leading ideological seminary, mockingly proposing an SEZ reserved for unreformed Maoists: 'Couldn't you establish a special economic zone for leftists? . . . Salaries would be low, you could rely on coupons, you would have to stand in line to buy everything and suffer everything else that goes along with leftism . . . If we actually set up [such] a place . . . would anyone want to go?'[7] Five years later, a Beijing university economics professor, Shang Dewen, even suggested that the SEZs might be turned into laboratories for free elections and other political reforms.

At the start of the reforms, the leftists' accusations were all the more telling because the geographical pattern of the new zones seemed deliberately or otherwise to mimic that forced on the Qing dynasty by the Western powers and their gunships in the mid-nineteenth century.

China's Manchu emperors had repeatedly rejected the applications made by a succession of Western ambassadors to open the country's doors to free trade. Most famously, the Emperor Qianlong dismissed a delegation led by Lord Macartney in 1793, saying in a letter to George III: 'As your Ambassador has seen for himself, we possess all things. I set no value on objects strange and ingenious and have no use for your manufactures.'

The West's naval and trading powers had become increasingly frustrated by Chinese restrictions on trade. The Portuguese, the first to venture so far east, had obtained a toehold at Macao but by 1760 all European trade was still restricted to one port, Guangzhou (Canton). Foreigners were not allowed to live there, however, except during the trading season from October to March, and they had to deal exclusively with a monopolistic guild of merchants called the Cohong. Not surprisingly the system led to numerous disputes.

After the failure of Macartney's embassy tensions rose. In an effort to redress the imbalance in trade, foreign merchants began to sell increasing amounts of opium grown and manufactured in India, despite the fact that it was illegal to import the drug into China (one of the main reasons being that it was seen to be a threat to the thriving local opium industry). The imported opium was kept in 'factories' or warehouses built on the small island of Shamian (Shameen), in the Pearl River outside the city of Guangzhou. Increasingly alarmed by the outflow of silver in payment for imported opium and aware that it was endangering the economy, in 1838 the Emperor appointed a high official called Lin Zexu to stop the illegal trade. Lin's confiscation and destruction of 20,000 or more chests of opium marked the beginning of the First Opium War which concluded with

China's defeat at the hands of the British. In 1842 the two countries signed the Treaty of Nanjing (Nanking). Britain failed to obtain permission to open an embassy in Beijing but by its terms was ceded the island of Hong Kong. Further, China agreed to open five cities to direct trade: Guangzhou, Fuzhou (Foochow), Xiamen (Amoy), Ningbo (Ningpo) and Shanghai. Soon afterwards the United States and France demanded and obtained a similar treaty but with extra provisions that included the right of foreigners to employ Chinese and learn the language, and the right to be judged according to their own laws.

Inside these ports, the Chinese granted the foreigners what were called 'concessions', a piece of land on which a consulate, warehouse and merchant house could be built. In these tiny communities, the British and other foreigners could live under their own laws, a principle known as extraterritoriality. Of the first five treaty ports only Shanghai really prospered and it was there, in 1854, that the Imperial Maritime Customs Service was established by foreign consuls to ensure that all foreign traders paid the same duties, as stipulated in the treaties. The Customs Service, largely run by the British, eventually extended throughout the treaty ports and gradually became the decaying Manchu empire's most important source of tax revenue. Within a decade of its establishment it was employing 400 foreigners and 1,000 Chinese. By 1916, there were 41 customs ports and 35 offices, and the service was even responsible for running China's postal system. Its activities were only eventually curtailed by the Japanese invasion of China and the outbreak of the Second World War.

Despite the Treaty of Nanjing and the expansion of its provisions by treaties with the Americans and the French, British merchants remained unsatisfied. The opening of the coastal treaty ports had not led to any great increase in trade. Pressure on China to open its doors further resulted in 1858 in a second Anglo-Chinese war in which China was once again defeated and forced to grant further concessions. Britain and other Western powers were to be allowed to open embassies in Beijing. The preaching of Christianity was to be permitted, as was travel by foreigners throughout China. Lastly, a further ten treaty ports, four along the Yangtze and another six on the coast, were to be opened.

Subsequently, when the imperial court attempted to renege on the treaty, a joint British and French force fought their way to Beijing and in revenge burnt down the imperial summer palace, the Yuanmingyuan. In the Convention of Beijing (Peking) which followed, China affirmed the earlier treaty, agreed to pay indemnities and make Tianjin a treaty port, and ceded to Britain part of the Kowloon peninsula that faces Hong Kong Island.

Among the new treaty ports was Shantou which became one of the first SEZs, while Tianjin, Haikou on Hainan Island and Pagoda Island near Fuzhou were all to be among the fourteen coastal cities to which Deng Xiaoping extended special privileges in 1984.

Under the Chefoo Agreement of 1876, the British opened up cities further and further inland. Some were along the Yangtze River such as Yichang (Ichang), Wuhu and, in 1890, Chongqing (Chungking) in Sichuan province. When there was resistance, as at Yichang, gunboats were deployed. Wenzhou was added on the coast but also Simao in the hills of Yunnan, Suzhou and Hangzhou in the Yangtze delta, Yuezhou in Hunan and Samshui in Guangdong. Many of these never prospered and some were soon shut, like Yuezhou which opened in 1899 only to close two years later.

As China became weaker the Western powers became more aggressive, competing with each other to acquire concessions. At the close of the nineteenth century, Russia, Japan and Germany, latecomers at the table, demanded equal treatment with the British and others. The acquisition of a new concession by one European country encouraged fresh demands by its commercial rivals. Germany took control of Qingdao in 1896, Russia seized Lushun (Port Arthur) and in 1898, Britain demanded Weihaiwei in Shandong province and a 99-year lease on Hong Kong's New Territories.

Nevertheless, though they competed for commercial advantage, the Western governments sought by and large to preserve the Manchu empire intact. There was to be no scramble for China as there had been for Africa. The great dream in China was to gain control of what was perceived as a vast market of some 400 million customers. Sir Henry Pottinger, the earliest governor of Hong Kong, was only the first to promise undreamt-of prospects when he told the British in 1843 that he had opened up a whole new world to trade, so vast 'that all the mills of Lancashire could not make stocking-stuff sufficient for one of its provinces'.[8]

Of all the treaty ports, Shanghai was to be by far the most successful. Initially, it benefited from its proximity to the areas that produced tea, silk and porcelain for export, but soon its position at the mouth of the Yangtze became significant. As the interior was opened up to Western trade Shanghai grew into the most important financial and industrial centre in Asia.

The International Settlement, as its British and American concessions were collectively known, grew up outside the original Chinese city and became China's most important window on the world. Its colleges and universities allowed Chinese to learn about the West, its medicine, religions, technology, architecture, management and fashions. China's industrial revolution flowered here as did cinemas, independent newspapers, writers and thinkers. Shanghai lacked nothing that the modern world could offer and its futuristic architecture rivalled anything to be found in London or New York.

Once, while walking through Shanghai's old French Concession, I came across the rather suburban-looking house of Sun Yat-sen, the father of the Chinese Republic. It seemed much like the sort of house in which I had grown up in London. In the kitchen there was a gas cooker. Even in 1920, it seems that Sun and his wife were cooking with gas, a convenience not introduced to most British homes until some decades later. In Beijing gas cookers only became common in kitchens in the 1990s.

Throughout the treaty ports Western businesses relied to a greater or lesser degree on Chinese partners and so there emerged a class of Western-educated Chinese merchants and professionals who bridged the two cultures and became known as 'compradors'.

Official efforts by the Chinese government to learn from the West and modernize were only partially successful. In the wake of the Second Opium War under what became known as the Self-Strengthening movement, fostered by men such as Li Hongzhang, Chinese were sent abroad to acquire Western technology and learning. New arsenals were built, naval and military academies were established, the Chinese fleet was transformed and the first Chinese-owned shipping company, the China Merchants' Steam Navigation

Company, was launched. The scope of the Self-Strengthening movement, however, was limited, little attention being paid to Western political systems, and those who promoted the movement had to do so in the face of intense opposition from conservatives at court.

By contrast Japan responded much more vigorously to the arrival of Western traders in the middle of the nineteenth century. After the Meiji Restoration of 1868, it sent students abroad and quickly copied Western technology and borrowed from Western culture what it thought useful. In 1894, Japan seized control over Korea, formally a Chinese vassal, and defeated the North China Fleet. At the Treaty of Shimonoseki signed the following year, Korea became independent, albeit under Japanese protection, Taiwan and the Liaodong peninsula were ceded to Japan, and China was forced to pay an indemnity and open up four more inland ports.

Within the Chinese imperial court, the debate between modernizers and conservatives continued. In 1898 the young Emperor Guangxu launched the Hundred Days Reform movement, a programme of more radical reform proposed by a number of scholars such as Kang Youwei and Liang Qichao who advocated educational change, reform of the civil service examination system, the establishment of a Western-style university in Beijing, and budgetary and administrative reform, changes underpinned by the belief that 'Chinese learning should remain the essence, but Western learning should be used for practical development.' Many of these modernizers' attitudes and ideas were not very different from those of Deng Xiaoping. For example, they proposed encouraging overseas Chinese to return home to contribute their skills and capital to building up China's industrial base. The reform programme proved short-lived, however. In a *coup d'état* in September that year the Empress Dowager Cixi had the Emperor imprisoned and some of the reformers arrested and executed in Beijing.

The increasing foreign presence in China was also to have adverse consequences. In 1899 and 1900 a series of concerted attacks on missionaries and railways, both powerful symbols of the West, developed in what became known as the Boxer rebellion. The uprising culminated in a siege of the foreign legations in Beijing that was lifted only by the arrival of an international force. The Empress Dowager, who had supported the Boxers in the hope that they would free China of foreign influence, fled the capital and China was forced to pay a heavy indemnity.

After the Boxer rebellion it became clear that the Chinese government under the Qing dynasty was doomed. At the same time, external pressure on China continued as Russia and Japan vied for control of Manchuria as a potential sphere of influence. In 1911, as a result of an uprising that began in Wuhan, the Qing dynasty was overthrown. In 1912 the Republic of China was established with Sun Yat-sen as its first president.

From then until the victory of the Communists in 1949, China was beset by a lack of control at the centre, but on one point most Chinese were agreed. The treaty ports were a symbol of China's humiliation at the hands of foreign powers, a humiliation that became embodied by the myth that there was a sign at the entrance to a small public garden on Shanghai's Bund that declared 'No dogs and no Chinese'.

Perhaps ironically, just as concerted resistance to foreign influence in the form of strikes and demonstrations began to develop in the 1920s and 1930s, particularly in Shanghai, it became clear that the treaty ports had outlived their usefulness. So much of China was by then open to travel and to trade that their *raison d'être* had passed. As it was, events overtook them. In 1937 Japan invaded China and occupied Shanghai and most of coastal China. After Japan's entry into the Second World War most foreign residents were interned by the Japanese. By the time a Sino-British treaty formally restoring the treaty ports to China was signed in January 1943, they had in practice already disappeared.

China had never technically relinquished sovereignty over these treaty ports and the new Communist government that came to power in 1949 believed it was not bound by any terms agreed under what it called the Unequal Treaties that had followed the Opium Wars and subsequent scramble for concessions. But, for reasons no one has ever fully explained, Mao's troops did not march into Hong Kong after 1949. A British governor, complete with cocked hat and feathers, continued to rule Hong Kong until the 99-year lease on the New Territories ran out. Even at the height of the Cultural Revolution, and despite its intense xenophobia, it was clear that Beijing wished to retain its window on the world. The British colony continued to serve the same purpose as it had when it was first founded in 1842, as a place where Chinese and Westerners could do business. In the 1970s, as had been the case at the time of Macartney's mission in 1793, those who wished to conduct trade with China were only permitted to travel up to Guangzhou to attend the country's sole trade fair once a year. For the rest, China's door was closed.

Nevertheless, Hong Kong survived this sudden isolation and prospered. Capitalists who had fled China in 1949 re-established their businesses in the colony. Some indeed had had the foresight to ship their textile machinery to Hong Kong in advance of the Communists' victory. Other refugees had arrived with little more than the clothes on their backs and became an instant source of cheap labour as Hong Kong began to industrialize.

Over the next decades, the colony's newest arrivals flourished. So too did entrepreneurial dynasties and companies that could trace their origins back to the days of the Opium Wars: the Hongkong and Shanghai Bank, Swire, Jardine Matheson, Butterfield, Hutchinson, Whampoa and Kadoorie.

In addition to these British commercial houses or *hongs*, there were also enterprises that dated back to Li Hongzhang's Self-Strengthening movement such as the China Merchants' Steam Navigation Company or the Bank of China, as well as names like the Wing On Department Store, once the most reputable in Shanghai, and branches of the great capitalist families of Shanghai such as those led by Y.K. Pao, T.Y. Chao and C.Y. Tung that prospered in shipping. The first Chief Executive of Hong Kong after its return to China in 1997, Tung Chee-hwa, is a member of the latter dynasty. And it was overseas Chinese such as these who, in the 1980s, responded to Deng's call to invest in the Shenzhen SEZ.

At the end of 1980, Xinhua claimed there were already 490 enterprises investing in Shenzhen of which 329 were factories making woollen knitwear, garments, toys, plastic and silk flowers, radio cassettes and building materials, or vehicle and machine repair shops. Those who had made their fortunes in property in post-1949 Hong Kong also responded to Deng's call and grasped the new opportunities to build housing, hotels, restaurants and factories, and later ports, motorways, bridges and airports.[9]

Investors in Shenzhen and the other three SEZs benefited from various incentives: they paid only 15 per cent of their profits in income tax (state-owned enterprises were later taxed at 33 per cent) and they could apply for exemption from duties on equipment, raw materials and transport vehicles. Exports were also exempt from duties for the first five years and eventually all trade with Shenzhen was free of duty.

The vehicle for these investments was the joint-venture company in which the Chinese party provided the land while the foreign partner was in charge of manufacturing, transport, sales and marketing. The latter also provided most of the capital while the Chinese ensured the supply of cheap, union-free labour. Goods could move freely in and out of the SEZ, but the movement of people into the zone was strictly controlled, sometimes to the fury of mainlanders who wanted to visit and found that they were treated as if Shenzhen was a new foreign concession. Yet within two years, Hong Kong newspapers began speaking of an 'exodus' of factories and jobs across the border.[10]

Deng's original hopes for the SEZs, however, remained unfulfilled. Though it prospered, Shenzhen attracted little in the way of modern technology in its first two decades, and the other zones did not even prosper greatly. Xiamen, in particular, despite the fact that its territory was increased from under a square mile to over 50 square miles after 1984, attracted only a handful of investors in the 1980s.

Still, though the zones might not attract modern technology, Prime Minister Zhao Ziyang, in a key speech made in 1988, recognized that cheap labour might prove a draw to investment: 'Labour-intensive industries are being moved to areas where labour costs are low. At this moment our coastal areas should be very appealing since they offer cheaper yet qualified labour, better communications and infrastructure, and particularly the capacity for scientific and technological development. These are our strong points. We can funnel in a large quantity of foreign investment if we do our work well.' With their large populations, the coastal areas should, he added, 'give top priority to developing labour-intensive industries'.[11]

As such, the strategy was undoubtedly successful. The coastal regions attracted 85 per cent of foreign investment (and in the 1990s China attracted the bulk of foreign investment channelled into developing countries). The 120,000 foreign-funded companies, employing nearly 10 per cent of the urban workforce, accounted for 47 per cent of the country's foreign trade. In Guangdong, the figure was 54 per cent and in Tianjin as high as 70 per cent. It is, however, probably fair to say that China has attracted no more than its fair share of investment from multinational companies. Most investment has come from overseas Chinese, many of whom use Hong Kong as their base. By 1995, investment from Hong Kong was put at US$63 billion, or two-thirds of all foreign investment.

According to its first Party secretary Li Hao, Shenzhen was 'a miracle created by China in its socialist modernization'. A rural back-water of just 30,000 rice farmers had been transformed into an industrial zone with a population of 3 million. In its first eleven years, the zone's authorities spent US$5.12 billion developing 27 square miles, including 9 industrial areas, 50 residential sectors, a large airport, a railway station, 7 harbours, 4 land ports, 180 miles of high-ways and 210,000 telephone lines.[12]

There was, however, another, darker side to Shenzhen. It and other zones such as Hainan Island were used by mainland companies mas-querading as joint ventures that were backed by the children of senior government officials. In one scandal which came to light in 1985, it was discovered that such companies had imported into Hainan 89,000 luxury cars and 3 million television sets, as well as video recorders and motorcycles, in deals worth US$1.5 billion. And even legitimate businesses in Shenzhen were described by one visitor as 'a dense hodgepodge of tindery sweatshops and cheap architec-ture'. She went on to paint a depressing picture: 'As you walk across the border from Hong Kong ... the senses are attacked from all sides.

Huge billboards advertise Remy Martin XO, Marlboro County, an international golf-course and beeper machines. The stink of the polluted Lohu River competes with the constant concussion of pile drivers at construction sites. Outside the train station child beggars, babies hanging from their arms like rag dolls, run alongside new arrivals, grabbing their sleeves. Painted girls in miniskirts or tight pants linger on the curbs, eyeing the arriving Hong Kong businessmen. Ramshackle, overcrowded workers' dormitories, some with no running water, line the roads heading out of town. Down a traffic-jammed main artery, a huge billboard pictures China's ageing leader, Deng Xiaoping, hovering over the city like a god as he exhorts the masses: "Stick to the Communist Party's line, 100 years unwavering."[13]

The vast majority of the factories are staffed by young peasant women, and Shenzhen's hotels and nightclubs are packed with girls waiting for customers. Many of the thousands of managers and technicians from Hong Kong or Taiwan who run factories in southern Guangdong have acquired mistresses. Some Hong Kong men have ended up leading dual lives with two families and two sets of children. Shenzhen even has its own concubine village with kept women living in cheap apartments near a border crossing at Huangbeiling.

All in all, the lifestyle enjoyed by foreign businessmen in the zones who live in heavily guarded villa parks bears more than a passing resemblance to treaty port life, despite the fact that the majority are not Westerners but overseas Chinese. Many are Taiwanese and some were among the 2 million mainlanders who fled to Taiwan with the KMT forces in 1949. In the 1990s, Taiwanese investors formed a second wave of investment in Guangdong. Within just five years the prefecture of Dongguan north of Shenzhen had 4,000 companies making everything from computer components to shoes to petrochemicals, and by 1998 there were 25,000 Taiwanese employing perhaps 2 million people there.[14]

Many of these factory-owners have taken pains to disguise their ownership and to dodge the responsibilities that go with ownership. In one survey a third of the companies listed as being from Hong Kong were actually found to be Taiwanese. Others registered in places such as the Virgin Islands so that obscure Caribbean islands accounted for nearly 10 per cent of investment in China in 1997. In the first nine months of that year this amounted to US$6 billions' worth of business.

By operating outside the law so much of the time, however, many Taiwanese became vulnerable to blackmail by crooked cadres. Others were abducted by gangsters. Between 1991 and 1998 about 60 disappeared or were killed and another 127 were kidnapped or otherwise detained.[15]

Working conditions in these factories seem little better than in the days of Shanghai's silk mills, then a byword for exploitation and maltreatment of workers. Talking is usually forbidden. To go to the toilet or drink a glass of water requires a permission card. Sexual harassment is common and punishments can involve beating, confinement or cancellation of wages. Arriving late can mean half a day's wages are docked. The girls work twelve-hour shifts with two days off a month, and they sleep eight to ten crammed into a dormitory room which is locked at night to prevent theft.

In addition, workers in the SEZs lack the protection of any legal safeguards because two-thirds of them are hired without the right *hukou* or work permit. Completely at the mercy of those who have smuggled them into the SEZ or who employ them, they are powerless to act when their wages turn out to be lower than promised or when they are not paid at all. Few have formal contracts or health or unemployment insurance. If they marry or become pregnant they are generally dismissed.

As in the 1920s and 1930s in Shanghai, most are young peasant girls. In 1998 altogether 4 million women worked in the Pearl River delta. Almost half of the 607,000 people living in the Zhuhai SEZ are migrant workers and of these 80 per cent are women aged 16 to 25, according to Tan Shen, a senior researcher at the Chinese Academy of Social Sciences. Many of them labour in some of the biggest shoe factories in the world, producing sports shoes for internationally known brand names, as well as garments, household gadgets and electrical appliances.[16]

Although many of the multinationals operating in Shenzhen observe reasonable standards and have tried to enforce better health and occupational safety standards, they still sub-contract work out to smaller factories that do not. Local government, the only body that might be expected to enforce safety, is often the local partner in a joint venture so conflicts of interest are common.[17]

Even the installation of such mundane things as panic bars on emergency exits can become a source of dispute, with the Chinese partner refusing to spend further money. Apo Leong, a researcher for the Hong Kong-based Trade Union Education Centre, blames low safety standards on greedy overseas Chinese: 'The bosses know how to get around the loopholes and give government officials benefits as trade-offs for all kinds of permits without actually complying with the law. Most of the bosses have their eye on profits only. Their plan is to get as much as possible in three to five years, so safety is one of the many non-profit-making sectors that is sacrificed.'[18]

An Australian academic, Anita Chan, has found an explanation for the severe military discipline imposed on the workforce – the managers are often former army officers from Taiwan or South Korea and the Chinese officials are also ex-NCOs who share the same attitudes. 'In some Taiwan-owned factories the owners fly in retired army officers to impose a martinet discipline on both mainland workers and Taiwanese staff . . . Female job applicants are ordered to stand to attention as if they are applying to join the army, are told to run a mile and then to do as many push-ups as they can within a minute.' Those who pass the test are then drilled in platoons for three days. She also found that Taiwanese businessmen scoff at what they consider to be the slack management practice of local Hong Kong-owned firms. 'I was told that corporal punishment is common in . . . many of the factories owned by Taiwanese and Koreans.'[19]

In 1995 the Zhuhai Labour Bureau took action against the head of a South Korean electronics factory who reportedly kept her workers on duty continuously for more than twenty-four hours. Some fell asleep during a ten-minute break and were ordered to kneel in front of her while others had to keep their hands raised in the air for ten minutes. In another Korean-run factory, a woman worker was locked inside a dog cage together with a large dog and publicly displayed in the factory compound.

Things were no better in the north. In the same year the *Worker's*

Daily reported that 600 female workers had staged protests at the South Korean Li Da factory in Qinhuangdao, Hebei province, demanding shorter hours, higher wages and the right not to be beaten or insulted. They also wanted a labour contract because they were being forced to do overtime in excess of the thirty-six hours a month stipulated by law. The company responded by firing the ringleaders and punishing the others.[20]

In Weihaiwei, Shandong, the same newspaper found that in South Korean factories workers were having to do enforced overtime to meet deadlines. Some factories had implemented piece-rate payment and then reduced the payment for each piece to force the workers to work longer to get a satisfactory wage. Only two enterprises paid their employees US$84 a month; the average was just US$50. The newspaper said trade union officials were being bribed to turn a blind eye to those foreign investors who failed to implement labour regulations.[21]

The worst examples of a disregard for the welfare of workers, however, came to light after a series of factory fires in the Pearl River delta. In one incident in November 1993, 87 workers were killed when the Zhili handicrafts factory caught fire and collapsed. The Hong Kong-funded factory had built a separate hostel building, unlike some companies who chose to save money by building workers' dormitories on top of the plant, but the factory's locked gates, barred windows and blocked exits made escape difficult. Later two firemen were charged with accepting bribes from the factory and the Hong Kong manager Lo Chiu-chuen was jailed for two years. In June 1994, 11 workers died and dozens were injured when the Xie Cheng toy factory, which had been built without permission, collapsed.[22] Then, in 1995, a fire broke out at a factory which made Christmas decorations after a worker left a candle burning and fell asleep. The fire trapped at least 1,000 workers sleeping in dormitories. There were 21 deaths and 108 injuries.[23]

In response to such cases Chinese leaders issued decrees tightening up health and safety regulations, and from January 1995 all foreign-run factories were obliged to permit the operation of a branch of the state trade union. Unofficial trade unions are outlawed. At the same time, however, many provinces were quick to issue tough new regulations to prevent workers from striking. All industrial action now has to be approved by the government-controlled union, and the overriding interest of most local governments is of course to boost foreign investment and exports. Unsurprisingly, despite the central government's efforts at ameliorating conditions, reports of workers dying in fires or suffering abuse have not stopped.[24]

Government efforts to enforce minimum health and safety standards in 1995 coincided with criticism of the SEZs on economic grounds. The Chinese economist Hu Angang argued that the SEZs were being unfairly subsidized by taxes levied on the rest of the country.[25] Enterprises in Guangdong retained most of their profits while Shanghai's state-owned enterprises delivered theirs to the government. In addition, Shenzhen could keep all of its foreign exchange earnings and Guangdong province 60 per cent of its foreign exchange earnings but Shanghai handed everything over to Beijing.

Most damaging to Deng's concept of the special economic zones, however, was evidence that the fantastic growth rates reported after his southern tour in 1992 were the product of a bubble economy. When the bubble collapsed after 1995, the country was left to face a mountain of debts, from which it has not yet recovered, and acres of empty and unwanted buildings.

The bubble began when Shenzhen, which had already had an unofficial stock exchange, won government approval to open an exchange on an experimental basis in December 1990, just two weeks before the official opening of the Shanghai securities exchange. Other areas, including Beijing, Shenyang, Wukan and Zhengzhou, as well as Haikou, the sleepy capital of Hainan Island, soon followed suit in a race to become the country's main financial centre.

Initially, Shenzhen listed just five companies whose shares shot up. In August 1992 rioting erupted when over a million people queued to buy shares in a new issue. The *South China Morning Post* reported what was happening: 'Police with cattle rods and batons battled to keep order last night as thousands of Chinese thronged to Shenzhen for the chance to buy shares in a wave of get-rich-quick fever. China's capitalist revolution went mad with a deluge of people hoping for a chance to buy shares in the city's stock exchange.'[26]

Queuing had started on the Saturday although the application forms for the new issue were not distributed until the following Monday. That evening tens of thousands marched through the streets protesting at the way in which the application forms had been distributed.

Shenzhen's mayor Zheng Liangyu was sacked and the authorities closed in on some of those who had profited from the stockmarket frenzy. One case involved Peng Jiandong, a 32-year-old who in 1991 had listed a textile company, the Shenzhen Champaign Industrial Company. With the capital raised, he bought himself a US$2 million home in a Sydney suburb, a sheep and cattle ranch in Wagga Wagga, a US$5.6 million seaside mansion in Hong Kong and a fleet of luxury cars. The Chinese police abducted him from a hotel room in Macao and he was sentenced to sixteen years' imprisonment for embezzlement. However, he had acquired Australian nationality, and by international standards he had not been given a fair trial. In circumstances strongly reminiscent of the treaty ports' exercise of extraterritoriality, his case became a diplomatic issue. He was released seven years later just before President Jiang Zemin paid a state visit to Australia.

Nevertheless, Shenzhen weathered the storm to become one of only two legal stock exchanges in China. Haikou was less fortunate. There many who had bought shares, issued loans or invested in property schemes lost heavily and in 1995 the stock exchange was closed. In 1999 the losses linked to Haikou's property bubble were estimated to amount to 39 billion yuan (US$4.7 billion).[27] The island as a whole has also been left with 750 million square feet of empty buildings and another 129 million square feet of half-completed buildings. Haikou alone has enough empty space to house an extra half a million people and across the island tropical vegetation is gradually taking over rows of half-finished villas. Tens of thousands who swarmed into Hainan to make their fortune in what was described as the new Hong Kong have been left penniless. By 1997 the island's population had dropped by 200,000.

The Hong Kong recipe was not so easily repeated, even if one was a Hong Kong tycoon like Yu Yuanping. In 1990 his company,

Kumagai Gumi (HK) Ltd (formerly the subsidiary of a Japanese construction corporation), took out a 70-year lease over 10 square miles of neglected coastline on Hainan to build a free port from scratch. Visiting the site five years later was a surreal experience. After speeding along a deserted motorway, I entered the zone through a high fence and arrived at a 36-floor skyscraper. From the roof, I was shown the neat roads laid out amongst the deserted miles of scrub and red ochre earth.

'In another ten years, there will be a modern city all around us with factories and homes for 400,000,' promised its Hong Kong manager, Terry Wong, breezily.

Inside the perimeter fence, which was eventually to enclose 27 square miles of land, the Hong Kong tycoon was free to operate like a colonial governor. He could sell land as he pleased, abolish duty on imports and exports, issue visas to new arrivals and sell goods at half the normal sales tax.

It was not to be. Although the company has spent heavily on building a new harbour, a power station and a customs house, no one has bought the land or established new sweatshops.[28] Instead of labour-intensive industries, Hainan has had to settle for becoming the centre of China's sex industry. There is nothing hidden or discreet about it, either. This is a government-backed industry. Prostitutes tout for customers outside and inside Haikou's best hotels. In Sanya, a fishing village at the southern end of the island that grew almost overnight into a town of 500,000, tens of thousands seem to be engaged in the trade. A new customer arriving at the door of one of the numerous nightclubs is automatically asked to select a girl before sitting down to watch a floor show featuring Thai transvestites. Even on the beach, pairs of girls stop and accost any man walking around unaccompanied.

Across the straits separating Haikou from the mainland, the story is much the same. At Beihai, one of the original fourteen open coastal cities and formerly the treaty port of Pakhoi, the houses of former merchants have become brothels. Heavily made-up Hunan country girls in black diaphanous tops and cut-off jeans sit around outside waiting for customers. Here too the property bubble burst, leaving dozens of empty and deteriorating developments – rows and rows of

Mediterranean-style villas complete with balconies, fountains and life-size statues of naked Greek goddesses and Roman heroes.

Further east along the coast is Zhanjiang, suffering from the same blight but better known for its smugglers. This is the headquarters of the PLA Navy's South China Fleet whose commanders have reputedly grown fabulously wealthy in recent years. As Hainan Island and the coasts of Guangdong and Fujian were on the front line during the Cold War, the navy 'owned' almost all the property worth having. It is therefore hardly surprising that it too became caught up in feverish real-estate speculation and involved in every conceivable racket, if only as a sleeping partner.

In 1998 the extent of the navy's involvement, and that of local Party officials, became clear. An anti-smuggling campaign launched by Beijing provided the first official confirmation of the scale of what was happening in Zhanjiang when it was revealed that smuggling was costing the state over US$10 billion a year in lost customs revenues. The quantity of goods involved was staggering – as many as 100,000 cars were reported to be smuggled in each year. Perhaps it was fitting, therefore, that when Zhanjiang's Party chief, Chen Tongqing, was given a life sentence for his involvement, he was tried at the theatre complex which for years had served as the marketplace for smuggled luxury cars. Some 600 other officials were also arrested in a sweep launched after the Prime Minister Zhu Rongji descended on the coast much as Lin Zexu had done in the days of the opium smugglers.[29]

The rackets that were revealed were every bit as heinous as those that had made Shanghai notorious in the 1920s and 1930s. Chen Tongqing had auctioned off lucrative posts, among them the chairmanship of the municipality's construction and planning committee, and had acted as godfather to the local triads. He had also involved the heads of the port authority, the customs and the police in running a huge operation which turned Zhanjiang into an unauthorized free port. 'Boss Chen and the gangsters were like a family, as close as fish and water,' reported the *China Reform Daily* in a breathless account of how Chen, together with mobsters like Big Ears Wang, had imported duty-free cars, crude oil, diesel, processed sugar, textiles and electrical and electronic parts.

One of these gangsters, who was subsequently tried and executed, was a former local peasant called Lin Chunhua. The *People's Daily* revealed that in one year alone he used a fleet of forty-four tankers, some of which he owned, to bring in oil and diesel equal to one-tenth of China's official imports. Every day hundreds of smaller tankers would line up outside the refinery to distribute the cut-price diesel all over southern China. Chen was only 33 when he was shot, but fifty cars filled with his supporters accompanied his corpse to its grave.

The head of the Zhanjiang customs, Cao Xiukang, was apparently seduced by 'three extremely beautiful mistresses', including a Shanghai-born beauty nicknamed the Smuggling Queen, who were supplied by triads. The Smuggling Queen's accomplice was a Hong Kong businessman, Li Shen, who regularly bought the drinks at a karaoke bar opposite the customs house and drove a dark blue Mercedes Benz 600 with the number plate 1111.

These gangsters settled their scores in public. In one case a shoot-out at a restaurant left four dead and nineteen wounded. Big Ears Wang, who smuggled goods using the local fishing and shrimping boats as a cover, intimidated people by severing their tendons with a meat cleaver or chopping off their fingers.

Visiting Zhanjiang in 1999 after these reports were published, I found many of the details confirmed by locals who added more information that had not been revealed in official press coverage. According to them it was actually the PLA that ran the docks, supplied transport and operated hotels and massage parlours. The press had reported that Zhanjiang's disgraced Party secretary 'did not care about progress but just lusted after sex and drink', but the available evidence suggests that he and his fellow officials squandered government money on numerous ill-conceived projects and that everything they invested in had failed – a brewery, an electronics factory, a bowling alley, a car factory, a textiles plant, an oil refinery, several sugar refineries, a beach resort and a hi-tech special development zone.

The Sanxing Autoworks was a case in point. On paper, the Zhanjiang authorities had invested one billion yuan (US$120 million) in a joint venture with Mercedes Benz to produce commercial vehicles. In reality, the plant had never managed to make a single vehicle of its own but instead had imported Dodge minivans duty-free as kits. All the factory did was unpack them and screw on the company's distinctive logo, then sell them on at a huge mark-up.

Smuggling on this scale poses the same problems as it did for the Qing dynasty which ended up relying on foreigners to run its customs service. And while the current central government has trouble collecting customs duties and protecting uncompetitive domestic industries, foreign governments are increasingly concerned about the pirates who are smuggling illegal immigrants into the West. Some treaty ports thrived on shipping out indentured labourers to work on the railroads of the American West, the sugar plantations of Hawaii or the rubber plantations of Malaya. Now tens of thousands of labourers are being smuggled out to America or Europe in ships operated by gangs based in Wenzhou.

The new-style SEZs and coastal cities are now dominated by the investments of overseas Chinese billionaires who are conscious of the legacy of shame that treaty port colonialism has left behind. A rhetoric of patriotism clothes the deals they negotiate, although they have yet to make Deng's vision of creating models of new technology and advanced management a reality.

Shantou, one of the original SEZs, is an example. It may have developed into another hotbed of smuggling but it lives in the shadow of its richest son, Li Ka-shing, the property developer who is Hong Kong's richest man and who was at one point the sixth richest in Asia. He started life as the penniless son of a wartime refugee from Shantou who arrived in Hong Kong and struggled to make a living as a teacher. Now, wherever you go in Shantou, people talk of what Li has built – the university, the church, the hospital, the bridges, the power station, the container port, the motorway, the new housing estates, the shopping centre and the factories.[30]

'Mr Li is the pride of the Chaozhou [Shantou] people,' declared Xu Deli, the Party secretary of Shantou. 'President Jiang Zemin has praised him as a true patriot.' At Shantou University, built of course by Li, visitors are shown a video in which he emotionally declares that 'My only true purpose is to contribute what I can to my home town, my nation and my motherland. It is my life purpose.'

The same would probably be said by the Indonesian Chinese tycoon Mochtar Riady of the Lippo group who has taken out a lease on 14 square miles of coastline near his birthplace at Putian in Fujian province. Another Indonesian billionaire, Liem Sioe Liong, is also building a new city and industrial zone in his ancestral home in Fuqing in the same province.

Good intentions are not enough, though, as Singapore's leader Lee Kuan Yew discovered. Lee was granted a concession outside the famous city of Suzhou not far from Shanghai which he promised to turn into a new Singapore, a model society with hi-tech industries operated with investment from multinationals. Singapore obtained a 70-year lease, and investment of US$30 billion was planned for a new city of 600,000 people. However, though his advice on how to deal with China has won the ear of many a Western leader, in 1999 Lee was forced to admit that after investing huge sums, the project had failed and the Singapore government was pulling out. He had acted with the personal backing of President Jiang Zemin but the Suzhou government had done everything to obstruct the project and favour its own separate industrial zone. Lee could not hide his astonishment at the sharp practices of the Suzhou officials and lashed out at the corruption in China, likening it to a powder keg that was set to explode.[31]

He must, however, have regretted turning down China's initial offer to help develop Shanghai's Pudong. This, the grandest of all the schemes that got underway in 1992, is an attempt to build a new version of Shanghai on the opposite bank of the Huangpu River. Pudong is now the biggest of all the SEZs. It covers an area of 200 square miles and some 2 million people are supposed to move there and work not just in export processing plants but in the Lujiazui financial centre, a free trade zone and a hi-tech park.

President Jiang Zemin and Premier Zhu Rongji, who have both served as Shanghai's Party boss, are determined to ensure that Shanghai is again transformed into the 'dragon's head' which will help open up the interior and encourage growth along the Yangtze valley. By 1999, US$29 billion had been poured into modernizing the area's infrastructure, partly financed by government funds raised by selling leases on prime property sites. This dwarfs the sums spent on

Shenzhen but Shanghai claims it has already attracted investment promises worth US$37 billion. Dozens of multinationals have invested in Pudong, among them General Motors which alone has spent US$1.5 billion on a modern car plant.

Even so, it will be many years before anyone can judge whether or not the Communist Party has succeeded in resurrecting Shanghai's past glory. Half the completed property still awaits tenants, and the American economist Milton Friedman has speculated on whether Pudong will become 'a state monument for a dead pharaoh, just like the pyramids'.[32] As Friedman complained after touring Shanghai in 1993, China's rulers are still obsessed with big government, grand plans and giant state-run industries. The next chapter describes how, in attempting to realize these aims, the state has mortgaged China's future.

6

The Iron Rice Bowl

THE GUARDS HAD gone and one could walk unopposed through
the factory gates and into the silent yards. Until the spring of
1996, 7,000 workers had streamed through the same gates each
morning to feed the tireless spindles and shuttles but now there was
barely a murmur to be heard, just a small group of men engrossed in
a card game on a bench in a small garden.[1]

'It's closed,' muttered one of them, barely looking up from his
hand. 'Shut down. Two months ago.'

The Shenxin No. 9 Mill, perhaps the oldest factory in China, had
fallen silent for the first time since 1878. No newspaper had reported
the closure or the lay-offs that had followed, and the old men in the
garden would not be drawn into conversation.

'Should have been done years ago,' said a younger man who came
past pushing his bicycle. 'Some of the shuttles were so old, I heard
they put them straight into a museum.'

Then he snorted a short, sour laugh. The shuttles, made in Lan-
caster, had been bought, second-hand, by Rong Zongjing, the founder
of the wealthiest family in China. Now a bust cast in iron with the dates
1873–1938 inscribed beneath it stands in the garden. Although Rong
was China's most successful capitalist – at its peak in the 1930s his firm
operated thirty of Shanghai's hundred textile mills – a grateful Communist Party had wanted to acknowledge his contribution towards
modernizing China. The Rongs had been no friends of China's hard-
pressed proletariat but they had helped build Shanghai, a city which
boasted it could clothe half the nation, into an industrial giant.

Around Shanghai, one can still see the vast palaces that the Rongs built themselves, islands of architectural glory in the shadow of the concrete and glass towers rising all around. Once I explored one of them, a mansion in Jugendstil with a parquet-floor ballroom and a banqueting hall with gilded mirrors that gave out on to lawns and rhododendron bushes. Inside, the officials of some obscure department were drinking tea and slowly reading newspapers in partitioned offices. Buckets stood on the teak floor to catch water from the leaking roof, and a dim light filtered through sagging, dust-laden curtains that shrouded the magnificent mullioned windows.

When, in the 1930s, so much of China's industry was in the hands of foreigners, especially the Japanese, the Rongs' efforts to build up the country's industrial strength marked them out as patriots, even in the midst of violent struggles between capital and labour. In Shanghai, where the Japanese alone employed 50,000 textile workers, hatred of Japanese and other foreign capitalists fostered the growth of the Communist Party.

In February 1925, after the Japanese owner of the Naigai No. 8 Cotton Mill was found beating one of his Chinese female workers, the rest went on strike and workers from twenty other Japanese textile mills joined in. Four months later, Gu Zhengzhong, a worker at the Naigai No. 7 Cotton Mill, was reportedly killed by a Japanese capitalist. The protests, encouraged by Communist agitators such as Liu Shaoqi, culminated in a rally which brought 200,000 students and workers out on to the streets.

The event is commemorated in a frieze along the bottom of the Monument to the People's Heroes in Tiananmen Square, in Beijing, and a life-size statue dedicated to the sacred memory of the murdered worker was erected at his former workplace, then renamed the Shenxin No. 4 Mill, after 1949. Yet when this factory too closed in 1996, there were no protests, not even a petition by the workers or a report in the newspapers. Shanghai's Communist Party had resolved that sentimentality should not stand in the way of profits or its plans to shut down an industry which employed half a million people.

In place of factories such as these, Shanghai's cranes were busy building new shopping malls, office buildings and villas. On the site of another factory, I found a large hall opening off the street where hundreds of men and women stood about silently watching the numbers change on a gigantic electronic screen.

'Shares,' explained one of them, a neat-looking woman of about 60. 'They're stir-frying shares.'

Mrs Chen was not one of those speculating in stock prices (colloquially known as 'stir-frying shares'). She just had nothing much else to do with her time, she said. She had worked at the No. 1 Cloth Factory and took me to see it. Inside, all the machinery had been stripped out, leaving a wide empty space. A few exhortative slogans in faded red were still visible on the bare walls.

'The factory was owned by a capitalist, Deng Zhong, who fled to Hong Kong before Liberation, taking all his money with him,' she recalled. 'I was just 16 years old when I started here. I remember how bad things were before Liberation.' Her speech changed its rhythm and she now began to speak with authority. 'Before Liberation we had to work twelve hours a day. There was only half an hour to eat lunch and go to the toilet. The bosses were always punishing you for the slightest infringement of other rules.' When her workplace became the No. 1 Cloth Factory, the Party had made her a member. She must have said the same thing at a hundred meetings to remind workers of the changes that the revolution had brought. 'After Liberation, life was much better, we only worked eight hours a day,' she concluded.

Under Communism, Shanghai's textile factories became models for the cradle-to-grave social welfare system that China copied from the Soviet Union. The factory, referred to as the *danwei* or work unit, guaranteed housing, food, clothing, pensions, education and health-care for its workforce. In return the workers, in their role as the van-guard of the revolution, had only to show their loyalty by taking a leading role in endless meetings and political movements. Even when, in 1987 and 1989, the Party's hold on power was threatened by Shanghai students' demands for democracy, Shanghai's leaders, Jiang Zemin and Zhu Rongji, could still summon workers from these state factories and send them out on to the streets armed with clubs.

Mill workers had long preserved a tradition of radicalism. Wang Hongwen, a member of the Gang of Four who attempted to seize power after the death of Mao, was a textile worker at the No. 17

Cotton Mill, and it was he who took charge of the Shanghai Workers' General Headquarters which directed the Cultural Revolution throughout the Shanghai area, when textile workers took the lead in persecuting class enemies and ransacking and destroying the homes of the bourgeoisie.

'Now an overseas Chinese property developer has bought the site,' said Mrs Chen. 'Soon it will be demolished and turned into a shopping centre.'

Mrs Chen accepted an invitation to lunch but by then her confidence had seeped away and she said little more. She was receiving a pension and was housed by the state. She would get by. It was just that there seemed to be nothing to do and, as we left the restaurant, she became glum and shook my hand feebly. An empty afternoon stretched before her.

When Deng Xiaoping launched his reforms in the late 1970s, Shanghai was still China's industrial powerhouse and generated the lion's share of central government revenues. Perhaps that is why the factories, nationalized in the 1940s, were never returned to their legal owners after 1979. In compensation, the youngest scion of the Rong dynasty, Rong Yiren (nephew of the founder Rong Zongjing), who had stayed behind in 1949 while the rest of the family scattered around the world, was given a new and lucrative post. He, who had once held the honorary post of deputy textile minister but had disappeared from sight during the Cultural Revolution, was now appointed the founding president of China's new international finance house, the China International Trust and Investment Corporation (CITIC). Later, Deng even made him Vice President of China and in the early 1990s sent his son, Larry Yung (who anglicized his name), to Hong Kong. A branch of the family had fled to Hong Kong in 1949, and there Rong Yuan set up the Da Yuan and Nanyang cotton mills which laid the foundation for Hong Kong's post-war rise as a manufacturing centre for textiles and garments. As the chairman of CITIC Pacific, Larry Yung took stakes in key companies to build up a Communist *hong* in the former colony, and he acquired a personal fortune along the way. In 1997, *Forbes* magazine listed him as the wealthiest man in China who owned, amongst other property, an English country house with 335 acres in East Sussex.

The 1990s were less kind to Shanghai's textile industry. With their outdated machinery and expensive workforce, the factories could not survive increasing competition from the new rural enterprises and SEZ sweatshops. Though China imported over US$5 billion of textile equipment between 1990 and 1995, and though by 1995 it was the world's biggest textile exporter, with exports worth US$38 billion, three-quarters of Shanghai's textile factories were losing money and facing debts of 2 billion yuan. The same story was repeated at other state-run factories across the country.

In a bid to reposition its economy by creating new industries in Pudong that would concentrate on bio-technology, new materials, micro-electronics, shipbuilding, cars and telecommunications, Shanghai decided to jettison almost the entire textile industry. Instead of the textile proletariat, it would be home to fashion designers and couturiers. The city also sought to recapture its position as a financial centre and as the leader in education and the arts.

Around 400,000 textile workers, mostly middle-aged and female, lost their jobs as the city began to transform itself into a service centre. The state media put out morale-lifting stories of how such women found a new life. One reputedly started up a very successful business washing and preparing vegetables for the new rich. The reality was rather different. Most found themselves unemployable in the new economy, for they had grown up during the Cultural Revolution and had never received a real education. During the same period in all about a million members of Shanghai's industrial workforce of 3.6 million lost their jobs. And the picture was much the same across the country. The state sector employed around 100 million, the entire urban workforce. By 2000, 30 million had been laid off and another 20–30 million are expected to lose their jobs over the next three years.[2]

State-owned enterprises (SOEs) such as these Shanghai textile factories had formed the backbone of the centrally planned economy set up after 1949 and consisted of three types: the pre-1949 factories concentrated in the former treaty ports and those built by the Japanese during their occupation of Manchuria; the 154 major industrial complexes built with Soviet aid during the 1950s; and the so-called Third Line factories built in the interior during the 1960s and 1970s to enable China to survive a nuclear war with the Soviet Union.

Central government ministries ran these factories according to five-year plans but each province also had its own system of SOEs, and so did many counties. The result was acute fragmentation. Instead of a handful of enterprises in one sector, China often has a hundred or even a thousand such enterprises. The 1980s and 1990s exacerbated the problem because then those state enterprises that were successful not only expanded their capacity but also branched out into new areas. This was especially true of defence industries which could only survive big cutbacks in orders by switching to the production of consumer goods.

The Communist Party, however, retained an unshakeable belief in its ability to plan the future systematically. In the 1950s, it had created the first of a series of blueprints for the industrialization of China, and although these five-year plans were overruled during the Great Leap Forward and suffered from the disruptions of the Cultural Revolution, the system still remained in place in the 1990s.

The Chinese state minutely organized and controlled what happened in every factory through a bureaucracy of a hundred ministries in Beijing and their subordinates down the administrative hierarchy. Journalists from the Soviet bloc who returned from touring state-sector plants in China would marvel at how orders were so much more rigidly observed by Chinese factory managers than by their counterparts in the Soviet Union or Poland. A manager in China would not even move a piece of machinery or reassign a worker without written permission from Beijing. The state took on the task of forecasting all needs and establishing the supply and distribution of absolutely everything. Every sock, every screw, every potato was either in the plan or it could not exist.

Judged by their own lights, the 300,000 SOEs were extremely successful in producing vast quantities of basic commodities such as iron, steel, coal and cotton of which China became the world's biggest producer. Unfortunately, this was achieved in the face of a total disregard for quality or cost. In addition, the state sector proved hopeless at responding to market needs and quite unable to innovate.

At the Flying Pigeon factory in Tianjin, for example, the workers continued to produce a bicycle that was a copy of the 1932 British Raleigh bicycle. It came in only one colour, black, but was still regarded as the Rolls-Royce of Chinese bikes in the 1980s, its only rival being an identical bike called 'Forever'. People waited years to acquire a Flying Pigeon bicycle because, like everything else, it was rationed, distributed on the say-so of a Party official. Almost all Chinese products – watches, sewing-machines, motorcycles – dated from a similar era, the only comparatively modern products being those produced for the military, such as Soviet-designed tanks dating from the 1950s or rockets and nuclear weapons.

When I visited the Flying Pigeon plant in 1996, over a third of its 20,000-strong workforce had been laid off. The rest received wages only erratically because production was suspended for part of each month.[3]

'The truth is we are bankrupt,' said one of the workers as he walked his bicycle up and down the street. In a pannier on the back he had some fish he had caught and was now trying to sell. He predicted with some confidence that the management would continue to shed workers until the factory became profitable.

'When a factory slowly starts closing like this, we call it *huang le* or "yellowing", like a leaf in autumn,' he explained, enjoying for a moment the small satisfaction that comes from explaining a complicated technical term to a newcomer.

By the 1990s people were no longer buying Flying Pigeons because there were hundreds of factories started by rural enterprises or foreign investors that were making better models at a lower price. Competition was fierce. China's annual demand for bicycles was just 30 million but the country's total capacity was nearly 70 million. Half the major companies were losing money and selling their products on the world market at any price, which led the European Union and Canada to impose anti-dumping restrictions.[4]

The bicycle worker turned fish-seller said he still had his iron rice bowl. One of the lucky few whose living standard was guaranteed by the state, he was allowed a subsistence wage of 200 yuan (US$24) a month, a rent-free flat and access to a school for his child. At the back of the plant were the four-storey red-brick blocks of flats that were typical of the housing built in the heyday of the SOEs. If the Flying Pigeon factory hung on long enough, he could retire at 55 or 60 on a pension almost as good as his former wage. The trouble was that for many now, neither wages nor pensions were being paid because many factories no longer existed except in name.

In Tianjin, it was usually the pensioners, not the laid-off workers, who took the lead in organizing protests during this period. Outside Tianjin's Fireproof Materials Factory, some 2,000 pensioners had staged a sit-in and then decided to block the road in the hope of forcing the state to pay back wages and pensions.

'It is always the pensioners because everyone thinks they have less to fear from the government. The police wouldn't dare arrest them,' explained one worker in a whisper. We quickly moved away from the factory gates in case there were plainclothes agents watching. Even though there were protests every week, everyone was too frightened to give their name and even feared saying the word 'protest' out loud, let alone 'strike'.

'We are just petitioning the state to help us. We are not against the state,' insisted the man. Then he bent his head and added slyly, 'Besides, how can you strike if there is no work to do?'

The problem posed by the pensioners is unlikely to go away. In the mid-1990s a large number of SOEs had as many pensioners on their books as workers. In cities like Shanghai and Tianjin, where industry had long been established, the financial burden of maintaining these pensioners was crippling. In 1997, some 70 million SOE workers across the country were supporting 24 million pensioners. The financial burden of supporting Shanghai's pensioners was equal to the city's entire GDP.[5] In the late 1990s, about 120 million people, or roughly 10 per cent of the total population, were aged over 60. By 2020 that figure will have risen to 16 per cent. By the middle of the century, one in four Chinese, that is 410 million, will be over 60. 'China will have a high-income economy's old age burden, with a middle-income economy's resources for shouldering it,' a report by the World Bank has warned. In urban areas the problem is especially acute because by then every third person could be a pensioner.[6]

As long as China lacks a national pension fund, each SOE will have to bear the responsibility of supporting its own retired workers.

The system is failing many pensioners because so many SOEs, especially those in the rust-belt, have ceased production or only continue to exist on paper, and the pensions have stop being paid. Shenyang in the north-east admitted in 1995 that one in five of its 560,000 pensioners was no longer receiving a pension.

Shenyang lies at the heart of China's rust-belt with a concentration of heavy industry built up in the 1950s and linked to China's massive industrial-defence complex. In the last decade everything that could go wrong with the SOEs has gone wrong here. At the PLA's Red Dawn Factory, the cancellation of orders for tanks and aeroplanes in the 1980s led to the dismissal of half its 20,000 workers. The remaining workforce was making consumer goods, a sector in which, like most SOEs, it was uncompetitive. The workforce, unused to the demands of competition, could not be made to work hard. A World Bank survey of five industrial cities in China concluded that Shenyang had the worst record of labour productivity, half that of Shanghai. In a city of 4 million, it was employing a million peasants to do the actual work.[7]

Those factories established by the Japanese in the 1930s in the Tiexi district, such as the New China Printing Plant or the Rechargeable Battery Plant, were the first to close down.

'It used to be that when sirens sounded at the end of a shift there would be thousands pouring on to the streets. Now you can't see anyone,' explained a helpful taxi-driver who took me on a tour of all the deserted factories in 1997.[8]

Tiexi's No. 4 Rubber Products Factory and the Daily Chemical Materials Factory had been put out of business by prisoners at the Dabei prison complex. Behind its barbed wire and high brick walls, the prison had put its 160,000 inmates to work making boots, shoes, soap and cosmetics, but by the mid-1990s, even prison labour was no longer cheap enough to compete with rural industries.

'The prisoners don't go to work any more, they now stay in their cells,' the taxi-driver said, and then added with a note of glee, 'even the guards and supervisors are now sitting at home without pay.'

Those plants built in the 1960s had also closed down. An industrial zone, dubbed the Avenue of Losses by the locals, consisted of mile after mile of silent, empty factories and blocks of the inevitable red-brick workers' flats. Behind the barred gates of the giant Shenyang Steel Plant, the statues of heroic workers stretching their hands to the sky no longer seemed triumphant but imploring.

The grass growing over the railway sidings testified to the decay which set in after 1992 and accelerated in 1995. In the 1980s, throughout China, even badly managed factories could make good profits. Demand was high and so whatever was surplus to the state plan could be sold. Then, as competition grew, even the badly managed could make profits simply by selling their raw materials, obtained cheaply under the plan, at a free-market price. But by the early 1990s, when the state gave up its fruitless efforts to plan the economy and determine the price for every product, plants were free to sell whatever they wanted to whomsoever they wished and the chain of supply that linked the SOE economy to a complex web of interdependency quickly unravelled. Every factory unit sought the best price on the open market and everyone demanded to be paid at the market rate for delivering raw materials or components. Soon the whole system seized up in a chain of unpaid debts, the SOEs owing each other some 900 billion yuan of so-called 'triangular debts'.

Managers unused to independent decision-making also borrowed recklessly to expand in all directions. By 1997, even the *Workers' Daily* was describing the SOEs as a 'bottomless pit' with debts totalling 4 trillion yuan. They absorbed 70 or 80 per cent of the loans handed out by state banks and soon their non-performing loans totalled hundreds of billions of dollars, enough to cripple the entire banking system.[9]

In Shenyang, workers were forced to subsist on handouts of just 129 yuan (US$15) a month. Soon there was a steady procession of small groups of nervous protesters who turned up outside the municipal Party headquarters to present a petition for payment of back wages or pensions, hoping that eventually an official would emerge from the imposing red-brick edifice that the Party had built for itself and agree to order an emergency handout. Other workers took to crime, forcing the authorities to deploy an extra 1,000 police on the streets. There were so many bank robberies in Shenyang that the city imported armoured cars to transport cash, and a spate of murders of taxi-drivers led the city to install an expensive satellite positioning system in each taxi to reassure drivers that help could be obtained quickly.[10]

In Liaoning as a whole, the authorities reckoned that half the province's 10 million SOE workers had lost their jobs in the 1990s. Much the same thing had occurred in Jilin province to the north where in Changchun, the provincial capital, an unofficial curfew was imposed after a gang committed a series of robberies armed with hammers.

China's northernmost province, Heilongjiang, however, was perhaps the worst affected. When I visited the province in the autumn of 1997, it seemed as if everything had shut down. Seventy per cent of Harbin's 4,000 SOEs were effectively if not legally bankrupt. A third of the 900,000 workers had reputedly been laid off, though locals claimed the real figure was far higher. In the province as a whole, the Party admitted that one in five of its 8 million workers had not been paid and that more than a third were under-employed. In city after grimy city, workers said the reality was still worse – up to 60 per cent of the urban population was either unemployed or not being paid.[11]

Perhaps surprisingly, there was no atmosphere of rebellion, no sign that something like the Polish Solidarity movement was springing up. Independent trade unions were strictly forbidden. The local population was largely composed of migrants in whom habits of dependency and passivity seemed to have become deeply ingrained. At the Jiangbei Sugar Refinery, which had once processed sugarbeet, none of the 2,000 workers had done any work for years. A succession of managers had come and gone but the plant could not compete with cut-price imports smuggled in through ports in the south such as Zhanjiang. In the last two years, the workers had struggled along without either their 150-yuan subsistence allowance or a 100-yuan pension but no government official wanted to declare the factory bankrupt because it had accumulated debts of 400 million yuan.

Among the men who loitered outside the gates or sat on stools playing chess in front of the standard apartment blocks there was only one issue: how to force the government to acknowledge its responsibility without triggering a violent backlash. On four separate occasions, the workers had dispatched around a thousand pensioners to stand in front of the provincial government offices.

'We shouted "We want to eat" for five hours. An official came out and told us it had nothing to do with the government but I can't understand that,' said a grey-haired man in a thick blue padded jacket. 'I've worked here all my life.'

The government did not want to dissolve the enterprise and thus assume responsibility for its debts. And as long as the Jiangbei Sugar Refinery maintained its by now nominal existence, each worker still had a right to his company flat and pension.

I was taken to see one of the flats. Inside it was small and cold, just two barely heated rooms and a narrow space for cooking. The air held the smell of years of frying winter cabbage in cheap rapeseed oil. On the staircase, the inevitable winter cabbage was piled up next to a worn black bicycle. A heap of coal-dust briquettes used for heating and cooking lay outside the entrance by a pile of pinkish cinders. We stood there for a moment and my companion poked at the cinders with a stick, wondering whether to confide in me.

'It's the pension fund that's the problem,' he said at last. 'We don't know if it is still there. There's a rumour it has gone, stolen by the last manager and his son.'

Inside the factory gates a delegation of eighty workers were holding talks with the management, but if the talks failed he did not think there would be any trouble.[12]

'No one dares go too far. China is not like other countries where there are protests and fighting,' he said, and his voice, hitherto a whisper, suddenly became querulous. 'What would be the use? They always arrest the ringleaders who then disappear.'

He could not leave Harbin to find work elsewhere, and as long as he had this place to live in and believed the government would help him, he could survive. Instead, he tried to supplement his income, standing on street corners selling bits of old equipment or other goods. The Harbin government claimed that 200,000 redundant workers had found new 'jobs' but this mostly consisted of such peddling which brought in only a few extra yuan a day.

Harbin was fortunate by comparison with other towns in the province which were dependent on a single enterprise such as a coalmine or a timber yard. All over the region, big timber mills had shut, throwing tens of thousands out of work, because massive logging had exhausted the once vast virgin forests.

Jiamusi, the biggest town north of Harbin, which had once been developed by the Japanese, was a depressing sight. Every one of the main employers – the timber mill, the factory which made coal-mining equipment and another which built big tractors – had shut down. It was said that some 300,000 were unemployed. Along the potholed streets, people shivered in the autumn cold, trying to sell something – a few plastic lighters, a pile of apples or a cardboard box full of winter underwear. Many factories tried to unload their unsold inventories by paying their workers in kind. Others indulged in a kind of cannibalism. In front of the timber yard where 4,000 had once worked, I ran into one of the former managers squatting in front of a display of scrap metal, piping, screws and clamps laid out on the pavement.

'When they sacked me, they said I could take some of it away,' he said, and then he laughed sardonically. 'And that's the deputy chief accountant.' He pointed to a man down the street who was perched on a stool in front of his shoe-shine brushes. 'See, he's still wearing his medals.' On the front of his jacket, the ex-accountant wore two medals made out of heavy bronze with a red star in the centre. They were the medals awarded by the state to model workers.

Jiamusi had attracted some new investment and so was better off than mining towns such as Hegang. The town has about a million inhabitants and is an hour's drive from Jiamusi, along a brand-new highway. Police-manned checkpoints at either end note down the names and identity-card numbers of all travellers. In fact the police seemed omnipresent in both Jiamusi and Hegang. Some drove brand-new Pajero jeeps. Others patrolled the streets on new bicycles. In Hegang, the police stood at the corners of all major intersections wearing helmets and carrying submachine guns.

The city had been hit by a wave of violent crime and people told of how a guard had been killed when thieves made off with 200,000 yuan taken from the colliery's safe. On bulletin boards outside the offices of the state prosecutor, I found a row of death penalty notices each marked by a large red tick, showing that the sentence had been carried out. The real reason for the suffocating police presence, however, was not crime but the fear of industrial unrest. The mines were bankrupt. Half the miners had been laid off and the other half received their wages erratically and then only after long delays. All around the city groups of workmen with shovels or bicycle carts waited, hoping to be hired by the day. On many occasions, the miners had gathered in the middle of the town, linking arms and blocking traffic to try and force the government to pay their wages. In other coal-mining towns such as Jixi or Shuangyashan, the miners had lain down on the railway tracks, blocking trains for days at a time.[13]

Some time after my visit, I met the Party secretary of one of these towns, Jixi, who was attending a meeting in Beijing. 'What can I do?' he said, shifting around in his armchair and searching the hotel room for a better answer. 'We are never paid for the coal we deliver.'

The state-run industry was owed billions of yuan from its equally stricken customers in the state sector. The collieries tried to sell their coal elsewhere but it was too expensive to compete with the coal produced by over 80,000 small mines operated by local governments or private individuals. They produced as much as half of China's coal. In 1992, the Ministry of Coal declared a net loss of nearly 6 billion yuan and unveiled a plan to lay off a million miners. Five years later, the ministry proudly declared that the industry was back in profit, but a year later it admitted that this had been the result of an accounting sleight of hand. Instead of counting unpaid deliveries of coal as losses, the ministry had recorded them as profitable sales. There was still no cash to pay wages.[14]

In Jixi, the Party secretary later said, he had 'encouraged' 17,000 miners to take up farming. The neighbouring town of Shuangyashan had sent 50,000 redundant workers to the countryside. Harbin had similarly dispatched 200,000 former workers and another 300,000 migrant workers. Yet this was no solution either for the coal industry or the rest of China.

The SOE problem became even more intractable after 1997 when the Asian financial crisis helped puncture the country's economic boom, resulting in a slump in demand and a loss of confidence. In the boom years, industry experts had confidently predicted that demand for coal would continue to rise over the next thirty years. Yet by 1998, the coal industry had 200 million tonnes of surplus coal stockpiled, equal to 20 per cent of annual demand, and accumulated debts of 26 billion yuan (US$3.2 billion). Industry experts now forecast that output, which has peaked at an annual 1.34 million tonnes, will drop by 40 per cent in the coming seven years and that demand will fall to just 800 million tonnes a year.[15] There has, however, been one unexpected benefit. Heilongjiang, like other parts of the country, has suddenly found itself grappling with a large surplus of electricity, and heavy industrial centres like Shenyang, once notorious for their air pollution, are now able to boast of their environmental achievements. The mayor of Shenyang, Mu Suixin, said Shenyang now enjoys cleaner air than Beijing and he talked with wild optimism of attracting tourists to his city.

With hindsight, it is easy to see that China has missed several favourable opportunities to grasp the nettle of SOE reform. At the Thirteenth Party Congress in October 1987, the reformist leader Zhao Ziyang pushed for the separation of state ownership and management, and proposed farming out many of the state's small enterprises to the private sector under the same contract responsibility system that had helped the peasants raise agricultural productivity. Zhao also proposed that professional managers be allowed to take charge of factories and that Party secretaries should confine themselves to housing and other social welfare issues. He called on the state to limit itself to regulating the market, and for enterprises to be guided by market forces. His advisers touted other slogans such as 'Small government, big market' and 'Small government, big society'.

With this encouragement, many voices began to suggest that certain ideological shibboleths should be discarded. Why not privatize the bigger SOEs and turn them into joint stock companies? Others proposed that change should come through an immediate deregulation because the economy could not function for long without massive corruption if a market economy and a planned economy tried to co-exist. Political and economic conditions were favourable. Price controls on many goods had been lifted and the reformers had widespread political support. China's economy was growing strongly and the country enjoyed international support. At that moment Shenyang had been chosen to pioneer a bankruptcy law and one factory, the Shenyang Fireproof Materials Factory, was permitted to close down. Yet when I tried to visit it, people felt such shame that no one in the city would give me directions or admit to knowing where it was. Shenyang was also the first city to try running a stock exchange in which the shares of a few companies were listed on a blackboard.

The moment passed, however, and after Zhao's fall during the Tiananmen protests of 1989, the Party strengthened its control over the factories. Shenyang's stock exchange closed and there were no more bankruptcies. After Deng's southern tour in 1992, the debate was resurrected as more and more state enterprises were allowed to list on the new domestic stock exchanges in Shenzhen and Shanghai, and issue 'A' shares restricted to Chinese investors. Certain state companies issued 'B' shares which were available also to foreign buyers. Then Chinese enterprises began backdoor listings in Hong Kong and went on to list so-called 'H' shares, those listed and traded in Hong Kong. Finally, as economic growth in the Chinese economy hit record levels, many SOEs began to list on overseas stock exchanges where investors became convinced that a market of 1.2 billion people had such vast potential that annual growth rates of 13 or 14 per cent could be sustained almost indefinitely.

Such optimism proved misplaced. The classic example of what went wrong was Beijing's Capital Iron and Steelworks, known as Shougang. Deng Xiaoping visited it in 1992 and praised it as a model for the transformation of the state sector. Its chairman, Zhou Guanwu, a long-standing associate of Deng, obtained a backdoor listing in Hong Kong and, with the cash in hand, announced that Shougang would quadruple its steel production capacity. The chairman sent his son, Zhou Beifang, to Hong Kong where he eventually listed six separate companies which, by 1995, had a combined market capitalization of US$12 billion. The son had gone into business with the second son of Deng Xiaoping, Deng Zhifeng, and when the two teamed up with the Hong Kong property tycoon Li Ka-shing, no one dared gainsay them.

Shougang, which had produced around a million tonnes of steel a year in the 1980s, now doubled, then tripled production and drew up plans to boost capacity to 20 million tonnes. With the billions of dollars of capital raised by the two princelings, the company expanded in every possible direction: into iron-ore trading, metal trading, shipping, real estate projects in Hong Kong and on the mainland, computer components and telephone accessories. It even went into banking, founding the Minsheng Bank. In the process it acquired 262,000 employees, 199 factories, 47 domestic affiliates, 27 joint ventures and sales offices in 18 countries. It shipped an entire steel plant from the United States, and it acquired an iron ore mine in Peru for which it reputedly paid four times the going price, as well as land in Beijing on which to build shopping centres and villas.

The managers of this vast and sprawling conglomerate, the state bureaucrats, behaved as if they were Western tycoons who had created a fortune. They bought fleets of Mercedes and went on holiday to Las Vegas. They took out golf-club memberships, bought villas, ran mistresses, raced horses and were always seen dressed in Italian suits and speaking into their mobile phones.

Where Shougang led, all the other giant steel enterprises followed, raising money through the stock market and quadrupling the country's steel production capacity to 190 million tonnes. Yet even at the height of the boom, demand never exceeded 100 million tonnes, and since about 80 per cent of Chinese-made steel does not meet international quality standards, China simultaneously became the world's biggest steel importer.[16]

Even the steel which Shougang did make and sell proved unprofitable because its customers were locked in the triangular debt chain. Whereas in 1993, the industry as a whole had made record profits of 29 billion yuan (US$3.5 billion), five years later, when China was the world's biggest steel producer, profits were down to just 2 billion yuan (US$240 million). Unsurprisingly, overproduction had led to a collapse in prices.

For Shougang, the end came in 1995 when Deng Xiaoping fell into a terminal coma and his political opponents made their move.

Shougang's chairman Zhou was summarily dismissed and his son was arrested and subsequently given a suspended death sentence. The government cancelled all the projects aimed at increasing the company's steel capacity as well as a string of other investment projects including a coalmine, a cement plant, a port and office blocks. A new management was brought in which admitted that Shougang was largely to blame for Beijing's terrible air pollution because the plant had failed to invest in even the minimum pollution control equipment. It also announced plans to dismiss 30,000 of its 50,000 steelworkers and to spin off all its subsidiary units – the company bakery, the car pool, the cleaners, the security guards, restaurants, hotels, printing presses, power plants and television stations, even its opera troupe.

Ironically, the failure to exploit the benevolent climate of the first half of the 1990s had left the SOEs even less capable of surviving in the marketplace. China now had 1,600 steel producers when it needed just three or four. Moreover, the example of Shougang did nothing to dampen the enthusiasm of many SOEs which, though hopelessly bankrupt, continued to list on the stock exchange. Hong Kong in particular showed a feverish interest in buying these so-called 'red chip' stocks. 'Red chips ... are often controlled by Chinese government agencies and thus have strong *guanxi* or connections in China that allow them to buy assets at bargain prices,' reported the *South China Morning Post* in explaining the popularity of these share offerings.[17]

Many SOEs made their share offerings more exciting by announcing plans to shed surplus workers but this was offset by the government's insistence that profitable SOEs such as Shanghai's Baoshan Steelworks take over their ailing brethren. Baoshan was ordered to merge with an older steel plant, Shanghai Metallurgical, which had 130,000 workers (producing the same amount of steel as Baoshan's 10,500), and to take over responsibility for its pensioners as well as its workers. Such mergers – often portrayed as the injection of assets at bargain prices – rendered even the most efficiently managed SOEs unattractive propositions.[18]

Even as the Asian financial crisis struck, hopes that the Party could keep the commanding heights of the economy under its control were promoted at the Fifteenth Party Congress in 1997. The Party resolved to retain state control of major SOEs and the Prime Minister Zhu Rongji announced that within three years the majority of SOEs would be turned around and made profitable. To help their recovery, the Party ordered the closure of many competing TVEs, including 50,000 coalmines, citing health, safety and environmental considerations.[19]

Efforts to deal with the smaller ailing SOEs in Shenyang proved how difficult this was. The mayor of Shenyang, Mu Suixin, toured southern China trying to find buyers for the factories but most backed off when they found they would have to shoulder the burden of the retired workforce. Mu even toured London, Rome, Paris and Tokyo, offering to sell the factories for just one yuan.[20]

Just why he found no takers became clear when the story of the Shenyang Micro-electric Factory, with 1,000 workers and debts of 37 million yuan, came to light in 1998. Its manager, Cheng Wen, agreed to buy the company for one yuan but as soon as the workforce heard the news, they immediately started to organize petitions and protests. The company's Party secretary, Yan Fengcheng, led workers in blocking traffic and staging sit-ins outside the Party headquarters. He accused the manager of stealing the company's equipment and transferring it to a factory set up under the name of his son. The dispute lasted six months. Cheng eventually triumphed but when production resumed there were jobs for just 200 who naturally did not include Party secretary Yan.[21]

Another case involved a foreign company trying to restore the health of a bankrupt SOE, the Harbin Ballbearing Plant with 15,000 workers and 9,000 pensioners. The Hong Kong-registered company Sunbase International Holdings was accused of diverting the SOE's most valuable assets into a joint venture, leaving the state to shoulder all its liabilities. Although the *Economic Information Daily* newspaper complained that the state had lost control over a billion yuan's worth of state assets, the new owners (probably local officials who had registered a front company in Hong Kong) still failed to make profits, and unsold stock piled up.[22]

The unclear ownership rights of SOEs and their assets did much to foster such corruption and thwarted many attempts to turn enterprises around. A State Assets Law passed in 1993 was supposed to help transform the SOEs into independent legal corporations, in which state holding companies would exercise overall control of state assets but leave day-to-day management to professionals hired under fixed-term contracts. As with so many TVEs, however, it proved impossible either to dismiss a bad management team or prevent the theft of a firm's most valuable assets. According to official statistics, of the 2.8 trillion yuan invested in SOEs by 1990, assets worth a third of this sum had been stolen, wasted or misused.

Many local Party committees also deliberately tried to profit from this asset-stripping mentality by packaging their best assets together in a conglomerate and promising to inject fresh assets later on. Beijing Enterprises, which included a brewery, a hotel and a toll road, sparked a frenzied enthusiasm among investors in Hong Kong who unwisely assumed that the *guanxi*, or political connections, of the Beijing Party would guarantee rich pickings later on. When Shanghai Industrial listed, its share price rose sixfold although the only common factor in its assets – a shopping centre, a cigarette factory and a car parts plant – was that all of them were owned and managed by Party cadres who proceeded to make very healthy paper profits.

In theory, the public listing of SOEs is supposed to make their managers more profit-oriented and responsive to the needs of the shareholders. Yet, with few exceptions, outside shareholders have remained in the minority. In practice, the capital raised is often used to cover the debts of other SOEs, and the interests of minority shareholders are ignored. A telling case was that of the Qingdao Brewery which makes the country's best-known brand of beer. After it had issued H shares in Hong Kong in 1993, investors discovered that the money was not being used to expand production. On the contrary, the brand saw its market share steadily shrink while the management paid off the debts of other enterprises within the group, none of which had anything to do with selling beer.

The next logical step in restructuring the SOEs would be complete privatization, but though this was much debated during the 1990s it was repeatedly rejected by the Chinese leadership on ideological and practical grounds. Certain industries which had remained a state monopoly, such as tobacco, power generation or telecommunications, continued to be highly profitable and a prime source of government revenue. By that time, central government revenue as a percentage of GDP had fallen to well under 10 per cent. The government, which had relied on the profits from SOEs to finance its budget spending, was now in a difficult position. It could not gather taxes from the loss-making sector as in the past and it had given sweeping exemptions to investments made by overseas Chinese. It also had difficulty extracting taxes from other parts of the economy, and was beginning to have to rely on foreign-run joint ventures for its tax revenues. Further moves to dilute ownership over the profitable sectors were therefore strongly resisted. At a plenary meeting in 1999, the Central Committee of the CCP, the primary decision-making assembly, decided to strengthen rather than weaken Party control over the SOEs and to 'enhance the primacy of state-owned businesses in the national economy'.[23]

At the same time, immense efforts were made to bolster the SOEs. The government forbade companies from competing to lower prices on certain products such as television sets by mandating a minimum price. The *People's Daily* encouraged a rally on the stock market. The Party introduced a new tax on individual bank deposits in the hope of persuading people to buy more shares in 900 listed SOEs. The central bank kept cutting interest rates to make it cheaper for SOEs to pay interest on their debts. Yet no matter what was done, the Chinese economy was trapped into a deflationary spiral. With most industries operating at around 60 per cent of their capacity, prices continued to fall throughout 1998 and 1999. So did profits.

By the end of 1999, the percentage of SOEs running at a loss had risen from 40 per cent in 1998 to 50 per cent. In Shenyang, the figure was 55 per cent. As SOEs absorb around three-quarters of the loans issued in China, the four main state banks were saddled with 'non-performing loans' and were technically bankrupt. The only thing red about the state sector was their finances. Just how bankrupt the SOE and state banking system had become, however, depended on whom one asked.[24]

Chinese bankers claim that only a fifth of loans are 'non-performing' but Western economists using international accountancy standards believe that the real figure may be closer to half. In other words, the state sector may be saddled with bad debts of US$300 billion. To this must be added all sorts of other SOE liabilities such as pensions, unpaid wages and the debts which SOEs owe each other. This might bring the total domestic debt burden closer to US$500 billion. Certainly, the interest payments alone which SOEs owe banks were reported in 1999 to be a combined US$55 billion. In fact interest repayments had become so large they absorbed as much as 70 per cent of the operating income of SOEs.[25]

By the end of the 1990s it was therefore obvious that the listed SOEs were neither making profits nor effectively reforming themselves with the help of the capital raised. In the summer of 1999 the Prime Minister Zhu Rongji tried to talk up China's domestic stock market in the face of plunging profits and low dividends but the strategy failed. At the end of the year, China announced that seven steel firms would be allowed to go bankrupt, including the Shenyang Steel Company which had in fact stopped production years before.[26] Some of the ninety-three state coalmines were also formally declared bankrupt. At the same time China began the process of writing off the bad debts of the SOEs. Angang, China's biggest steel producer, transferred bad debts of 6.8 billion yuan (US$820 million) to several so-called asset management corporations which lightened the burden of its debt interest payments by US$60 million a year.[27]

However the Party tries to juggle the debts around, they will sooner or later have to be written off, the banks will have to stop directing capital at the SOEs, and what remains of the state sector after bankruptcy will probably by privatized in one form or another. Creating new jobs is essential, and for that the Party is having to look, however, disdainfully, at the private sector. It is, as the next chapter describes, a very painful concession.

7

The Pig that Fears to Become Fat

IN MARCH 1999 a small group of legislators from Henan province found themselves discussing an ancient question: should there or could there be such a thing in China as private property? Earlier that year the National People's Congress had formally amended the Constitution to recognize at least the existence of the private sector, but this could only be the start.

'The amendment just doesn't go far enough,' complained one official, who argued that the American Constitution should be taken as China's model. 'What we need are explicit guarantees protecting private property.'

Throughout the imperial period, the state had always asserted an absolute right to control the life, liberty and property of its subjects, but Mao's government was the first to make the issue a moral cause. After it came to power in 1949 it quickly expropriated the property of both rich and poor in a rush to realize Marx's goal – the abolition of private property. Now, those who had grown rich since 1979 both wanted and feared the enshrining of the individual's rights over those of the state.

Out of the hubbub of voices, the sharp tones of the president of Zhengzhou University raised a point that silenced the rest. 'Then what would stop people from claiming the property they lost to the state after Liberation? After the French Revolution, children of the nobility could still claim their property under Napoleon,' he reminded his listeners.[1]

As Party cadres became property-owners during the privatization of the SOEs in the 1990s, many began uneasily to contemplate Proudhon's dictum that all property is theft. Although the Chinese Constitution has been frequently revised, one article, no. 12, remains unaltered. It insists that socialist publicly owned assets are sacred and that public ownership can never be diluted. If that were to happen, the Chinese Communist Party's name, Gongchang Dang, which means literally 'The Party of Public Assets', might have to go.

'If large amounts of state assets are indiscriminately transferred to individuals, and ultimately concentrated in the hands of just a few, then our socialist system will lose its economic foundation,' President Jiang Zemin had warned in a speech shortly before the National People's Congress met in 1999 and amended the Constitution. 'Some people abroad mistakenly believe that China wants to engage in privatization, and some of our comrades have developed a similar misunderstanding.'[2]

The amendment to the Constitution that was finally adopted, after much debate, redefined the status of private enterprise. Instead of being a 'complement' to the socialist market economy, it was now recognized as 'an important part' of it, and protection of 'the legal interests and rights of the private economy' was promised.[3] (Under an earlier amendment made in 1988, the text had avoided the word 'private' in favour of the much vaguer expression, 'individual' economy.)

The Chinese word for private is *si* which has negative associations with selfishness, while *gong* denotes the public good. Workers in SOEs are called *gong ren* or 'public people', that is people working for the common good, not petty interests. Under Mao, large public notices everywhere had urged people to 'Strike hard against the slightest sign of private ownership' or to 'Smash the private and [Soviet] revisionism.' Even after they had been stripped of all their property, Mao had still treated all capitalists and landlords as incurable criminals. Class warfare would never be over, he believed, because even if the state owned all property, people could still be guilty of 'thought crimes'.

Lenin had claimed that 'small-scale production engenders capitalism in the bourgeoisie daily, hourly and on a mass scale'. And Mao reminded the Chinese in his Little Red Book of quotations that 'the spontaneous forces of capitalism' are always ready to re-emerge even among the poorest peasants. Indeed, under Mao, many peasants were arrested just for growing vegetables in their own backyards, considered to be private plots, or for trading some tobacco or undertaking carpentry.

Modern capitalism existed only fleetingly in China during the Republican period, after the imperial system had collapsed in 1911. When Mao came to power, he was not slow to launch a campaign against first the Three Antis and then the Five Antis, directed at those businessmen and industrialists who had not fled China. The Three Antis campaign started in 1951 following the Suppression of the Counter-revolutionaries campaign and targeted Communist Party members, officials and managers who were guilty of three vices – corruption, waste and obstructionist bureaucracy. The Five Antis campaign which started in Shanghai in 1952 targeted the bourgeoisie. Mirroring the campaign against landlords in the countryside, its victims were accused of bribery, tax evasion, theft of state property, cheating on government contracts and stealing state economic information. In February 1952 alone, there were over 3,000 struggle and criticism meetings held in Shanghai and several hundred thousand letters of denunciation sent in by employees. Once the terrified 'capitalists' had confessed, the state seized all their property.

In the years that followed, the campaign was extended to just about anyone who could be described as owning a business, be it running a tea shop, a market stall or a restaurant, sewing on buttons in a tailor's shop or even just pulling a rickshaw. All private endeavour disappeared and by 1959 so had private property. The peasants handed over even their pots and pans to the communes while city-dwellers 'voluntarily' began to do the same, donating everything from works of art to metal bedsteads which were melted down as part of the national steelmaking drive.[4]

Just how difficult it has been to reverse this attitude to private property and private enterprise can be illustrated by the life of Nian Guangjiu. The son of a poor peasant from Anhui province, he was arrested in 1956 as a 20-year-old for running a fruit and vegetable stall in the rich Jiangsu town of Wuhu and imprisoned for 'speculation' and 'trading'. For the next twenty years, with his record now seemingly permanently marked, he drifted in and out of labour camps and communes. Then, when Mao died in 1976, Nian set up a new business selling melon seeds. Within a few years he had three employees. By 1984, he was employing 103 people and had become wealthy.

Throughout this period, as each leftist campaign came and went, he would be arrested, investigated and fined for corruption. After Tiananmen, Nian's fortunes sank to their lowest ebb. He was arrested and charged with 'corruption' and 'the misuse of public funds'. His business was closed and his assets confiscated. He was then held without trial until May 1991 when he was sentenced to three years' imprisonment for 'hooliganism'. Then, in 1992, when Deng Xiaoping embarked on his southern tour, Nian was released. 'He was a changed man, no longer extrovert and talkative but reserved and taciturn,' one Chinese newspaper reported.

Nian struggled to restart his business again until in 1997 the Fifteenth Party Congress formally endorsed the concept of a mixed economy. Soon the barely literate entrepreneur had opened outlets across the country and on National Day in 1998, the Party selected him as one of ninety-six 'Heroes of Reform'. He was fêted in Beijing as a guest of the state and told the press: 'The Party has given us an umbrella of protection. We no longer need to fear. Now we can really get to work.'[5]

Though Nian's story would appear to have a happy ending, those who have embarked on private enterprise are still vulnerable to the unpredictable whims of the Party. Even Deng Xiaoping, despite his exhortation that 'to get rich is glorious', himself launched a campaign against 'economic crimes' in 1982. And the Party has still not adopted legislation that would enshrine the principle of the inviolability of private property or accord it equal treatment by banks, courts and tax-collectors, despite the astonishing growth of the private sector in the last two decades.

The size of the private sector is a matter of some controversy. According to some statistics, in 1999 China had a million private businesses that employed 13.5 million people and a further 31 million so-called self-employed households. Others claim that there are 30 million private firms employing 70 million people, and that there are at least 10 million Chinese each worth a million yuan.[6]

Whatever the figures, the rich can be roughly divided into three groups: peasants who were allowed to start 'sideline' businesses after 1979; largely self-funding small-time 'petty bourgeois' in the cities; and semi-corrupt Party officials, who are probably the wealthiest of all. Each group operates along the blurred and shifting line dividing what is merely unauthorized from what is forbidden, but Party officials are as much to blame as anyone for undermining faith in the fairness of a market economy.

When I first came to China in 1985, most of the 'rich' people were still the peasants. Early each morning, through my window overlooking the Avenue of Eternal Peace in Beijing, would come the putt-putt-putt sound of tractors pulling small carts laden with fresh vegetables or fruit. The less successful arrived on carts pulled by donkeys, and their cries of encouragement could be heard along streets then still devoid of cars. They were heading for 'free markets' where they could sell what they grew in their private plots. Many had ingeniously adapted their Flying Pigeon bicycles to be able to transport live fish, chickens or pigs on their panniers. While Mao was alive, the Party had issued strict regulations limiting each household to one pig and so many chickens or ducks. Now its officials suspiciously monitored checkpoints at the entrance to the city, and squads of inspectors carefully checked prices and weights in the free markets, convinced (as were many Beijingers) that every transaction involved one person cheating another.

Unsurprisingly, at the start of Deng's reforms, the peasants had been wary of embarking on any form of private enterprise, so from 1980 the Party began to hold up examples of '10,000 yuan' households for public recognition. Nian with his 'Idiot' brand melon seeds was one; an 18-year-old peasant girl called Wang Zhaomei, who reportedly became rich by growing and selling fresh flowers, was another. After her story appeared she was bombarded by letters and for a while received as many as seventy visitors a day. The first peasant to buy a car in China was another girl. Sun Guiying had started to rear chickens. 'She can now drive her silver Toyota around to make business contacts and promote egg sales,' explained the *Beijing Daily* which declared her a Zhuang Yuan, in imperial times the title awarded to a Confucian scholar who had passed the highest examinations.

Soon certain villages and even whole districts began to specialize in particular products or set up large-scale wholesale markets. In the county of Xinmin in Liaoning province, tens of thousands of house-holds specialized in eggs. Indeed China's biggest private company, the Hope Group, was started by a family that went into breeding and selling quails' eggs.

In the cities, those who dared to start up a private business began by offering small services – repairing bicycles, patching clothes or opening a tiny hole-in-the-wall type of restaurant. In Shanghai, for example, Gu Dehua started tailoring in his family's tiny flat after being unemployed for three years. He learned his trade from his father who had run a tailoring shop until 1956, when he was forced to join a collective.

One of the first private restaurants to open in Beijing was the Xiao Xiao Jiu Jia (the Little Little Restaurant) which the Liu family started in their front room. There were just five round tables at which every-one sat on stools to eat. The food was brought straight from the kitchen next door. When it opened in 1980, television cameras recorded the event and thereafter it was always full.

Mrs Liu, a large round woman, did the cooking. Her husband, a thin shrimp of a man, waited at table.

'The only trouble is people see how well we are doing,' observed Mr Liu, emerging one lunchtime with a plate of *gongbao jiding* (chicken, peanuts and red pepper). 'And their eyes go red.' In China envy is not green but red, and Mr Liu seemed to spend a lot of his time smiling and bobbing and handing round packs of cigarettes to any minor official and his friends who came in.

'They just order a meal and then walk out without paying,' he said, 'and there's nothing I can do about it.'

Such individual household enterprises are known as *getihu*. In the early days of reform those who operated them were considered to be lower down the social scale than anyone who worked for the state. Many also still bore the stigma of belonging to one or other of the categories of people singled out by Mao as class enemies. Some *getihu* were started by former political prisoners released under one or other of the general amnesties that Deng announced after he came to power. After decades in camps, such people could not find proper jobs in state *danwei* when they returned to the cities. Fearful of attracting attention, they strove to keep a low profile. 'The wise man shuns fame just as the pig fears becoming fat,' Mr Liu was fond of saying.

One of the few exceptions to this rule is Liao Changguang, China's 'hotpot king', who has built up a nationwide chain of restaurants and who drives around Chongqing in a flashy white Mercedes.

'Life was unfair when I was young. I never had a chance to stay at school and I became a Red Guard at 13,' he recounted in a recent interview.[7] 'When I was 18, in 1969, I was sent to a remote village in Sichuan to be re-educated by peasants. Then I worked in the rice paddies for five years.'

After Mao's death in 1976, Liao seized the chance to return to Chongqing and began to work as an electrician in a state-owned enterprise, installing cables and power switches.

'I was lucky to get back', remarked Liao when I met him in 1999, 'but it was pretty hard work and boring. There was no competition but it was secure. I wanted freedom and took a lot of sick leave and hung out with my mates and quickly became interested in business.'

He hired two street children to help him sell shoes. 'We bought shoes from the state-owned department stores downtown and sold them at a market a few blocks away. I made two or three yuan a pair,' he said. He was soon earning 300 or 400 yuan a month from this side-line, as against his electrician's monthly salary of 32 yuan.

His next scheme was to buy black-and-white televisions that had been pawned by gamblers desperate for cash, and sell them on to peasants, making a profit of 20 yuan on each sale. Then, in 1981, he left his job as an electrician, borrowed 3,000 yuan from his mother-in-law and set up a clothes stall in a free market. His wife, who had worked as a designer at a shoe factory, also left her job to help him.

'Such a move was unheard of in those days. Not many people understood why I wanted to smash my iron rice bowl. And in those days it was quite hard to leave an SOE. I had to beg my way through layers of contacts to persuade my boss to let me go,' he recalled.

In the first month, the clothes stall produced a profit of 2,000 yuan. A year later the Liaos bought three big woks and six tables and opened a hotpot restaurant. The fiery pepper-laden stew that they served was such a success that by 1989 they had expanded to three restaurants.

'It took us seven years to earn 100,000 yuan but now the money comes quicker,' Liao said. By 1999, the rather grandly named company Chongqing Cygnet Diet Culture Group had 5,000 employees and 40 subsidiaries, with an annual turnover of 100 million yuan and profits of some 30 million yuan. Now the Liaos have set their sights on turning their Cygnet brand into the McDonald's of China.

'But we need to invest in politics,' stressed his wife as she sipped tea in the vast lobby of one of Beijing's plush hotels. In one year alone they had donated over a million yuan to good causes, building schools in poor mountainous areas and sponsoring dance ensembles to entertain troops stationed in border areas. Now the Liaos were attending the National People's Congress as the first private businessmen to represent Chongqing.

The first fortunes in China invariably came from the supply of basic necessities – food, drink and clothing – and more often than not were made by 'educated youths' who had returned to the cities after 1979. Yang Zhenhua was but one example. After twice failing the entrance exam when the universities reopened, he set up a street stall selling clothes.

'It was easy. The government had more unemployed youth than it knew what to do with, so it encouraged them to go into business,' he recalled. Yang, who lives in Dalian, in the north-east, prospered by becoming the first local to travel south to Guangdong where the latest fashions from Hong Kong could be picked up. With the profits, he branched out and started a private bus company.

By the second half of the 1980s, however, entrepreneurs from a different background were emerging. The Party began to encourage state employees to go private or *xia hai*, meaning to 'plunge into the sea'. The most famous example was a Mrs Guan Guangmei, a Party member in the coal and steel town of Benxi, Liaoning, who leased eight bankrupt state shops to distribute rationed vegetables. Within two years she had earned over 44,000 yuan, creating what the Party newspapers hailed as the 'Guan Guangmei phenomenon'. In 1987 she was a star delegate at the Communist Party Congress, much to the disgust of its hardline Maoists.

In the first decade of reform, private businessmen of whatever background still swam in a sea of bewildering rules and regulations. Peasants had to circumnavigate the restrictions on long-distance travel and come to terms with the protectionism of local governments. In many parts of the country, local officials blockaded roads to prevent farmers from selling their goods in other provinces. Jiangxi province, for example, battled with its orange growers who wanted to sell their fruit in neighbouring Guangdong's free market, where prices were higher, rather than to the Jiangxi provincial fruit-juice plant.

However, the biggest handicap was the plethora of regulations that prohibited private businesses from hiring more than five workers. To get round this obstacle, wily entrepreneurs were forced to exploit the system. Zhang Guoxi, at one time said to be China's richest man, managed to build up a wood-carving business in Jiangxi province by hiring handicapped carpenters, having discovered that the state granted numerous incentives to those who employed the disabled. When I visited Zhang in the late 1980s, he employed over 2,000 people to carve wooden furniture. He also owned a huge house next to a ten-storey office block that rose straight out of the paddy fields and towered above the little town of Yujiang.

Over a dinner of stewed snakes prepared by his chef, Zhang told how he had left school at the age of 11 and become a carpenter. Through a chance meeting, he won a commission to carve a Buddhist statue of the goddess Guanyin for believers in Japan. Soon other commissions followed and he was able to hire extra hands. Later he branched out into carving panels, chests, tables and other goods for the export market. 'Now I would like to become the first man in China to own a private jet,' he concluded.[8]

Others exploited the minority regions' exemption from restrictions on private business and tax incentives. One of the most famous was Rabia Kader, a Uygur housewife who in 1977, with capital of just 100 yuan, began a little buying and selling. In 1980, just after her eighth child was born, she embarked on a gruelling tour of China's big cities.

'At the time I hardly spoke Chinese at all. I just brought together buyers and sellers and even cooked Muslim food for Islamic businessmen,' she recalled. Within a couple of years, she had opened a small shop in Urumqi, the capital of Xinjiang. Ten years later she owned a shopping centre spread over an area of 75,000 square feet. 'The centre is only part of her fast-growing property, trading, agricultural and manufacturing interests grouped under the umbrella of her Xinjiang Arkider Industrial and Commercial Corporation,' reported the *Financial Times* which interviewed her when she visited London.[9]

Zhang Guoxi and Rabia Kader had each found one way round the system. Elsewhere individuals might take over a collectively owned village and township enterprise and in that way bypass restrictions on how many workers a household enterprise could hire. As a result the most unexpected people revealed an entrepreneurial drive to build up a successful business and they emerged from backwaters all over China.

In 1988, with the reformers still in charge, the status of private entrepreneurs peaked and the Party press showered praise on them. The *China Daily* reported with some pride that the country had 22 million people who were 'very rich' and many who were actually millionaires. And it was at that point that the Constitution was amended to recognize the private economy as 'a complement' to the 'socialist public economy'.

Such was the change in climate that the Party even began to contemplate the admission as Party members of private businessmen. Guangdong was the first to do so when, in 1987, it instituted 'political thought training for private business people' in which candidates were instructed in ideology, professional ethics, education and the function of private workers within the state. Nationwide, some 2,400 were eventually accepted into the Party, though in Beijing, where the municipal Party organization was distinctly unenthusiastic, fewer than ten were allowed to become members.

One of those repeatedly turned down as a Party member was Liu Xigui, a peasant from the outskirts of Shenyang in Liaoning province who ran a trucking company with over 600 vehicles. He had raised his start-up capital by selling his own blood and then investing the money in an old truck. Liu was generous with his profits, giving away half a million yuan to local schools and welfare organizations, and even after his third application for Party membership had been rejected, he was determined to sound reasonable: 'The Communist Party is not like other parties. It is strict and solemn. It assesses a person to see if their politics are up to scratch.'

However, as Liu was well aware, no business could prosper without strong Party affiliations: 'Without political position, you have nothing. I am good at making friends and the more friends you have, the more avenues are open to you.'[10]

In the 1980s, doing even the simplest things – making a phone call, renting a hotel room, buying a train ticket, eating in a restaurant, finding a taxi – involved navigating innumerable obstacles. To do so everyone needed a mutual support network of *guanxi*, or political connections, and the use of those connections was termed 'going through the backdoor', or *zou hou men*.

At the time China's economy was dominated by shortages of everything from coal to electricity, from trucks to railway wagons, all of which were invariably distributed according to some form of bureaucratic rationing. In a bureaucracy that still regulated the market, an official could make life either easy or impossible. Peasants who wanted to transport their eggs or watermelons to the city needed to find a means of transport, then some fuel, then an entry permit and then a hawker's registration card. The only way to get all this done was to have a friend or relative in the right office. Naturally, all this fixing involved a great deal of gift-giving and banqueting to help oil the wheels of friendship.

As collective, joint-venture and private factories sprang up, they too needed access to power, raw materials or transportation which were often state monopolies supplying SOEs according to the plan. At the same time the SOEs were slowly allowed to produce more than in the plan, and so had a surplus to sell on the open market.

Wheeler-dealers known as 'briefcase companies' became the means by which buyers and sellers could trade. If, for example, a light industrial factory in Guangdong needed coal, a briefcase company might buy coal from a state coalmine in Inner Mongolia, find some means to transport it, say on wagons leased from a steel enterprise to a PLA port, and then engage a navy vessel to ship it south. Such deals, of course, also involved sweet-talking innumerable officials to get umpteen chops, the official stamps that constitute the bureaucracy's main currency.

The Party's propaganda machine constantly inveighed against the extravagant wining and dining that was generated by the practice of *guanxi*. Gift-giving is in fact a traditional part of Chinese social intercourse but the Party had prided itself on eradicating this social custom in the interests of austerity. During the 1980s, the *People's Daily* repeatedly published new regulations specifying the number and type of dishes officials could order when entertaining each other – the maximum was judged to be four dishes and one course of soup – though a proposal to levy a banquet tax was dropped.

As the market economy expanded alongside the centrally planned economy, the opportunities for sheer profiteering, known as *guandao*, became ever greater. In the state-run economy, the prices of both commodities and finished products bore no relation to market prices. It was all too easy to buy goods cheaply from the state sector and sell them dearly in the marketplace. The Communist Party repeatedly launched political campaigns to stop this happening, Deng's 1982 campaign against 'economic crime' being but one example. On each occasion officials would be singled out for public humiliation and sometimes even executed.

For bureaucrats who became involved in such deals, trust and confidentiality between partners were paramount. For foreign businessmen, already treated with considerable suspicion, operating in such an environment was awkward. At first they might be asked to provide simply gifts of imported cigarettes or envelopes containing cash, but within a year or two there would be requests for colour television sets or video tape recorders. As the scale of the foreign investment projects became larger, so the gifts became correspondingly more generous. Businessmen might be asked to leave the keys to a new car behind on the table as they left a banquet or to arrange for the children of important officials to study abroad.[11]

Unsurprisingly, a great many officials grew wealthy from exploiting their *guanxi*, and those who flaunted their wealth most ostentatiously were those who had the best *guanxi,* the children of top Party officials. Such ostentation provoked a great deal of public anger and a public opinion survey published in one domestic magazine, *Outlook*, concluded that the rampant abuse of power by officials, in particular embezzlement and the taking of bribes, constituted a grave threat to public order.[12]

The Party campaigns that were launched in the mid- and late 1980s, targeting the most privileged, were an attempt to respond to such anger. In February 1986 the children of three top officials in Shanghai were executed, though this provoked a severe backlash. Many within the top echelons of the Party called for a halt to such ruthless gestures, fearing such action might plunge the Party into a round of tit-for-tat political purges.

In 1987, the Ministry of Supervision, which had been abolished in 1959, was resurrected and given a staff of 15,000 to investigate corruption, and a 'hotline' was set up, on which citizens were invited to ring up the ministry and inform on acts of corruption.

Then, in 1988, a new campaign was launched, Deng Xiaoping reportedly saying, 'We must begin our surgery close to home.'[13] That year forty-two companies run by the children of high cadres dubbed *gao gan zi di* or 'princelings' were shut down. Even Deng's own son, the paraplegic Deng Pufang, became the victim of this crackdown. His China Kang Hua Development Corporation, which benefited from its special tax-exempt status as an offshoot of the China Welfare Fund for the Handicapped, was ordered to divest itself of its subsidiaries and stripped of its precious import-export licence. In two years the company had done deals worth US$670 million. Nevertheless, despite all the rhetoric about 'killing one to teach a hundred' and 'killing the chicken to scare the monkey', and the occasional netting of 'a big tiger' – a minister of astronautics, the governor of Jiangxi

province and the governor of Hainan Island – it was mostly the little
tigers who were investigated.

Quite how extensive corruption had become was hard to establish
but the leftist faction tried to use the issue to discredit both reform
and the new private sector. 'The corrupt are a minority . . . but they
destroy the prestige of reforms and open policy and damage the
interests of the state and the masses,' declared the *People's Daily*.[14] As
the conflict between reformers and Maoists approached a crisis
during the Tiananmen protests in 1989, the *People's Daily* took a
defensive tack, arguing that 'corruption is an inevitable accompani-
ment of social progress'.[15]

During the nationwide pro-democracy protests of 1989 that culminated in the demonstration in Tiananmen Square many of the
marching students carried aloft banners attacking official profiteering which was linked in the public's mind with inflation. It was all too
easy to assume that sharp hikes in the cost of many staples, after controls were lifted by the reformers, were the result of corrupt officials
driving up prices. Public support for political reform was therefore
tinged with ambiguity. Some argued that an open political system was
the only way to combat corruption but the government later claimed
that many Chinese wanted tighter controls and 'stability', a word
used incessantly.

Among the most ardent supporters of the student protests were
getihu who banded together in 'dare-to-die' squads and raced around
Beijing on motorbikes, organizing resistance to the army. Many
donated food and drink to the protesters. A few, like Wan Runnan
who had founded one of China's first computer companies, the
Stone Corporation, gave generous financial support. In fact
Tiananmen demonstrated how, for the first time in forty years, the
private sector was capable of wielding political influence and consti-
tuting something like an opposition to the Communist Party.

In the aftermath of the protests however, the Party instigated a
large-scale investigation of private companies and started yet
another propaganda campaign, accusing them of evading taxes and
selling pornography. 'Self-employed traders and peddlers cheat,
embezzle, bribe and evade taxation,' wrote the new Party chief, Jiang
Zemin. Even the children of private businessmen were attacked. A

survey published by the *China Education Daily Survey* found that 'many of their children are often involved in fighting, drinking alcohol, gambling and reading pornographic materials. Eighty per cent of them are tired of collective activities and duties. One student paid his classmates to do classroom cleaning for him for the whole year.'[16]

According to official figures, out of 14.5 million private companies, a million were closed and their owners' assets confiscated during this period. At the same time the Party also cracked down on other businessmen who tried to parlay their wealth into political influence. For instance, the Uygur businesswoman, Rabia Kader, was arrested after her husband, a scholar of Uygur history, fled, having been accused of fomenting anti-Chinese and pro-independence protests.* Lastly the Party also decreed that, in order to preserve its 'purity', in future no private businessmen would be allowed to join and those who were already members would be placed under strict supervision.[17]

The biggest pro-democracy protests had been in southern China, particularly in Hong Kong where a million people took to the streets, and where many overseas businessmen had sent money and helped those democracy activists who fled China. For a while the growth of a pro-business and pro-democracy political movement financed by the overseas Chinese business community looked a strong possibility. Deng Xiaoping's southern tour in 1992 and his bid to encourage greater foreign investment and instigate a new round of reforms were also a calculated attempt to nip this new movement in the bud. It proved highly successful. The frenzied economic boom unleashed by further reforms sucked in a huge new wave of overseas Chinese investment, and support for political opposition quickly faded away.

Though Jiang Zemin had started his rule after 1989 by issuing decrees forbidding the children of officials from taking part in business and promising to open the bank accounts of Party members to

---

* In 2000, Rabia Kader was sentenced to eight years' imprisonment on a charge of breaking the law on state secrets. The accusation was based on the fact that she had sent newspaper clippings to her husband in America.

inspection, Deng soon reversed these decisions. Indeed, as has already been seen, one of his own sons quickly went into business with the Hong Kong tycoon Li Ka-shing and listed numerous subsidiaries of the steel company Shougang on the stock exchange.

Within China, the Party press once again hailed private businessmen, although this time not for breeding rabbits or opening small restaurants but for speculating in land, stocks, bonds, commodity prices, foreign exchange and futures contracts. One of the most famous model investors was Yang Baiwan, known as Millionaire Yang, who made a fortune trading in government bonds. A Shanghainese whose education was disrupted by the Cultural Revolution, he had ended up in the late 1970s as a warehouse watchman earning 68 yuan a month. Initially he tried selling electric wire in the countryside through the novel method, for China at least, of direct mail. His wife ran the business while he hung on to his job. With the money earned, the couple then began to buy government bonds which were being offered with a guaranteed return of 15 per cent. Soon they noticed that there was a difference in the prices at which the government sold state bonds, depending on the intended customer. Simply by buying and reselling such bonds, it was possible to make a profit. 'I must have been the first Chinese to notice this. At the time, people who wanted to buy government bonds at all were rare. Most people bought them because the government forced us to. But for me, this situation provided an opportunity,' he later recalled.[18]

Yang borrowed as much money from relatives as he could and rode around town on a bicycle, buying bonds from one counter and reselling them at another. He then discovered that bonds in the countryside were sold at a lower price than in the city so he began to go to the villages and buy up their allocations. Sometimes he bought bonds for 70 yuan and sold them for as much as 100 yuan.

After the crackdown that followed the Tiananmen protests, he became worried and decided to declare his wealth. Entering a tax office, he told an astonished clerk that he had earned a million yuan, an event which marked the start of his fame. As China's stock markets took off, Yang moved out of bonds and into stocks and then sold before the first crash came in 1995 when the government stepped in to cool an overheated economy. He subsequently became a professor of economics at the Shenyang Financial Management Institute, touring the country and giving lectures to as many as 7,000 at a time. In 1998, Xinhua reported that he was now living in self-imposed seclusion, glued to a computer screen in his home in Shanghai. 'I haven't been downtown in ten years and I don't participate in recreational activities,' he told the news agency. Instead he works at home, an ordinary flat, trading on markets via his computer and telephone.[19]

After 1992 others became instant millionaires by speculating in property. Chen Yuguang, the son of poor Sichuanese peasants, who had done time in prison, arrived on Hainan Island with only the clothes on his back. Five years later, he had made a fortune by persuading the PLA Navy, which controlled the best property, to lease some of it to him so that he could build luxury villas, hotels and offices. At the height of the Hainan property boom, Chen boasted he was worth US$150 million. Dressed in a white jogging suit, he described to one journalist how he had donated a tennis court for Zhongnanhai, where the leading cadres live in Beijing, and was now a tennis partner of Li Ruihuan, a member of the Politburo Standing Committee, the apex of Party power.[20]

On Hainan Chen built himself a five-storey castle modelled on Disney World with turrets and towers all in white. Inside was another tennis court, this time air-conditioned, as well as a swimming-pool and running-track. Visitors were equally amazed by a huge plaster copy of Rodin's *The Thinker* in the entrance hall, an enormous eagle carved over a double staircase and an interior graced by rows of classical pillars.

Another example of those who made money in property at this time was Li Xiaohua, the first man in China to buy a Ferrari. His start in life came with a chance meeting on a Beijing bus when he was unable to pay the bus fare. A fellow passenger took pity on him and paid the fare herself. She turned out to be the daughter of a senior general, and their brief encounter led to marriage.

Li was another rusticated urban youth who had spent years on a farm in the north-east before being allowed back to Beijing in 1978 where he started peddling watches made in Hong Kong. He was arrested and given a two-year stint in a reform-through-labour camp, but on his release he went back into business, investing 3,000 yuan in a machine that made iced drinks which he sold on the beaches of Beidaihe, a popular seaside resort. His first fortune came when he won the sole franchise in Japan for a hair-restoring potion invented by a traditional Chinese doctor from Wenzhou, Dr Zhao Zhangguang, another of China's famed multi-millionaires. The 101 Lotion was an enormous success in China in the 1980s and did well in Japan. Li bought each bottle for US$1 in China and sold it for US$10 in Japan.

A few years later he set up a company called the Huada Group, moved to Hong Kong and invested in property at the bottom of the market. By 1998, his group claimed to embrace 33 companies in 16 countries and regions and to employ 8,000 people. It also now owns office blocks in Beijing, two holiday resorts outside the capital, a ski resort in the north-east and a car racing club.[21]

Li's political connections provide essential protection. In 1990 he donated a million yuan to the Asian Games which Beijing hosted just after the Tiananmen crackdown. His offices are full of pictures of him shaking hands with members of the Politburo Standing Committee as well as vice premiers and current and former Western leaders.

When the post-1992 bubble burst at the end of the decade, the collapse in property prices led to the downfall of many self-made private businessmen, among them the colourful Mou Qizhong. The son of a prominent businessman in Wanxian, a river port near Chongqing, and the maid of his third wife, Mou had initially worked in a glass factory. During the Cultural Revolution he co-authored a book entitled *Where is China Going?*, as a result of which he was arrested and sentenced to death as a counter-revolutionary. The sentence was never carried out because Mao died the following year, but Mou was only released from prison in 1979. The following year he borrowed some money to buy clocks from a local munitions factory and then sold them in Shanghai. Arrested again in 1983, this time for 'speculation', he was released a year later. His next business venture was importing refrigerators from South Korea, with which China then had no diplomatic relations, and selling them to consumers in Beijing.[22] However, he shot to fame when in 1992 he brokered a huge barter deal with Russia in which four Tupolev passenger planes were exchanged for 500 railway wagons full of thermos flasks, shoes, clothes (including 600,000 pairs of socks) and other consumer goods.

In 1989 he had been the first businessman to voice support for the Communist Party just as the military was about to crush the students in Tiananmen Square. This earned him essential political support and access to state bank financing which he used to underwrite all kinds of often half-baked business schemes – the purchase of a Russian aircraft-carrier, the blasting of a 30-mile pass through the Himalayas to let in warm air, the leasing of Russian satellites, and the acquisition of real estate to build a special economic zone at Manzhouli on the border with Russia. When the latter, used as surety for his bank loans, proved to be worth far less than the 10 billion yuan he claimed, his creditors closed in. By 1999, he was in prison again facing a lengthy sentence for fraud.[23]

In common with most other private entrepreneurs operating in the 1990s Mou had had difficulty in raising credit, for China's banking system is devoted to financing local, provincial and central governments and all their SOEs and makes no provision for private companies. The stock markets are similarly skewed towards financing SOEs and only a handful of non-state companies have been authorized to issue shares.

Within the state sector, at the lowest level, the 55,000 rural credit co-operatives originally set up before 1949 to enable farmers to borrow money, have become in effect the state banks of local Party organizations that funnel money into real estate schemes and rural enterprises. At the highest level, provincial governments such as Guangdong have set up trust and investment corporations that also channel borrowings into property and factories, thereby adding to China's surplus capacity.

Those businessmen operating outside the government structure are, like Mou, forced to borrow money at very high interest rates, often as much as 30 per cent a year, through unregulated private banks and trust funds. In the countryside, these latter are known as *jijin hui,* and they have had the effect of draining capital out of the countryside and away from farming into urban areas. In the wake of the property collapse at the end of the 1990s most small townships in China were left with property companies that had tens of millions of yuan's worth of non-performing loans.[24]

Many of those who created fabulous fortunes in the 1990s did so by setting up trusts that promised investors wildly ambitious rates of return. As long as fresh investors could be found, these rates could be achieved but once the supply of new money ran out the entire pyramid scheme would collapse. In one widely publicized case, the Great Wall Machinery and Electronics Company issued bonds worth more than a billion yuan to over 100,000 people who believed they were guaranteed an annual return of 24 per cent. When the company defaulted nineteen officials were arrested on a charge of corruption and a vice minister was executed. An even bigger scheme which collapsed was the Xinxing Conglomerate based in the city of Wuxi, Jiangsu province, which had promised investors an annual return of 50 per cent a year and which had attracted investment funds worth 3.2 billion yuan from local governments, state enterprises and individuals. Although the scheme was ostensibly set up by a 58-year-old retired worker, some reports later claimed that Beijing's State Security Ministry – the secret police – was behind it.[25] Perhaps the most widely known case, however, was that of the Guangdong International Trust and Investment Corporation (GITIC) which had attracted foreign investors. When GITIC was allowed to go under in early 1999 it had debts of US$4.7 billion.

The failure of such schemes as these, the collapse of the property market, and the demise or unprofitability of many TVEs – coalmines, tanneries, shoe factories – generated a great deal of unrest. In 1998 angry investors in the failed Xinguoda Futures Company, another scheme that had collapsed, even marched to Tiananmen Square and the gates of Zhongnanhai, demanding compensation after the directors disappeared with a billion yuan. The company had claimed to invest in green-bean futures contracts and its 10,000 investors had expected to double their money in two years.[26]

Across the country that autumn, investors who had placed their life savings in various trust companies panicked and fought with police as they staged protests outside government offices or blocked railway lines. Local governments were forced to promise that they would repay small investors, and the cities of Chongqing and Tangshan announced that they had each set aside 1.5 billion yuan to ensure 'social stability'. Private banks in the countryside are thought to have accumulated bad debts of between 100 billion and 170 billion yuan. The rural credit co-operatives, with 1.2 trillion yuan's worth of peasant savings, were also technically insolvent since their liabilities exceeded their assets.[27] The few private businessmen who survived did so only because they had had the foresight to get out of property or stocks before the market collapsed.

Only a handful of entrepreneurs in the mid- to late 1990s managed to find legitimate ways of raising capital to fund expansion. One was the Orient Group, founded by Zhang Hongwei, which in 1994 was the first private company to be allowed to list shares. Later, it was also the first privately owned firm to obtain a loan from the World Bank's International Finance Corporation.

The story of Zhang's life follows a familiar pattern. His father, a teacher, was condemned as 'rightist' in the 1950s. As the son of a class enemy, Zhang was then exiled to the countryside. Unable to receive an education and barred from any normal career, he began by organizing a construction gang of peasants to work in Harbin, in Heilongjiang, before moving into the border trade with neighbouring Russia. His Orient Group now has investments in many sectors but Zhang is well aware that the backing of the Party is paramount in conducting a successful business. 'You have to take part in politics because politics and business are interrelated. The non-state-owned sector has to be represented in the political arena. In China doing business is different from doing business in other places: you only spend 30 per cent of your effort on business. The other 70 per cent is spent on dealing with all kinds of inter-personal relationships.'[28]

Entrepreneurs like Zhang, Mou or the 'hotpot king' Liao have complained that they are barred for ideological reasons from obtaining loans or buying out bankrupt SOEs. Yet life for entrepreneurs within the Party is often equally fraught. A telling example is China's

1. Deng Xiaoping, architect of China's reforms, stares out from a billboard: increasingly, however, such billboards advertise the products of a consumer society

2. A town in the poverty-stricken province of Shaanxi, held to be the original birthplace of Chinese culture and the homeland of the Han people, as the Chinese now refer to themselves

3. High-density housing in overcrowded Shanghai: Deng Xiaoping's reversal of Maoist ustification policies allowed tens of millions to try and make their way back to the cities

4. Balancing the burden of China's burgeoning population: the one–child policy
introduced in the 1980s has proved a failure

5. A farmer ploughs his paddy field: such peasants probably constitute the largest
unenfranchised group in the world

6. Speculating in stock prices of state-owned enterprises, or 'stir-frying shares' as it is
olloquially known: the public listing of state-owned enterprises has, however, done little
to improve their profitability

7. Workers on a state-owned motorcycle production line in what was once a military factory, part of the vast empire of the People's Liberation Army: attempts by the military to diversify into commercial activities have had mixed results

8. Workers at a button factory in Wenzhou: thousands of such small dingy factories have brought prosperity to this former treaty port on the southern coast of China

9. The return of Western companies to China after an absence of forty years has once again transformed lifestyles

10. A newly built department store in Shanghai, once the capital of the ultra left: consumerism not Communism is now raising living standards

11. A collective factory in Shanxi: the industrialization of the countryside has had a devastating effect on the environment

12. The consequences of ecological mismanagement: pumping out water from the Yellow River which runs dry for part of every year

13. People's Liberation Army soldiers go through their paces: despite their diminished political role, the modernization of China's armed forces is still a top priority

14. Unemployed men while away the hours in a public park in Shanghai: state-owned enterprises are shedding tens of millions of workers

15. Schoolteachers and their pupils in the Baiyangdian marshes, Hebei province: though the characters printed on the wall read 'Education', in the countryside it is a low priority, and most rural teachers struggle to earn a living

16. Xie Jinhao, a Miao barefoot doctor in Guangxi province, displays his qualifications and his vaccines: like education, however, rural healthcare is in crisis and preventative medical services are in decline

17. A statue of Mao Zedong in a temple within the memorial park in his home village in Hunan province: despite the privatization of the economy, Mao continues to be deified

18. Police attempt to control crowds queuing to buy stock options in Shenzhen: these riots in 1992 heralded the start of a new round of economic reforms

19. Bao Tong, the political aide to Zhou Ziyang who fell in the wake of the Tiananmen demonstrations of 1989: despite years in solitary confinement Bao, like many other members of the intelligentsia, continues to believe that the Party can reform itself

20. The arrest of a suspect is shown on state television in the aftermath of Tiananmen: the ruthless crackdown on dissent that followed the pro-democracy demonstrations put an end to political reform and plunged China into isolation

21. A parade of condemned prisoners is used to reinforce the state's authority: China executes more people than any other country in the world each year

22. The annual ritual of the National People's Congress at the Great Hall of the People in Beijing: though the NPC is nominally the highest law-making body in China, real power remains concentrated within the secretive institutions of the Communist Party

23. Jiang Zemin reviews the People's Liberation Army at the fiftieth anniversary celebrations of the People's Republic of China on 1 October 1999: the trappings of a modern head of state are juxtaposed with the symbols of imperial authority as Jiang passes the marble balustrades of the Forbidden City

'tobacco king', Chu Shijian, who turned his Red Pagoda cigarettes into the country's best-selling brand. In 1979, Chu started as general manager of a small factory in Yuxi, an obscure town in the south-west province of Yunnan, which made various local brands of cigarettes. Staff and workers all earned less than US$25 a month and the factory handed its profits over to the state.

From the early 1980s, with money in their pockets for the first time in decades, everyone in China began to buy cigarettes, and demand for popular brands soared. Through his own initiative, Chu began to promote Red Pagoda all over the country until it became so popular that a pack sold on the open market at twice the official fixed price. Distributors even began stumping up bribes just to gain access to supplies of Chu's Red Pagoda cigarettes. Yet all the while the company only had to report income from sales made at the official price. By 1996, Red Pagoda was churning out 100 billion cigarettes a year and reporting an income of US$2.3 billion while the state was still paying Chu an official salary of only US$250 a month.

Then, in 1996, the axe fell. Chu's commercial empire suddenly came under investigation when his boyhood friend, Pu Chaozhu, Yunnan province's Party secretary, was ousted. Chu was arrested, charged with corruption and expelled from the Communist Party. An account in the *People's Daily* accused him of pocketing US$1.7 million in bribes, and his wife and daughter were also implicated.

Precisely what had happened to the company's profits is unclear. Some money was certainly spent on new housing for the company's 5,000 employees, and a gleaming skyscraper was erected as the company's headquarters. Chu himself allegedly diverted US$145 million in profits into various bank accounts and it is thought that some money was sent abroad after his son took charge of the company's overseas operations in Singapore. Overseas dealings were extensive because the company exported huge quantities of cigarettes merely in order to smuggle them back into China and thus avoid paying a heavy domestic sales tax.

When Chu learned of the warrant for his arrest, he tried to flee. He was caught attempting to cross the border into Vietnam, and his wife and daughter were also seized. The daughter died in prison, apparently committing suicide, and the parents were also imprisoned.

The son in Singapore survived. In reporting the case, the *New York Times* concluded: 'There barely exists a large company in China today that does not have hidden accounting, secret decision-making, tiny salaries and lavish perks for managers, all of them invitations to greater financial impropriety. Corruption is now so endemic in China's businesses, that no one can accurately see where it begins and ends.'[29]

Whatever the extent of Chu's culpability, his case demonstrates not only the potential for corruption but also the insecurity of property in China. Most companies keep multiple sets of company accounts that make it impossible to decipher true revenues or profits, and few businesses feel secure in their ownership of property. Indeed it has been estimated that every year nervous businessmen move over US$20 billion abroad.

When it comes to intellectual property rights, the lack of protection is even more damaging. China now wants to build up its 'knowledge economy' and copy the Silicon Valley recipe of venture capital funding small hi-technology start-ups. Yet such is the extent of piracy of trade marks, brands, software and technology of all kinds, that anyone engaged in any creative activity, be they a musician or a scientist, has little chance of becoming wealthy. And if they do, envy soon marks them out as potential victims, vulnerable to accusations of corruption in the next political campaign.

An example is Professor Wang Xuan and his wife Chen Dangqiu of Beijing University who invented a computer programme to print Chinese characters on laser printers. After 1979, the programme formed the basis for the commercial success of one of China's top technology companies, the Founder Group. In 1958 Wang had joined a small team making China's first computer, the Red Flag, out of vacuum tubes. When the Great Leap Forward started that year, the team's leader, Professor Dong Jiebao, a man who had returned from the United States out of a sense of patriotism, was persecuted and committed suicide. Wang replaced him but during the nation-wide famine that ensued, he almost starved to death when he lost his precious grain ration tickets. He survived but fell ill and all work on the computer stopped. A few years later, during the Cultural Revolution, he again came close to death when his father was labelled a 'rightist'. Wang himself was beaten up for listening to the BBC World Service and, as he later confessed, he came close to committing suicide.

Eventually he and his wife were allowed to stay at home where they worked on developing a computer language, ALGOL 60, which could be used in domestic computers. In 1972 he began to look for a way to input Chinese characters on a Western keyboard. Three years later he completed a proposal but was so weak from malnutrition that his text had to be read out by his wife. Eventually the proposal was listed as a key state project and the couple were allowed to work on it.[30]

Wang's software was soon being used by printers throughout China and in the late 1980s he established the Founder Group, which eventually listed in Hong Kong where its shares shot up. As the company's chairman Wang himself held stock options worth US$5 million. Several years later, however, the company began to lose money as others pirated its technology. The Party secretary of Beijing University, which holds a majority of the shares, used the opportunity to dump Wang, still aged only 62, and replace him with Party officials.

In similar circumstances many of the engineers from the Chinese Academy of Sciences who created China's other successful hi-technology company, the Legend Group, which dominates personal computer sales, were also ousted. The reorganization came just as the company began to issue shares to its employees although the state retains complete control. As its founder and chairman, Liu Chuangzhi, said with a small smile at a *Fortune* business conference held in Shanghai: 'I am not a capitalist but I would like to become one.'[31]

The Communist Party might not have changed its name by the end of the century but many ordinary people had become proud property owners and the once banished statues of the plump God of Wealth were being worshipped again.

8

The God of Wealth

THE WEDDING OF the Wangs took place down a cramped little alley, close to the Qianmen Hotel in Beijing. The bride looked graceful in her white wedding dress but the groom, wearing a Western-style suit for the first time, did not. He kept grinning foolishly, fingering either the red tie hung outside his pullover or the label sewn on the outside of his jacket sleeve.

There were dozens of guests who looked at us with the same mixture of curiosity and trepidation that they would have given a rare and possibly dangerous animal. 'When foreigners come, it brings good fortune,' the groom kept reassuring them.

After contributing our gifts – two bottles of local grain spirit and cartons of imported 555 cigarettes – we joined the other guests seated around small collapsible tables for the wedding feast. We too felt awkward.

Our presents were added to a display of more impressive gifts – a new imported colour television set, a stereo cassette-player, an eiderdown and bedding decorated with black-and-white pandas, enamel washbasins, a large alarm clock and a collection of aluminium pots and pans.

'Can they understand what we are saying, do you think?' asked one wizened old man loudly, as he looked at us and nudged his companion.

The Wangs lived a few hundred yards away from where I had stayed in the first months after arriving in China in the autumn of 1985. Out on a walk one day, I had ventured down their alleyway, known as a *hutong* in Beijing, and the groom had invited myself and two friends to his forthcoming wedding.

In those days it was a rare and daring gesture. No foreigner could go to a Chinese house without first obtaining permission from the Public Security Bureau. And likewise no Chinese could enter a foreigner's home or even a hotel like the Qianmen without registering. Everyone feared that any evidence of contact with a foreigner would later be used against them in some campaign or other. Years of such political campaigns, in which anyone with a foreign connection or even a relative abroad was suspected and very often persecuted, had left a deep-seated fear.

'I was afraid to talk to you at first. I thought there would be trouble later,' said Mrs Wang after she was married. 'The neighbours said it was dangerous to mix with foreigners.'

But in fact after the Wangs' wedding, I kept getting invited to more weddings by their friends, so many in fact that I eventually grew tired of spending Saturday afternoons drinking endless toasts and eating dishes of congealed squid or sea cucumber. My role as a social trophy began to pall.

It seemed that everyone was getting married in China in those days. People born during the baby boom that had followed the famine of the early 1960s were now in their twenties. In fact half the country was under the age of 30. The tens of millions of 'urban youth' who had been sent to the countryside in the second half of the 1960s had returned to the cities and now they were in a hurry to make up for lost time. Indeed the early 1980s were a time for families. The Communist Party had abandoned its goal of destroying the 'bourgeois' family. Chinese television deliberately showed Deng Xiaoping surrounded by his children and grandchildren at Chinese New Year.

Millions of families that had been split apart during the last thirty years, dispersed to labour camps, exiled to the countryside, seconded into army units or sent to work on industrial projects in the interior, were now reunited. They returned to live in bare, shabbily furnished apartments, or, like the Wangs, in a crudely built shack erected when a larger courtyard house had been subdivided. Most had no running water or individual toilets or bathrooms and daily life was thus still very collective. The Chinese called it 'eating from the common pot' but there was at last room for private family life; and with the advent of the free markets there was now an alternative to the endless queuing at state outlets.

Some hoped that Deng's reforms might go far enough to permit a restoration of the old pre-1949 life with its big families living under one roof, numerous social and religious festivals, temple fairs and traditional gift-giving. In Beijing an attempt was made to revive some of the temple fairs with their foodstalls and street entertainers but after thirty years of neglect they could not be brought to life so easily.

At one wedding I sat next to a man in his late sixties. He was almost bald and dressed in blue thickly padded cotton clothes against the winter cold. In the slow and rather courtly way that Beijingers who grew up before 1949 still speak, the elderly wedding guest recalled how life had been lived in the past: 'There were seventy people including servants, where I grew up. And at Spring Festival there were many rituals – the offerings to the Kitchen God, the blessing of the God of Wealth.'

The Kitchen God made his report to heaven on the goings-on of each member of the family and was sent on his way with melons, cakes, candied fruits and firecrackers. A picture of Cai Shen, the God of Wealth, was also found in all homes, and his favours were requested on the third day of the New Year holiday. The Communist Party still frowns on such superstitions and they are virtually banned in cities.

'Now, it is just eating and drinking, just showing off,' said the old man, smiling a little, as another plate was placed on top of those that already covered the table in front of us. 'Still, it is better than the 1970s, when it was forbidden to eat anything at all. Then the Spring Festival lasted just a day and people prided themselves on how little they ate or drank.'

The Wangs each earned a paltry salary, 30 or 40 yuan a month (around US$10 at the time), from their state jobs. He was a driver for a state company and she worked in an office. Even so, they were keen to display what wealth they had, though anxious that it would not be enough to impress foreigners.

'And how much do *you* earn?' each wedding guest would ask me. Comparisons are never more odious than when it comes to incomes. 'It is hard to say,' I would usually mumble, before explaining, if pressed, how at home two-thirds of my income went on tax, rent and services as they were much more expensive than in China.

Deng's political programme of reform, dubbed the Four Modernizations and launched in 1979,* offered the immediate prospect of *xiao kang* or small prosperity, meaning enough to eat, drink and wear, and that within twenty years per capita GNP would quadruple to reach US$800.[1] No longer were the Chinese to sacrifice everything for the state: now they could amass some wealth for themselves. Within fifteen years, private consumption would become the driving force behind economic growth. Still, understanding how much disposable income Chinese had in 1985 was difficult. Their tiny salaries were never taxed and hardly any of their income was spent on housing, electricity, water, transport, schooling, health, pensions and so on. Moreover, many of them looked at their income in terms of the household. Pooled household savings for a television set or some similar purchase could accumulate quite quickly.

Some households also had substantial savings. For many years, there had been nothing to spend the money on, especially for those banished to the countryside but still earning their old salaries. A third complicating factor was that when people mentioned their salaries, they omitted all the bonuses which their work units handed out. These were often worth more than the salaries themselves. Most units handed out cash but many also distributed ration tickets for, say, a much sought-after Flying Pigeon bicycle and, more regularly, supplied deliveries of fish or pork, boxes of fresh fruit or some other luxury.

What was not spent on eating – half of consumer spending – was mostly spent on clothes. When I first arrived in Beijing almost everyone seemed to be dressed in army surplus clothing – olive green plimsolls, baggy olive green trousers, thick olive green cotton padded coats or, in summer, white nylon shirts and grey trousers. But,

---

* The Four Modernizations referred to Agriculture, Industry, Science and Technology, and Defence.

gradually, the young began to appear in fashionable clothes – jeans, T-shirts, dresses and high-heeled shoes.

Party elders were horrified at the results of the first wave of consumerism and reacted with the launch in 1983 of a campaign against spiritual pollution. Consumption for its own sake, without even the blessing of ritual or tradition, was felt to be deeply immoral. Under pressure Hu Yaobang, the diminutive Party Secretary who had just been the first to welcome private entrepreneurs into Zhongnanhai, the leadership's complex in Beijing, and who had suggested that the Chinese ought to switch to using knives and forks, performed a complete volte-face. He lashed out against 'wasteful extravagance', 'Epicureanism', hedonism and those who 'indiscriminately advocate the worship of foreign things', and joined the chorus of veteran revolutionaries pressing for a return to 'the spirit of bitter struggle and hardship'. Editorials called for thrift and self-sacrifice, and praised those who voluntarily handed over their surplus money to the state. At the same time, the Party targeted those who wore bell-bottom jeans as 'decadent', calling them 'hoodlums' and accusing them of 'blindly imitating the Western capitalist way of life'. In some places, the Party even mobilized its Youth League members to patrol the streets in search of the wearers of flared trousers and to wield scissors against those with long hair. In some cities, the municipal government printed notices warning that young women with long hair would not be allowed into government buildings.[2]

Anything that was redolent of self-gratification in preference to the glorification of the state, such as body-building competitions, beauty contests or fashion shows, became an ideological battleground, sometimes permitted, sometimes banned, and the battle was couched in virulent nationalist terms. When the state ordered people to buy something, it called them 'patriotic treasury bonds' or 'patriotic winter cabbage'. Those who wanted to acquire foreign goods were therefore branded as 'traitors', and Maoists accused young people of foolishly thinking that 'even the moon is rounder in the West'.

The dispute harked back to the first decades of the twentieth century. In the 1930s, Japanese goods had flooded China, and this influx was seen by many Chinese as part of a deliberate strategy to turn China into an economic colony and founder-member of Japan's 'Co-prosperity Sphere'. The experience left a bitter legacy. Buying domestic goods instead of foreign imports was not seen as protectionism but as a matter of survival. In the mid-1980s, Beijing students even staged a march in Tiananmen Square, protesting at the 'second Japanese invasion' and the flood of Japanese TVs, cars and other goods entering the country.

To prevent the reforms from being thrown off course, Deng intervened in 1984, declaring that it was nonsense to say that 'the poorer we are the more revolutionary we are'. Socialism did not have to be equated with poverty. Nevertheless, the opening up of China allowed the Chinese their first glimpse of the outside world for thirty years, and for many that was profoundly unsettling. Everything foreign seemed better and in fact usually was. Old feelings of inferiority resurfaced. Some in the Communist Party wanted to whip up nationalist feelings and a fear of foreigners to deflect those who questioned the Party's record and its legitimacy.

Even so, everyone yearned for something foreign. In one of the first 'foreign' restaurants, situated at an intersection off the Avenue of Eternal Peace in Beijing, I found young people trying to eat bread and jam with chopsticks. Outside the Friendship Store, one of the handful that sold imported goods, Chinese could only enter with a special ticket, and buying anything imported required foreign exchange certificates, the second currency with which foreigners were obliged to pay.* That, however, did not stop them from coming to look.

For most people, however, the nearest they could get to buying something foreign was to drink Coca-Cola or smoke imported foreign cigarettes. The first entered the country legitimately: the

---

* The official script, the *renminbi* or people's currency, is not a hard currency and ordinary Chinese could not use it to buy imported goods without special permission. Foreigners could exchange their money for foreign exchange certificates (FECs). All goods and services available to foreigners were priced in FECs which allowed China to charge higher prices and obtain foreign exchange from visitors.

second were mostly smuggled in and, since they were therefore untaxed, were cheap enough to be affordable. Even now China may still be the fastest growing market for Coca-Cola, despite the fact that in the 1980s alone sales grew by 30–40 per cent a year. By the mid-1990s, the company had 23 bottling plants and 23 per cent of the market.

'They view us as American but also as local,' said the Chairman of Coca-Cola, Roberto Goizueta, after a trip to China in 1995. 'Coca-Cola is ours but to them it is also a symbol so that to become more like Americans they consume Coca-Cola.'[3]

Foreign goods not only became a status symbol but also quickly earned a reputation for reliability, thereby highlighting the inadequacy of domestic goods. Everyone had stories to tell of locally made television sets that did not work, batteries that leaked, shoes that fell part, beer bottles that exploded, alcohol that blinded drinkers, patent medicines that killed patients. In 1985, the Party was forced to set up a Consumer Complaints Office to which people could appeal when they had bought faulty domestic goods.

In the early days it was generally impossible to buy what one wanted so people settled for what they could find. There were very few shops and even when they were open they rarely had what they were supposed to stock. My abiding memory of what shortages meant came when I invited guests to the Peking Hotel's Peking Duck Restaurant only to find it had run out of Peking duck, and that was the only dish on the menu.

As time went on plenty of other restaurants offering Peking duck sprang up, since this was not a government monopoly. The telephone service and the post office were a different matter. Calling a central government ministry from the Qianmen Hotel replicated the experience of 'K' calling the Castle in Franz Kafka's eponymous novel. After a series of clicks and whistles, the phone at the other end would ring and ring until a distant interplanetary voice would brusquely answer '*Wei*?' ('Hello?') In order to confirm that contact had been established, one would reply with another '*wei*' down the crackly line. This exchange might go back and forth a dozen times until, usually, the phone line would be abruptly and mysteriously severed. Traditions of secrecy were such in China that everyone seemed determined to avoid revealing what department one had reached. The process would then have to start again and, since phones were unmanned during the statutory two-and-half-hour lunch break, making a successful phone call might take a whole day.

At the Qianmen Hotel, one of the handful open to foreigners in the early and mid-1980s, the telex machine was turned off outside office hours so it was virtually impossible to receive a message from Europe or North America. The only alternative was to go to the International Post Office which made available a handful of international telex lines. In 1986, the whole country had just 1,862 international telephone and telex lines, and in the cities there were just 3.4 million phone lines or one telephone for every 159 people. Even in the capital, Beijingers had to wait up to sixteen years to have a phone line installed. And yet between 1981 and 1986, more phone lines were installed – 1.81 million – than during the whole period from 1949 to 1976.

Other public services were no better, although the 1980s saw a phenomenal expansion in the state bureaucracy. During the Cultural Revolution, the number of ministries had shrunk to thirty but in the 1980s it grew to at least a hundred, to which were added new offices such as that handling patents. Much of the growth in consumption in the 1980s was fuelled by state spending on new offices, cars, desks, chairs and telephones. Indeed, China became one of the world's biggest importers of cars although many of them were smuggled or imported tax-free, a privilege granted to joint ventures.

In the countryside in the 1980s, the biggest consumer item was housing. For the first time since the Great Leap Forward the peasants were able to spend their savings on building new homes. The old mud and straw cottages were pulled down and gave way to brick and tile houses. About 60 per cent of villages lacked electricity at the start of the decade but this quickly began to change as small local generators were installed. Peasants also bought themselves lamps, vacuum flasks, stoves and small tractors.

In the cities, housing remained state property. Like that of the Wangs, most homes in Beijing could best be described as slums. Little new public housing was built in the 1980s and when families needed more space, they would simply tack on a ramshackle shed constructed out of odd bits of wood or spare bricks to create an extra room. From close up much of Beijing soon came to resemble a temporary refugee camp.

Conditions in the high-rise flats, mostly dating from the 1950s, were no better. The lifts often failed and always closed down before ten at night. The lights on the staircases never worked and people had to store a winter's supply of 'patriotic cabbage' on the stairwells and balconies. All that was available in the way of living-room furnishings were strange and ugly sofas, high-backed, made of plastic and apparently stuffed with rocks.

At night, the streets quickly emptied (not until the mid-1980s was street-lighting introduced). Even motor vehicles were forbidden to turn on their headlamps. In winter, once the crowds of cyclists had returned home, Beijing was deserted. There were no bars or discothèques, few concerts or football matches, almost nothing to do once the restaurants had shut. Most towns possessed only one bookshop and even in Beijing there were no more than a handful. In the absence of anything else to do young people sat around in the public parks and in winter went skating.

The only major source of popular entertainment was the state television, and the import and production of television sets therefore became a priority. In 1979, the government shipped in several hundred thousand black-and-white television sets from South Korea, a country with which it had no diplomatic ties. To satisfy increasing demand, China then began to import, largely from Japan, television, set assembly lines and components. It also started the first car production plant in Shanghai, a joint venture with Volkswagen. Still, the consumer market for such items was flooded by imports.

In 1987 and 1988, when price control on many commodities was lifted, the cost of basic goods such as soap, kerosene, salt and matches shot up and China's inflation rate rose to at least 30 per cent. Many people panicked and began to hoard goods, convinced that it was better to turn their savings into something durable, like a Japanese TV set, or at least to exchange their savings for foreign currency. At the time foreigners were forever being confronted by Chinese who would sidle up in the street and say, in mangled English, 'Schange maney?'

The God of Wealth

Those with the right *guanxi* who had access to foreign exchange certificates or hard foreign currency were much envied. They included most of the Party élite who could buy imported luxury goods distributed through unmarked commission shops. Yet by the end of the 1980s, the first signs of the consumer boom of the 1990s were already becoming evident. There was a general outbreak of what can only be described as 'spivdom'. Young men with slicked-back hair, sporting gold watches and Hong Kong-style suits with flared trousers, and smoking American cigarettes could be found in the first private bars that opened. Beijing's *jeunesse doré* did not, like the average Chinese, have to pester foreigners to teach them how to disco-dance. With access to imported films and Hong Kong television programmes, they already knew exactly what to do.

On the eve of the Tiananmen protests in 1989, the first two Kentucky Fried Chicken outlets opened. Other Western companies such as Proctor & Gamble were also making inroads into the domestic market, driving domestic producers of soap and shampoo to the wall. After the Tiananmen massacre, however, the economy went into free fall, Beijing's private bars closed and most foreign companies withdrew. Then, in 1992, Deng Xiaoping's southern tour ushered in a period of feverish growth.

The consumer explosion quickly lifted sales of household goods. In 1997, a Gallup poll revealed that 90 per cent of Chinese homes now possessed a TV set, and even in rural China, 84 per cent of households possessed one, even if it was just a black-and-white set. In the cities, nearly 70 per cent owned a refrigerator, 82 per cent possessed a washing-machine, 33 per cent a pager and 22 per cent a video cassette-recorder. Living conditions, however, remained unchanged. A survey of urban households by the Sofres Media Establishment found that over 70 per cent of households lacked hot water and 60 per cent did not have their own bathroom.[4]

Food still accounted for half of consumer spending but an enormous change in eating habits had taken place with the Westernization, or globalization, of Chinese tastes. The first McDonald's in China opened in 1990. By the end of 1999 there were nearly 500 outlets. Many other companies followed suit and by the mid-1990s, a new outlet for one or other of the American fast-food chains was opening every week.[5]

The Chinese, who in the 1980s still invariably drank green tea, also began in the 1990s to drink coffee. Maxwell House, Nestlé and other makers of instant coffee established production in China and spent heavily on advertising, and the drink began to be served regularly on domestic and foreign flights. A survey of twelve cities conducted in 1998 found that 32 per cent now drank coffee at least once a year and fresh coffee distributors such as Starbucks began to open up.[6]

Beer was another Western beverage whose consumption increased dramatically. In the ten years to 1995, consumption grew at an average annual rate of 18 per cent, attracting 60 foreign breweries into the market. With an annual average per capita consumption of 16 litres, the Chinese were still far behind Hong Kong with 30 litres or Japan with 55 litres, but even so China had become the world's largest market for beer.[7]

Chinese consumers also developed a taste for icecream which, along with most other dairy products, had hitherto been almost impossible to buy in China. In the 1990s, the market grew by 20 per cent a year and in Beijing alone, consumption doubled in just three years. Still, to attain such growth companies had to make a heavy initial investment. Unilever's subsidiary, Walls, found it had to give away refrigerator boxes and carts free to vendors before it could sell its brands; and manufacturers of entirely new foodstuffs such as frozen yoghurt face an even bigger challenge in persuading the Chinese to try their goods.[8]

At the same time many Chinese abandoned their traditional sweets, such as the mooncakes passed around at the autumn Moon Festival, and began to buy chocolate. Consumption doubled to 22,000 tonnes in the six years to 1994, with imports capturing a fifth of the market. Soon foreign companies were investing in domestic manufacturing. Mars was the first in 1993, followed by Cadbury Schweppes and M&Ms, and sales have since continued to grow by nearly 20 per cent a year. Interestingly, foreign manufacturers have adjusted their products to suit Chinese tastes, Cadbury's, for example, making a slightly less sweet chocolate.[9]

Western products almost entirely new to Chinese palates have also found buyers. The Chinese, who rarely ate potatoes in the past, began to acquire a taste for potato chips. Sales of wine soared. Even cheese, which the Chinese are generally thought to dislike intensely, is now produced in China and eaten, if only on pizzas. Indeed one German company, Hochland, has even developed cheeses flavoured with banana or strawberry in the hope of persuading the Chinese to acquire the taste.[10]

Similarly, many wheat-based products – biscuits, cream cakes, various kinds of bread and pastries and most of all instant noodles – have become very popular too. Perhaps not surprisingly, Taiwanese companies have dominated the market for instant noodles. In 1992, one such company, Tingyi, opened its first factory in Tianjin. Within four years it had forty-eight production lines making its Master Kang brand noodles, and by 1998, China as a whole had 1,800 producers who together accounted for 33 per cent of sales world-wide.

Apart from food and beverages, another fast-growing area has remained toiletries and cosmetics. Throughout most of the 1990s the market grew by 30 per cent a year. By 1997 it was worth US$2 billion, and some industry experts forecast that it may well have risen to US$22 billion by 2013.[11]

The effort required by Western companies to develop the Chinese market has been considerable. The country is vast and its communications still poor. Food manufacturers in particular have had to create, virtually from scratch, the means to transport frozen food from one part of the country to another.[12] At the same time the introduction of Western consumerism has brought about a change in Chinese habits and customs. Chocolate manufacturers now promote St Valentine's Day, and McDonald's have encouraged parents to bring their children to their restaurants for birthday parties, a novelty in China.

Those foreign companies who set up business in China soon commanded a dominant share of their particular market. For example, a Hong Kong research company, Frank Small & Associates, has estimated that by 1996, foreign multinationals held 60 per cent of the colour TV market, 79 per cent of the shampoo market and 84 per cent of the carbonated soft-drinks market.[13]

The world's retailing giants have also arrived in China. The first foreign retailers were allowed to set up shop in 1998 and others soon followed – Carrefour from France, Wal-Mart from America, Metro from Germany, Ikea from Sweden, Makro from Holland and Isetan, Sogo and Ito-Yokaido from Japan. Their presence has in turn sparked off a retail property boom. Beijing, which had just one major department store in the early 1980s, boasted eighty by 1998, with still more on the drawing-board. Shanghai now has seventy department stores each covering over 30,000 square feet. Competition between them is fierce, one store going so far as to hire an actor to impersonate Mao and attract customers, a move that caused uproar.[14] Such competition has also encouraged the state to urge domestic companies to set up their own department stores and supermarket chains, and the dingy state distribution shops and the unhygienic street markets have all been earmarked for closure.

By the end of the 1990s, Beijing had become a very different city, crowded with cars, illuminated at night by neon lights, with streets of private bars and new office blocks and shopping malls. When I went back to the Wangs' *hutong*, I found it had been demolished to make way for a shopping mall. The Wangs themselves were among the half million Beijingers who have been moved out of the centre of the capital, and the enterprises in which they and many others worked have either been closed or relocated as well.

Now Beijing is fast earning a reputation as a shopper's paradise, especially for visitors. Foreign exchange certificates have been abolished and the different prices for foreigners and locals have been phased out. Anyone can now go to the Friendship Store although with the arrival of so many new shopping malls in the city, generally only tour groups shop there. Most visitors, however, prefer to browse through the nearby Silk Market where clothes, toys, shoes and carpets, whether fake brands or the genuine article, can be bought at a fraction of the price they would cost in the United States or Europe.

The consumer boom has not, however, been plain sailing. Worried by the speed with which foreign companies were capturing large parts of the domestic market, in the mid-1990s the Chinese government mobilized a counter-attack. In 1995, legislators submitted a petition demanding that the government restrict the expansion of Coca-Cola and Pepsi, and the authorities began to promote struggling domestic soft drinks makers such as Jianlibao. In response to pressure from public opinion, too, Coca-Cola set up a joint venture with the Ministry of Light Industry to produce a new domestic brand made from fruit called Tian yu Di or 'Heaven and Earth'.[15] Even so, the new domestic brands have struggled to match the marketing and organizational skills of their foreign competitors.

The government also publicized reports by Chinese nutritionists who argued that eating fast food such as hamburgers was bad for children's health. 'Most foreign fast foods consist of lots of meat and few vegetables, and the cereals in them are too refined to retain Vitamin B which is very helpful for the development of children's memories,' Dr Chen Xuecun informed Xinhua. And he warned that once a child acquired the habit of eating at McDonald's, it was hard to shake off.[16] McDonald's in turn argued that they were creating jobs and that, besides, competition was healthy and would raise standards.

China's efforts to compete on the fast food front were no more successful than they had been where soft drinks were concerned. The Ministry of Internal Trade issued guidelines and produced a national development plan for the fast food industry, earmarking seed funds and supporting, amongst others, the Ronghuaji or Glorious China Chicken Company as a competitor to Kentucky Fried Chicken. 'It is not exactly an equal competition,' complained one of Ronghuaji's senior executives, Hu Xingquan, in 1997. 'We are a six-year-old child in the business and KFC is a sixty-year-old veteran. KFC has reached levels of capitalism that we cannot match. They advertise heavily on television but we have not done so this year.'[17] Such domestic start-ups also failed to match the Americans in management, cleanliness, efficiency and above all in consistency. By the turn of the century, Ronghuaji was struggling to keep a dozen outlets going but KFC was fast approaching its target of operating 500 outlets.

The only real rival to these foreign fast food chains was started not by the government but by two Chinese-American entrepreneurs.

The California Beef Noodle King serves fast-food noodles and rice-based dishes. Unfortunately, the two founders fell out and went to court, a turn of events which has inevitably damaged the company's growth prospects.[18]

Occasionally, China has tried to exploit the competition between rival foreign giants. In its battle against Fuji for market share, Kodak won the all-important support of the central government by investing US$490 million in taking over three ailing mainland manufacturers and promising to invest a total of US$1 billion, to include the building of a brand-new plant in Xiamen.[19]

In some areas, however, domestic manufacturers have begun to stage a comeback. Although many parts of China had imported production lines by the mid-1990s, the domestic market is now dominated by just a handful of big Chinese manufacturers such as Changhong and Konka. Similarly the Chinese personal computer company Legend dominates the domestic market. At the same time some countries such as Japan have moved out of the domestic production of TV sets and other household goods altogether as their currencies have appreciated.

Other Chinese companies, having acquired the necessary knowledge through joint ventures and come to dominate the domestic market, have gone on to compete successfully abroad. Haier and Kelon, manufacturers of refrigerators, air-conditioners and water-heaters, are but two examples. Many companies had no choice but to expand overseas. In 1997 China had the capacity to make 36 million television sets a year but annual sales amounted to only 15 million. The same was true for air-conditioners. Capacity was 13 million but sales reached just 7 million.[20]

Too often, however, those Chinese companies that did manage to compete became the victims of their own success. A boom-bust pattern of expansion, proliferation and then consolidation was repeated in many industries. The production of cashmere will serve as one example. In the 1980s, there were just 10 state-run processing plants in China. Ten years later there were 2,600, each competing to buy the goats' wool. Domestic herds grew by 9 per cent a year but even so China had the capacity to process three or four times the amount of wool produced. In 1998, when the supply of finished cashmere products exceeded demand by about 40 per cent, prices collapsed across the world and shepherds in Inner Mongolia began to cull their herds.

Many Western companies have also had cause to regret their wildly optimistic expectations about both the size of the Chinese market and its potential. In the mid-1990s the world's car giants, backed by their governments, scrambled for the privilege of investing billions of dollars in new plants in China. With growth rates of between 30 and 40 per cent a year being achieved, such investment seemed a safe bet. Ford predicted that private car sales alone would reach one million per year by the start of the new century. Volkswagen, with over half the market, doubled its capacity to 600,000. But by the close of 1999, sales of saloon cars had stuck at just over half a million. The company then more soberly predicted that by the year 2010 a maximum of 20 million Chinese would be able to afford to buy a small car.[21]

At the end of the 1990s it was a strange experience to speed down one of the deserted motorways built earlier in the decade and gaze out of the window at peasants pulling a wooden plough across their plots. Many of the cars that stopped at the toll gates were waved through toll-free because they belonged to Party or military units. Once I got a taxi to take me along the new motorway linking Chongqing to Chengdu, the only two big cities in a region with a population of 110 million. For hundreds of miles, the road was empty.

'The lorries won't pay the tolls. They prefer to take the old road,' explained my driver. When we reached the outskirts of Chengdu, he forced me to get out quickly with my luggage. 'If they catch me with my Chongqing number plates here they'll kill me,' he explained before hastily turning round. Local taxes and fees of various kinds discourage people from driving even from one part of a city to another, and local protectionism has also prevented cars made in one area of the country from being sold in another. Shanghai only buys Volkswagen cars, Wuhan only those made by its French joint venture with Citroën.

Although China has spent heavily on motorways, airports and

aeroplanes, this has largely been for the convenience of a narrow élite. The construction of urban mass transport systems is only being undertaken slowly, even though many people believe it unlikely that most Chinese will ever own a car.[22]

The outskirts of the cities have also witnessed the growth of luxury villa developments, many of which were built in the boom of the mid-1990s. But such housing, like the cars, is beyond the pocket of most Chinese consumers. By 1997, the SEZs had an oversupply of housing that could last ten years. In Shanghai about 40 per cent of residential housing was standing vacant at the end of 1998 even though rents had been falling steadily for several years.[23] Much of the considerable investment in new housing was aimed at the very top end of the market despite a pressing need for low-cost housing. In that area, as in other sectors, the development of a housing market has been dogged by confusion over the ownership of existing property, land rights and restrictions on resale, and by poor construction quality and the difficulty of obtaining mortgages.

The failure of the housing and car markets to develop their full potential has prompted some experts to revise downwards their assessment of how wealthy the Chinese have become. At the end of 1999, China's annual GDP per capita was calculated to be just under US$700, not far off the target of US$800 set by Deng but still low compared to an average of US$3,200 for eastern Europe, US$3,500 for Mexico or US$5,000 for Brazil.[24]

A Gallup poll conducted at the end of 1999 found that urban Chinese account for 70 per cent of the country's wealth, with a mean annual household income of US$2,500. The annual average income of rural households was US$870. Per capita peasant incomes had actually fallen since 1997 by US$200 to US$240 a year, and some experts at the Ministry of Agriculture thought even this estimate was too high.[25] This concentration of wealth in the hands of a minority is also illustrated by a number of other figures in circulation, although their reliability is questionable: just 40 million people own all the shares in some 900 listed SOEs, and 38 per cent of the 6 trillion yuan in personal bank deposits is owned by just 3 per cent of those with savings accounts.

Widely differing calculations for the growth of China's economy over the twenty-year period of reform have also been made. Some claim that China averaged growth rates of 10 per cent a year, almost better than any other nation.[26] Others believe it was about 7–7.5 per cent in nominal terms but, allowing for inflation, probably closer to 5 per cent, on a par with India and similar developing countries.[27]

Chinese economic statistics are notoriously unreliable and elastic but nothing can disguise the extraordinary explosion in communications which has taken place, far exceeding all expectations, even those of optimistic foreign investors.

In 1985, China announced plans to install 30 million telephone lines by the end of the century, but the target kept being raised by surprised planners until it finally reached 140 million lines, the government declaring that it would continue to install 12 million new lines a year until, by the year 2020, there would be 40 phones for every 100 people. By the end of the century, there were still only 3 or 4 telephones per 100 villagers but 80 per cent of urban homes had one. By 2020, China could reach the level of 50:100 seen in many richer countries in the mid-1990s.[28] Radio paging services also grew rapidly, from 3,000 subscribers in 1987 to 87,000 by 1991. Nine years later two-thirds of urban homes possessed one. In the same period China became the fastest growing market for mobile phones, with 26 million subscribers by the end of the century. Half of all urban homes also had a VTR or DVD player and 86 million people had access to cable television.

Huge expectations are also building up about the potential of the Internet. Personal computer sales reached 2.5 million in 1997 and over 3 million in 1998, and it has been reported that China now has more than 8 million Internet users. Some believe that the growth in Internet services will eventually match that witnessed in telecommunications. A technology conference organized by *Fortune* magazine and held in Shanghai in 1999 inspired further predictions. China could have 33 million subscribers by the end of 2001, and 60 million subscribers and 40 million personal computer owners by 2003. Edward Tian, the President of China Netcom, claimed that there might even be up to 100 million online users of computer networks by 2003, while

Nicholas Negroponte, an expert on the Internet, predicted that within twenty years the most widely spoken language on the Internet will be Chinese and that China will have the world's most advanced digital education system.[29]

Advances in broadband and wireless technology may also mean that many urban Chinese will have access to low-cost and ultra-fast transmission of data which will in turn mean that global media companies (and individuals) will be able to sell and transmit their products – films, books, magazines, newspapers or newsletters – without even being present in the country. That free flow of information may well undermine China's highly centralized political system.

Since the start of the reforms, the Communist Party has waged a desperate rearguard action to prevent individuals from gaining access to information or being able to distribute it independently. For years, overseas calls were monitored and international letters opened, and no one was allowed to use office fax machines without permission. Indeed in 1993, the state outlawed private satellite receiver dishes and clamped down on the illegal ownership of fax machines. All books published in China are censored and periodically the state launches a crackdown on broadcasters and publishers, closing those that have strayed from Party control. Major efforts have also gone into blocking the broadcasts of the BBC, Voice of America and Radio Free Asia, and those caught passing on information of protests or strikes to the outside media have been arrested and severely punished.

China continues to stop foreign publications from being freely distributed within its borders. The few publications available for sale in the shops often have offending articles torn out. Even in 1999 when the *Fortune* conference was held, copies of *Time* magazine's special edition devoted to the fiftieth anniversary of the People's Republic of China were confiscated because the magazine contained articles by exiled dissidents. Very few media-related joint ventures are permitted, and those that have been have tended to be apolitical (for example, Hachette's fashion magazine *Elle* which launched a Chinese edition as early as 1988). The state has permitted only ten foreign films to be shown in China and severely restricts the broadcast of foreign television programmes. An exception has been sport – many Chinese have become avid fans of foreign soccer teams.

The state's efforts have to a large extent failed. As fax machines and the cost of phone calls have become cheaper, so it has become harder to stop people from writing, printing or distributing what they wish. Restrictions on imported films have been undermined by the pirating of videos which also makes them extremely cheap to buy. Anyone can now watch almost anything they choose at home on a VTR machine or DVD player and there is nothing the state can do about it. The consequences of such piracy have been devastating for China's writers, film-makers, musicians, singers and other performers, and even the official Chinese media, with its relentless diet of Party panegyrics and dreary reportage, has become vulnerable to competition.

The 'Westernization' of China against which Maoists raged in the early 1980s is becoming a reality. When in 1999, the Chinese government backed Disney's decision to build a Disneyland in Hong Kong, largely intended to profit from mainland visitors, few Chinese intellectuals demurred and many Beijingers, young and old, actually welcomed the news. Zhang Meini, professor of children's literature at Beijing Normal University, argues that the fairy stories on which Disney draws have been a part of Chinese culture for over a century now and are not seen as especially foreign or threatening: 'It is not an invasion. Disney's cartoon figures belong to the cultural heritage of all mankind. We should absorb this heritage.'

Before the turn of the nineteenth century, China possessed little in the way of children's literature, apart from didactic stories to illustrate Confucian four-character phrases instructing children on ethics and behaviour. Then, after the collapse of imperial China, many writers began to translate and publish Western classics including fairy stories.[30] In the great literary upsurge of the 1920s, some of China's greatest contemporary writers translated or composed children's tales – among them Zheng Zhenduo, Ye Shengtao, Mao Dun, Yan Wenjing and Shen Congwen, who rewrote *Alice in Wonderland*, calling it *Alice in China*. Tin Tin, Beatrix Potter and Winnie-the-Pooh, the tales of Hans Christian Andersen and the Brothers Grimm, even Mickey Mouse became as familiar to Chinese children as to their contemporaries in the West.

From 1964 Mao and his circle of ultra-leftist intellectuals banned all fairy stories, Chinese or foreign. 'They were not revolutionary enough,' recalls Professor Zhang. 'The slogan went: men of old and all kinds of animals could fly in the sky but not workers, peasants and soldiers who are never mentioned.'

However, since 1970, when Snow White and the rest were formally rehabilitated, Chinese children in nurseries and kindergartens have been brought up on everything from Mary Poppins to Little Red Riding Hood. Books for children, almost entirely based on foreign works, are now the most profitable part of the domestic publishing industry. It is therefore hardly surprising that the Chinese are now becoming avid consumers of the global entertainment and information industry.

A new generation of Chinese is now coming to adulthood who will be comfortable as part of the 'global village' and who will increasingly share a similar lifestyle and education to those elsewhere. At least in the big cities, it is possible to see the emergence of a Westernized élite that eats at McDonald's, shops at Ikea, is entertained at home by Disney and communicates via the Internet with the rest of the world. Many of those under the age of 40 in the next decade seem destined to take out a mortgage, save up to buy a small car, take a holiday abroad, invest in an independent pension and life savings scheme, pay for private education and worry about financing healthcare. These people may only form a small proportion of China's total population, perhaps no more than 20 per cent in the next ten years, but in actual numbers a consumer market of between 60 and 150 million is still substantial by any standard.[31] What no one can be sure of is what will become of the rest of the Chinese who earn US$250 or less a year. They are surely still at least a generation or more away from anything other than a fragile subsistence economy, and many of them still struggle to obtain basic education and health services, as the next two chapters explain.

9

Guttering Candles

To reach the village of Tian Zhuang, the boatman punted his craft through a maze of waterways between thickets of reeds that grow taller than a man. In the autumn, when the reeds turn green and golden, the locals cut them down, heap them on to their wide, flat-bottomed boats and take them back to the village. There they are dried and woven into mats and baskets. Once the reed-cutting industry brought wealth to the half a million people who live in the Baiyangdian marshes but plastic has cut the demand for reedmats and this is now an area of poverty.

The marshes in Hebei province are just three hours' drive from Beijing along a new six-lane motorway, but at the height of the Cultural Revolution, when the children of imprisoned senior Party officials were exiled here, it took days to reach Tian Zhuang. These 'educated youths' were put to work cutting reeds or teaching in the school for five or six years. Nearly thirty years later, a cheque for US$30,000 arrived from America, sent by an anonymous donor with instructions that it should be spent on helping local teachers.[1]

'It was quite a surprise. At the time I was earning so little, I couldn't even pay for the education of my youngest,' said Tian Zhengsheng, the 55-year-old schoolmaster who was the first to benefit. A stooped bony man whose grey jacket hung around his shoulders, he gave a shy smile to his latest visitors and looked tolerantly at the crowd of grinning urchins clustered outside who were trying to look in through the window. 'And I can still remember the one who sent it. It took him quite a while to get used to our life of hardship but he learned how poor the peasants are and how much poorer are the *minban* teachers.'

Teacher Tian, who received 250 yuan (US$30) from the donation, had himself spent only a few years in school and is one of the 3 million untrained teachers, known as *minban*, who struggle to educate some of China's 235 million schoolchildren. One in four of the world's schoolchildren is Chinese and they are taught by some 14 million people, making it at once the world's biggest and most under-funded educational endeavour.

Several hundred children attend Tian's school and it is financed entirely by the villagers. In the unheated classrooms built around a big yard, there are rickety desks and stools but the school is too poor to pay for proper blackboards, and so a wall painted black is used instead. In one of the classrooms, a young teacher is telling the story of Isaac Newton, the apple and the discovery of the forces of gravity. When her pupils see me they giggle and shout out a 'hello' in English.

On the brick walls of the classroom hang portraits of the four bearded Chinese sages responsible for the 'Four Great Inventions' attributed to Chinese civilization – paper, the compass, gunpowder and printing. They have replaced the four bearded Westerners – Marx, Engels, Lenin and Stalin – who used to hang in Chinese class-rooms. Patriotism rather than Marxism is now the order of the day and in the school yard there is a flagpole around which each morning the national anthem is sung at a flag-raising ceremony. Even so all the children still join the Red Pioneers, the Communist version of the Boy Scouts, and swear an oath both to love the motherland and to sacrifice their lives to defend Communism.

The young teacher, dressed in a tracksuit that is the fashion of the day, is one of China's 800,000 *daike* or substitute teachers, who earn just 5 yuan a day. The *minban* teachers earn 200 yuan a month plus whatever they can make from farming. Another of the younger teachers, who like everyone else in the village is called Tian, says his wife earns an extra 100 yuan a year by weaving reeds into mats and then he describes his finances in detail. He can scrape by as long as nothing goes wrong but a few years ago his father became sick, poisoned by the fumes of a coal stove, and then he suffered a stroke. Soon the son had run up debts of over 3,000 yuan in medical fees.

'My colleagues had to help me, giving me money every year to buy clothes and a pair of shoes,' he said, looking down at the floor. We followed his gaze down to his worn black leather shoes.

After the funding of education was localized in the late 1980s, the local county government became responsible for paying the teachers' wages and started to levy fees. In Tian Zhuang, the families pay an annual tuition fee of 50 yuan. Textbooks cost another 100 yuan a year. In many poor areas, education revenues are insufficient and wages are often paid half a year late and sometimes not at all.

The younger Tian was only saved from destitution by a donation of 5,000 yuan from a national charity, the Candlelight Project, that sprang up after Beijing television produced a documentary on the impact of such a donation on the lives of poor teachers in rural Hebei. It showed scenes of moving poverty and devotion. Some teachers had died, leaving their families crippled by debts. Others described how their wives had left them when they refused to give up teaching.[2] The charity takes its name from a verse composed by Li Shangyin, a poet of the Tang dynasty, to describe the devotion of teachers, comparing them to 'the silkworm spinning silk unto death, the candle that sheds light until it gutters and dies'.

The poverty of almost all China's teachers is a legacy of Maoism. Even after twenty years of reform, the education system is handicapped by 10 million teachers who still need to be retrained and by decrepit, ill-equipped buildings. Many ambitious targets have never been met. A decision to phase out *minban* teachers throughout China by the year 2000 is here the responsibility of officials at Baoding, the local prefectural government headquarters. As is so often the way in a bureaucracy, they have skirted the issue simply by relabelling. *Minban* teachers are now either categorized as *daike* teachers or given a new label of 'local government state teacher'. However, to qualify as a state teacher, referred to as a *guoban,* the younger Tian explains, he would have to pay 8,000 yuan to attend a training course: 'It is not worth it because if I became a state teacher then I would stop being a peasant and so lose my land and the little money that that brings. And as a state teacher, I still wouldn't be paid.' The story is much the same for the *guoban* teachers themselves, many of whom are owed months of back wages.

It is hard to account for the neglect of education in a nation famed for the antiquity of its culture, its veneration of teachers and its devotion to the written word. What is certain is that immense damage was inflicted on education during the Cultural Revolution when teachers were beaten and often killed.

'They were all listed as enemies along with landlords, counter-revolutionaries and bad elements. Many of them were beaten here but no one was killed,' explains the older Tian with embarrassment.

It is difficult to get at the facts now, but from unguarded conversations it is clear that many teachers did die. A few weeks before visiting the marshes, I had travelled down the Li River to Guilin, in the southern province of Guangxi, where the local guide, a Zhuang minority woman, talked about her childhood memories: 'I'll never forget it. I saw my teacher bleed to death after being attacked with choppers.' Like most people in the countryside at that time, she grew up without learning to read or write because the schools were either closed entirely or taught only Maoist slogans or 'work study'. In the countryside, that meant helping on farm jobs such as mucking out the pigs.

In *Scarlet Memorial*, the writer Zheng Yi, describing the same period, records how teachers in five counties in Guangxi province were murdered and eaten. In all 100,000 'class enemies' were killed in Guangxi, the victims including the staff of local hospitals and others with higher education or those who had relatives abroad.[3]

To replace qualified teachers and doctors, the Communist Party introduced untrained peasants as 'barefoot doctors' and unqualified peasant teachers, those who after 1979 were renamed *minban* teachers. The communes paid them with workpoints. When China formally abandoned the communes in 1984, however, the central government did not introduce proper funding for rural schools, though at the same time it set itself ambitious targets to reduce illiteracy and provide seven years of compulsory education for all by the end of the century. Poorer places such as Tian Zhuang with its 500 schoolchildren were still struggling to achieve this target in 1999.

Education remains China's biggest challenge and an area in which the Communist Party has singularly failed its people. In a table drawn up by UNESCO in 1995, China ranked 119th out of 130 countries in terms of its per capita spending on education, allocating only 2.3 per cent of its GDP. Though this was an improvement on the 2 per cent spent in the wake of the 1989 democracy movement, despite oft-repeated promises that spending would reach 4 per cent, China had still not reached even 3 per cent by 1999. By comparison, developed countries spend on average 5.3 per cent of their GDP on education and the majority of developing countries 4.1 per cent.[4]

State spending on education has in fact quintupled over the past twenty years in absolute terms, reaching 119 billion yuan (US$143 billion) by 1998. Between 1978 and 1994, the number of institutes of higher education doubled to 1,080 and student enrolment more than tripled. Yet UNESCO ranks China only 103rd out of 131 countries in the number of university graduates per 100,000 inhabitants.[5] The 1982 census found that only 0.87 per cent of the workforce had received higher education. In the 1980s and 1990s only 2 per cent of the population attended university compared with over 50 per cent in the United States.[6]

A century ago, in the last decades of the Qing dynasty, mass education was one of the causes pushed by reformers who hoped it would 'save' China. The first students sent to study abroad went to the United States in 1870. Later, Americans became closely involved with the establishment of modern schools and universities, often run by missionaries, all over China but especially in the treaty ports. Much of what China paid to the United States after the Boxer Rebellion as reparations was subsequently spent on building some of China's most famous institutions such as Yenching University, the site of what is now Peking University, the nation's leading centre of higher education. By the time of Mao's victory over the Kuomintang in 1949, Protestant colleges alone were teaching 12,000 Chinese students a year, or one in every ten students being taught. Education in China was thus closely linked with the complete Westernization advocated by some Chinese in the 1920s. That fact alone may explain

Mao's distrust, even hatred of Chinese intellectuals and why so many were murdered during the Cultural Revolution.

The education movement of the first half of the twentieth century was part of a deeper search for a cultural renaissance and a profound rejection of the past – 'the cannibalistic Confucian society' as the writer Lu Xun labelled it. Central to the Confucian system was the use of ancient Chinese characters. In imperial times, the state recruited just a few thousand scholars who had passed examinations that required a mastery of this antique script. The fact that 90 per cent of the population was illiterate at the turn of the century was blamed by reformers on the retention of this system, and many argued that China could not modernize without radical changes to the way in which education was conducted.[7]

The first Chinese university was founded during the Hundred Days Reform movement of 1898, and in 1905 the imperial examinations were formally abandoned. China's first ruler after the collapse of the Qing dynasty in 1911, General Yuan Shikai, pushed for compulsory and free primary schooling for the male population. The debate about what to retain and what to discard culminated in the May Fourth movement which erupted in 1919 when students gathered in a huge demonstration in Tiananmen Square in Beijing. The demonstration began as a reaction to the Treaty of Versailles at the end of the First World War. Many were angry that Germany's territories in China were not handed back, but rather given to Japan, and for the first time the students who protested in Tiananmen established themselves as a political force. They went on to form a student union which regularly petitioned the government. At the time, the government was spending 80 per cent of its budget on the military. Students demanded that it spend more on education, a dispute that continues to this day.

The May Fourth movement led to a cultural sea change. China abandoned classical Chinese – the equivalent of Latin – for writing and embraced vernacular Chinese, known as *bai hua*. Reformers also introduced Western notions of grammar and punctuation, and the Western numerical system. Writers, too, began to imitate Western literary styles. However, although some proposed abandoning the use of Chinese characters altogether, they were retained because the characters allow Chinese to communicate with each other even though they cannot understand each other's speech (some linguists argue that China has at least eight major linguistic groups aside from the minority languages). Republican China also adopted a standardized form of spoken Chinese, known as *guo yu* – literally state language – which was based on the Beijing dialect and which foreigners used to call Mandarin Chinese.[8] In the wake of these reforms the country was therefore ready for the era of mass communications and mass education which was ushered in by the advent of modern printing and broadcasting technology. The 1920s saw a tremendous outpouring of both literature and journalism. The KMT encouraged the expansion of higher education and in the 1930s it abolished university fees altogether. For the first time in Chinese history, too, education became available for girls.

However, Chiang Kai-shek's government increasingly concentrated its resources on the military as it sought to control a country rent by warlords, Communist guerrillas and a Japanese invasion. In the absence of adequate government funds many educational institutions resorted to levying all kinds of fees and, as student anger and frustration grew, the Communist Party found the universities a rich recruiting-ground. In response the KMT tried to re-establish political control over academia and, as the Japanese occupied more and more of China, many universities relocated first to the KMT capital at Nanjing, then to Chongqing and other cities in the southwest.

After Japan's defeat in 1945, when the universities moved back to Shanghai and Beijing, the crisis in funding grew worse, with students unable to afford fees and professors struggling to collect their salaries. Students in Shanghai used the KMT's failure to fund education as a focus for anti-government protests and complained that Chiang Kai-shek's government had cut education spending to just 3.6 per cent of total expenditure. Among the protesters was Jiang Zemin.

At the time, Jiang was studying engineering at Jiaotong University which proposed making many of its staff redundant and closing all but the engineering department. In 1946, he turned out to show support for a delegation heading for Nanjing, the KMT capital, on thirty-five trucks to deliver a petition. The supporters chanted: 'End the civil war! Cut military spending! Increase education spending!' The first protests were successful: the authorities handed out grants to 10,000 students unable to afford the fees. That summer the students themselves raised money for impoverished professors with a fund-raising movement called 'Respect Teachers'. A second delegation was then organized to push for more education funding, but this time KMT troops were turned out and many of the protesters were beaten up. Soon afterwards, Jiang formally joined the Communist Party.[9]

In the first years following the Communist victory, the Party was praised for opening schools, launching literacy campaigns and stabilizing the funding of higher education. The new system abandoned the American-influenced style of education and became a replica of the Soviet system. An Academy of Sciences and a Writers' Union were established; teachers had to follow the exact timetable and hours of Soviet universities; and everyone brought up under the old system was forced to attend rigorous and punitive ideological remoulding sessions. All this spelt the end of notions of academic or financial independence from the state.

The Communists also readdressed the question as to whether or not Chinese characters should be replaced by the Latin or Cyrillic script. In the end, it was decided to retain the characters but to simplify them so as to make them easier to learn. (Basic literacy requires a knowledge of 1,000 to 1,500 characters. An educated person would be familiar with 5,000 out of more than 50,000; a university graduate would be familiar with 10,000–25,000.) At the same time, the Communists abandoned the Wade-Giles system of phonetically rendering the sound of Mandarin using the Roman alphabet and adopted instead the *pinyin* system. This is why Chinese outside China, who did not follow suit, write their characters differently and still romanize Chinese according to the Wade-Giles system.* Mainlanders use simplified characters, *jianti zi*, introduced by the Communists, while the rest of the Chinese world uses *fanti zi*, traditional characters.

The decision to stick with characters has made it harder for the

---

* In 1999 Taiwan decided to switch to the *pinyin* system.

Chinese to make use of modern inventions such as the typewriter, the printing press, Morse code and the telegraph. A printer has to memorize the whereabouts of thousands of typeface characters in order to assemble a page of type quickly. Sending a telegram requires the substitution of every character with a four-digit code. Receiving a telegram requires the reversal of the process at the other end. This makes it harder for an individual to send a message without the co-operation of a government-run office. Only since the spread of the photocopier and the fax machine in the 1990s has the state's grip on the transmission of information weakened.

The Party's investment in the education system soon faltered. In the Anti-Rightist campaign of 1957 close to a million students, teachers and other intellectuals were persecuted. The start of the Great Leap Forward the following year foreshadowed the collapse of the whole economy and the suspension of schooling in much of the country. Much worse was to follow. During the Cultural Revolution schools became embroiled in 'making revolution' and teachers were persecuted. Universities were shut down entirely for five years and then only reopened to admit workers, soldiers and peasant students. By 1977 when the first entrance exams were being held, a whole generation of Chinese had received no education or professional training.

Despite all this the Party claimed that its education policies were a great success, boasting in 1975 that elementary school attendance had reached 98.4 per cent. Many foreigners were impressed. The influential economist Professor J.K. Galbraith toured Chinese schools and universities that year and compared them favourably to those in the United States.[10] Tony Benn, a minister in the British Labour government of the time, was also impressed by what he saw on a visit and claimed that Britain had a lot to learn from China.

As in so many other areas, Mao's death marked a turning-point. The following year Fang Yi, a member of the Politburo, launched a savage attack on Mao's education policies. He castigated slogans such as 'Study is useless', or ' The more knowledge you have the more reactionary you are', and the claim that 'The basic theories of natural scientists are fabrications by bourgeois scientists of the West'. And he singled out as an example of the bankruptcy of Mao's educational theories a student, Zhang Tiesheng, who had been widely praised in

1974 for handing in a blank sheet of paper at the end of his university entrance examinations. Fang Yi recognized that China's science and education were in a parlous state and admitted that China had not awarded a single degree or doctorate for thirteen years.[11]

In what proved to be the first of many over-optimistic plans, he went on to reveal that a team of 1,300 experts were drawing up a new education programme with new textbooks and and a bigger budget. At the same time he promised to introduce nine years of compulsory universal education by 1985 and to restore the status and living standards of teachers.

In 1982 China held its first national census under the government of Deng Xiaoping. It revealed that half the population, some 519 million people, were illiterate or semi-literate. In response, a massive literacy campaign was launched but the resources devoted to education remained firmly stuck at 2.5 per cent of GDP. China's underfunded system could not cope with the combined pressures of a baby-boom generation entering the classroom, educated youth who had now returned from the countryside and wanted to make up for lost time, and the demand for adult and vocational education.

Much hope was pinned on night classes and the new medium of television universities. Then, in 1985, a new plan was drawn up. This time 10,000 experts were consulted and it was now forecast that compulsory universal education for nine years would be achieved by the end of the century. The new plan, entitled 'The Reform of China's Education System', was no less optimistic than its predecessor, promising that by the year 2000, 10 million students would graduate each year.[12]

In the atmosphere of political reform in the late 1980s, the Party also promised to give the universities more independence, shifting power away from the Party committees to the university president and allowing senior administrators to be chosen by a committee of faculty members. Mandatory ideological study was to be phased out and stultifying teaching methods were to be changed. The universities of Jiaotong in Shanghai, and Qinghua in Beijing, and the Hefei University of Science and Technology were singled out as guinea pigs. The Party also decided to permit 20 per cent of classroom time to be devoted to discussion and questions.[13]

In Hefei, there was an immediate upsurge in student unrest when in 1986 an outspoken astrophysicist, Professor Fang Lizhi, was elected as university vice president and began to criticize the shortage of funds and urge students to take part in the election of the university's representative to the local people's congress. Political unrest spilled over into the universities in Shanghai and Beijing. In a nice twist of fate, Jiang Zemin, then Party secretary of Shanghai, was heckled when he went back to his alma mater where he faced an audience of students who attacked the government's record on education.

By the following year, the true extent of the crisis in education was made clear by the liberal wing of the Party. At the National People's Congress in March 1988, the *People's Daily* quoted teachers who complained that their spending power was a tenth of what teachers had had before 1937.

'Education has been neglected for years. Attacks and insults against teachers happen constantly. We are the worst-treated profession in China with an experienced teacher getting less than a graduate starting work. Our housing is dreadful, with several generations living under one roof. When we are ill, we cannot get the medical treatment we need. Many teachers die in middle age,' wrote one teacher, Fang Ming.[14]

University teachers still earned less than manual workers and often lived in smaller flats, with living space below the national average. Even the prestigious Peking University was running short of funds and things were worse in many other colleges where officials refused to grant doctorates to their staff because, by recognizing higher qualifications, they would have to pay higher salaries.[15]

A few months later the Minister of Education, He Dongchang, revealed some even more devastating statistics: China was short of over 5 billion square feet of classroom space; over 300 million square feet of existing school buildings, often borrowed rooms in old temples or warehouses, were rated as dangerous; less than 10 per cent of secondary and primary schools had the equipment they needed; rural teachers often had to wait six months for their wages; 70 per cent of teachers were either untrained or unqualified; and only 60 per cent of children managed to finish primary school.[16]

At the same time, the issue of education became politicized. He Dongchang's damning report could be construed as a direct attack on the conservative Li Peng who, as the candidate of the hardliners, had just been made Prime Minister. He had earlier served as Vice Premier and minister in charge of the State Education Commission and it was he who had set ambitious targets for primary and tertiary education, despite the fact that there was no money available. The state had increased spending by 70 per cent in the 1986–90 five-year plan but doubled the number of colleges. In 1986 China had also adopted a law on compulsory education but it was left to local governments to foot the bill. By 1991, 88 per cent of total funding for education was coming out of local government coffers.

In the absence of government funding, teachers had to moonlight and schools became self-financing. In the Mao era, many schools had run factories or farms as part of the work-study policy. In 1987, China boasted that its 650,000 schools ran enterprises with a combined turnover of 9 billion yuan and profits of 1.7 billion yuan. Yet there was a grotesque side to this. Newspapers reported how in Hunan teachers ordered their students on to the streets to sell apples. In Shanghai teachers themselves were found peddling boiled eggs and icecream. In some schools teachers touted for business on behalf of insurance companies and publishers, and local governments levied fees to cover the cost of textbooks. The more fees that were levied, the more children dropped out. And the best teachers often resigned, going into business themselves or becoming local government cadres.

At the next meeting of the National People's Congress in 1989, the education issue became even more politically charged. At a press conference, a *Guangming Daily* reporter openly challenged Vice Premier Li Tieying to explain why China's per capita spending on education of 42 yuan was the second lowest in the world. 'The backward situation of education has not been changed,' Li admitted, conceding that it had 'not been properly dealt with in the process of reform, opening up and modernization'. He was probably echoing Deng who had reportedly acknowledged that 'Our greatest failure in the past ten years was lack of sufficient education development.'[17]

It was not only the teachers who were frustrated and bitter. A generation that had suffered so much under Mao now hoped that at least their children would have a better chance in life. Yet the vast majority of state funding was concentrated on a handful of schools known as 'key institutions'. These referred to 7,000 primary schools, 5,200 middle schools and 96 universities, all of them in a handful of large cities. The children of a privileged élite therefore went to a key state kindergarten and then a key primary school so they were best placed to pass the entrance exams that earned them a place in a key middle school.

The 11-plus exam had been abolished during the Cultural Revolution. When it was reinstituted after 1979, it put enormous pressure on children and their parents. Even in the 1980s there was only room in the junior middle schools for a quarter of the children aged between 11 and 14, and there were only enough university places for 2 per cent of the 25 million children born in 1966.

Newspapers frequently reported distressing tales of children who committed suicide or who had been beaten and abused by parents desperate for them to succeed at all costs. In 1986, Shanghai tried to dispense with the system of key schools, saying that students who were turned away developed an inferiority complex and a sense of shame. The city also tried issuing regulations requiring parents to limit the amount of time their children devoted to homework.[18]

Yet even those who did get into university, a virtual guarantee of a senior job in the bureaucracy, were angry and disappointed. The government admitted that conditions in a fifth of the colleges failed to meet its minimum standards. At Peking University, students complained about the terrible food in the canteens, the cramped living quarters in which they slept six to a dormitory room with bunk beds but no space for a desk, and the very restricted library opening times.

These frustrations boiled over during the 1989 protests in which the students and their professors joined forces and deliberately evoked the traditions of the May Fourth movement. The student-led demonstration on 4 May 1989 involved a million people in Beijing who carried slogans and even sang songs first heard seventy years earlier. The students also set up their own Autonomous Student Federation to function like the earlier student union, but while in 1946 Chiang Kai-shek had at least received a student delegation,

Deng refused to do so and finally ordered the army to retake the city, killing some students and imprisoning many others.

Not only did the 1989 protests fail to unseat the government but education deteriorated still further. Jiang Zemin, now promoted to General Secretary of the Communist Party, cut the education budget and increased military spending, exactly the policies he had gone out on to the streets to protest against in 1946. Then Chiang Kai-shek had cut education to 3.6 per cent of government spending. Now China's expenditure on education fell to its lowest level, accounting for less than 2 per cent of GDP in 1992.[19] Peking University professors were ordered to re-educate themselves through labour and could be seen weeding the grass on campus, and students from certain universities in Beijing and Shanghai had to spend a year in army camps undergoing intensive indoctrination. By 1995, a million college students had gone through some form of military training programme, although only some ended up spending a whole year in camps. Unsurprisingly, applications to Peking University and Fudan University in Shanghai dropped sharply.

Over the next five years the entire education system was restructured to stiffen ideological education. Deng retracted his admission of failure in 1989, claiming he had meant that ideological education was the biggest shortcoming of his reforms. In schools, the stress was now not so much on Communism as on patriotism. All schools were ordered to hold daily flag-raising ceremonies at which students should assemble to sing the national anthem. During a series of Patriotic Education campaigns soldiers toured the schools giving lectures, and the cult of the soldier-martyr Lei Feng was revived.* Government propaganda conveyed a picture of China surrounded by enemies constantly manoeuvring to impoverish the country and to divide its people and territories. 'Education is the fundamental project in the construction of the Socialist Spiritual Civilization,' explained the *People's Daily* in 1997, 'and the aim of our Spiritual Civilization Construction in schools is to foster Patriotism.'[20]

The shortage of government funds led to an acute crisis as the

------

* Lei Feng, a private soldier who selflessly sacrificed himself for others, was first turned into a national model in the early 1960s.

drop-out rate in primary schools reached 35 per cent or some 8 million children. In poor rural areas these were usually girls. At the end of 1992, rural teachers were owed 340 million yuan in back wages, and their salaries were still lower than those of workers. One newspaper, the *Guangming Daily*, reported how in southern China teachers had stopped classes in order to train pupils as professional mourners at funerals and had then hired the children out at 5 yuan per head.[21]

In the face of a lack of government funding, other means of financing education have had to be found. An increasingly large amount now comes from commercial activities. The Xiantao Teachers' College in Hubei province runs a foam packaging plant, makes surge power generators and operates two soft drinks factories and a printing plant. The same college also runs a shop, a kindergarten and a night school, and it charges its students tuition fees. Well-connected universities such as Beijing have set up highly successful companies, like the computer giant Legend, and talk of creating science parks. Between 1991 and 1995 alone school enterprises expanded annually by 33 per cent and brought in 300 billion yuan (US$36 billion) in profits.[22]

A second strategy has been to rely on charity funding efforts such as the Candlelight Project. To help schools in poorer areas where the drop-out rates are so high, the Party first launched the Hope Project. It raised money to build schools from big domestic and foreign companies. The first was built in 1991 after floods in Anhui province and it is claimed that within five years over 60,000 Anhui children had been brought back into school. This was followed by the Spring Bud programme, directed at helping girls in poor provinces to return to school. The following year the Spring Love Operation mobilized 500,000 students to offer voluntary teaching as part of their patriotic education. Women, who make up 70 per cent of the country's illiterates, were a special target.[23]

In 1993 the government started a campaign to bring down the illiteracy rate to 5 per cent by the year 2000 among people born after 1949. Backed by donations from UNESCO, the World Bank and bilateral aid donations, the state enlisted 50,000 cadres to run the pro-gramme. It worked in the usual way, with districts being set quotas which are apparently always met. However, many doubt whether those recorded as successfully completing a course have in fact done so and can read 1,500 characters. It seems more likely that progress has been a case of 'two steps forward, one step back', with three or four million leaving the ranks of the illiterate each year but another two or three million joining.[24] For example, children born outside the one-child policy are usually excluded from state schools as are the children of peasants who have moved to an urban area. In Beijing alone there may be 100,000 such children, although some do attend special schools for migrant workers' offspring.[25] In general, no one knows how many children are outside the school system but it is probably over two million.

The biggest obstacle to universal literacy may still be the retention of Chinese characters. The literacy drive has fostered fresh discus-sions about finding easier ways of writing Chinese using *pinyin*, or of designing methods to make memorizing the characters easier. Yet the state still expects all the children of minorities to master Chinese characters in order to move through the education system and does not encourage the use of existing scripts such as Tibetan or Mongol, or support special alphabets for other groups like the Miao, men-tioned in Chapter 1. Many schools run by religious or ethnic groups such as those in Tibetan monasteries have been shut down. The education system serves to assimilate minorities, not to encourage a separate identity, but this hinders the children of 10 per cent of the population from taking advantage of even the limited higher educa-tion opportunities that are open to them.[26]

Mastering the Chinese script is so much more difficult and time-consuming than learning an alphabet that one often wonders whether the enormous enthusiasm for learning English is not linked to a rejection of the old Confucian culture. It is thought that 200 million, or one out of every six Chinese, are studying English, and Chinese Central Television has broadcast sixty series of teaching programmes. Children start to learn the subject at school in their fourth year, and over 2 million college students take the compulsory College English Test, set by the Ministry of Education, annually.[27]

A third means of relieving the shortfall in state education funds has been the toleration of private fee-paying schools. The first were set up in the late 1980s and by the end of the 1990s there were 50,000.[28] In the early 1990s there was said to be a new one opening every day. Known as 'aristocracy schools', many of them were boarding schools which required downpayments of up to 200,000 or even 500,000 yuan, as well as hefty fees. They were particularly popular with the *nouveaux riches* of Guangdong where forty boarding schools were set up, many of them joint ventures with the local authorities. In a mid-1990s leftist backlash, Li Lanqing, an education minister, attacked them for 'fostering an aristocracy' and creating social divisions, and accused them of putting profits before public welfare.[29]

This mood did not last long, however, and other specialist schools soon appeared, among them the first all girls' school since 1949 and others that offered military training or all lessons in English, even at kindergarten level. Some senior officials even began to send their children abroad to be educated in American or English boarding schools.[30]

The most curious reaction against this 'Westernization' of China's youth is the Sheng Tao School outside Beijing which is the first primary school since 1949 to teach the pre-1911 Confucian curriculum. The private boarding school is funded by Xia Jingshan, a wealthy Chinese painter living in America, and named after Ye Shengtao, an early education reformer who wanted to combine the best of East and West.

When I visited the school in 1999, a little girl, Jiang Shan, stood up in front of a class of 7-year-olds, put her hands behind her back and recited verses from the *Book of Songs*, composed in the first millennium BC. On the blackboard were the traditional Chinese characters that have not been taught on the mainland for over forty years. In front of a visitor, she stumbled over the unfamiliar pronunciation.

'When you get them young, their memory skills are better and they can manage with little effort,' explained the headmistress Liu Yinfang. The sixty-six children will have memorized the five classics of the Confucian canon – including the *Book of Changes* and the *Analects* – well before they can understand their meaning.

The day starts at 6.30 in the morning with martial arts exercises taught by an expert from the Shaolin Academy, and the pupils go on to study painting, calligraphy and Chinese opera. One of the school's founders is Ye Zhisan, the son of Ye Shengtao, and the children perform his compositions of classical Chinese poems set to Western classical music. The school seems to have a pleasant and relaxed atmosphere. The deputy director, Wang Zhiyuan, a bearded scholar of classical Chinese in his late thirties, was dressed not in a gown but in green cords and a tweed jacket, and was anxious to explain the philosophy behind the school.

'It has all been pretty controversial,' he admitted. 'People in China wanted Westernization but it has gone too far. Our idea is to cultivate children to be carriers of our traditional culture.'

We stopped at one of the classrooms where there was a row of small computers. The children are taught computing and English because the parents insist upon it but Wang wants them to realize a different aim. 'Ultimately, we need to train an élite to preserve traditional Chinese culture. There is no point in preserving ancient texts and artefacts as dead objects in museums if there is no one left who is capable of appreciating their meaning.'

The little girl, Jiang Shan, is an unlikely beneficiary of all this. She had been rescued from summer floods along the Yangtze in 1998 after being found by soldiers clinging on to the branch of a tree above the raging waters. Her mother and three of her six siblings had drowned.[31]*

Country schools in Jiang Shan's former village and those run by the *minban* teachers in Hebei are now essentially private fee-paying schools. It is not a system that benefits the poor and the politically powerless. Rural fees amount to as much as 300 yuan a year for primary schools and 1,000 yuan for secondary schools, and many peasants cannot afford to pay. Local officials who levy fees and taxes to fund the schools are often accused of wasting or embezzling the money, and many people complain that too much of the money is absorbed by an overstaffed bureaucracy. In Hebei, those running the

---

* Many other families in the same village had more children than is permitted or recorded. 'The village was big,' said Jiang Shan. 'There were a lot of children and in school each class had more than seventy pupils.'

Candlelight Project say that half or even 70 per cent of the education administrators should be sacked.[32]

In the richer urban areas, the decline of SOEs and the rise of
unemployment have also put education beyond the reach of many.
An independent survey carried out in Chongqing in 1998 found that
only half could afford the fees of between 150 and 380 yuan a term.
Many families had to borrow money from relatives or friends, or
donate blood to raise the money. Another survey in Zhejiang
province revealed that nearly 70 per cent of teachers believed their
income to be too low. Repeated government promises to raise the
living standards of urban teachers have not been kept.[33] Figures in
the mid-1990s showed that one in five had no housing, 800,000 had
housing problems, 420,000 had no access to state housing and
370,000 lived with just 43 square feet per person or less. Many teachers were unable to find spouses and if they did, they could not get
married because there was no housing available.[34]

For parents too, even the wealthy, the system remains a nightmare
as the education minister Li Lanqing has admitted, likening it to 'thousands upon thousands of people trying to cross a single log bridge'.
There are just 2 million university places for 47 million middle school
students, and survey after survey has condemned urban children for
being overweight and short-sighted because they spend ten hours a
day studying poorly printed books in dim classrooms.[35]

Parents complain that from the age of 4 or 5, children have no free
time and are pushed beyond their limits. Too many suffer from sleep-
lessness and depression, and nervous breakdowns are not uncom-
mon. A picture emerges of shy, depressed, lonely swots unable to do
anything except pass exams. A survey in Heilongjiang found that
many were unable even to tie their own shoelaces or dress themselves. 'Some 90 per cent knew how to play the piano and 70 per cent
could recite Tang dynasty poems but they know very little about day-
to-day life,' complained a newspaper report.

In the late 1990s, the government became enamoured with the
idea of creating 'a knowledge economy' in China and launched
another effort to transform education and again try to align it with
the American system. Huge neon signs across Shanghai proclaimed
Jiang Zemin's slogan – 'Restore the Country through Education and

Science' – which sounds strikingly like a May Fourth movement slogan.

Hidden away behind one of the Victorian stone façades off a busy road in the heart of old Shanghai, I visited Mrs Mao Peiyan's primary school which is a pioneer of new teaching methods. The marked decline in the number of schoolchildren in Shanghai as a result of the one-child policy has had a beneficial effect. 'We used to have an average of at least fifty pupils in a class. Now there are around twenty-two so the teaching is changing,' explained Mrs Mao. The severe rote learning and discipline which have drawn much criticism elsewhere are here being replaced with a fresh desire to generate creative thinking: 'Now we want to encourage more questioning and more interactive teaching.'

However, not everyone has managed to adjust to the new ways. 'Some of the teachers had to go,' said Mrs Mao. 'They couldn't adapt to the new system.'

Teachers who want to keep their jobs have had to pass an exam to prove that they can use a computer and know how to access the Internet. A new rule forbidding classes from being taught in the local Shanghainese dialect has meant that almost all those over the age of 40 and trained during the Cultural Revolution are being forced out. The city that issued edicts limiting the hours a child should spend on homework, and where parents hire hotels rooms so that their children can study in peace, is now making its teachers, not its children, pass exams. The 11-plus exam has been abolished and with it the system of key schools. Instead everyone is supposed to attend their nearest junior or senior middle school.

'The children are much happier now – and freer. The atmosphere is so different, everyone enjoys school now,' said Mrs Mao. Outside, we could see a class marching to the computer lab dressed in bright red tracksuit uniforms. 'Of course, the parents complain about the fees for computers and the Internet.'[36]

At most of Shanghai's thirty-nine universities, I found the same mixture of fear and a new-found freedom. A wave of closures and mergers were underway, accompanied by job cuts and redundancies among faculty members, but for the students, change was for the better. At St John's College, founded in 1879 by American

Protestants, a student strolling amid the beautiful lawns and ivy-covered buildings stopped to talk.

'It is not so easy to find a job now,' he said, 'but we are free to go and do what we want.'

In 1989 university students' fees were paid by the state which on graduation assigned them jobs. Ten years later, the state does neither. The cost of the fees, around 10,000 yuan a year, is borne by the parents, and students like Liang Bochun from Guizhou must find their own employment afterwards.

'Not many people where I come from can afford the fees,' Liang said. Half the university places in Shanghai used to be reserved for Shanghai students, and once the baby-boom generation has graduated, the universities will be free to select their students. Cities such as Shanghai, Beijing and Shenzhen are already competing to attract graduates and are now offering students from the provinces a *hukou* as soon as they find themselves a job.

'That's easy enough,' Liang said. 'Banks are offering starting salaries of 3,500 yuan a month.'

Salaries this high are nearly double what his professors earn. At Tongji University in Shanghai, founded by Germans in 1907, the young German-educated president Wu Qidi sat in a new white building donated by Siemens and complained about the government budget.

'We need much more money from the state, we are still far too poor,' she said. 'We need a third more money than we are getting.'[37]

Under her management, the university already has to raise half its revenue from tuition fees, donations, foreign government grants and contracts negotiated with commercial enterprises. This is perhaps the country's prime centre for architecture and engineering, and many faculty staff are hired as consultants on civil engineering projects or lured away by the offer of higher salaries in the commercial sector. The result has been a severe shortage of teachers.

'Over a quarter of the faculty staff are already past the retirement age but we have to ask them to stay on,' she said. While the older professors are being asked to stay on until the age of 70 to enjoy what is called 'a second golden period', younger academics are put on an accelerated promotion ladder.

The Cultural Revolution left a huge generational gap in the academic world. In 1996, China had 4 million scientists and technicians over the age of 60 of whom 800,000 were in senior positions. The Chinese Academy of Social Sciences has even considered closing because 85 per cent of its 4,000 experts are due to retire before the year 2005. Often, too, the younger academics emigrate. In 1997, Beijing University's physics department complained that a third of its graduates had left the country and that the top 500 brains in the field are now living in the United States. The brain drain is reaching huge dimensions because most of the 300,000 students who have gone abroad since 1980 have not returned.

'Millions of accountants, book-keepers, linguists, computer experts and agricultural technologists are desperately needed,' lamented the country's deputy education minister, Chen Zhili, in 1997.

The country's spending on vocational training is also so inadequate that most foreign investors have had to set up their own training institutions in order to hire not just managers but qualified people at every level. In terms of graduates, China was reportedly short of 7.5 million graduates between 1990 and 2000, and the forecast for the next decade is a shortfall of at least 10 million.[38]

China is now in the awkward position of trying to expand higher education opportunities with few resources. The Ministry of Education has cut the number of university disciplines by more than half to 300 and has begun to merge universities and colleges into bigger units where teachers will have to work longer hours and teach more students.

Tongji University, which was the first to try out the reforms by absorbing two other colleges, now has 24,000 students. The two colleges which disappeared – the Shanghai Urban Design College and the Construction Materials College – were both formerly run by ministries. Altogether some 300 higher education institutions operated by SOEs or ministries are being merged or made independent of Beijing. The changes, however, have met with considerable opposition. A recent attempt to merge the famous universities of Beijing and Qinghua met with vigorous protests and has been abandoned. In 1999 students in Sichuan province boycotted classes and tried to demonstrate against plans to merge the South-west University of Politics and Law, where many senior legal officials are trained, with the far less prestigious Chongqing University which is much easier to get into.[39] China is moving ahead however with its plan to build up 100 'key' universities and create 10 'world-class universities', among them Tongji, by the year 2005.

University teachers, who customarily taught for just three or four hours a week, are now being required to teach for twenty hours, as is common in the United States. At another of Shanghai's famous universities, Fudan, a merger with the Shanghai Medical University and the Shanghai Foreign Languages University has created an enormous institution with 28,000 full-time and 8,000 part-time students. The reform means that whereas Fudan University previously had a ratio of one teacher to seven students, it will under its new guise have a ratio of 1:20, and it is laying off 2,000 ancillary staff who will be assigned to independent service companies.

For students, the changes are making life easier. Where once they had to pass entrance examinations in six subjects to join a humanities course and seven to join a science course they are now required to take exams only in Chinese, mathematics, English and one other subject of their choice. Within a few years, universities may be free to set their own entrance examinations. China also now has its first private university, Sanda, set up in 1996 in the new industrial area of Pudong, and many others are planned to satisfy the demand for higher education. At the same time moves are afoot to increase the number of post-graduate students to as many as 120,000 per year in the future.[40]

More important has been a shift in education philosophy which has been driven by China's fear of falling behind the 'knowledge-based economies' with their high-technology, information-driven small companies funded by venture capital.

'We think our students study too much and end up with poor personalities and low communication abilities. We are now pushing KAP – Knowledge, Ability, Personality,' said Professor Wu. Reports from elsewhere in China bear out her concerns. Some of China's best science students have reputedly been unable to pass even basic tests in written Chinese.[41]

Western companies such as Nokia, Motorola, Ericsson and Microsoft that have set up research centres in China have even started their own in-house MBA courses. Instead of the learning-by-rote customary in Chinese universities, these courses are designed to encourage creative thinking, discussion and analysis. Chinese officials also foresee that interactive teaching could be spread via the Internet as a means of offering better educational opportunities to those in rural areas, in other words the majority who are now excluded from the best teaching. The future may therefore see the spread of American-derived educational techniques throughout China which, in the long term, may bring about profound social changes.[42]

Sadly, though, a century of change has left China with an education system that will, at least in the immediate future, become even less egalitarian than it ever was. In particular, the privatization of education means that children from rural China will have less chance of gaining a university place than ever before. Even urban families have difficulty in affording annual university fees of 10,000 yuan. While the state is proposing to establish bursaries for students from poor families as well as a system of student loans, for rural children these represent further obstacles along an already difficult path. The demographics of China, whereby most rural families have two or three children and urban families just one, make it inevitable that higher education will be restricted to less than 2 per cent of the population for decades to come.[43]

10

Barefoot Doctors and Witch-doctors

SMALL AND WIRY, Xie Jinhao looked the picture of a barefoot doctor as he set off for his mountain village in Guangxi. He tightened the strap of the box of vaccines slung across his shoulders and smiled the broad smile of youthful optimism.

'I can help people if they let me,' he said, and then he turned and walked across a wooden suspension bridge high above the river. On the other bank, a path meandered past the school and up into the hills where small settlements of Dong and Miao peoples are scattered.

The villages of Rongshui county, with their picturesque wooden houses, straddle the border between Guangxi and Guizhou provinces. Here a battle for people's hearts and minds is being fought, a battle in which the barefoot doctors are steadily losing ground to the shamans, or witch-doctors.[1]

'People prefer the witch-doctors. No one comes to see me for treatment. They only come if the shamans can't do anything. I even cost less. Their fee is 4 yuan and a meal for a consultation but I don't ask to be fed,' Xie complained when I interviewed him in 1999.

A Maoist innovation, the barefoot doctors received three or six months' health training and were intended to bring minimal health care within reach of the poorest rural communities. Xie's father had been a barefoot doctor before him and he himself had just received three months' training by Médecins sans Frontières (MSF), the international aid group. But in the village in which he lived there were now four or five practising shamans.

MSF had just restored a clinic in the local township of Danian which lies at the end of a dirt road, six or seven hours' drive from the county centre. Danian is just a cluster of grubby buildings around a market square where the bus stops and turns round. Here the peasant women, still dressed in their traditional bright blue and mauve embroidered dresses, come down from the hills to buy and sell. The new two-storey clinic building, an island of shiny white bathroom tiles, is rarely visited by the women, however. On any given day there are just a handful of patients and most of the beds in the three wards lie empty. One of the clinic's doctors is a young ethnic Miao, Yan Qincheng, who recently graduated from medical college and now feels well-equipped to win back the confidence of the people. 'We are in competition with the witch-doctors but they will see we are better.'

Yan says that the villagers have stopped attending the clinic, first set up over thirty years ago, partly because the cost of treatment is prohibitively expensive and partly because they have lost faith in Western medicine. Now those that come do so only as a last resort.

We went to see one of his patients, the month-old son of a 30-year-old village woman. Standing next to his wife at their child's bedside was her husband who had just undergone a compulsory vasectomy. It had been done without anaesthetic, he muttered in a low tone, and it hurt. His wife spoke with reluctance, but after some prodding she admitted to first having consulted a shaman in her village.

'They certainly possess magical powers,' she whispered. 'They will go into a trance to divine the illness and then summon a spirit to help. Sometimes they will also kill a chicken or an ox,' and she rolled her eyes back, mimicking the trance of a medium.

MSF have also restored and re-equipped a much bigger hospital twenty miles down the road at Gongdong, now staffed by a French couple and a doctor from Benin who trained in Beijing. The hospital is supposed to serve a catchment area of 110,000 people and should by rights be crowded day and night, but when I visited it was almost deserted.

'Our biggest problem is first to restore people's confidence in the healthcare system,' explained Dr Marcel Roux, an energetic Frenchman who spearheaded the decision to channel resources into the project in Rongshui county. He believes that much of rural China is experiencing a crisis in healthcare: 'The level of healthcare is less than basic. Even healthcare in Africa is better. There people are organized and there are good African physicians and health workers, but in China, they don't have the knowledge, the structure or the people to make it work.'

His views come as a shock to those familiar with the romanticized view of Mao Zedong's barefoot doctors who helped make China a model for healthcare in the developing world.

Dr Roux said it took him and MSF a long time to gain access to enough rural villages to find out what was really happening. He recalled his experience of visiting the prefectural capital, Liuzhou, in 1996 when it was struck by floods, and of offering to supply emergency aid, MSF's speciality: 'We dined with public health department officials who never even told us there was an outbreak of cholera in the city. We only learned about it after hearing a public announcement on television.'

Many other foreign aid workers have been equally astonished at finding public hospitals empty during an emergency. The explanation is simple. Few of those who need help can afford the fees. In 1978, a fifth of the national health budget was spent on rural areas. In 1993, only 4 per cent was going on caring for the poorest quarter of the population who must pay for themselves.

In 1996, when the state drew up new policies, it was revealed that 90 per cent of the peasants are not covered by any form of health insurance. In urban areas too, where so many state-owned enterprises are losing money, fewer and fewer people are covered by adequate insurance. The employees of the state and of state-owned enterprises used to benefit from a free and relatively well-funded social welfare system. The cost of all medical treatment, whatever its standard, was borne by the work unit. Now, growing numbers struggle to afford the cost of drugs and private treatment. In one of the world's last Communist countries, healthcare has become a pay-as-you-go privatized industry, or as one researcher, Charlotte Cailliez of the School for Advanced Social Studies in Paris, has put it, 'The state has simply withdrawn from healthcare in rural China.'[2]

When Dr Roux was first taken to see the hospital in Gongdong he found it a ghost hospital with broken and rusty equipment dating back to the time it was built in the early 1960s: 'The biggest danger to a baby being delivered in the operating-room was not infection but the roof falling in,' he said. 'That was why there were only two or three patients a day. Now there are at least twenty to thirty.'

Things were no better in Danian's clinic before it was rebuilt. It had survived without electricity or water supplies for years. Elsewhere many rural hospitals are deep in debt and, as MSF discovered in Rongshui, staff are owed months of wages. In order to earn a living doctors and nurses have turned to growing vegetables and rearing chickens and pigs, although the primary source of income for rural and urban hospitals is the profit to be made from the sale of medicines.

At the Danian clinic, the senior doctor is Shi Rongsheng, an ethnic Miao trained in the 1970s. He earns 475 yuan (US$57) a month. 'I could earn ten times as much if I moved to the city. Other people have done it,' he said, though he showed no signs of wanting to leave. Compared to local villagers who earn as little as 200 or 300 yuan in a whole year, he was well off.

He gave another quiet smile when asked about his own medical training. It probably did not last very long. With the universities closed during the Cultural Revolution, and Western-trained doctors the victims of persecution, no one could have received a high level of training.

'Even the proper doctors in rural cities have poor qualifications, perhaps just a year of training twenty years ago,' said Dr Roux. There is also some doubt as to whether things have improved in recent years. Though only 43,000 doctors graduated each year in Western medicine in the 1980s, the authors of one World Bank report recorded a 'puzzling increase' in the number of Western-trained doctors reported by Chinese statistics.[3] 'There are many fake doctors in China and too many others with little training,' concluded Dr Roux.

In 1975 China claimed that it had 1.6 million barefoot doctors, one for every 400 rural inhabitants, but these were of much the same standard as the village *minban* teachers. After 1981, the state began to refer to them as 'village doctors' before finally abolishing the title 'barefoot doctor' altogether in 1986. Many of them abandoned their posts when the communes were abolished because they were no longer being paid. The better qualified migrated to jobs in the cities and newly graduated doctors usually refused to work in rural areas, especially poor ones like Rongshui.

In the early 1980s village doctors were required to pass a formal examination. Those who did so received a certificate. Those who failed became known as village health aides. A Ministry of Public Health survey in 1990 found that China had 776,000 village doctors, 455,000 health aides and 470,000 registered birth attendants. The majority of village doctors were male, with no more than junior middle school education and generally with less than a year of training. Some were actually illiterate. Since 1978 the ratio of recognized doctors in rural areas had fallen to one for every 700 people and there was just one dentist for every 50,000 people.[4]

Dr Shi believed that the health of the villagers was better under Mao when regulations on public hygiene were rigorously enforced. Now diseases that had apparently been conquered in Rongshui, such as tuberculosis, hepatitis, dysentery, intestinal worms and Japanese encephalitis, are making a comeback. Elsewhere, leprosy, cholera and typhoid are spreading.

The old clinic at Danian, a brick building behind the new clinic, is now being used as an isolation unit for tuberculosis patients. They are, however, only being cared for there because MSF has agreed to pay their medical bills. Others suffering from the disease never show up. However, even official statistics report that China has around 6 million cases and 900 deaths from tuberculosis each year.

With the rural healthcare system in the state it is, there is no working system to collect reliable data on the renewed spread of disease. Many deaths from such diseases are not recorded simply because the patients have never visited a local clinic. In addition many children are not registered by their parents because they are in breach of the policy on birth control and they are unlikely to be immunized. 'We suspect the immunization rate is not 80 per cent but 60 or even 30 per cent,' remarked Dr Roux.

Before setting out with his vaccines against rubella and measles young Xie Jinhao had explained that in his village many people had seven or eight children. The villagers fought a constant war with local family planning workers who were trying to enforce a two-child policy. After 1980, the minorities were allowed to have as many children as they wanted as a concession, but in the 1990s, the authorities had gradually tried to bring them into line with the rest of the country, forcing the women to be sterilized after they gave birth in a hospital or increasingly requiring the men to agree to a vasectomy. Those who ignored the restrictions had their houses pulled down and their animals seized in an effort to extract fines as high as 10,000 yuan.

The huge efforts made to hide the coercive birth-control policy became evident when we went to visit a barefoot doctor, trained by the MSF, who lived an hour's walk away. We found a local girl who could speak standard Chinese and the local language and who agreed to come and translate. Accompanied by a French doctor we set off early next morning only to find that a mysterious young man had silently attached himself to our group without introducing himself.

The doctor in Ya Guang village, Xie Pengfei, lived in a big wooden house with a balcony overlooking the valley. On the ground floor he kept his animals and farming tools. Upstairs he lived in rooms graced by a pleasant breeze. Xie had had one year of medical training and said his job was to prescribe tablets and injections for minor illnesses and to refer more serious cases to the township clinic or the county hospital.

'I charge 1.2 yuan for an antibiotic tablet but if the patient has a severe cold then I give an injection which costs 10 yuan,' he explained. Many patients liked to be put on a drip which he said was considered the most effective treatment.

As we talked about his cases, Xie kept looking for approval to our unknown companion who, whenever the conversation turned to a sensitive issue, spoke up and took control. Even here the secret police kept a close watch on what was said. Still, it soon became clear that most of Xie's treatments were ineffective. His patients, who earn perhaps 300 yuan a year, can rarely afford to buy enough tablets to complete an antibiotics course.

'Earlier this year, I had a patient, a 54-year-old man, who fell sick and became paralysed from the waist down,' Xie recounted, over the misgivings of the official. 'I think he had rheumatism. His family finally took him to the prefectural hospital in Liuzhou. They sold all their timber and animals, borrowed money and spent thousands of yuan on treatment but he died anyway. The family is still in debt.'

The staff of a hospital usually first find out how much a patient can pay before deciding on any treatment. Local peasants are required to pay a deposit of 1,500 yuan and sometimes as much as 3,000 yuan or they are refused admission.[5] It is therefore not surprising to find that a major cause of poverty in both the villages and the cities is healthcare. Families borrow heavily and privately, often at exorbitant interest rates, to pay for medical treatment.

All too often, too, the wrong medicine is prescribed. Dr Roux recalled one case of a child with diarrhoea who died after being treated with atropine, a drug used in anaesthesia, and World Bank studies report that as a matter of routine village doctors prescribe intravenous solutions of amino acids for fatigue, antibiotics for non-bacterial infections and adrenocortical hormones and multiple antibiotics for common colds. Some village clinics stock as many as a hundred different drugs. In general, every time a patient visits a doctor an average of 2.3 drugs are prescribed, and almost all drugs are in any case available over the counter without a prescription. National spending on drugs, especially new and imported drugs, has grown so quickly that it now accounts for 52 per cent of total health spending, compared to between 16 and 40 per cent in most developing countries.[6]

In 1995, the Ministry of Public Health reported that 2.5 million patients admitted to hospital each year died after having been prescribed the wrong medicine and that 100,000 died from violent reactions to drugs. In addition the indiscriminate distribution of drugs, especially excessive dosages of antibiotics, has been blamed for robbing as many as a million children of their speech and hearing.[7]

The prohibitive cost of Western-style treatment and its misuse have gone hand in hand with official encouragement of 'folk medicine'. In the 1950s, the Communist Party led a ruthlessly implemented campaign to arrest shamans and prohibit their activities as 'superstition', but in the 1990s, they were officially redesignated as 'traditional med-icine practitioners' and the state turned to sponsoring traditional Chinese medicine and training doctors in its use. A report by Xinhua in 1996 boasted that 'following a decade of efforts to develop tradi-tional therapeutic methods, Guangxi has become one of the country's leading herbal medicine production bases . . . Medical research departments in Guangxi have collected more than 50,000 folk recipes . . . and researchers have found nearly 5,000 well-known folk doctors with proven folk medicine skills across Guangxi.'[8]

At the same time the state advocated the practice of *qigong* and other traditional forms of martial arts exercises. Unwilling to pay for the medical treatment of the ageing population, they encouraged the people to help themselves. Every morning in parks and public spaces across China, groups of generally elderly or middle-aged women can be seen engaging in mass callisthenics, often performing the move-ments recommended by *qigong* masters who claim to have acquired superhuman powers and to be capable of curing seemingly incurable diseases such as Aids and cancer. (The word *qi* refers to the inner force that is believed to exist in all living creatures.) The most successful *qigong* sect, the Falun Gong, attracted tens of millions of adherents in the late 1990s after its leader, Li Hongzhi, promised his followers that if they adopted his system of exercise they need never take medicines or go to hospital for treatment.

Added to his mixture of Daoist and Buddhist thought was the claim that he could save the world from the various forces threat-ening it, from modern technology to extra-terrestrial beings. His adherents included family members of leading figures in the Politburo, as well as of PLA generals and other senior officials, and the credulity he encouraged went hand in hand with belief in UFOs and recourse to fortune-tellers.

Even senior Party members became enamoured of the idea that Chinese *qigong* masters hold the key to a system of knowledge that is beyond the understanding of Western science. The Party only reversed its view in 1999 when it launched a campaign to crush Falun Gong after Li Hongzhi had organized 15,000 followers to assemble in protest outside the leadership compound of Zhongnanhai in Beijing to demand state recognition.

This reluctance to trust Western medicine is prevalent throughout Chinese society, even amongst the educated and the powerful. Hospital 301 in Beijing, where Deng Xiaoping and many other senior leaders were kept alive until well into their nineties, employed the latest Western medical technology. However, its director, Li Qihua, was a strong advocate of *qigong* and encouraged many masters to visit Zhongnanhai to demonstrate their powers to ailing octogenarian generals. He was also responsible for employing a series of fake doctors who allegedly possessed magical powers, such as Zheng Xiangliang, who claimed to have X-ray vision, and another who said she could use her ear to diagnose internal illnesses. Ironically, Deng himself finally died as a result of an infection which spread throughout a ward as a result of basic inattention to routine procedures.[9]

Similarly, China's top rocket scientist Qian Xuesen was a fervent advocate of the use of *qigong*, believing that if these forces could be understood and harnessed, China would witness a new revolution in science. This extraordinary retreat from real science, in what amounted to nationalism combined with credulity, echoed the days of the Cultural Revolution when the Chinese media was full of false reports of the miraculous achievements of barefoot doctors who could reattach severed arms without using anaesthetic.

At the start of the twentieth century Western empirical science and medicine were embraced in an attempt to rejuvenate the nation both figuratively and literally. The Chinese feared they had become a race whose physical health was markedly inferior to those of other countries, especially Western nations, and who might lose a Darwinian survival-of-the-fittest competition between the races. Echoing early reformers such as Liang Qichao who wrote panegyrics to the Han race, extolling it as a yellow race superior to other Asian peoples, a 1920s middle school textbook taught that: 'Mankind is divided into five races. The yellow and white races are extremely strong and diligent. Because the other races are feeble and stupid they are going to be exterminated by the white race. Only the yellow race competes with that race. This is so-called evolution.'[10]

The founder of Republican China, Sun Yat-sen, made racial

nationalism one of his Three Principles of the People, arguing that the Chinese people are 'a single, pure race'; and researchers tried to define the Chinese race by investigating blood groups or cranium types, or even culture. The founder of the Communist Party, Chen Duxiu, thought, for instance, that Westerners were individualistic but Chinese communalistic; Westerners emphasized struggle, Chinese tranquillity; the East was spiritual, the West materialistic.

At the same time many books on eugenics appeared that proposed ways in which to purify the Chinese race. The reformer Kang Youwei advocated the establishment of state pleasure hotels where selected young people could mate, the prenatal education of children and the sterilization of the disabled and the mentally deficient. A Chinese Committee for Racial Hygiene, founded by Dr Pan Guangdan, the father of Chinese eugenics, sprang into existence and it put into practice the beliefs of those like the influential reformer Tan Sitong, who held that 'If we pay attention to the science of racial advancement, each generation will be superior to the last; through endless transformations, it will give birth to another race.'[11]

This desire to make the Chinese race fitter and stronger was evident across the political spectrum. As students Mao Zedong and many of his fellow activists trained their bodies, obsessed by the belief that there was a connection between their physical prowess and the strengthening of China's military might. The KMT promoted a New Life movement, launched in 1934, which included mass callisthenics aimed at creating 'a strong race and a strong nation'. (Even in the 1990s, China launched a National Fitness Programme which claimed that upgrading sports in schools was vital 'for the prosperity and strength of the nation'.)[12]

When the Communist Party came to power, it embarked on a series of patriotic health campaigns especially directed at exterminating 'the four pests' – birds, rats, insects and flies. Other campaigns targeted specific health problems such as the snails in rice paddies which spread schistosomiasis (snail fever). Mass campaigns to improve sanitation by the digging of public latrines and to make the boiling of drinking water commonplace helped control many diseases, in particular tuberculosis, a leading cause of death, typhoid, neonatal tetanus and leprosy.

By contrast, since Deng came to power in 1978, statistics suggest that there has been a decline in public sanitation. In 1997, 400 million still lacked access to safe water and 76 per cent lacked access to safe sanitation. Five years earlier the World Bank reported that there were 'substantial parts of China where the decline in diseases has slowed or even been reversed'. Snail fever has returned, as has tuberculosis. In the mid-1990s the number of Chinese infected by hookworm parasites was put at 200 million, and 90 per cent of poor children were thought to be infected. China also topped the league of nations with the most cases of diarrhoea among those under the age of 5.[13] Even so, people now live longer and the average height of the Chinese has risen by an average of just over an inch each decade.

In truth it is difficult to make comparisons between the two eras. Statistics from the Mao era, compiled at a time when ideological fervour was all-prevailing, are deeply suspect. The same is also true of the 1980s and 1990s, although for different reasons. One Western researcher, Giovanni Merli, who has tried to test the reliability of data in Zibo near Shandong province, has commented: 'In the evaluation of the quality of Chinese demographic data, both Western and Chinese scholars agree that Chinese birth and infant mortality systems suffer from severe under-reporting, and that censuses, surveys and registration systems are complicated by respondents failing to report births and infant deaths.'[14]

The performance of Chinese officials is evaluated according to the population statistics which are reported for their area. It is therefore hardly surprising that immense efforts are made to report low infant mortality rates, to such an extent, indeed, that rural areas report figures that are low even when set beside those of the richest countries such as Japan, Sweden, Finland or Singapore where nearly twice as many births take place with the help of trained doctors and midwives as in rural China.

Control of the growth in population lies behind this deception. In the 1950s Mao had rejected the advice of demographers such as Professor Ma Yinchu that China's population should be controlled, and within a few years he had turned against all 'experts', including demographers, doctors and geneticists. Mao termed birth control a bloodless genocide and his followers attacked eugenics as an 'imperial tool of domination' and condemned both psychology and psychiatry. By the early 1970s, the economy was struggling to feed and clothe a rapidly expanding population. In the following decade, the one-child policy was introduced first in the big cities and then throughout the country in an attempt to curb the burgeoning population explosion that Mao's policies had fuelled, with the aim of reducing China's population to 700 million by the year 2030.[15]

In consequence, although state spending on rural healthcare has declined sharply over the last two decades, the family planning service, with 300,000 full-time workers and 80 million volunteers, has been relatively well funded. The vast and coercive machinery was responsible for 8.7 million abortions in 1981, 12.4 million in the following year and 14.4 million in 1983. That year there were also 18 million insertions of uterine devices and 21 million sterilizations.[16]

Even when, in 1984, the campaign was relaxed in response to often violent opposition by peasants, there was still one abortion for every two births. The policy was then amended to permit two children if the first was a girl or handicapped and the target for the year 2000 was adjusted from 1 billion to 1.2 billion. However in 1989, articles appeared warning that the relaxation was a mistake and that the target would be missed. The baby boom which had followed the famine of the early 1960s meant that after 1985 over 12 million women were being added to the child-bearing population each year. The numbers peaked in 1989 and 1990 when women aged between 15 and 44 accounted for a quarter of the population.[17]

In the much tougher climate after 1989, the state launched another big drive in which 10 million people were sterilized in one year. The campaign had the effect of lowering the birth rate sharply. By 1992 it had reached 18.24 per thousand, for the first time below the replacement rate. In terms of the child-bearing population, the crest of the wave passed in 1996 since when restrictions have been relaxed a little.[18]

The population campaigns are one reason why infant mortality figures are so unreliable and why a question mark hangs over data on the ratio between the sexes. China reports significantly higher infant mortality rates among girls than among boys. According to a 1995 sample census, it is 39 per thousand for girls compared to 30 per thousand for boys. In some places such as Guangxi province, the infant mortality rate is reported to be as high as 82 per thousand for girls compared with 34 per thousand for boys.[19] Female infanticide may be one reason. Another, the increasing availability of ultra-sound machines, especially in the 1990s, has encouraged selective screening and may have contributed towards the reduction in the number of girl births. The 1992 census indicated that there were 118.5 boys born for every 100 girls whereas the global average is 105 boys for every 100 girls. Reports in 1993 spoke of 12 per cent of female foetuses being aborted and 1.7 million girls unaccounted for each year.[20]

It is possible that some girls are simply not registered when they are born but if such an imbalance really does exist, China will have 10 million enforced bachelors by the year 2020 and eventually as many as 70 million if trends continue. The government has, in consequence, repeatedly issued urgent notices forbidding clinics from using medical checks to identify the sex of unborn children.[21]

The traditional preference within China for male children has received further impetus in recent years because of the lack of any social security system in rural China, and especially the absence of health insurance. It is now all the more important for peasants to produce a son who will inherit the land and provide for his parents in their old age. Customarily, girls marry out of the family, so a couple without a son may face a difficult future.

The severity with which the one-child policy has been enforced has varied with time and also with geography. In the early 1990s rural cadres were executed for having accepted money to issue a birth certificate for a second or subsequent child. Now, however, negotiated fines seem to have become acceptable in the event of a second or even a third birth.[22] Sometimes, too, it seems that the poorer an area is, the more lenient the state has tended to be in enforcing its family planning policy. It was most strictly enforced in Shanghai, the richest city, which in 1993 became the first city in China to record negative population growth. In such urban areas, the cost of caring for the growing numbers of elderly will therefore inevitably fall on the state. Within a few decades, China's medically vulnerable population – below the age of 5 and over the age of 50 – will increase from 38 per cent to 60 per cent of the working population.[23]

In poor and minority areas such as the county of Rongshui, implementation of the one-child policy has generally been fairly lax, which has led to complaints that the 'quality' of the Chinese nation has suffered. 'The growth of the population has been twisted in an abnormal way. While the number of offspring of the illiterate has soared, those of the intellectuals has dropped,' complained one writer in an article that advocated exempting intellectuals from the one-child policy.[24]

In rural China, evidence linking poverty to large families has been used to justify state eugenics policies and to legitimize measures to reduce the high rate of birth defects common in poorer areas.

Those who live in infertile mountainous areas are prone to a number of diseases that are peculiar to China. Victims of Keshan disease, which results in heart failure and death, suffer from the absence of selenium in the soil. Two to three million people, many of them Tibetan, suffer from Kashin Beck disease in which the lack of another mineral affects the bones of victims who develop claw-like hands, bulging knees and gnarled limbs.

The Chinese on the loess plateau are also plagued by illnesses that are directly linked to their environment. Shanxi province has the highest rate of birth defects in the world, sometimes attributed to water and air pollution and sometimes to the lack of Vitamin B and trace elements in the diet. Out of every 10,000 babies born, 180 suffer from neural tube defects and 444 from various other defects. In fact China has the highest rate of neural tube cases in the world, 80,000 to 100,000 being recorded each year.[25] In addition, the Ministry of Public Health estimates that iodine shortages are responsible for over 12 million cases of mental retardation. Lack of iodine hinders brain development and causes goitres, a swelling of the thyroid gland. Recent research shows that the shortages may be more widespread than was once imagined and that perhaps as many as 400 million are threatened. Many victims reach adulthood with lowered intelligence and the problem is particularly severe in provinces such as Gansu, Shaanxi and Shanxi where there are whole villages of retarded peasants.[26]

As elsewhere in the world, the poor are more likely to be ill, and their children suffer in consequence. Infant mortality rates are four times higher in the poorest quartile of the countryside than in coastal regions. A joint report published in 1997 by the Chinese Academy of Preventative Medicine and UNICEF revealed that 39 per cent of all rural children suffer from lower than normal growth rates as a result of malnutrition. Further, more than a quarter of pre-school children in rural counties suffer from anaemia, rickets or other illnesses related to vitamin and protein deficiencies. In addition inadequate nutrition is blamed for the death of 310,000 infants each year.[27]

Despite such clear evidence of the effects of environmental factors on health, many experts in China have preferred to seek causes elsewhere – in particular, and not always with justification, among inherited genes. Though Mao banned genetics research, two years after his death the first conference of the China Genetics Institute was held which helped encourage research into the heredi-tary causes of some of these health problems.

Publications such as *Population and Eugenics (Renkon yu yousheng)*, issued by the Population Research Centre of Zhejiang Medical College in Hangzhou for a general audience, continue to advocate that genetically fitter elements of the population, such as educated urbanites, should be encouraged to have more than one child while the state should take measures to check dysgenic trends in the coun-tryside. In 1988 Gansu province became the first to pass a law pro-hibiting mentally retarded people from having children. Officials there complained that the province had 270,000 retarded people who were breeding 2,000 retarded children a year. Since then Liaoning, Zhejiang and Henan provinces have passed similar laws.[28]

At a further national eugenics conference held in 1989 officials reported that China had 30 million genetically defective people whose maintenance was costing society up to 8 billion yuan a year, which prompted Chen Muhua, a senior family planning officer, to declare that 'eugenics not only affects the success of the state and the prosperity of the race but the well-being of the people and social sta-bility'. A subsequent legislative drive culminated in 1995 in a National Eugenics Law, later renamed the Maternal and Infant Health Law in response to public outrage abroad. It authorizes officials to carry out pre-marital check-ups to see if either parent suffers from a serious hereditary, venereal or contagious disease in order to prevent 'inferior births'. If the official deems it necessary, he can order sterilization or an abortion.[29]

Many Chinese also share a belief that something must be done to improve the nation's gene pool which is felt to be too small. Centuries of inbreeding have supposedly resulted in a population in which 30 per cent suffer from some sort of hereditary handicap. According to one expert, Frank Dikotter, the Chinese government has actively fostered the perception that it is the duty of the state to intervene in the intimate lives of its subjects both to restrict population growth and to improve the 'quality' of the Chinese: 'The medical knowledge dispensed in eugenics campaigns is not designed to enable informed individual choices in reproductive matters, but to instil a moral message of sexual restraint and reproductive duty in the name of collective health. Eugenics promotes a biologising version of society in which the reproductive rights of individuals are subordinated to the rights of an abstract collectivity.'[30]

The definition of a hereditary handicap is sometimes extended to cover minor defects such as a harelip or cleft palate. Some evidence suggests that children born with them are routinely left to die. A Human Rights Watch report released in 1996 also claimed that there is an official policy to allow handicapped children to die even though they have been placed in the care of state orphanages.[31]

Some Chinese also believe schizophrenia to be a hereditary illness. Indeed, all mental illness carries a strong social stigma in China and treatment, if it exists at all, is poorly funded. Under Mao, psychiatry in any form was written off as the invention of bourgeois capitalism. As a result, even in 1999, psychiatric hospitals continued to be underfunded and tied to old-fashioned practices that relied on outdated therapy.[32] China has 16 million mentally ill patients but only 110,000 hospital beds in 575 hospitals and clinics. Even so, 40 per cent of those beds remain empty because people cannot afford the fees. Only an estimated 30 per cent of schizophrenic patients are treated and less than 5 per cent of those who suffer from depression are helped. China also reports the highest suicide rate in the world, it being estimated that 350,000 kill themselves each year, making it the leading cause of death among people aged between 15 and 35. And

China is the only country in the world where a higher rate of suicide is recorded among women than among men.[33]

As with education, state spending on health has shrunk steadily since 1979. Although the central government's health budget has gone up in absolute terms, as a proportion of total spending it had shrunk from 32 per cent to 14 per cent by 1993. By the late 1990s only 4 per cent of the recurrent health budget came under the direct control of the central government. At the same time, total health spending rose from 2.3 per cent of GDP in 1980 to 3.2 per cent in 1987 and is expected to reach 5 per cent of GDP by the year 2010.

Spending on health increasingly benefits an ever narrower class of people. There are nearly twice as many hospital beds serving the cities as there are the countryside, and in most cities the ratio of beds to population exceeds that in Western countries. Eighty per cent of health spending goes on big city hospitals which have spent lavishly on acquiring modern equipment such as computerized tomographic (CT) scanners. By 1986 China had 170 such scanners and Beijing alone had bought 34, despite a shortage of qualified technicians to operate them. Seven years later, the country as a whole had 1,300 CT scanners and 200 magnetic resonance imaging machines, and hospitals in Beijing alone had more of these machines than the whole of Britain.[34]

Most of the state's expenditure on health is devoted to providing for just two groups of people – 25 million government officials and 75 million SOE workers. The Labour Insurance System covers half the medical fees of SOE employees and a separate scheme covers all the bills of state cadres. In addition insurance schemes run by collective enterprises cover another 50 million workers. Two-thirds of public health spending is therefore devoted to caring for just 15 per cent of the population. Between 1978 and 1992, the cost of healthcare for state employees rose by 700 per cent and on a per capita basis by 450 per cent.[35]

More worryingly still, fewer and fewer resources are devoted to preventative medicine which perhaps accounts for the recent upsurge in hepatitis, tuberculosis and other infectious and endemic diseases. Most health spending goes on treating China's urban élite for the sorts of ailments – heart disease or cancer – that plague people in far richer countries. In a nation of 320 million smokers, epidemiological surveys have concluded that of the 300 million males under the age of 29 in 1998, at least 100 million will die of causes related to tobacco. By the year 2050, annual deaths from smoking could reach 3 million.[36] Motor vehicle accidents, which kill some 85,000 a year, have also become another leading cause of hospital treatment.

AIDS too may reach epidemic proportions. China reported 100,000 cases of HIV infection at the end of 1995 and triple that number three years later. Some fear that at this rate there could be 10 million cases by the year 2020. In addition to drug addicts, who may number over 10 million, and fast-growing numbers of prostitutes, the infection is spread by blood donors. As a result of a strong cultural aversion to donating blood, some Chinese hospitals have to buy as much as 90 per cent of the blood that they need. An illegal trade in blood donations which often depends on blood sold by people who are carrying the disease is blamed for spreading infection among both volunteers and the sellers of blood themselves through the use of insanitary equipment. In 1998 the state introduced a law banning the trade in blood products.[37]

China is also spending too much on buying drugs. The cost of medicines has risen a hundredfold, in some cases two hundredfold, since 1990 when China deregulated pricing. Spending on drugs accounts for over half of all health spending and is blamed for health costs rising at a rate of 35 per cent a year. China's pharmaceutical industry, with a turnover of 100 billion yuan in 1995, has become wildly profitable and, as prices have risen, many companies have ventured into the production and sale of fake or substandard medicines.[38] China's pharmaceuticals market has grown by an average of 18 per cent a year since 1978, making it among the fastest-growing in the world. In 1997, US$8 billion worth of Western medicines were sold and consumption is likely to reach US$12 billion by 2001.[39]

As state subsidies to hospitals have been repeatedly cut, profits from the sale of drugs have become the main source of hospital incomes. By the late 1990s, such profits financed as much as 60 per cent of hospital budgets – sometimes even 90 per cent – and padded the meagre salaries of state doctors. Many doctors also readily accepted kickbacks. The state has found it difficult to control the commerce because local governments, their pharmaceutical companies and the hospitals all share a common interest in pushing expensive drugs.[40] The profits are even greater when doctors prescribe imported drugs. Most patients have more faith in foreign brands than in domestic drugs because there are so many locally produced fakes. Imported or joint-venture drugs account for half the prescriptions in big cities, and China spends up to US$3.5 billion a year importing medicines. As even doctors in big city hospitals earn just 1,000 yuan a month, they are inevitably grateful if foreign companies offer gifts, free flights to international conferences or the donation of furniture and new equipment. The central government has slowly been trying to re-establish controls over the industry by banning the import of some drugs and restricting insurance coverage to 1,156 drugs. It also wants to divide drugs sales into those obtainable only by prescription and others approved for over-the-counter sale.[41]

Attempts have been made to address the issue of healthcare but progress is slow. As part of its overall strategy, announced in 1996, the state aims to increase government health expenditure to 5 per cent of GDP. In urban areas, it plans to create a national medical insurance system that will replace those operated by work units which depend on the variable economic fortunes of companies. Enterprises are to contribute 10 per cent of each employee's salary to an outside fund, while employees will contribute 1 to 2 per cent of their own wages. This means that even if an SOE goes bankrupt, its employees will continue to be protected by medical insurance.

As the government tries to lower drug prices and control spending on medicines, hospitals are raising their charges for operations and other forms of treatment which are currently set at below cost. Income from the sale of medicines and from treatment is to be accounted and administered separately, and profits from the sale of medicines are to be placed under the exclusive control of local health administration departments.

In 1996, Beijing also announced a plan to set up peasant co-operative medical insurance schemes and refinance the rural clinics.

For example, the Guangxi Public Health Bureau is allocating 10,000 yuan to each country to help restart village co-operative clinics. Yet the case of Rongshui shows how little is actually being achieved. There the MSF team has also drawn up a shortlist of essential drugs and is helping to retrain local staff, but in most of the countryside there is no such outside help.

The peasant medical insurance scheme is not working either. Rongshui villagers are supposed to contribute 5 yuan into a fund to insure themselves against emergencies costing more than 200 yuan but Dr Roux doubts whether such a scheme will ever work: 'It has existed since 1997 but the villagers don't want to put any money into it. Some don't trust it at all. Besides, if there are just two emergencies, all the money will be used up.' His colleague, the Miao doctor, doubted whether any significant change would be seen in poor rural areas for a long time to come.

Providing affordable healthcare is certain to remain a major political challenge. Many urban as well as rural families bankrupt themselves trying to pay for the treatment of family members, and the fact that most public money is spent on only a fraction of the population breeds resentment. It is an odd complaint to make of a Communist state but health and education are the two areas where most Chinese experience a lack of state intervention and a need for public services. It is in those areas too that the intelligentsia, described in the next chapter, have yet to regain their skills and influence.

II

The Stinking Ninth

THERE IS MUCH to admire about Chinese intellectuals but also much that is less admirable. Many of those who joined the Communist Party have attempted to marry the most archaic and cruel traditions of Chinese political thinking with the digital era, and some still continue to justify the resulting horrors in the name of a patriotism that is often sister to an ugly racism and brother to a crude xenophobia. Equally disturbing is the deep-seated worship of power and tyrants that many Chinese, regardless of their educational level, seem to share. It is all too common in China to hear professions of admiration for Hitler, Stalin, Lenin and Mao as well as the most brutal Chinese emperors because they were strong men. A reverence for power, the scorning of moral scruples, the embrace of the dicta-torship of the proletariat in preference to the values of individual liberty, even by those who became victims of Mao, all draw on a deep-rooted idolization of the state. Past horrors and mistakes do not seem to have weakened a servile belief in the ultimate benevo-lence of the state and a willingness to grant it unlimited powers.

Yet other Chinese intellectuals have retained a remarkable sense of patriotism and personal honour through the most extraordinary trials and humiliations and have remained loyal to the ideals of the May Fourth movement of 1919 that followed the collapse of impe-rial China and that was dubbed the Enlightenment. (The leading newspaper for the intelligentsia is still called the *Enlightenment Daily* (*Guangming Ribao*).) Prominent intellectuals who spearheaded the forces of change in the 1920s, such as Hu Shi, sought to bury the cruelties of Confucian society and promote Western humanist and Christian values, and the movement led to arguably the most open society China has ever witnessed. For the first time in history, in the 1920s and 1930s, Chinese could join political parties and participate in elections, read an open press and seek justice from an independent judiciary.

Even so, when offered a choice, many preferred Stalinism with all its lies and secrecy. Those Chinese intellectuals who travelled to the Soviet Union in the 1920s and 1930s somehow failed (as did many Western intellectuals) to see the reality of the mass famines, the labour camps, the secret police, the show trials and the rest. And those who could not leave China and instead travelled to Mao's soviet in Yan'an, the enclave in Shaanxi province established after the Long March in 1934, proved equally willing to submit to a form of self-delusion, disregarding the purges, the forced labour and the executions that took place there.

What went wrong in China in the twentieth century is a question which underlies much intellectual life. Some blame Chinese culture. Others single out the Chinese intelligentsia. Mao himself developed such a contempt for Chinese intellectuals that he called them 'the stinking ninth' category of social undesirables, and he had no compunction in destroying his liberal critics or even those Marxist intellectuals such as Chen Boda who had served him for decades and had even helped pen his thoughts.

Zhang Xianliang is convinced that the intellectuals were not the victims of Communism but helped build it. Zhang was arrested whilst a university student for publishing counter-revolutionary poems in 1957. He then spent twenty-two years in labour camps, an experience he describes in *Grass Soup* and *My Bodhi Tree* which are based on diaries he kept at the time.[1]

When I met him during one of his rare visits to Beijing in the mid-1990s, he described how his fellow-inmates in the camps – respectable professors, teachers and engineers – spied on one another and betrayed each other to their guards and interrogators, and how in struggle sessions, intended to 'educate' criminals, they would join in a mass beating of one of their fellows even though they knew their turn might be next.

'They lied, sneaked and betrayed each other all the time. They stopped at nothing to try and prove their loyalty to the Party. There was no solidarity, no attempt to retain any humanity. Everything, all human relations, were twisted,' he said. 'For all their high-flown ideals, they behaved with grovelling servility.'

Each of his fellow prisoners believed that in their case a mistake had been made by an essentially benevolent Party, that somehow they could perform some act that would prove their loyalty beyond doubt, that they would be redeemed and permitted to serve the state again.

As we talked, Zhang made it clear that he did not consider himself to be a dissident and that he had no particular desire to expound his views to newspapers. In fact he did not expect any great change in the future because he believed the behaviour of Chinese intellectuals betrayed their essential weakness. After reading books by Alexander Solzhenitsyn about life in the Soviet *gulag*, or those of Primo Levi about the Nazi concentration camps, he had become convinced that the Chinese respond differently in comparable situations.[2]

This belief that 'the Chinese are different' is widely held in China and is invariably the final card in any discussion about the prospects for political reform – 'You don't understand, our culture is different.' Whatever the truth of the matter, it is certainly possible to argue that Chinese intellectuals have always belonged to a caste whose role has been to advise the ruler of the state. By comparison, Russian intellectuals, many of whom were men of action, believed in a grand moral mission beyond serving the state.[3]

The archetype Chinese intellectual is Qu Yuan who lived from 343 to 289 BC and whose memory lives on. (It was astonishing to see middle-aged protesters marching along Beijing's streets during the 1989 democracy protests with placards saying 'Qu Yuan! Your lament is not forgotten.') Several centuries after his death, a biographer described Qu as 'a virtuous minister of the Chu [kingdom], who was banished because of a slander. He wrote the poetic lament *Li Sao*

(*On Encountering Trouble*), ending with the words "Enough! There are no true men in the state: no one understands me." Then he threw himself in the river and was drowned."[4] A national festival now celebrates his death with dragon boat races when people also feed sticky rice balls wrapped in leaves to the fishes to prevent them from eating Qu Yuan's body.

Qu Yuan's complaint that the ruler, surrounded by deceiving and flattering courtiers, had ignored his sound political advice took place at a key moment in Chinese history during the Warring States period, when the Chu kingdom was about to be defeated by the rival Qin state, which would go on to unify China under the First Emperor.

During the Warring States period, the various rulers were advised by scholars who proposed different and competing political systems. A number of schools of political thought emerged, in particular the Confucianists and the Legalists, who often borrowed from one another. The period is generally referred to as one in which 'a hundred flowers bloomed and a hundred different schools of thought contended'. When, in 1957, Mao responded to the death of Stalin, the acknowledged leader of world Communism, by proclaiming the Hundred Flowers campaign, Chinese intellectuals naïvely took this as an invitation to debate political and economic reform. This brief period of free speech was soon followed by the Anti-Rightist campaign in which those who had unwisely spoken out were arrested and sent to the camps. Zhang Xianliang was among their number, as was Dai Huang, then a young journalist at Xinhua, the state news agency.

Dai had spoken out at a Party cell meeting about the deification of Mao and the excessive privileges given to cadres which he complained were fostering corruption. After being arrested in 1957 and denounced as a 'rightist' he was dispatched without trial to a labour camp in the Great Northern Wilderness in Heilongjiang province. His wife divorced him and during the famine of the Great Leap Forward, like Zhang Xianliang, he survived by eating wild grasses, field mice and seeds, though his weight fell from 14 stone to just $6\frac{1}{2}$ stone. In 1960, he was allowed to return to Beijing and wrote an account of what he had witnessed in the Great Northern Wilderness but in 1962, when the tide turned yet again, he was 'struggled' and given a two-year labour reform sentence that was preceded by five years in various prisons around Beijing. Then, in the Cultural Revolution, he was sent to the countryside in Shanxi province for re-education through labour. During this period his sister died of tuberculosis, his elder brother was 'struggled' to death and his mother died. His daughter by his first marriage was given to another family to raise. In 1962, he had remarried. After his re-arrest his second wife had to raise their two daughters alone. When he eventually returned the girls barely recognized him. His story is not untypical.

When I met Dai Huang in 1998, he was living in a small apartment near the centre of Beijing in the compound of Xinhua. He was still writing and his autobiography *Nine Deaths, One Life: My Progress as a Rightist,* which recounts how he narrowly cheated death in the camps, had just been published.[5]

In addition to his autobiography, he had just written a biography of Hu Yaobang, the liberal Party leader whose death in 1989, following his dismissal two years earlier, had triggered the 1989 protests.[6] In it he describes how in 1978 Hu had struggled to grant an amnesty not only to the intellectuals, 'the stinking ninth', but also to 30 million others who had been persecuted because of their background – landlords, rich peasants, even reactionaries. Since this persecution had also extended to all those related to the individual, perhaps 200 million people were affected. In Dai Huang's own case, the lives of 300 family members were blighted. They were criticized in various campaigns, barred from attending schools or universities and prevented from joining the People's Liberation Army (PLA) or the Party.

Dai Huang's book further describes how Deng Xiaoping had been put in charge of the Anti-Rightist campaign of 1957. In 1981, the Party delivered a verdict on that event and others, known as 'The Resolution on Some Historical Questions of the Party since the Establishment of the Country'. It did not go so far as to admit that the campaign was a mistake, merely that it had been 'broadened' too widely.

'According to Party documents, only 96 were originally targeted but the campaign was expanded to cover 552,912 people. So this was "broadened" by a factor of 5,000!' Dai Huang remarked. 'This is worse than Chiang Kai-shek who in 1927 massacred Communist

Party members, saying it was better to kill a thousand than let one go free.'

Mao had in fact set a quota for the Anti-Rightist campaign: 5 per cent of China's 5 million people classified in their identity documents as educated should be persecuted and each work unit had to fill its quota. In fact, Dai believes that far more people were affected than those listed in the Party documents, perhaps another 200,000 or 300,000. 'There were tens of thousands of people, who, though not openly declared rightists, were put under supervision as rightists,' he said. 'Actually, it is now impossible to calculate the total number of victims. You have to remember that many people who were sent to the countryside as rightists were never rehabilitated and their cases have never appeared in the records.'

Indeed even after the 1979 amnesty, many people who had been sent to the countryside for re-education were still there. 'In one place I went to in Henan province, over 700 rightists had appealed for help. I had to go to the Party Secretary of Henan to try and get them released. In parts of the country, where bad men are in power, such rightists were not permitted to leave,' he explained.

Every day, his postbag was full of letters of gratitude from those who had benefited from his campaign. He pulled a small envelope out of a bundle and unfolded the thin pieces of paper on which a series of tiny characters had been drawn. The author Shao Yanxing had written to him: 'Without eyewitnesses like us, the younger generation won't understand how much blood and tears lie behind the word "redress". They won't know about the battle between justice and evil.'

Despite his experiences, however, Dai Huang seems at peace both with himself and with his commitment to Marxism and the Communist Party. He had joined the Communists' Fourth Route Army at the age of 16 and as a journalist had covered the Korean War and the defeat of France in Vietnam: 'My generation believed that we intellectuals are the backbone of the country.' Even now, however, he is firmly wedded to the Marxist conviction that 'history' is a force in itself. He also believes that the Communist system can be reformed and that Mao's brutal reign was somehow an aberration.

In Dai's view the Anti-Rightist campaign is important because it was the first great mistake of the Communist Party and it led to many others: 'After the Anti-Rightist campaign no one dared say anything and that was the biggest disaster. That led straight to the deaths of 30 million in the famine [during the Great Leap Forward] and then to the Cultural Revolution.' Another book that appeared at the same time, *Crossed Swords* by Ma Licheng and Ling Zhijun, quotes the estimate of Marshal Ye Jianying that the Cultural Revolution alone accounted for the lives of another 20 million people.[7]

Zhang Xianliang's view of his fellow intellectuals would seem to be confirmed by the fact that very few of the victims of the Anti-Rightist campaign or other campaigns have actively protested against the labour camp system. The most prominent example of one who has is Harry Wu, also imprisoned for twenty years, who later moved to the United States and set up a foundation to expose the Chinese *gulag*. He has repeatedly travelled to China to film the inmates of labour camps and been rearrested, only to be released after considerable diplomatic pressure.

Other Chinese writers who chose to stay in China, such as Dai Qing, have gathered evidence to show that, contrary to what Dai Huang believes, the Anti-Rightist campaign was by no means the first 'mistake'. The thousands of intellectuals who flocked to Mao's base in Yan'an in the 1930s and 1940s, including the actress Jiang Qing whom Mao later married, were also victims of a system that imprisoned or killed those who dared to speak out.

In particular, Dai Qing had researched the fate of a writer, Wang Shiwei, who had joined the Party in 1926 and translated the works of Marx, Engels and Lenin. His fate remained unknown until the 1990s, when Dai Qing unearthed the details of how he was arrested, tortured and imprisoned for five years in a squalid jail before being beheaded. As in 1957, Mao had encouraged those attending Yan'an's Marxist-Leninist Research Academy to speak out and offer constructive criticism to the Party. Among those who put up posters and delivered speeches at meetings was Wang Shiwei. In 1942 he wrote an open criticism of Mao's leadership and the Party's system of privileges in *Wild Lilies*.[8]

In the crackdown that followed the period of free speech, many thousands of intellectuals and Party members were tortured to force them to admit to being Trotskyite revolutionaries or Nationalist spies. Among them was the author Ding Ling, then already the most famous woman novelist of her generation. Her husband had been shot by the KMT and she had spent three years under arrest before escaping to Yan'an. There she was made arts editor of the *Liberation Daily* but fell foul of Mao.

In 1942 Mao gave a series of instructions, later known as the 'Talks at the Yan'an Forum on Literature and Arts': 'There is in fact no such thing as art for art's sake, art that stands above the classes, art that is detached from or independent of politics. Proletarian literature, and art . . . are, as Lenin said, cogs and wheels in the whole revolutionary machine.' And he went on to make it clear that he thought the only role of intellectuals was to be like 'oxen for the proletariat and the masses, bending their backs to their tasks until their dying days'.[9]

However, even these purges at Yan'an were not the first that Mao had conducted. At his earlier base in the Jingangshan soviet in the early 1930s, some 5,000 were executed in a purge now known as the Futian Incident. Among those who narrowly escaped death was Hu Yaobang himself.

Yet in the 1930s and 1940s, many Chinese intellectuals preferred to join organizations such as the League of Left Wing Writers or the National Salvation Front that attacked the KMT for its censorship and lack of political freedom. Even now it is rare for Communists like Dai Huang to admit that they had been better off under the KMT than under the Communists. Before the establishment of the Republic in 1911, China had only seven newspapers but by 1935, when Mao arrived in Yan'an, there were 910 newspapers and more than 900 periodicals as well as independent publishing houses, film studios and radio stations. It was during this period that the greatest works by China's most famous twentieth-century writers – Ba Jin, Shen Congwen, Lao She, Lu Xun, Qian Zhongshu – were written. Little of comparative worth has appeared since 1949. So it is hard to explain why, even after the Anti-Rightist movement, Marxism should still have exerted such an overwhelming attraction.

Ding Ling was arrested again in 1957 and spent a further twenty-one years undergoing various forms of hard labour to 'reform her thoughts', yet her son grew up as a fanatical Maoist. As the writer Lao Gui, he describes in *Bloody Dusk* how he came to be a Red Guard in Inner Mongolia. Like Zhang Xianlang's fellow inmates, he went to great lengths to prove his loyalty to the Party and to Mao, volunteering for the hardest assignments, and beating up impoverished herdsmen for being 'capitalists' and 'landlords' because they owned some cattle and horses. Even in the 1980s, Lao Gui retained a belief in the ultimate reformability of the Communist system and in 1989 he wrote a petition in his own blood during the Tiananmen protests.[10]

The number of former Red Guards who for many years continued to claim to be Marxists and then became democracy activists is surprising. Wang Xizhe was one of three dissidents who in 1974 put up a famous anti-government wall poster in Guangzhou. The Li-Yu-Zhe poster, as it was called, advocated democracy and the rule of law. Arrested and imprisoned, Wang nevertheless continued to speak of his belief in Marxism. Another example is the famous dissident Xu Wenli, who in 1979 edited the *April Sixth Forum*, one of the first independent magazines published since 1949. He advocated socialism for China in the belief that the Party could be reformed and guided towards a real social democracy.

Why is it then that such people still retain their faith in the system? Perhaps one reason lies in the extraordinary success of the Communist Party's propaganda in deceiving not only Chinese but also foreigners. American journalists who visited Mao in Yan'an in the 1940s returned convinced that Chinese Communism was primarily an agrarian reform movement and that they had seen a real democracy budding. Many Tibetans, Mongols and other peoples similarly believed that if the Communists won power they would, as promised, be given the freedom to secede.

A strong commitment to democracy and direct elections was in fact a major element of the CCP's political programme right up until its seizure of power. In 1941, Deng Xiaoping was among those who stressed the importance of having a directly elected assembly for a Provisional Border Region, a territory then under Communist control: 'We Communists always oppose a one-party dictatorship and don't approve of the Nationalists having a one-party dictatorship. The CCP certainly doesn't have a programme to monopolize political power because one party can only rule in its own interest and won't act according to the will of the people. Moreover, it goes against democratic politics.'[11] And at the Seventh Communist Party Congress in 1945, Mao himself spoke of the prospects for a coalition government in which he too promised that the Party would not impose a dictatorship of the proletariat and that it was not opposed to private capital or property. He also insisted that the Communists wanted freedom of political and religious belief.

It is doubtful whether those close to Mao ever believed in his sincerity in professing such beliefs, and many of them have continued to play a leading role in suppressing intellectual freedom and dissent since his death, even though they themselves have undergone periods of political persecution.

General Yang Shangkun ordered the troops into Beijing in 1989, while Wang Zhen and Hu Qiaomu were responsible for a succession of campaigns against intellectuals in the 1980s.* Deng put Wang Zhen, a barely literate ex-railway worker, in charge of the Central Party School, and he appointed Mao's former secretary, Hu Qiaomu, as head of the newly established Chinese Academy of Social Sciences.

Together with Deng Liqun, the man responsible for the Propaganda Department, these men crushed the 1979 Democracy Wall movement when dissidents put up posters in the centre of Beijing calling for democratic freedom. A priority was to stop the dissidents being able to publish anything and so retain a tool which had proved so effective in the past: 'During our struggles against Chiang Kai-shek, we took advantage of the loopholes in the law on publications established by the Nationalist government to advance our legal struggle. At present we must avoid allowing others to take similar advantage in turning what is illegal into something that is legal and employing it against us. So that they can't have any place

---

* It was Yang Shangkun, Wang Zhen and Hu Qiaomu who ordered the execution of the writer Wang Shiwei in 1947.

to register their publications we must outlaw all of them,' Deng Liqun explained to the officials in charge of the Propaganda Department.[12]

Though Deng Xiaoping, on the eve of his visit to the United States, had given a qualified blessing to the Democracy Wall Movement in what was christened the Beijing Spring, and even as the horrors of Mao's misrule were being revealed and Hu Yaobang was pushing through an amnesty for intellectuals, Hu Qiaomu and Deng Liqun drew other lessons from the past. The slightest sign of independence among intellectuals had to be stamped out and the shoots of the Beijing Spring were quickly crushed. In particular, Wei Jingsheng and Xu Wenli, who had put up posters and published independent journals, were given severe prison sentences.

In 1983, the hardliners launched another political movement, this time against 'spiritual' pollution. Among the targets were new authors such as Zhang Xianliang who was criticized for advocating individualism and a Western exploration of the self. Yet with the patronage of Hu Yaobang, many intellectuals including Dai Huang still remained convinced that the Party finally had the right leader and that it could be reformed. Hu helped to establish influential liberal think-tanks and encouraged intellectuals to circulate proposals on reform at least within the Party. The Party even encouraged experiments in multi-candidate elections for local district congresses in Beijing. Among those who stood as candidates was Wang Juntao who had been arrested for taking part in protests that had taken place in 1976. Then huge crowds had gathered in Tiananmen Square after the death of the Prime Minister Zhou Enlai, in what developed into an anti-government protest that was suppressed with violence. Later Deng reversed the official verdict on these protests, deeming them to be against the Gang of Four who had tried to seize power after the death of Mao.

Wang Juntao is one of the few intellectuals who have tried to operate outside the system. Together with another influential figure, Chen Ziming, he set up a non-official social science think-tank in 1986, launched a non-Party journal, the *Economics Weekly*, and established the Opinion Research Centre of China to carry out independent opinion polls. The Party later accused both men of being the 'black hands' behind the Tiananmen protests of 1989. Foreign organizations such as the Ford Foundation have also helped nurture independent thought. The financier George Soros underwrote a Fund for the Reform and Opening of China and offered to spend US$1 million a year on an international cultural exchange centre. A few of the emerging semi-private enterprises, notably the Stone Corporation, have also tried to provide funding.[13] Most intellectuals, however, have preferred to operate within the system.

Despite Deng Liqun's best efforts, there has since 1978 been an explosion of information within China. The number of registered publications has jumped from 150 to over 4,000. In the more vibrant and less orthodox south in particular, dozens of publications such as the *Shenzhen Youth News* provide an outlet for liberal ideas.

Hu Yaobang was the first to encourage a freer press and to comment on what was called 'the dark side of society', saying it was not necessary for all articles to be positive. In the face of the traditional view of the journalist as 'the mouth and tongue of the Party', the *China Daily* even ran an editorial in 1988 that declared: 'To protect artistic freedom what needs to be done first of all is to prevent interference from above in creative activities – such as telling writers what to write and arbitrarily sticking political labels on their works.' For the first time, too, China even had a Minister of Culture who was a liberal writer, Wang Meng. His deputy was the actor Ying Ruocheng who appeared in the film *The Last Emperor*, albeit as the head of a Communist-run prison.[14]

In the 1980s, the battle between liberals and hardliners was marked by reversals and sudden changes of fortune on both sides, with Deng as the final arbiter. The key battleground was not the future, about which the Communists were always confident, but the past. Who would control history's judgement?

A central issue was the Cultural Revolution, a period which all the senior leaders could not help but agree represented a terrible mistake. Deng's new policies required that intellectuals should be allowed to explain the crimes of the Gang of Four and the economic disasters of what were referred to as 'the ten years of chaos'. At the Chinese

Academy of Social Sciences, the liberal scholar Yan Jiaqi published a lengthy history on the Cultural Revolution.[15] The 82-year-old novelist Ba Jin lobbied to establish a museum like that at Auschwitz to ensure that later generations did not repeat such mistakes. He feared that the harmful effects of the Cultural Revolution would take generations to eradicate. Even Deng Pufang, the eldest son of Deng Xiaoping who had been thrown out of a window during the Cultural Revolution and was paralysed as a result, backed a publishing house, Huaxia, that printed works on the Cultural Revolution, including a collection of essays entitled *History in Deep Contemplation*.[16]

Exposures of the Cultural Revolution were often barely disguised vehicles for attacks on Mao and the entire elderly generation of Marxists, and almost all bemoaned its effect on the younger generation. An article in the *People's Daily* by the Party Secretary of Hubei, Gao Yang, complained: 'The young people I meet now have little knowledge, cannot write Chinese properly and cannot think logically. Moreover, their behaviour has become savage. It is said this comes from the Cultural Revolution, but young people who were hardly born in those days also behave in a savage way ... Our cadres, elderly cadres excluded, did not receive proper training. They are rude and do not know how to express themselves, how to write a proper report, how to carry on a discussion.'[17]

The feeling that something had gone terribly wrong developed into a conviction that the root causes were to be found deep in Chinese culture and history. The Taiwanese writer Bo Yang wrote a book entitled *The Ugly Chinaman* that subsequently became a bestseller, and in it he posed the question which many wanted to discuss: why was it that both the Communists and the KMT had imprisoned so many independent thinkers, including himself: 'I got to thinking about how and why fate led me to where I am. I sought answers in Chinese history books. And I found my own problem was not unique. All through history many Chinese ended up in prison like myself. I realized then that it was not an individual problem. There must be something wrong in our national character and at the very heart of our culture.'[18] Chinese culture, he delighted in telling everyone who came to see him in Taipei, was nothing but a vat of putrefied soy sauce giving off a horrible stench: 'Even if one were to place a fresh peach in a soy sauce vat full of putrescent brine, it would eventually turn into a dry turd.'

A six-part television series first broadcast in 1988 traced the madness of the Cultural Revolution back to the earliest origins of Chinese civilization. Scripted mainly by Su Xiaokang (who fled the country after the events of 4 June the following year), *He Shang* or *River Elegy* deplored China's antique and inward-looking culture and the slavish behaviour of its intellectuals. The latter had always attached themselves to their rulers and had yet to become an independent social group with a separate identity.

The series' title referred to the Yellow River, the cradle of Chinese civilization, and it attacked the whole legacy of the First Emperor, Qinshi Huangdi. Mao had deeply admired him and the totalitarian dictatorship he established, and gloried in his identification with the most famous tyrant in Chinese history who had ended the original 'Hundred Flowers' period. After the Anti-Rightist campaign was over, he declared: 'We have outdone Qinshi Huangdi more than a hundredfold . . . People always condemn Qinshi Huangdi for burning books and burying alive Confucian scholars and list these as his greatest crimes. I think, however, that he killed too few Confucians . . . All those Confucian scholars were indeed counter-revolutionaries.'[19]

At the end of his life, Mao even ordered the country to study the achievements of the Qin Emperor and the totalitarian political philosophy of his Legalist advisers. The campaign lasted for three years until Mao's death in 1976. In the 1980s, Chinese students still read textbooks that justified the Qin dictatorship and explained that 'under such circumstances, it is necessary to employ measures to unify people's minds in order to consolidate unity and prohibit reactionary activities that use the ancients to criticize the present'.[20]

The Qin Emperor had followed the advice of the Legalist philosopher Han Fei who advocated eradicating all traces of free expression or free association: 'Any ruler who wants to govern his state must eliminate the formation of groups . . . to rule the state all [independent] associations must be wiped out. If they are not wiped out, then people will congregate in crowds . . . Within the state of a wise ruler, there are no books and manuscripts. Educational instruction comes from the law. There are no recorded sayings of the former sage kings, the state officers are the teachers . . . Those whose hearts are different and who advocate private learning are opposed to the present trend . . . Their action must be prohibited and their groups must be dispersed.'[21]

Under this political system, as under Mao's, the ruler was the sole arbiter of the moral code and his bureaucrats the only authorized teachers of the state philosophy. The Qin state also recognized 'thought crimes' so that even the expression of wrong thought or criticism was severely punished as an act of rebellion. A web of spies and informers and a system of mutual surveillance ensured that those who knew of a crime but failed to denounce its perpetrators were equally harshly punished.

Soon after the death of the First Emperor in 206 BC, rebellion erupted. After a civil war, a new dynasty, the Han, came to power and established an empire that lasted for generations. Indeed the Chinese still refer to themselves as the Han people. Some Chinese scholars argue that under the Han dynasty Legalism continued to be the guiding philosophy but that to make it more palatable, Confucianism, the more benevolent approach which the Qin Emperor had sought to destroy, was proclaimed. This was summed up in the four-character phrase *ru wai, nei fa* – 'Be Confucian on the outside but follow Legalism on the inside.'

Confucianism stood for a style of government in which the power of the centralized state was balanced by the rights of a feudal aristocracy and tempered by the requirements of rites and traditions. An orthodox form of Confucianism, known as neo-Confucianism, was elevated to a state religion during the Song dynasty after AD 1100 which above all stressed obedience to the Emperor in the Three Bonds: the Emperor is the master of his subjects, the father is the master of his sons, and the husband is the master of his wife.

However, others argue that all dynasties that succeeded the Qin retained essentially the same legal system and a bureaucratic machine that attempted to enforce absolute state censorship and operate a controlling propaganda apparatus. All this was lumped together in the 1980s and termed 'feudalism', although in European history the word denotes a quite different society with a powerful aristocracy, a strong church and an often weak monarchy. Moreover, feudal China, unlike feudal Europe, lacked the earlier traditions of the Greeks and the Romans with their civic and democratic culture. In China the state had never funded marketplaces, theatres or senate houses where people could freely associate, or encouraged the study of public oratory in schools.

As people sought to discover why China had moved from the Enlightenment at the start of the twentieth century to the totalitarianism of Mao, the Marxist state was compared with the 'feudal' state of the Qin Emperor. 'The May Fourth movement in 1919 shook feudalism but did not uproot it. In the following decades, feudalism was largely ignored but it found its expression in the "Cultural Revolution" under new circumstances. We hope that a probing and systematic study of Chinese feudalism will be conducted to understand its influence on Mao Zedong's thought in his later years and its relationship to the ultra-leftist mentality,' explained the *China Daily*.

As the works of intellectuals of the 1920s such as Hu Shi became available once more, many agreed that the only way out of the grip of history was to adopt Western political ideas and this became a major theme of many who contributed to the short-lived Democracy Wall movement and its successors. One activist, Ren Wanding, wrote in his nineteen-point manifesto, pinned up on the Wall in 1978, 'We must draw not only on Western science and technology but also on Western traditions, democracy and culture.' His China Human Rights League, which consisted solely of Ren and a few friends, was easily snuffed out and he was given a four-year prison sentence but similar ideas continued to circulate even among the highest levels of the Party.

The older generation of revolutionaries and Marxists sought to defend Marxism-Leninism by claiming that they were defending traditional Chinese culture. When the conflict between the two wings of the Party came to a head and Hu Yaobang was dismissed in 1987, it was the hardline octogenarian Wang Zhen who vehemently refuted Hu's belief that the Party had failed the people: 'I must point out that in the past few years bourgeois liberalization has been rampant. One manifestation has been to contradict the great history of our people and say that everything Chinese is bad and everything foreign is good. This is completely wrong.'[22] At the same time propaganda organs such as the *Beijing Review* attacked Hu Yaobang for advocating 'complete Westernization' and for arguing that China must 'learn from Western science, technology, culture, politics, ideology, ethics and all other things'.[23]

A few months later, during the anniversary of the May Fourth movement, Wang Zhen declared that the lesson of history is that 'only Marxism can be the correct ideology to transform China' precisely because it had led the people to fight feudalism and imperialism. The following year he also condemned the television series *He Shang* for 'attacking the valuable cultural heritage of the motherland'.[24]

Deng Xiaoping chose to follow a middle road. Despite the terrible things that had happened during Mao's 'ten years of chaos', he relied on the argument, given in an internal speech, that 'We cannot adopt Western ways because if we do, it will mean chaos.'[25] This twist in the rationale for retaining the 'feudal' system matched what Lu Xun, a writer much admired by the Communist Party, had observed in 1927: 'Chinese culture is a culture of serving one's masters who triumph at the cost of the misery of the multitude. Those who praise Chinese culture, whether they be Chinese or foreigners, conceive of themselves as belonging to the ruling class ... Almost all those who praise the old Chinese culture are the rich residing in the [foreign] concessions or other safe places.'[26]

In 1987 Hu Yaobang was replaced by Zhao Ziyang who continued to support the drive for change and established an Office for the Reform of the Political Structure led by one of his secretaries, Bao Tong. Under Zhao's protection, intellectuals continued their attacks. In October 1988, artists swathed part of the Great Wall in white bandages to symbolize the infirmity of China. An exhibition of propaganda photographs, exposing the machinery of deception, showed how images of Party leaders had been airbrushed out of existence after they had fallen from power. A famous photograph from the Korean War of a woman offering her breast to succour a soldier who had fallen in battle was revealed to be two photographs imposed one on top of the other.[27]

An exhibition devoted to avante-garde art in February 1989

deliberately satirized the message of Mao's Yan'an Forum talks, that the only sanctioned purpose of art is to convey the messages of the rulers. At the Central Academy of Arts, rooms were decorated with huge inflated breasts and penises, and artists sat on a pile of straw, pretending to hatch eggs and wearing paper vests bearing the words 'No reasoning during incubation so as not to disturb the next generation'. The closing act of surreal political theatre was real. A posse of police wearing helmets and armed with machine guns stormed the exhibition after another artist fired two bullets into her sculpture of a telephone box.

The strongest challenge posed by the intellectuals, however, came from Professor Fang Lizhi, the elected Vice-President of Hefei University where reforms in higher education were being undertaken. He organized a petition, signed by seventy prominent intellectuals, that called on Deng to release all political prisoners. On the seventieth anniversary of the May Fourth movement, in 1989, he said it was time that China's intellectuals, cowed for so long by decades of persecution and humiliation, spoke out. The Chinese people had to demand political rights, not wait for them to be given by their rulers: 'We are always considering our own innate rights as some kind of charity.' More petitions followed and Fang insisted: 'We have been cheated before, we won't be cheated again.'[28]

In the student protests in Tiananmen Square that followed Hu Yaobang's death on 15 April that year, many petitions and wall posters returned to the theme of feudalism, the legacy of the Qin Emperor and the unfulfilled hopes of the May Fourth movement. Students deliberately mocked the Party for wrapping itself in the mantle of the Chinese emperors by pretending to be scholars delivering a memorial to the Emperor and kneeling down on the steps of the Great Hall of the People until officials came out to receive it. In the carnival atmosphere that sprang up, fear of the state evaporated and its rulers were openly ridiculed. In the most striking moment, Chinese television showed the Prime Minister Li Peng being mocked and scolded by students on hunger strike in a meeting at which he attempted to patronize them.

After the PLA's occupation of Beijing on 3 June, Zhao Ziyang disappeared from public view, his assistant Bao Tong was imprisoned, the student leaders were hunted down and Fang Lizhi took refuge in the American Embassy. The rebellion by the intellectuals had been crushed.

In the ensuing decade, the debate has not moved on. Intellectuals have tried but generally failed to find some independent space within the system. Every few years, publishers have been ordered to re-register. In 1995, the state vetted 8,000 periodicals and 2,000 news-papers. Censors searching for subversive messages have examined everything from slogans on T-shirts to poetry magazines. The pro-paganda machinery has returned to its traditions. When it high-lighted the heroic role of the PLA in combating the floods of 1998, it included repeated showings on television of a grateful peasant woman offering milk from her breasts to an exhausted soldier, who had apparently been stung on the head by a bee.[29]

A flood of operas, films, television programmes and articles have held up a succession of model plumbers, bus conductresses, peas-ants and cadres whose merit is that they have sacrificed themselves to serve the state. These have been accompanied by campaigns prais-ing Confucianism because 'the disappearance of social norms, the death of morals and the disintegration of traditional values have brought about a moral crisis'.[30] Attempts have also been made to justify the crackdown on the media, regarded as necessary because, as the state news agency put it, 'the industry could otherwise become a mere money-making machine rather than something serving to improve the moral standards of people'.[31]

The state has reasserted its traditional right to serve as the sole moral arbiter and its officials to be the only teachers. It has also con-tinued its efforts to suppress or destroy traditional beliefs and customs. Most art is devoted to artificial festivals such as the celebra-tions of Army Day, Teacher's Day, Women's Day and National Day, while the main traditional festivals, such as that celebrated at Chinese New Year, are marked only by three- or four-hour television per-formances praising the Party. The performers may dance in folk cos-tumes or sing in a traditional form but the aim is to praise such abstract ideas as 'the spirit of the Fifteenth Party Congress'. Even historical dramas are only televised in order to suit the state. A new television dramatization of the novel *Outlaws of the Marsh* (whose plot resembles that of *Robin Hood*) ends with the rebels choosing to abandon their independence in order to serve the Emperor.

The few remaining dissident voices have tried to counter-attack by undermining the Party's moral authority. When, in 1995, the United Nations held a 'Year of Tolerance', the elderly dissenting physicist Xu Liangying released a typical petition that appealed to the authorities 'to put an end to China's practice over thousands of years of punishing people for thinking, speaking and writing' and that attacked the Party on the grounds that 'corruption has become a wind blowing through the country, and the trading of money for power, the embezzling of public funds and other phenomena of corruption are found everywhere. We must do everything possible to remove and strictly punish those who are bringing disaster to the nation and its people.'

He and many others now outside the country continue to push the argument that only a democratic system where all are equal before the law can bring corruption under control. Without democracy the Party cannot realize its slogan of 'ruling the country by law'.

In response, the official propaganda machine has kept up a sustained attack on Western political systems, Western democracy, human rights and individualism. British attempts to introduce an elected government in Hong Kong before its return to China in 1997 were heavily criticized and when Taiwan held its first open parliamentary and then presidential elections in 1995 and 1996, China fired missiles and condemned the elections – the first successful such exercise in a Chinese state – as a money-driven, Mafia-dominated farce.

The state's propaganda is often openly xenophobic and couched in nationalist tones, harping on past injustices or imagined slights, and it has continued to issue books such as *China Can Say No*, a diatribe against the United States, and to resurrect the atrocities committed by Japan before and during the Second World War. The accidental bombing of the Chinese Embassy in Belgrade in 1999 by American bombs during the Kosovo conflict was a godsend to the Party.

The dissidents' fight to control the memory of the nation has now shifted from the Cultural Revolution to the 1989 massacre, with a string of petitions and letters calling for a reassessment. Yet their access to the media is still very limited and the dissemination of their views relies chiefly on foreign broadcasters such as Voice of America or the BBC. The Internet may change that if the Party proves powerless to control access to it.

The state has certainly proved powerless to stop many other recent changes such as the growth of underground churches or the Westernization of popular culture. The depoliticization of so many aspects of life means than on any given day one can switch on the television and see on one channel a programme of ballroom-dancing lessons and on another an earnest professor recounting the history of musicals from *West Side Story* to *The Sound of Music*. Many taboos on once forbidden subjects and books have been lifted and ordinary Chinese are now knowledgeable about the relative merits of such things as British soccer stars or Italian tenors.

Yet the Party still manages to prevent intellectuals from organizing themselves in the form of a political party, a non-government organization or even a discussion group. Han Fei's warnings on the need to forbid free association continue to be taken very seriously. In 1997 the Democracy Wall activist Xu Wenli judged the time ripe for the establishment of a China Democratic Party which briefly managed to form a network of 200 branches across the country. All its leaders were subsequently given long prison sentences.

Xu had embarked on this hazardous course because he had given up earlier hopes that the Communist Party would reform itself, saying that it was no different from the imperial rulers: the ideal of the Qing dynasty, 'one family under heaven', had been replaced by that of 'one party under heaven'. Indeed, far from moving towards accepting even the existence of another political party in Taiwan, it was attempting to bring the KMT and other parties in Taiwan under its control.

A common tactic of intellectuals trying to exert some influence has perversely been to demonstrate the hollowness of the state's claims to 'rule by law' by being imprisoned. When Xu Wenli or others have been arrested, they have been held, sometimes for years, without trial, without even necessarily being charged. And those trials that do take place are held without any real pretence at observing the laws of criminal procedure.

In October 1996 the veteran dissident Wang Xizhe and the literary critic Liu Xiaobo issued a joint letter calling on the Communist Party to honour its pre-1949 promises to guarantee all political freedoms after it won power.[32] The letter also called for the impeachment of Jiang Zemin and accused him of having violated the Constitution because he had declared that the PLA is under the 'absolute leadership' of the Party not the state. Liu was imprisoned without trial and Wang fled to the United States.

Shortly before the tenth anniversary of the 1989 Tiananmen protests I received an anonymous dissident's letter that declared: 'They have brainwashed the people by saying "Although the system is not perfect, the solution is not to break it but to repair it." But in fact for everything to be really free, it must be broken and rebuilt.' Such a belief in radical solutions is nevertheless rare among intellectuals. The majority believe that reform is a historical inevitability and that the Party will one day be bound by the laws it passes. Even Bao Tong, the former political secretary of Zhao Ziyang, emerged after seven years in solitary confinement unshaken in this belief. In 1998, on the ninth anniversary of the Tiananmen protest, not long after he had been released, I went to visit him. When I asked if my visit would endanger him, he replied, 'The Constitution guarantees freedom of opinion so I cannot get into trouble. This interview will be a test of that and the principle that everyone is equal before the law, including those in power.'

In 1989 Bao had been detained on his way to a meeting in Zhongnanhai and taken to Qincheng Prison. Only three years later was he shown an arrest order, tried in a one-day trial and given a seven-year sentence for leaking state secrets and inciting counter-revolution. The light in his cell was never turned off and he was allowed only one visit every two months. Even after his sentence expired he was kept in an unofficial prison for another year.

Over lunch cooked in his flat's tiny kitchen, he talked about his life. He had joined the Party in 1949 and ten years later had witnessed at first hand the horrors of the Great Leap Forward. His protests in

1959 led to him being condemned as a rightist. His wife, who had also visited famine-stricken regions in Henan province where millions had died, had stayed in the Party. An embarrassed silence greeted my questions about the famine before Bao added gently, 'She is still a Party member.' Bao's own failure to bring about change had not shaken his loyalty to the Party either. 'It was better to do something and keep the momentum going than do nothing,' he insisted. 'Our Party could have carried out its own reforms in its own time.' Bao had pinned his hopes on one man, Zhao Ziyang, just as Dai Huang had believed in Hu Yaobang.

Bao Tong is no longer allowed to give interviews and has, like Zhao Ziyang, remained under house arrest. To an outsider his continued belief in the Party as the only vehicle for change is astonishing but perhaps it is also realistic. Whether the Chinese and Western political traditions can be blended in China remains to be seen. Yet it remains an irony that the suffocating and sterile embrace of the state that has hopelessly weakened the country's cultural vitality has also left it vulnerable to the spell of imported and largely Western culture. At the same time, the failure of the revolt in 1989 has left the military as the most powerful political caste, as the next chapter discusses.

12

Secret Empire

WHEN CHINA AND the Soviet Union were preparing for a nuclear Armageddon in the late 1960s, over 100,000 workers and their families were brought from all over China to a remote valley in the Taihang mountains on the border of Shanxi and Hebei provinces. Here they set about building Factory 5419, designed to produce T54 tanks.

Wang Zhizhong arrived at the factory in 1970 as a fresh-faced engineering graduate from Peking University. Then there was just a dirt track running through the impoverished villages scattered around the base of the wooded mountains.

'We believed war was coming so we had to sacrifice everything to defend the country against an invasion,' he recalled as he sat in front of a large new desk in his office. Through the window behind him lay the vast and silent yard of one of the factory's subsidiary plants which had once employed over 5,000 men to make engine castings.[1]

Marshal Lin Biao, at one time Mao's chosen successor and head of the army, had reacted to the pitched battles fought in 1969 between China and the Soviet Union along the Amur and Ussuri Rivers by ordering the construction of possibly the world's biggest tank factory. Factory 5419 was only one of many built at the time but in one year alone it was capable of supplying 2,500 tanks.

Ironically, it was the Soviets themselves who had been responsible for showing the Chinese how to make tanks. In the 1950s, the Soviet Union had built 156 major industrial complexes in China in perhaps the biggest transfer of technology in history. A third of these projects were devoted to enabling Mao to equip his forces with jet fighters, battleships, tanks and missiles. The Soviets had built another giant tank factory, code-named 617, in Baotou, Inner Mongolia, which could make 1,000 tanks a year but this lay only a hundred miles from the front line, the border with the Soviet-run People's Republic of Mongolia. The Baotou factory now supplied the experts, the technology and the machinery to help start the new plant.

The original plan envisaged building twenty-two factories and a power plant scattered over three counties to protect them against bombing, as well as the roads and railways to connect them. In addition, the workforce needed housing, schools, a hospital and shops. Yet by the time Mao died in 1976, the money had run out and Deng Xiaoping began to cancel defence procurement orders. Planned output was then scaled back to 500 tanks a year but finally, in 1984, even before the complex was ready to start full-scale production, all orders were cancelled. Indeed, only a handful of the outdated tanks were ever built.

'At most we managed to build six battle tanks a year,' Wang said, and added with a smile, 'but the Iran-Iraq war saved us. We supplied tank parts to both sides.' A tall northern Chinese, he seemed more at ease than others with the past. Someone had always come along to sink more money into the project and now an American company had taken him on when it decided to modernize the plant to make commercial engine castings.

Another engineer, Gao Ruoqin, a Cantonese, was less sanguine as he showed me around the complex. Altogether, he reckoned the state had invested the equivalent of US$3.5 billion in the tank complex.

'It is such a pity, such a waste,' Gao muttered as we stood before two towers made of red brick, their windows broken, the branches of a tree poking out through one. 'It's a coal gasification plant', he explained. 'We designed it ourselves, but it never worked either.'

Down the road, and at the end of another valley spur, stood the main tank assembly plant, a low building that stretched for half a mile in the lee of a steep buff by a river. There was almost no one inside apart from a handful of workers standing around a turret which would eventually be fitted on to one of the four tanks that now constitute the plant's entire annual output. Elsewhere, we found several other men tinkering with the interior fittings of two motor-coaches, which represented the assembly plant's effort at switching to civilian production.

Each factory was now responsible for its own economic survival. Wang, the veteran of a succession of failed commercial ventures, showed me glossy brochures full of pictures of golf buggies, a sight-seeing vehicle for funparks, heavy-duty clutches, radiators, train axles and other unidentifiable metal widgets. In the 1990s, the complex had been taken over by the China International Trust and Investment Corporation (CITIC) which managed to find a partner, a Singaporean company that sank US$300 million into a production line for making diesel engines. Almost inevitably, the new enterprise failed.

'We now have debts of 2 billion yuan and wages are three or four months behind,' said Wang. 'But it is the same story at 80 per cent of the military plants in Shanxi.'

Gao laughed when he heard what Wang had told me. He said that half the workforce had been laid off and the other half had not been paid for nine months.

When I visited Factory 5419 in 1998, it was reckoned that two-thirds of China's defence industry capacity probably lay idle. China's total battle-tank production had slumped to fewer than a hundred per year. In ten years, the country's vast military shipyards had built only six destroyers and thirteen frigates for the world's largest navy. However, though the PLA's procurement orders had been falling steadily since the late 1970s, it still possessed the world's biggest armoury – 10,000 battle tanks, 5,000 military aircraft and the world's largest fleet – all of it built with Soviet technology dating from the 1950s. Aircraft production had peaked in 1974 when 540 military air-craft were produced but by the mid-1990s just 80 were being made each year. Not a single bomber had been made since 1990.[2]

The vast military effort to counter the perceived Soviet threat probably bankrupted the whole Chinese economy in the 1970s. For the PLA's industrial-defence complex comprised not only several thousand gigantic 'backbone' projects but also thousands of other smaller *bingqi*, or military-run plants. Shanxi province alone built hundreds, including iron works, coalmines, textile factories and pharmaceutical plants to enable the province's economy to function in wartime even if it was cut off from the rest of the country. Some of these plants, including ordnance factories, were actually built inside mountains to shelter them from the expected Soviet nuclear attack. 'Should the Russians launch a nuclear attack and destroy every Chinese city, there will still be over a hundred million Chinese to carry on,' Mao declared.[3]

Indeed, one of the major differences that divided Beijing from Moscow at the time was Nikita Khrushchev's thaw with the United States and their combined efforts to lessen the threat of nuclear war. Mao believed that the bomb was a 'paper tiger', declaring to Khrushchev that it would not matter if China lost 300 million people in a nuclear war: the other half of the population would survive to ensure victory. In the same vein he told India's Prime Minister, Jawaharlal Nehru, 'China has many people. They cannot be bombed out of existence. The death of ten or twenty million is nothing to be afraid of.'[4]

Although China is generally presented as having been plunged into chaos during the Cultural Revolution, during that period Mao launched a series of ambitious measures to ensure the survival of his regime and the PLA no matter what happened. Starting in the early 1960s, much of China's economic strength was devoted to building what was called the third front. The first front comprised the defences along the coast facing Taiwan that were intended to counter the threat posed by the Americans. The second referred to the large-scale defence and heavy industry of Manchuria close to the Soviet border. The third, generally known as the Third Line, consisted of building or relocating from the coastal regions some 29,000 factories in the undeveloped interior at an estimated cost of US$54 billion.[5]

The undertaking has few parallels in history. Chiang Kai-shek had moved some factories up the Yangtze to Chongqing in the 1930s, and Stalin had relocated many factories to Siberia in order to resist Hitler's invasion. Neither of these efforts, however, matched the scale of Mao's undertaking. 'It was', conclude two Western scholars, 'the most daring and perhaps ill-considered industrial relocation plan that any country ever attempted. From the mid-1960s to the mid-'70s nearly half of China's budget went to Third Line construction.'[6]

At its peak, the Third Line employed over 16 million workers in addition to nearly 5 million troops in uniform. Enterprises in the Third Line included 75 per cent of China's nuclear industry, 60 per cent of its electronics industry and half the armaments and aerospace industries as well as 300,000 scientists and other experts employed in research and development institutes. Submarines were built far from the sea in Jiangxi province and torpedoes were tested at a research establishment built on the shores of Lake Koko-nor (Qinghai Hu) on the Tibetan plateau, almost as far from the ocean as it is possible to get on the planet.

The factories, airports, rocket-launching centres and much more were located in remote and inaccessible areas. Indeed, some Western academics believe that just building the necessary roads, railway lines and tunnels to link them together absorbed as much as 80 per cent of the funds allocated to the whole project. Huge efforts went into creating an underground military-industrial complex. Part of the Shanxi tank factory was built underground, for example, and Guizhou province with its hollow limestone mountains, employed 700,000 people in its subterranean military plants. Many of these factories are still functioning in their hollowed-out mountainsides. 'I've been in some of them in Shanxi,' Wang told me. 'They were terrible. Water leaked everywhere and it was hard to breathe. Many people died trying to build them as well.'

During the 1970s much of China's urban population was also put to work building gigantic underground nuclear shelters to protect the Party élite. Tourist guides in Beijing still take visitors to a textile shop in an old part of the city. Behind the counter, a button opens a trap door to reveal stairs to a separate subterranean world. A long escalator takes visitors down to a dank network of tunnels linking shops, restaurants, cinemas and dormitories with 40,000 beds. Wuhan has China's largest underground complex, covering 500,000 square feet. That of Shenyang covers 338,000 square feet. Still others were built in Guangzhou, Chengdu, Tianjin and elsewhere.

Underground shelters were built not only to house cities or factories but also to protect tanks, ships and aeroplanes. In the Western Hills outside Beijing, one can still come across caves cut out of the hillsides to shelter individual tanks, though they have now been abandoned. Another mountainside near the Ming tombs was exacavated to enable planes to shelter and take off unseen by the enemy. In Shandong province 25,000 men spent eleven years burrowing into the cliffs to create tunnels that could shelter both submarines and destroyers from a nuclear attack.

So vast is the PLA's secret empire that, even after the transfer to civilian use of an inventory listed in a 1998 national defence paper as comprising 101 airports, 29 harbours and docks, 300 special railway lines, 90 telecommunications cables, 1,000 warehouses and 22 million square feet of land, including many historical sites, it is still able to support the world's largest armed forces.[7]

It is not easy to explain why relations between China and the Soviet Union deteriorated so quickly in the 1960s, why fraternal assistance turned into enmity and fear. In the 1950s, Moscow had provided the technology and the Chinese the manpower to fight the Korean War. During that conflict China suffered a million casualties. The Defence Minister, Peng Dehuai, who had directed the fighting, was committed to transforming the PLA – which includes the navy and airforce, as well as the army – into a regular mechanized force on the Soviet model. However, after Peng criticized Mao's disastrous Great Leap Forward in 1959, he was purged. His successor, Lin Biao, made the PLA a more powerful political instrument than the Party itself, and a force that was prepared to fight a 'people's war'. The annual military parades were abandoned and rank and insignia discarded as the PLA became the 'chief repository of Mao thought' and, of course, of his military doctrines. 'It is still fundamentally true that it is men, not materials, that decide the outcome of war. If a war breaks out, we will mobilize the masses to swamp the enemy in the ocean of people's war,' explained a *Beijing Review* editorial even as late as 1982. Under the slogan, 'everyone a soldier', some 220 million Chinese were trained in the militia so that they too could play a role in luring an enemy into the interior and then destroying him.[8] Having over-seen the creation of this vast war machine for use against the Soviets, Lin Biao disappeared in 1971, dying in a plane crash while fleeing to Moscow after a failed *coup d'état* against Mao.

It is also hard to know how seriously Mao took his concept of a 'people's war'. During the Korean War, China did manage to offset the vast technological superiority of the largely American forces by relying on human waves of infantry equipped with just a few days' rations and a handful of bullets. The ratio of casualties suffered was perhaps 20:1 but the Chinese 'volunteers' were able to fight the UN forces to a standstill. On the other hand, China also spared no expense both in building up a huge armoury and in developing nuclear weapons and rockets. The first Chinese nuclear bomb was produced at Factory 221, now a city called Xihai in Qinghai province on the Tibetan plateau. Like other Third Line complexes it too required the construction of a new railway as well as roads, schools, farms and a power station in a remote area. Large-scale facilities to test nuclear weapons were also built at Lop Nor in the deserts of neighbouring Xinjiang province; and in the remote mountains divid-ing Yunnan from Sichuan, and in Gansu and Shanxi, the PLA estab-lished three rocket-launching sites. In 1964 China successfully tested a nuclear bomb and a decade later it launched its first satellite into space.

Mao's concept of a people's war was never tested in the defence of China but the state did expend enormous resources in support-ing Communist guerrilla forces operating abroad. China armed and trained insurgency forces from all over the world but especially those of neighbouring countries, notably Cambodia's Khmer Rouge but also guerrilla forces in Laos, Thailand, Malaysia and Burma. In south-east Asia as well as in African states such as Ethiopia and Somalia, the aid was part of Mao's attempt to supplant Moscow as the leader of the Communist bloc. By far the most significant intervention was in Vietnam. The PLA sent over 400,000 troops and enormous quan-tities of arms and grain to assist Hanoi. While some of this aid went to helping guerrilla forces operating in the south, much of it was devoted to developing the regular armed forces of North Vietnam.

However, of far greater long-term significance than hazy notions of a 'people's war' has been the extraordinary political powers that have accrued to the PLA since the 1960s. After the failure of the Great Leap Forward, Mao used the PLA to crush all opposition within the Party. Mao's quotations were selected and distributed by the PLA in the form of the Little Red Book, and when the Cultural Revolution began in 1966, the PLA helped the students, now called Red Guards, to make revolution by transporting them around the country in military vehicles and housing them in army barracks.

The Red Guards persecuted the backbone of the Party leadership, arresting, imprisoning and publicly humiliating top Party cadres. Mao called on the military to 'support the left' and PLA units began to distribute arms to support Red Guard factions. As the scope of their attacks widened to include veteran PLA generals such as Peng Dehuai and Yang Shangkun, the power struggle turned into a civil war, with some parts of the military siding against the radical Maoist factions. In many parts of the country, the battles were fought with tanks, machine guns and anti-aircraft weapons. The worst incident took place in Wuhan where, in 1967, the military regional command instigated a *de facto* rebellion that led to large-scale fighting between military units. Army units loyal to Mao triumphed and the PLA then established control over all the organs of the state. PLA officers were assigned to run all newspaper and broadcasting facilities and were put in charge of all ministries and provincial governments. In principle, tripartite commissions, known as Revolutionary Committees and comprising Red Guards, veteran Party cadres and PLA commanders governed all cities and provinces. In reality, it was invariably the PLA who wielded real power and by the end of the 1960s it was rounding up Red Guards and disarming and disbanding their forces. When the violent phase of the Cultural Revolution ended in 1969, the PLA became in effect ruler of China's provinces. By 1970 at least 60 per cent of the 158 Party secretaries of various ranks in the provincial Party committees were army officers, and at Politburo meetings 13 of the 25 seats were occupied by men in uniform.[9]

Construction of the Third Line gave the PLA command over the country's industrial economy and its scientific resources. The export of Mao's revolution abroad gave it the final say on foreign relations.

And in the border regions, the PLA was in charge of both defence and a *de facto* colonization policy. In the 1950s demobilized troops were sent to build paramilitary settlements in territories where there had never been significant numbers of Han Chinese, such as Yunnan, Tibet, Xinjiang, Hainan Island, Inner Mongolia and most of Manchuria. Over 100,000 troops were dispatched to Heilongjiang's Great Northern Wilderness to fell trees, drain marshes and establish the Daqing oilfields. With the troops went large numbers of political prisoners to labour in slave camps identified only by their military code number. The largest such institution to survive into the Deng era is the Xinjiang Production and Construction Corps, founded in the 1950s by PLA troops. By the 1990s, the *bing tuan* (or military regiment), as the organization is known, had 2.9 million members who accounted for 14 per cent of Xinjiang's population. The *bing tuan* runs whole cities such as Korla, operates factories, farms a third of Xinjiang's arable land and produces 40 per cent of the province's cotton.[10]

The PLA's power did not stop there, however. Throughout China it policed the cities and guarded the prisons, while in the countryside demobilized NCOs were invariably appointed to controlling Party posts in the communes when they returned to their villages.

By the time China's economy cracked under the strain of maintaining this vast secret empire, in the mid-1970s, per capita food production had slumped to near-starvation levels and the output of military planes and tanks had reached its peak. In a speech delivered in 1975 but not made public until many years later, Deng Xiaoping called for a halt to the growth of the PLA: 'The number of people in the army has increased greatly, and military expenditure has become an increasingly large proportion of the national budget, with a great amount of money being spent on food and clothing for personnel. More importantly, the army has become bloated and is not a crack outfit that will make a good showing in combat.'[11]

Deng himself was then a vice premier but he was also a former PLA political commissar. With the backing of Marshals Nie Rongzhen and Ye Jianying, he staged a *coup d'état* after Mao's death in

1976 by arresting the Gang of Four led by Mao's widow, Jiang Qing. The Gang of Four had themselves begun to build up an armed militia in the cities which they apparently planned to mobilize if an armed struggle broke out after Mao's death.

Once firmly in power Deng attempted to halt the momentum of the arms build-up, to cut down the size of the PLA (which peaked at 4.75 million troops in 1981) and to reduce its political influence. Instead he sought to direct resources away from defence and into the civilian economy, to defuse foreign policy tensions and to create a smaller army staffed by better educated and technically proficient men. (Some believe that Deng deliberately sent the PLA into Vietnam in 1979 not to teach Vietnam a lesson but to make plain the need for change. In the brief border war, the PLA was successfully resisted by Vietnam's border guards and militia, and suffered 20,000 casualties.)

Deng began a drive to replace the PLA's Maoist 'people's war' officers with a properly educated officer corps. In 1978, the PLA reinstituted an officer training programme. In the following year ten of the eleven most senior commanders were replaced. Early retirement was sweetened by generous housing allowances, cars and pensions. Some of those who had been trained by the Soviets at home or abroad were reinstated, including veterans who had served in the Korean War under Peng Dehuai, but on the whole the emphasis was on promoting younger men. Deng laid down strict age limits: corps commanders could not be older than 55, divisional commanders 45, regimental commanders 35, and battalion commanders 30. By 1983, the PLA was recruiting its first university graduates, and in December 1985, it merged three academies to create a new University of Defence. A sweeping reorganization of the PLA's structure was also launched. The eleven military regions were merged into seven, and the thirty-five group armies were reduced to twenty-four. Many provincial military academies were also closed down or merged.

Accelerated promotion for younger officers led the PLA to claim in 1986 that 25 per cent of its officers on the active list were graduates. Yet finding jobs for those forced into retirement was not easy. In the past officers had automatically been assigned senior positions in government units or state factories but as the market economy developed, factories wanted proficient managers, and officers had to settle for lesser positions. In 1986, it was also revealed that 60 per cent of the officers due to retire had refused to do so, complaining that they had not been given a decent alternative. Nevertheless, in 1988 Deng issued a decree that all officers who had served for thirty years or more, or who had reached the age of 50, must retire; and a solution to the problem of retirees was found by shifting millions of men and officers into an expanding public security apparatus. The People's Armed Police (PAP), a paramilitary police force, was established in 1983. Between 1986 and 1992, it absorbed one million servicemen. In addition, 22 per cent of those army officers forced to retire were allocated jobs as judges, lawyers, procurators or prison wardens.[12]

As the country's infrastructure was placed under civilian control and as the PLA withdrew from institution after institution, many took off their uniforms but stayed in the same jobs. The 170,000 men of the PLA Railway Corps became employees of the Ministry of Railways. The Shenyang military region alone handed over thirty-six railway lines to civilian control. The men of the PLA Capital Construction Corps, who had helped build Shenzhen, became civilians as did many teachers and doctors, nurses, actors, writers, journalists and propaganda officials. Then, in 1985, Deng formally announced that over the next two years China would demobilize a million soldiers. At the end of 1986, Hu Yaobang went further, saying that the Party intended to reduce the armed forces by 2 million. The officially reported defence budget was slashed in 1981 by 25 per cent to 16.8 billion yuan, or 16 per cent of the total budget, and continued to fall in real terms until 1988 by which time its share of the state budget had dropped to 8.6 per cent.

Deng and his reformist lieutenants, Hu Yaobang and Zhao Ziyang, not only cut the army down to size but also tried to diminish its status. In the new constitution promulgated in 1982, the PLA was nominally placed under the supervision of a civilian body, the Central Military Commission, supposedly elected by the National People's Congress. The military was also supposed to be run by a ministry, like any other organ of state, and to be subject to laws passed by the National People's Congress. In 1988, the PLA took the symbolic step of reintroducing the ranks and insignia that had been abolished twenty-three years earlier. Soon afterwards, some troops began to appear in new dress uniforms, reputedly designed with the help of the French *haute couturier* Pierre Cardin.[13]

The 'normalization' of the PLA and the formal restoration of diplomatic ties with Washington and its NATO allies gave China the opportunity to acquire new military technology. Ever since President Nixon's breakthrough visit in 1972, China had been treated as a key player in the Cold War. Its estimated million troops along the border with the Soviet Union tied down huge amounts of Soviet hardware – 600,000 troops, 7 tank divisions, 1,500 fighter planes, long-range bomber fleets, intermediate-range ballistic missiles and nuclear warheads. In addition, China had a fleet of 31 nuclear submarines and 410 surface vessels. All this reduced the might which could be deployed in a Soviet invasion of Western Europe, and in retrospect may have played a role in the eventual collapse of Eastern bloc Communism.

In the 1980s, China reduced the threat it posed to Western powers by cutting off aid to most of its Communist allies such as Albania, Ethiopia and North Korea, and by reducing support for Communist insurgents around the world. Consequently, the West began to encourage military contacts and allow China to acquire modern military technology. The policy was extremely controversial, especially since so much military technology could be used for both military and civilian purposes, and as China began to trade more openly with the West, it was also difficult to monitor.

China liked to stress that its vast military-industrial defence complex was turning away from weapons production towards manufacturing civilian goods. Journalists were taken to see the Xian Aircraft Corporation whose 18,000 workers had stopped making bombers and now produced meat-grinders, noodle-makers, pots, window frames, low-quality cranes and even noisy washing-machines. Thousands of other factories switched to making light industrial products or went into joint-venture partnerships.

Mercedes Benz linked up with the huge tank factory in Baotou to make lorries and coaches. The Changhong Machinery Plant in Mianyang, in the mountains above the Sichuan basin, found a partner in Japan's National Corporation and switched from making radar equipment to producing television sets.[14]

Some of these metamorphoses were very successful. The renamed Changhong Electronics Group became the biggest and most profitable colour TV brand manufacturer in China. The Jialing Industrial Company, a munitions plant first moved from Shanghai to Chongqing by Chiang Kai-shek, teamed up with Honda to make motorcycles. Another well-known brand, the Changan mini-sedan called the Alto, is produced at a former military plant, the Jiangling Machinery Factory, which formed a partnership with Suzuki. In 1994, China claimed that the proportion of its defence-industrial output destined for the civilian market had risen from 7 per cent in the 1970s to 80 per cent.

Even so, Western countries were made uneasy by the PLA's success in exporting military hardware and know-how, and some questioned the wisdom of supporting its entry into the commercial space industry. Chinese arms exports rose steadily in the 1980s, reaching US$3 billion in 1988, and China benefited in particular from supplying both sides in the Iran-Iraq War and from the sale of missiles such as the M-11 and nuclear technology to other nervous countries in the Middle East.

As China pressed ahead with reform in the 1980s and relaxed price controls, the price of raw materials used by the defence industries rose, pushing up the price of weapons. At the same time defence plants were running at well under capacity and were being forced to sell their products at a loss. Western experts calculated that the PLA's budget only covered 70 per cent of its requirements. Provincial governments, which were obliged to keep local troops supplied with grain and other necessities, baulked at doing so at below market prices, and the central government had to keep issuing decrees to force them to meet their responsibility.

In 1985, Deng Xiaoping issued a directive allowing PLA units to earn money to make up the shortfall in their declining budgets. PLA hospitals could now admit anyone willing to pay the fees.

Construction and engineering battalions could bid for contracts to build bridges, canals and roads or to lay pipelines and cables. The 600 farms run by the PLA to feed itself began to sell their surplus on the open market and diversified into profitable sidelines. The PLA Airforce (PLAAF) opened airports to civilian use and began to run its own civilian passenger flights which were soon carrying 2.9 million people a year. The Navy did likewise, transporting commercial cargoes and allegedly smuggling illegal goods.[15]

Yet the income from all this commercial activity did little to raise the individual incomes of many PLA troops and retirees. Before the 1989 military crackdown in Beijing, morale was low. As the PLA's prestige and power declined, generals complained that it was increasingly hard to recruit peasants. Girls no longer wanted to marry officers, let alone privates, as their privileges vanished. PLA recruits earned 10 yuan a month and the basic salary of even a colonel was only 200 yuan a month, while some peasants boasted of becoming 10,000-yuan households. As inflation rose sharply, retired officers also found they were unable to maintain their standard of living, and many were unable to find accommodation in the midst of a chronic housing shortage. The PLA had occupied many buildings in the 1970s and turned them into barracks but these were now being handed back to civilian control.

By the time students began to protest in Tiananmen Square in 1989, the PLA's image had changed to such an extent that it no longer commanded much respect. When troops first appeared on the streets of Beijing and failed to impose martial law, this disdain was reinforced. The peasant recruits dressed in their shapeless baggy trousers and canvas shoes became the objects of derision, and for weeks people stood around the army trucks and armoured personnel carriers parked on the outskirts of Beijing and berated the barely literate peasant boys.

The shock troops who entered Beijing on the night of 3 June were altogether different, so different in fact that many claimed the army had given them drugs to make them more brutal. It has not become clear what units they were drawn from but reportedly there were elements taken from different regional commands. The Beijing garrison was said to have refused to take part in the action and later some of its officers were court-martialled. It was also reported that the leadership selected troops for the assault and then kept them isolated from all news and indoctrinated them into believing that the capital was occupied by 'hostile forces'.

Like a sudden flash of lightning illuminating a darkened scene, the massacre of civilians on the night of 3/4 June and the arrest of the official head of the Communist Party, Zhao Ziyang, shattered many illusions about the PLA. It was clearly not a 'people's army' but the army of the Party, and loyal not so much to the Party as an institution as to a cabal of octogenarian revolutionaries.* Real power in the land lay in the Communist Party's Central Military Commission (CMC) rather than the civilian body of that name set up under the aegis of the National People's Congress.

After Tiananmen, Jiang Zemin was made Chairman of the CMC, the first civilian to hold the post, but, surrounded by power-hungry veterans, notably Generals Yang Shangkun and his brother Yang Baibing, it took him time to gain their loyalty. Immediately after Tiananmen, China's defence budget was increased by 50 per cent, and there have been further steep increases since. However, Jiang has at the same time continued to pursue Deng's policy of reducing the size of the PLA and transferring its resources to civilian control. A further reduction in the number of troops was announced in December 1991 and in the following April there was talk of cutting at least half a million or even a million troops over the next five years. In 1993, 53,000 officers were discharged and in 1994 another 50,000.[16]

How many troops have been demobilized altogether is not certain but by the mid-1990s, experts believed there were 2.9 million soldiers and a reserve and militia force of 1.2 million. Three of the twenty-

---

* During most of the crisis the PLA and its commanders disappeared from view. Later in 1989, Deng justified the clampdown by explaining that there had been a real threat of civil war. 'Turmoil in China will be unlike that in Eastern Europe or the Soviet Union,' he said. 'If it happens in China, one faction will control part of the army and the other, another part. A civil war could then erupt.' (Willy Wo-lap Lam, *China after Deng Xiaoping*, p. 201).

four combined group armies had been eliminated as had over thirty units at or above group army level. The heaviest cuts occurred among the infantry but even the airforce was reduced by 25 per cent. In 1997, following the death of Deng Xiaoping, Jiang Zemin announced a further reduction of 500,000 troops. By 2010, the PLA's manpower is expected to be between 1.75 million and 2 million, with around half a million troops on active service, roughly equal to the size of US forces in 1998. Whether this process of demobilization has actually reduced the burden on the exchequer is by no means clear. Many have continued to be transferred to the public security apparatus. By the end of 1997, it had some 4 million people on its payroll (the PAP alone is thought to number 1.8 million), making it considerably larger than the PLA itself.

Western experts also continue to debate the extent of the burden of China's defence spending. Many assume it is five or six times the figure declared in the annual budget and accounts, which means that it accounts for a far larger share of GDP than is the case in Western countries. The Stockholm International Peace Research Institute, for instance, considers that in 1996 China spent US$56 billion, or 5.7 per cent of its GDP, on defence compared to the United States which spent 3.6 per cent of its GDP.[17]

One reason for the confusion lies in the difficulty of distinguishing between the armed forces and the defence sector and its business interests. Some estimate that only 25 per cent of PLA ground forces actually serve in combat-ready units, perhaps just 275,000 men, and that the rest work in fields or factories. The PLA General Logistics Department alone employs 300,000 people in 250 factories processing food or making clothing and medicines.

In the early 1990s, as the domestic economy took off and there was further inflation, the PLA's financial crisis became more acute, despite its bigger budget. Jiang responded by authorizing the army to expand its business activities, with extraordinary results. The PLA General Staff Headquarters began to run an opulent five-star hotel, the Palace, in the middle of Beijing. An army barracks in another part of Beijing became the Hot Spot Disco where go-go girls gyrated in cages. The Second Artillery, the PLA's nuclear missile force, opened up a franchise of Baskin Robbins, the American icecream company, and the Guangzhou Military District HQ set up a stock-broking firm, J&A Securities, though that was closed down in 1998.

Big military units set up conglomerates such as the Poly Group, the Kaili Group and Norinco. Often run by the children of senior generals, they began to operate like successful multinationals. The General Logistics Department established the Xinxing Corporation which employs 100,000 people and has interests in every sector of the economy including chemicals, specialized steel, real estate, hotels and textiles. Its annual manufacturing revenues are estimated at 1.2 billion yuan and one of its most successful companies, the 999 Enterprises (Sanjiu Pharmaceutical) based in Shenzhen, which sells herbal medicines, is listed on the Hong Kong stock exchange. Norinco, the North Industries Corporation which operates many defence factories including Chongqing's motorcycle plants, is listed on the Irish stock exchange. Other units, such as Huitong Communications, have made use of military radio frequencies to launch themselves into businesses offering pagers and mobile-phone services. Western companies have been eager to set up joint ventures with such well-connected units and by 1997 there were 576 of them with a total capital investment of almost US$1 billion.[18]

Reports of the success of the military conversion have, however, begun to ring alarm bells abroad. The CIA has estimated that in 1993 the profits of PLA Inc. topped US$5 billion and were being ploughed back into the acquisition of new military technology. Warnings about the threat posed by PLA Inc. were also voiced in *The Coming Conflict with China*, published in 1997, whose authors worry that 'growing Chinese economic and military strength, linked to the nation's ambitions and to its xenophobic impulses, are making it more rather than less aggressive'.[19]

Some American experts, however, feel that the military conversion has been a failure and that the PLA remains a millstone around the neck of the economy. For example, defence plants such as those making munitions and small arms soaked up subsidies worth 20 billion yuan in 1993 – a year when the economy was booming – and 50 billion yuan in 1995. One study has concluded that 'The few successes are vastly outnumbered by the problems and potential bankruptcies. In markets where there is competition, the defence plants do not do well.' By the late 1990s, perhaps two-thirds of all defence factories were operating in the red, especially those making textiles and machine tools.[20]

In addition, half of the country's loss-making SOEs are reckoned to be former defence plants. In 1997, tens of thousands of unpaid workers at former Third Line textile factories in Mianyang and Nanchong in remote areas of Sichuan province went on the rampage.[21] To modernize such enterprises and help them to move out of the mountains and into 52 high-tech parks set up near cities or to the coastal ports, the government has launched two pro-grammes, the Torch Plan and the Spark Plan, to channel investment into new technology. Yet, as one authority has concluded, the strat-egy has not worked: 'defence conversion has been a disaster. And it is getting worse.'[22]

Shanxi's Factory 5419 was fortunate to be rescued by two American companies, Caterpillar and ASIMCO, which decided to invest US$98 million in one of the plants to supply engine castings to domestic and overseas buyers. Heading the conversion of the factory was a genial American, Ron Martin, who had worked for Caterpillar for thirty years around the world. The joint venture, which has created 500 jobs, has brought hope to the whole commu-nity, even paying for computers for the schools and hiring an American to teach English to the children.

'We were bankrupt. Nobody knew how to save this factory, it was hopeless. But the American Ma Ding [Martin] saved us,' one of the engineers told me, still wondering at the unexpected generosity and optimism of the Americans.

'It is true, no one else was willing to come here. When I first arrived in December 1995, they didn't even have enough money to buy coal to heat the guesthouse. It was so cold, I slept with my clothes on,' Martin recalled.

The guesthouse is now an oasis of American comfort amidst the cramped tenements of the workers. The handful of Americans have hot water, satellite TV, cellular phones and a large stock of imported provisions. In the canteen, Chinese co-workers spread peanut butter on their steamed buns with their chopsticks. Many have been sent to America on training programmes.

'We had to change the way people think and interact,' Martin said. 'There was no discipline, no motivation and terrible management. Now if we say we want this, it comes.'

His engineers were busy installing imported smelting furnaces, moulding lines and core-making machines. Yet despite all this activity vast areas of the factory were still going to be left unused, though the specially built military single-track railway line and its steam engines that link the site to the coast may eventually be put to work shipping finished goods. As for the rest of the tank complex, the central government had washed its hands of it and placed it, and its 100,000 inhabitants, in the hands of the local government. Local officials then declared it the 'Shanxi Huaxin Economic and Technological Development Zone' and offered investors five years of tax-free profits.

The likelihood that such investors will materialize seems slim. In July 1998, Jiang Zemin divested the PLA of its responsibility for all such factories, placing them instead under the control of a civilian body, the Commission for Science, Technology and Industry for National Defence (COSTIND). Those defence factories that still function as purely military manufacturing establishments are now concentrated under the wing of the PLA's General Armaments Department.

The PLA is also now supposed to be cutting its links with its profitable ventures, such as property-related joint ventures like the Palace Hotel. These ventures were often able to avoid paying normal business taxes and import duties and were in fact beyond the control of any civilian agency. In exchange for relinquishing these money-earners, the PLA has reportedly agreed to accept annual payouts of between 30 and 50 billion yuan as compensation while local governments have undertaken responsibility for the liabilities of the loss-makers, put at over 100 billion yuan.[23]

This move to divest the PLA of its business arm has been prompted by public indignation at the corruption spawned by the PLA and by the realization that few within the PLA have actually benefited from its business activities. In 1994 Jiang ordered all active service personnel to withdraw from business activities. At the same time newspaper editorials criticized the PLA for abandoning its fine traditions of 'plain living and hard struggle' in favour of 'mammon-ism, hedonism and individualism'. Xinhua singled out for praise the Second Artillery's missile brigade because its men refused to be entertained at local restaurants or bars and declined all invitations to go into business. Anger at the huge gap that had opened up between the living standards of enlisted men and those of senior command-ers led to army officers in the Beijing military region 'voluntarily' handing back 787 'excessively large' homes.[24]

Evidence of just how badly paid most troops are occasionally sur-faces in the press. In 1999 a survey of 163 officers in the East China Fleet found that most of them were deep in debt and resented the fact that they were earning far less than their relatives on civvy street.[25] Matters came to a head in 1999 when two senior officers were executed after being found guilty of selling state secrets to Taiwan for a total of US$1.6 million. The two officers had revealed details of the military exercises and missile tests carried out in order to intimidate Taiwan during its elections in 1995 and 1996.* In response Jiang Zemin froze all pay rises for the PLA.[26]

The PLA's efforts to project force and give credibility to China's aspirations to become a superpower have in the last two decades relied heavily on bluff. Once the Iran-Iraq War was over, the PLA's annual sales of arms fell in the early 1990s to around US$100 million. Some of China's customers such as Thailand complained openly about the poor quality and unreliability of arms they had purchased, and China's own efforts to modernize its weapons by building a new fighter jet and designing nuclear-powered submarines had by the close of the 1980s ended in failure. The military aviation industry, which had built up a capacity to produce perhaps 1,000 planes a year, was unable even to make the transition to civilian production despite repeated attempts to find foreign partners. China has had to rely on Boeing and Airbus to supply nearly all its commercial aircraft.

---

* These threats of force occurred in late 1995, when Taiwan was holding free elec-tions to the Legislative Assembly, and in spring 1996 at the time of the first free presidential elections.

China's military vulnerability, despite the plethora of planes, tanks and battleships, became all too apparent during the Gulf War in 1991 with the rapid and total rout of Iraq's invasion force in Kuwait. The Iraqi force was equipped with technology similar to that used by the PLA, as well as with a quantity of arms made in China. Unsurprisingly, China's huge arsenal began to be referred to as 'the world's largest museum for obsolete weapons'.[27] 'High technology has changed the way of fighting,' admitted General Liu Huaqing, vice chairman of the Central Military Committee, in June 1991.[28]

The Chinese airforce is hobbled by its lack of range and speed. Chinese pilots cannot even fly in bad weather because their radar screens are unreliable. Since the Gulf War, China has largely abandoned efforts to modernize its existing planes and has bought Russian Sukhoi-27 supersonic aircraft and S-300 air defence missiles and Israeli electronic reconnaissance technology.[29] It has also acquired French Mirage jets as well as helicopters and missile defence systems from the United States. The importance of strengthening the PLAAF became all the more apparent in 1999 during the Kosovo conflict. While Belgrade – with defence systems comparable to those possessed by China – managed to hide some of its weapons from NATO air forces, its air defences were unable to inflict a single casualty.[30]

The PLA Navy is similarly at a disadvantage. Although larger in terms of ships and manpower than the US Navy, it is tied to its coastal waters and seems entirely inadequate even for the mounting of an invasion across the 100-mile-wide Taiwan Straits. American commentators have talked mockingly of China having to launch a 'million-man swim'. In the 1990s, the Navy bought few domestic warships and, despite talk of building an aircraft-carrier, turned instead to the Russians for attack submarines and destroyers.

The infantry too is handicapped by what are termed its 'short arms and slow legs'. In other words, or so it is said, it can only move as fast as it can walk. Its low level of mechanization is one problem but poor communications and training mean that the PLA also has difficulty in co-ordinating different units and large bodies of troops. The PLA exercises directed against Taiwan in 1996 showed that only 10 per cent of the troops deployed could manoeuvre at any one time because of poor communications. At the end of 1999, Jiang Zemin launched a programme to centralize the management of the three armed forces in order to reduce logistical and communications difficulties.[31]

China has seen the military gap with the United States steadily widen in an era of 'smart weapons', and the embargo on weapons sales introduced after the 1989 Tiananmen massacre has made it difficult to acquire Western military know-how except by stealth. To remedy this shortfall China published a book detailing how agents should obtain military technology, especially from America, by accessing open or secret sources. *Sources and Methods of Obtaining National Defence Science and Technology Intelligence*, written in 1991 by Huo Zhongwen and Wang Zongxiao, specialists at the China National Defence Science and Technology Information Centre, declared that 80 per cent of what was needed could be obtained from available sources and it then went on to outline the covert methods to be used in obtaining the other 20 per cent. Anger at China's espionage efforts came to a head in 1999 when the United States Congress published the Cox Report which brought the issue to public attention amid claims that China had stolen nuclear secrets from the Los Alamos Laboratories in Nevada.[32]

In the absence of an up-to-date conventional arsenal, China's claims to great-power status rest largely on its nuclear weapons and missile forces. The technology was acquired at the end of the 1950s either from the Soviet Union or from the United States through the defection of a handful of scientists such as Qian Xuesen. He helped build the first missile, the Dongfeng-1, based on the P-2 designs given by Moscow in the 1950s. These in turn were based on the Nazis' V2 flying-bomb which both Russian and American scientists, including Qian Xuesen, examined after the Second World War. Since then China has continued to develop its missile technology and by 1999 had successfully test-fired the Dongfeng 31, an intercontinental missile capable of carrying a single 700-kg nuclear warhead. In a conflict, the PLA can also draw on long-range, medium-range and tactical missiles which can be fired from land-based mobile launchers or from submarines.

The size of China's nuclear arsenal is unknown but is thought to number around 300, including neutron bombs. China is also reported to have earmarked funds to develop second-strike capabilities in case of an attack as neighbouring countries such as India acquire long-range missiles and nuclear weapons. However, the future of China's missile arsenal has been put into question by the development of Star Wars-type anti-missile defence shields which may shelter some potential adversaries, including Taiwan, and destroy China's ability to strike first. China is therefore investing in space exploration, and plans to put a man in space and build a space station are intended to help China keep abreast of the big powers. The changing technology and growing cost of new weapons, however, pose the risk that China might be tempted to overstretch a limited budget to a dangerous extent.[33]

China plans to close the technological gap by 2010. To do so many expect that it will have to scrap four-fifths of its existing hardware and continue to reduce the size of its armed forces. And as the new technology becomes increasingly important, so the PLA will need to retire its older generals and replace the officer corps with university graduates. A very different PLA ought to emerge from these developments but its political role has barely begun to change.

As long as the PLA's primary role is to maintain the Party's monopoly of power and enforce its authority over the population, it is unlikely that it will become a professional and apolitical force as is the case in Western democracies. Jiang Zemin's anointed successor, Hu Jintao, another civilian with no military background, has been made first vice-chairman of the Party's Central Military Commission. Yet the process that was begun in the 1980s and interrupted by Tiananmen of putting the army under the supervision of a civilian government, as the Constitution specifies, has hardly begun in earnest. The PLA still functions in complete secrecy as a state within the state, answerable to no one but a handful of men at the top of the Party. It is even hard to make contact with the world's biggest army. It operates on a completely separate and secret telephone network, and foreigners are rarely taken to military installations or allowed to see PLA forces taking part in exercises. Outside China, the lasting image of the PLA remains its assault and occupation of Beijing in 1989. Within China, its true strength, its technological reach, its budget and indeed its function cannot be openly discussed. How much is being hidden can only be guessed at as long as the PLA remains fused with the Communist Party and is not subject to the scrutiny of a normal civilian government. The emergence of such a government, as the following chapter discusses, still lies in the future. The Party's chief instrument of power is a bureaucratic apparatus that is simply a mirror of the Party itself.

13

Tremble and Obey

THE NOISE EMANATING from the crowds of civil servants mingling in the thickly carpeted meeting halls as they attended the Third International Administrative Conference was a polite murmur. All the delegates were in suits except for Hou Jianling, department chief in China's Ministry of Personnel. He had put on his most formal attire, a well-cut dark blue Mao jacket and trousers, the jacket buttoned up to the throat, one of its breast pockets buttoned down, the other displaying three fountain pens whose silver clips shone faintly as if polished.

It was 1998. China was playing host to the International Institute of Administrative Sciences, the global union for civil servants, and Hou was one of the stars. The audience was listening to him outline China's long history of civil service examinations and the numerous regulations which were further perfecting the system.

Hou explained how his department, in charge of policy and the regulation of the civil service, had drawn up rules on nepotism, one in a series of new decrees designed to fight corruption. The regulations contained eighteen clauses that listed measures to ensure that officials could not employ anyone related to the fourth degree. They also listed the punishments to be meted out should the regulations be breached. In addition, Hou went on to explain how, in drafting the regulations, he had first examined the code of officials promulgated by the Qin dynasty, the Han and the Tang. He was particularly keen on the latter.

'In the Qin dynasty, the punishments were too severe, decapitation or branding and penal labour. Those of the Tang dynasty were more reasonable and comprehensive,' he said, taking off his horn-rimmed spectacles to polish them.

By the end of his speech Hou had described how he was creating a new administrative structure, governed by interlocking regulations, which by the year 2008 would give China a perfect system, and one more akin to a Western civil service. Instead of cadres there would be civil servants, and instead of *renzhi* – arbitrary rule by man – there would be *fazhi*, rule by law.

The work had begun in 1992 and had so far covered civil service admission exams, annual performance reviews, a new civil service school, a new wage system and the end of the job-for-life iron rice bowl. Since 1949, only 3,000 officials had ever been sacked. Now they would be severely, but of course fairly, judged on their performance. Officials would have to be honest too – even their incomes would have to be made public.

Hou rather relished the thought that with each new round of regulations, he was moving closer and closer to perfection. To his knowledge there had since 1949 been nine such reforms of the bureaucracy, and the number of ministries and departments had ebbed and flowed. Still, though the bureaucracy was being refined, at the same time it kept growing in size, and its very complexity brought new problems.

'There are now 35 million bureaucrats and it is certain that their numbers will keep growing,' he said when later we sat down together for an interview. And then, without admitting any contradiction, he added in the next breath that under new reforms, still being planned, the number of ministries was to be cut still further. Ten years before there had been 100 but by the year 2000 there would be just 30.

'By the time the socialist market economy is fully established, it will be possible to create a permanent government structure,' he declared, with such conviction that for a moment I believed him.[1]

Hundreds of thousands, perhaps millions of Chinese devote their lives to this never-ending, never-changing labour, drawing up plans, laws and regulations, gathering statistics and publishing investigative reports. No sooner has one round of change been effected than the cycle of meetings, regulations, inspection tours and decision-making begins again. Yet the Chinese bureaucracy seems such a product of pure enlightenment, designed on such rational grounds, that it is no wonder so many have admired it.

China can justifiably claim to have invented the first modern state with the system of national administration established by Qinshi Huangdi in the third century BC, under which state officials were appointed for the first time, though strictly speaking, civil service examinations were not introduced until the Tang dynasty (AD 619–907). In the state of Qin, under the influence of the Legalist school, the aristocracy was stripped of its privileges, and its sons were no longer automatically permitted to succeed their fathers in senior government posts. As the historian Sima Qian (145–?86 BC) explained, 'The Legalist school does not discriminate on the basis of closeness of personal relationship or status of noble lineage but makes decisions based uniformly on law. Thus the sentiments of kinship and respect are eradicated.' Rather, the ruler sought out talented scholars, appointed them on merit and promoted on achievement.[2]

A Legalist state was tightly planned and strictly utilitarian, regulated by laws that ordered every aspect of life and that were enforced by a code of graduated punishments. According to the Legalist philosopher Guan Zong (?–645 BC), 'The ruler is the creator of the law. The ministers are the keepers of the law. The people are the objects of the law.'[3]

The laws were explicitly coercive, as a later Legalist, Han Fei (280?–233 BC), noted: 'Laws are commands that are only displayed in government offices so that the people are aware in their minds what punishment or reward will be in store.'[4] Subjects were expected to obey the laws out of fear, not out of loyalty to the law-giver, respect for traditions evolved over centuries or because of a belief in a higher being.

Officials applied the law but they themselves had also to obey it: 'Officials are responsible for maintaining the law and performing duties but those who act in violation of the law of the king should be executed without the possibility of pardon: that punishment should also be extended to members of their families to the third degree,' recommended Shang Yang (?–338 BC), another of the early

Legalists.[5] Indeed, even the emperors of the last imperial dynasty, the Qing, ended their instructions to officials with the injunction 'Tremble and obey'.

Under the Legalist school, the ruler himself was above the law and so not bound by it but able to change it at will. There was therefore little distinction in ancient China between laws, regulations and administrative orders. By the same token the fixed legal code of punishments was not designed to place limits on the arbitrary power of the ruler but rather to enforce the implementation of his will. Officials were supposed to have as little personal discretion as possible in their interpretation of the law so that their actions would not be tempered by traditional morals, personal sentiment or initiative.

The Legalists also had a great deal of advice to give on how to run an efficient bureaucracy, one that would not develop interests of its own that it might favour over those of the ruler. Han Fei recommended that a ruler prevent his administrators from knowing too much and insisted that there should be no horizontal communication between different departments. 'The way of the wise ruler is such that one person is assigned to only one official post, and one official post is responsible for only one job . . . The hundreds of officials should have access [to the ruler], and the ministers should all converge like the spokes of the wheel with the [ruler at the] centre.'

This cold, rational and purely functional blueprint of statecraft bears a striking resemblance to the totalitarian governments of the twentieth century. Legalists aspired to create a state in which officials were impersonal tools in the hands of the ruler, and the common people were docile and obedient. Qinshi Huangdi is said to have wished to have subjects as close to automatons as possible, and the terracotta warriors found in his tomb are therefore a fitting symbol of his aspirations.

Naturally, many other influences have played an important role in shaping China's culture, not least of course Confucianism, but it is striking how the debt owed to the Legalist tradition is symbolically acknowledged by the current Chinese government. It ensures that all visiting foreign heads of state travel to the Qin Emperor's grave at Xi'an, but none are taken to Confucius's birthplace in Shandong nor to Wuhan, where the rebellion that led to the overthrow of the Qing dynasty and the birth of republican China began. Nor are the memorial hall in Nanjing to Sun Yat-sen, hailed as the father of modern China, or the school in Shanghai where the Communist Party was founded included in the official itinerary.

When, in 1997, President Jiang Zemin became the first Chinese leader to pay a state visit to the United States for almost twenty years, he started his tour symbolically by visiting Williamsburg in Virginia where the American Revolution began, and then stopped off in Philadelphia to go to Independence Hall where the Declaration of Independence was signed. When, the following year, President Clinton paid a return visit, his first stop was Xi'an where he posed among the terracotta warriors at the vast necropolis built by the First Emperor.

The reciprocal visits neatly mirror the contradictory philosophies underpinning the two political systems. The American Revolution began as a protest against the tyranny of arbitrary rule by the British sovereign George III, and the American Constitution seeks to impose a series of checks and balances to prevent future government administrations from impinging on the rights of the individual. Among these are the division of government powers between an elected president and elected legislative bodies, an independent administration, an independent judiciary with a powerful Supreme Court, an independent press and an obligation to ensure maximum transparency in decision-making. Some Americans assumed that Jiang's visit reflected a desire to learn from this system of government. The Chinese, however, regarded it as merely a polite diplomatic gesture. Jiang's government more closely resembles that laid out by the Legalists over two millennia ago.

After the fall of the Qing dynasty reformers introduced into China a new legal code, an independent judiciary, a free press, elected legislatures and decentralized government. By contrast, the earliest Communist-run territories, the soviets, developed along totalitarian lines, following the example of the Soviet Union. There the Party was the state, and Party members made up the secretive bureaucracy. Indeed, the most powerful bureaucratic apparatus in the Soviet

Union quickly became the secret police who were used by Stalin to purge the army, the bureaucracy and the Party of his opponents.

In China, the totalitarian state developed along different lines. From the 1930s, the Chinese Communist Party was fighting a civil war for territory and, despite the efforts of Communists trained by Stalin to extend the powers of a Chinese secret police, the military of necessity became the most important arm of the Party. Between the CCP's founding Congress in 1921 and 1928, its membership had grown from 57 people to 40,000, dominated by intellectuals but including some urban workers and peasants. After Mao took control of the Party in the mid-1930s, he stepped up the recruitment of soldiers into the CCP. By 1945, when there were 1.2 million members, the majority were from the People's Liberation Army and it was therefore hardly surprising that the new post-1949 administration was dominated by soldiers and demobilized soldiers. In contrast to the Soviet Union, where the NKVD and later the KGB remained supreme, in China the PLA became almost the executive arm of the Party.

Half a century later, the secrecy with which the Party meets and interacts with the world still reflects the traditions of the PLA in the days when it was an underground guerrilla force. The Party leaders hold their convocations in total secrecy each year at the PLA-run Jingxi Hotel in Beijing. Often such meetings are never announced and even when a decision is reached – a new leader chosen, a new policy agreed – a communiqué may appear only days later. Individual Party members are still routinely informed of the Party's decisions in the dead of night. Nor does the CCP have a listed address or headquarters although it must be one of the largest and richest organizations in the world with over 50 million members. Its administrative buildings, scattered around Beijing, are not marked in any way other than by the presence of armed soldiers, and Party members are expected, like the military, to act with unquestioning obedience.

After 1949 the CCP embarked on a massive effort to bring China under its control and to modernize it by establishing a minutely planned economy. The scope of this endeavour required a vast administrative machine and substantial numbers of trained and qualified bureaucrats. The task of taking a census and registering a population of over 500 million alone required considerable man-power. Everyone in urban China had to be issued with new identity documents and a file identifying his or her class background, and whilst the peasants were excluded from this *dang'an* system, as it is called, they too had to be assessed and given a class label. By 1956, CCP membership had grown from 1.2 million to 10.7 million, many of the new members drawn from the civilian population.

To establish control over the economy more than a hundred min-istries were set up. They were responsible for administering the five-year plans, determining the price and quantity of all goods produced and supervising their distribution. Within the system each official was assigned a place in the minutely stratified bureaucratic hierarchy, and such was the complete identification of Party and state that there was no real attempt to distinguish between officials of the govern-ment and members of the Party. Both were referred to as *ganbu*, or in English, cadres.

Since the entire legal and administrative structure of the KMT government had been rejected, the bureaucracy also had to set about drawing up a vast web of regulations and rules to cover every activ-ity. There was no criminal code and most laws were never more than unpublished internal regulations but a handful were made public, the first being the Marriage Law, though it soon became known as the Divorce Law because it was used by many to escape from an exist-ing marriage.

To administer the country the Party created in effect two parallel organizational structures. First there was the Party, which had its own constitution and its own rules and regulations. Its committees, con-gresses and cells were the ruling bodies, and within each unit the Party secretary wielded all real power. The Party was supposed to be a democratic pyramid with lower cells passing on their views and selecting representatives to attend ever more powerful representative bodies up to the Central Committee of some 300 members which met usually once a year to make key decisions. Every five years or so, there was to be a National Congress which chose the Politburo, a cabinet-style body which met once a week, though real power lay with the smaller Politburo Standing Committee.

In reality, there have been no discernibly fixed rules or permanent institutions during the last fifty years. From 1958 onwards, Mao paid almost no heed to authorized Party structures, and though after his death the Party attempted to restore a sense of organizational rules and procedures, Deng himself invariably ignored them whenever they were inconvenient. In much the same way, even the lowest-ranking Party secretary is, within his own domain, more or less a law unto himself.

Alongside this Party structure the façade of government was maintained, under which the same officials held different titles, not as Party secretary of a ministry but as its minister, not as Party secretary of a factory but as its director. Power, however, resided in the Party. The head of a province or a city was its Party secretary, not the governor or mayor. Certain bodies remained wholly in the hands of the Party, among them the Propaganda Department in charge of censorship and the United Front Department which organized the activities of non-Party collaborators.

Having declared that it wanted to establish a multi-party democracy when it was fighting for power, the CCP also retained eight other pre-1949 parties and even gave some of their members honorary positions such as a deputy ministership. The supreme law-giving body was deemed to be the National People's Congress, with several thousand members elected by similar bodies at lower levels. Advising it was an upper house of united front collaborators from outside the Party, such as former KMT leaders or religious leaders, called the Chinese People's Political Consultative Conference.

The Party also created a variety of non-governmental organizations to represent specific interest groups such as the All China Trade Union Federation, the All China Women's Federation and similar bodies for writers and scientists. Seemingly designed to transmit the will of the people upwards to the leadership, all these organizations in fact did the reverse and were used to convey the orders of the leadership downwards. Much the same was true of the Party organization, in which no one was elected and there was generally never more than one candidate for each post who had been selected by his superiors.

In 1958, however, this whole elaborate edifice was swept aside by Mao in his determination to propel China immediately into a state of Communism, bypassing the stages of socialism. With the launch of the Great Leap Forward, overnight Mao ordered the creation of the people's communes in the countryside and accelerated the pace of industrial growth. The bureaucracy's careful planning and regulation were to be replaced by a feverish effort by each person to promise to do more than was ever possible. There was therefore no longer any need for experts – Mao replaced them with loyal followers. There was still less need for laws – Mao's word was the only law that mattered. The Ministry of Justice was abolished and the State Statistical Bureau was subsumed within the Propaganda Department.

In future, Mao ordered, the Party was to admit only 'workers, former poor and middle peasants, or children of such families'. (The Party would not formally approve the membership of 'intellectuals' until 1982.) Mao did not trust the Party apparatus either and between 1961 and 1963, millions of cadres were sent to work in the villages to 'remould their ideology'.[6] Though during this period Party members often had privileged access to food and were largely exempt from having to perform forced labour, they nonetheless fell victim to the all-pervasive atmosphere of fear. Party members had constantly to reaffirm their loyalty by informing on others and to participate in 'struggle sessions', the ideology meetings that had now become part of daily life.

With the launch of the Great Proletarian Cultural Revolution in 1966, Mao seems to have set out to destroy the Party and government apparatus entirely, though much of what happened in the 1960s and 1970s is not yet fully understood and Mao's actions and intentions are still debated by historians. Whatever the case, in this period most of the governmental institutions established in the 1950s ceased to function altogether. The number of functioning ministries shrank to just fifteen and there were no more five-year plans. The rules governing Party affairs, even those regulating the Central Committee or Party Congress, were ignored. Insignificant bodies such as the National People's Congress did not meet at all. Most of the earlier intake of Party members were either imprisoned or sent to the countryside for 're-education', and the personnel of entire ministries or universities were rotated through labour camps, known as May 7th Cadre Schools after the date of a call by Mao for political re-education. At the same time, however, Party membership actually doubled and by 1969 there were 20 million members. The new members were usually fanatics who qualified for membership because they had the correct class background and low level of education.

Although the Cultural Revolution was later designated as 'the ten years of chaos', the mass persecution that characterized it in fact remained a profoundly bureaucratic and well-organized process. Each persecuted Party member (or non-member) was repeatedly required to write confessions, and to re-examine his life by composing a biography. To these personal records were added the accusations of others, and the reports filed by all neighbours and colleagues. Even children were asked to inform on their parents. Everything was written down, filed and stored away, an endeavour which employed literally millions of archivists.

By the time Mao died, Party membership stood at 39 million and the new rulers of the country soon began their own purge, another vast bureaucratic effort to weed out the 17 million recruited during the Cultural Revolution. In 1977, the Party shut down the organs of the Maoist inquisition, such as the Central Case Investigation Committee which had examined senior officials, and established its own. The Central Disciplinary Inspection Committee rehabilitated previously purged cadres and put on trial their persecutors. Ten of Mao's key followers were tried, whether or not they were still alive. The Central Party Rectification Working Leadership Commission, led by Qiao Shi under the rehabilitated veteran Bo Yibo, posthumously expelled Kang Sheng and Xie Fuzhi, two of those in charge of Mao's purges, as if their excommunication would affect them in the afterlife.

In all some 30 million Party members were judged, rehabilitated and compensated, a task which took ten years. The new regime required every member to re-register so that their qualifications and dossier could be re-examined, and many of the unfair accusations were removed from their files and destroyed. Those deemed to be 'rabble-rousers' who practised 'factionalism' or instigated armed violence were expelled. Some 6 million rural Party cadres condemned as leftists lost their membership as a result.

However, the process still left the Party with two problems – how to deal with those recruited under Mao who were often semi-literate and unqualified but who had not been expelled, and how to employ those who had been rehabilitated or who were elderly. In 1985, 15 million of the Party's 40 million members could not read or write and only a million had tertiary education. The Party began to send as many as possible to Party schools, some on courses that lasted for as long as three years, partly to reindoctrinate them but largely to educate them. At the same time, nearly 3 million rehabilitated cadres had to be found new jobs as did a million demobilized PLA servicemen. And each year hundreds of thousands of new graduates became automatically entitled to jobs in the state bureaucracy. After Hu Yaobang became General Secretary of the CCP in 1979, the number of officials grew by an average of 320,000 a year. By 1983 the bureaucracy was expanding at the rate of half a million a year and when Hu was forced to step down in 1987, his successor Zhao Ziyang oversaw the enrolment of an additional one million *ganbu* a year. By then, the number of ministries had risen to 50, the number of ministry-level organizations to 100, and the burden on state finances had increased by 23 per cent in just one year. The bureaucracy had spread its tentacles so wide that in the late 1980s, there was reckoned to be one cadre for every twenty-five people, compared to one for every ninety when the Communists had taken power in 1949.[7]

What had caused this extraordinary growth? After 1979, the Party sought to resurrect the entire state planning apparatus that had existed before 1958. New plans began to be produced and the new army of bureaucrats attempted not only to calculate the price of everything that was produced but to inspect it as well. Full-time inspectors, for example, patrolled the newly opened free markets, checking prices and issuing penalties. And it was not just goods that were planned. Over 300,000 officials were employed by the family planning services to try to ensure that the number of people born each year was also determined by a plan – a plan calculated by the same formulas and computers used in calculating rocket trajectories. Those who devised China's family planning programme now looked at the systems analysis methods pioneered in the United States by

Robert McNamara first at the Ford Motor Company and later, and notoriously, in the management of the Vietnam War.

'[In the 1980s] we tried to apply the methods of warfare to building socialism,' explained Li Junru, one of the Party's leading ideologists at the Research Centre of Party History, when I interviewed him in 1999. 'Now we believe Marx didn't want his followers to set about the detailed planning of a future society. A plan is just a goal for people to make efforts.' He went on to describe how, in the past, the Chinese had felt themselves to be on the brink of war and so had wanted a tightly controlled society. Now Li was all in favour of giving free rein to individual initiative, an admission which still shocked some of the western European Marxists who visited him, though it was obvious that planning had failed everywhere.

'When I visited the USSR, they used big computers to calculate and to draw very specific plans but you know they failed as well. The economy cannot be planned that way. We cannot say that this year we must produce so many computers or suits or shoes because people may not want them. We abolished this way of planning in 1995.'

Even so, in 1999 the state still employed 250,000 scholars of Marxism, evidence that many still believed state planning was important. At the prestigious Marxism-Leninism Institute of the People's University, the historian Xu Zhengfan, an elderly and noted expert on research into scientific socialism, said his fundamental beliefs had not changed: 'There is a law in history. Of course it is not as clear as those of physics, because human society is far more complicated, but it means the future can be predicted in a scientific way.'[8]

What the CCP has abandoned since 1979 has been the belief that China can change the nature of man himself and create a new socialist man devoted to serving the state and the common good selflessly, an altruist who disregards his own individual interests. The ideal citizen had been exemplified by Lei Feng, a humble soldier who reputedly wanted to be 'a rustless cog in the machinery of socialism' and around whom a cult was erected – even today a picture of Lei Feng still hangs on the walls of each Chinese school.

Xu Zhengfan admitted that such an ideal had been too abstract, too doctrinaire and unrealistic. 'You cannot make everyone altruistic, we cannot change hundreds of millions overnight. Mao once hoped all Red Guards, born in the new society, could be turned into new men but it turned out differently.'

Ironically, however, recognition of this fact has led the CCP to resort to the customary Chinese Legalist tradition of ordering society through a code of rewards and punishments. As individuals became free to pursue their own interests, so state officials began to draft laws and regulations and establish new bodies to enforce them. Suddenly there was a need for whole new tiers of bureaucracy to provide everything from health inspectors in private restaurants to a patents office, and these bodies sprang into existence side by side with the restored planning organizations. At the same time an entire policing and legal system had to be set up although the state was slow to create a legal code to regulate the emerging market economy. In the meantime, each part of the central bureaucratic apparatus drew up its own internal regulations. And, as central government revenues were outstripped by the growing bureaucratic machine, rapid decentralization occurred.

Every Chinese leader who has come to power since 1979 has tried to wield an axe against the multi-headed hydra that is the bureaucracy. Hu Yaobang's particular challenge was to force into retirement those elderly cadres who had been restored to their positions after the death of Mao. After 1982, he managed to get rid of 2 million, often those who had joined the Party before 1949, by setting new limits for retirement. Women now had to retire at 55 and men at 60. For those in senior positions the age limit was 65. Retired cadres were entitled to 70 per cent of their pay, and sometimes more was offered as an inducement to early retirement.

'What Hu did was go into an organization with 200 cadres and say you only need a hundred here. The rest should go and find new jobs,' one official explained. 'At that time the market economy barely existed so they could not go into business. All that happened is that these officials were kept on. They continued working in the same offices which were now renamed "consultancies" or "supervisory committees".'[9] These were known as 'mother-in-laws' and the greatest of them all was the Central Advisory Commission for elderly veterans who had been Party members for forty years. A third of the members of the Eleventh Central Committee of 1977 were moved into this body but were permitted to keep their office cars and secretaries and to attend plenary sessions of the Central Committee and influence policy and personnel selection. The Party reorganization or restructuring approved in 1982 still left it with an unwieldly structure: a Central Committee of 348 members, a Politburo with 28 members and a six-member Standing Committee, whose average age was 77. The veterans, known as the Immortals, were even older. They felt free to ignore the new Party Constitution and did so when, in January 1987, they pushed Hu Yaobang out of power. They then organized an enlarged Politburo meeting in which 23 of the 43 seats were taken by non-Politburo members.[10]

When Zhao Ziyang took Hu's place, he brought the average age of the Politburo Standing Committee down to 64 years and made an even more ambitious effort to change the nature of the Party administration, attempting to make it more democratic and insisting that there should be more than one candidate for each post, genuine secret balloting and real voting in the Politburo.

'We thought the political reforms should go from top to bottom, from inside the Party to outside. Zhao wanted more democracy inside the Party and he said the Party must obey the law before it asked ordinary people to do so,' recalled one of his chief aides, Bao Tong, in an interview after his release from jail in 1998. Bao Tong had been in charge of a Political Reform Leading Group which co-ordinated research but he admitted there was never a definitive blueprint: 'There was no plan but a philosophy. I think Zhao could only do as much as he thought Deng could tolerate, and he wanted to move forward step by step. Still, it was better to do something and keep the momentum going than do nothing.'[11]

In his report to the Thirteenth Party Congress, Zhao outlined some ideas to separate the Party from the government administration: 'We should work out different methods for managing personnel in different categories . . . This should be done in accordance with the principles of separating Party and government, separating the functions of government from those of enterprises and ensuring that administrators in charge of personnel have command of professional knowledge so that they will do their work more intelligently.'[12]

Zhao proposed the idea of 'small government, big market' to

reduce central planning and delegate more power to local administrations and enterprises. He also hoped to create a division between permanent civil servants and political appointees from the Party – Zhao's followers even wanted to educate Chinese cadres on how this would work by showing them the British television comedy *Yes Minister* which centres around the battles between an elected minister and his wily permanent secretary.[13] Within SOEs, he wanted to give managers more power and the Party secretary less, or to remove the latter altogether. In the countryside, the Party introduced village elections, and inside the Party the Central Disciplinary Inspection Committee began to expel ever larger numbers of errant members. At the same time, Zhao urged some checks and balances on the power of the bureaucracy – giving the media more independence and making the workings of the administration more transparent, a process called *tuminghua*.

Many perceived Zhao's efforts as an attempt to reduce the influence of the Party and matters came to a head in 1989 when demonstrations brought millions on to the streets in over eighty cities around China. The demonstrators were probably orchestrated and manipulated by Zhao's faction within the Party, perhaps because Zhao thought he could prove that his faction truly represented the will of the people. However, the PLA's intervention showed that popular support counted for nothing and that the word of the octogenarian Immortals counted for more than any institution or law. According to the Hong Kong historian Willy Wo-lap Lam: 'The Gang of Elders looked upon China pretty much as their fiefdom. Vice President Wang Zhen said it all when he noted soon after Liberation that "He who wins heaven and earth has a right to rule over it".'[14] In May 1989 when another of the Immortals, Chen Yun, spoke in favour of martial law, he expressed the same view: 'We are all old comrades who have struggled for decades for the creation and construction of the socialist republic. At this critical juncture, we seniors must throw ourselves into the effort to quell the rebellion.'

In the first eighteen months following the imposition of martial law in June 1989, the CCP instituted a large-scale witch-hunt for Zhao's followers and supporters. After 4 June most of the 48 million Party members had to re-register and submit to self-evaluations, self-criticism and struggle and study sessions, and work teams were sent to weed out those who had marched in demonstrations or were guilty of spreading or advocating 'bourgeois liberal thought'.[15] In the two years following 4 June, around a million cadres were dispatched to grassroots units to learn from the masses. During this Maoist rustication campaign, they reportedly reformed their thoughts by taking part in physical labour and a process of 'investigation and research'.[16] Some cadres were sent back to the Central Party School and other institutions for renewed indoctrination. By March 1993, the Party said it had expelled 33,400 members and had taken measures against a further 158,000 members. With morale plunging after the overthrow of Communist regimes in the Eastern bloc, many Party members were also sent to take part in ideological training camps to help bolster their faith.[17]

Amidst this shake-up the PLA strengthened its grip on the Party and increased its presence on the Central Committee so that it now accounted for 22 per cent of its members. Senior PLA officers who had hesitated to show their loyalty were purged, and the PLA and the Party now came under the control of the 83-year-old general Yang Shangkun and his brother and fellow general Yang Baibing who dominated the Central Military Commission. However, when Deng Xiaoping made a comeback in 1992 and relaunched the economic reforms, he was able to remove the Yang brothers from power and replace 300 officers loyal to the two veterans. And the power of the Immortals, irrespective of their policies, began to decline as each in turn shuffled off their mortal coil. In 1995, Deng himself fell into a coma from which he did not re-emerge, and he died in 1997 at the age of 92.

The passing of these men, coupled with the reforms that Deng had ushered in before power slipped from his hands, inevitably led to a sea-change. All the Party's institutions of control remained in place – the personal files, the *hukou* system of registration, the neighbourhood committees, the Communist Youth League, the Young Pioneers, the family planning system – but the minute supervision of daily life fell away. As more and more people became economically independent of the state, the state intruded less and less. The Party's once pervasive presence retreated still further. Already in the 1980s, the Party had stopped requiring citizens to attend daily ideological study sessions, limiting attendance to one meeting a week, usually on a Saturday. By the mid-1990s, even this single weekly meeting had been abandoned, and at the same time the state introduced the two-day weekend. The activities of Party cells in most organizations also fell off and even in the universities, which after 1989 were placed under tight supervision, Party members attended political meetings only once or twice a year.

The Party also tried to change in response to the protests against corruption and nepotism that had played such a role in the 1989 demonstrations. When Jiang Zemin took over from Zhao Ziyang, he ruled out any separation of Party from government and required officials to reaffirm their loyalty. Yet at the same time he also began to introduce a whole range of regulations governing the activities of officials to show that the Party could police its members without the democratic checks and balances called for in 1989. Officials were forbidden to employ relatives or engage in business and were obliged to reveal all sources of income to their superiors. One regulation issued in 1991 forbade officials from holding New Year banquets and restricted them instead to tea parties. Others forbade year-end bonuses, the distribution of shopping coupons and state-controlled commodities, the use of office cars, the holding of meetings in resorts, the purchase of mobile phones and many other run-of-the-mill forms of corruption. One propaganda campaign targeted officials in Hunan province for public criticism because, in 1990, they had spent three times more on entertaining themselves at banquets than they had on the province's education. Another campaign attacked spending on luxury cars. The *China Youth Daily* reported how in southern China, a Mercedes Benz could be found parked outside nearly every municipal or county office, and one province in the north-east was alleged to have bought 4,314 luxury cars in just five months at a cost of a tenth of its revenues.[18]

New regulations which in 1993 adjusted the wage structure of the bureaucracy showed how little, in theory, officials supposedly earned. In the 1950s, CCP members had been divided into thirty grades. On the lowest rung, a junior clerk earned 18 yuan a month while at the other end, Mao earned 540 yuan. In the interests of egalitarianism, the grades were reduced to fifteen during the Cultural Revolution. The new system also had fifteen grades, with middle school graduates at the bottom earning 155 yuan and the prime minister, in the first grade, earning a basic salary of 1,200 yuan (US$144). In practice the pay scales are far more complicated. Each rung on the ladder is subdivided into as many as ten ranks, and salaries are adjusted depending on bonuses awarded according to seniority, grade and rank. In addition these salaries exclude the cradle-to-grave welfare system which includes virtually rent-free housing and bonuses that far exceed in value the nominal annual salary.

Just as Hu Yaobang and Zhao Ziyang failed to halt the growth in the size and cost of the bureaucracy, so too did the government under Premier Li Peng. In 1993, the Ministry of Personnel ordered a 25 per cent cut in the 9.2 million Party and government staff over a three-year period. The number of various central government organs, which by then had risen to 171, was also to be cut back to 85. Li Peng's solution was to convert some ministries controlling industrial sectors into industrial corporations, associations or regulatory bodies. The Ministry of Light Industry became the General Association of Chinese Light Industry, the Ministry of Textile Industry, the General Association of the Chinese Textile Industry. And as the role of the State Planning Commission dwindled and economic central planning was abandoned, similar changes were expected among those departments responsible for electricity, coal, chemicals, building materials, electronics, machine building, the metallurgical industries, aviation, aeronautics, aerospace and telecommunications.

Yet somehow the number of bureaucrats kept on rising. 'The number of officials working for the central government went up by one million instead of falling by two million. The numbers in the Communist Party's central organs rose by 200,000 to 530,000. In the provinces the picture is much the same,' concluded Professor John Burns of Hong Kong University after studying the results of Li Peng's reforms. Research by Dr Jean-Pierre Cabestan of the French Centre on Contemporary China led to the same conclusion, although both experts admit that so little information is made available, it is hard to know exactly what is going on behind all the changing of names.[19]

By the time Zhu Rongji took over as premier in 1997, the number of central government bodies had risen to 200, and he complained that all these officials were literally consuming the state budget. One official magazine, *Outlook*, reported that 60 per cent of central government revenues went on staffing costs, the food bill alone amounting to 366 billion yuan (US$44 billion).

In yet another attempt to deal with this vast, bloated bureaucracy, in March 1998 Luo Gan, the senior official in charge of the State Council which groups together all central government bodies, announced a programme of ruthless reform, declaring that 'organizational reform is revolution'.[20] He proposed to reduce the number of ministries from 40 to 29 and to halve the number of central government staff to 4 million. The once mighty State Planning Commission was rechristened the Economic Development Commission with a staff of just 300. Some ministry-level organizations were turned into self-financing bodies. One such, the Sports Commission, has issued shares on the Shanghai stock market, and has raised 240 million yuan to be spent on new stadiums, swimming-pools and other state facilities which are to be managed on a commercial footing.

At the same time, attempts have been made to create a better educated, more professional administrative apparatus. The majority of ministers in the late 1990s had university degrees and their average age is 60 – not low, but a great deal lower than that of those in power in the 1980s. Many state bodies are also changing their style of work and becoming more professional and less ideological. The central bank, for instance, the People's Bank of China, claims it is being reformed along the lines of the US Federal Reserve, and some of its former duties, supervising banks, securities houses and financial markets, are now the responsibility of the China Securities Regulatory Commission.[21]

The crippling cost of subsidizing the world's largest bureaucracy should make more radical reforms imperative. Measured as a share of GDP, the state's tax revenues fell to below 10 per cent in 1998, one of the lowest rates in the world. The shortfall in revenues is felt particularly acutely outside Beijing where in 1999 more than half China's 2,000 counties were running a deficit. The surrounding province of Hebei reported in the mid-1990s that it had not been able to pay the salaries of a third of its staff. In Shandong all the county governments are reported to be bankrupt, and in Hunan 88 per cent were bankrupt in 1999 with combined debts of 6 billion yuan.[22]

One solution, repeatedly considered but never implemented, would be to dismiss many rural cadres. An experiment in 1991 found that in Zhuozi county, Inner Mongolia, it made no difference when 30 Party and government units were abolished and the number of cadres was cut from 700 to 300. In 1999, Beijing drew up plans to cut 60 per cent of its 6 million local government and Party staff and to halve the 60 government agencies which operate in most provinces.[23]

The sprawling, suffocating local bureaucracy is financed by illegal taxes and fees that are blamed for provoking much of the rural unrest endemic in China. Taxes are levied on everything from the slaughter of pigs to 'hanging-objects-from-the-ceiling'. In 1998 the central government reported that it had abolished 973 different 'taxes' that had so far raised 45 billion yuan (US$5.4 billion) and local governments had promised to abolish another 26,710 'random fees' which had hitherto raised 98 billion yuan (US$11 billion) a year.[24]

With the central government so short of revenue, however, local Party officials have little incentive to heed orders from Beijing. The Party leadership complains that Party discipline has collapsed in many rural areas. Even according to published statistics, 11 per cent of rural Party cells are considered 'regressive' and some officials have described most rural Party cells as 'comatose' or 'paralysed'. Counter-measures taken in 1999 involved sending 600,000 senior cadres to explain central policies to officials in rural areas in order to strengthen Party control. A further 15 million rural cadres attended training courses to improve their understanding of Party policies.[25] The shortage of government funds is even threatening centrally funded bodies such as the Family Planning Commission. By 1999 it had cut its staff by a third from the 300,000 it employed in 1992 and was unable to keep open the clinics that perform abortions and deliveries. To remedy the problem some experts have called for a *de facto* privatization of its activities.[26]

In an attempt to replace the revenues which once came from the profits of the SOEs, in 1993 the state launched a national tax system.[27] A new tax code has introduced a series of national taxes in the hope of replacing the plethora of local levies. Among them is a national tax on all enterprises regardless of their ownership, a value-added tax and a consumption tax. And, for the first time in Chinese history, individuals are being asked to pay income tax. Within three years of its introduction in 1996, income tax accounted for 4 per cent of total tax revenues. Though this is small beer compared to the average 40 per cent income tax contribution of developed countries, it may prefigure wider social changes. Individual taxation might, for example, help push the state into treating its subjects more like citizens with a right to representation.[28]

What is certain is that the state's refusal to contemplate genuine political reform since 1989 has severely hampered any progress towards creating an efficient and incorrupt administrative system. As John Stuart Mill, the nineteenth-century British philosopher, remarked in his essay *On Liberty* of countries such as China or Russia where the bureaucracy is all-powerful: 'No reform can be affected which is contrary to the interests of bureaucracy.' Even when a new dictator takes power, Mill points out that he must still rely on the bureaucracy to implement his commands: 'He can send any one of them to Siberia, but he cannot govern without them or against their will.'[29] Chinese leaders have repeatedly failed to reduce the crippling costs of the Party bureaucracy because they remain so completely dependent upon it.

At present rural cadres can issue commands and regulations that have the power of law and they have unlimited power to enforce regulations such as those on family planning and to deny villagers access to necessities such as fertilizers, seeds, fuel, work permits, schooling and travel documents. They can also sentence individuals to up to three years' hard labour without going through the courts. Even in cases where individuals have successfully managed to overturn a decision by appealing to the courts or petitioning a higher level of bureaucracy, Party officials retain unlimited powers to take their revenge.

Any rigorous attempt by Beijing to curb the ability of the bureaucracy to coerce the rest of the population into paying taxes or bribes, or to prevent them from diverting public funds into their own pockets or enriching themselves in other ways, would undermine the whole political structure. Nevertheless, some cautious steps towards limiting the unbridled power of the state and its officials by establishing a legal system are being taken and these are looked at in the next chapter.

14

The Rule of Law

SIX MONTHS AFTER his release from prison, the lawyer was still in shock. He sat hunched in a cheap coat, bewildered by the other hotel guests in smart suits and ties milling around the lobby of one of Beijing's five-star hotels.

One day Yang Weilin had suddenly found that he had crossed an invisible wall dividing this world from another that had always co-existed but that he had never seen properly. Now, he could barely believe he was out again.

'Nobody could help me. Although I was a lawyer myself, once inside, I couldn't even make contact with anyone outside and try to get another lawyer to defend me,' he said, no longer indignant but subdued, still afraid to attract attention to himself.

As he sat there, dishevelled and tieless, it was hard to picture him as the brash successful lawyer that he had once been. He had been defending a client in what had at first seemed a routine commercial dispute when suddenly he found himself thrown into a detention cell and accused of persuading witnesses to provide false testimony.

'I had the evidence to prove that my client was not guilty,' he said by way of explanation.

Now aged 48, he had started working as a part-time lawyer in 1983 when China was just beginning to build a legal system from scratch. Five years later, he had taken enough night classes to pass the exams and become one of Beijing's 3,000 registered lawyers. Within a few years, he was doing well.

'I used to earn 400,000 yuan a year. I had everything,' he said wistfully. His secret, as he admitted at another meeting, lay in the strength of his Party connections. His father was a retired PLA general. He himself was the friend of this leader's son, that person's brother. His wife came from another family of high-ranking Party cadres.

Yang had agreed to act on behalf of one of the partners of a joint venture that made industrial heaters. The state prosecutors had charged the partner with embezzling 120,000 yuan (US$14,500). Yang did his job and found four witnesses to testify that there had been no fraud and the receipts to prove his client's innocence. Then, before the case came to court, Yang himself was seized and thrown into one of the detention houses of the Beijing police that come under the supervision of the *gongan bu* or Ministry of Public Security.

'Conditions were very bad. The prosecutors kept trying to make me confess that I had committed a crime. They kept at me in shifts from 9 in the morning to 11 at night and would not allow me to eat or drink. They promised that if I confessed they would not bring the case to trial and I would be released,' he said.

Most prisoners succumb to such pressure and confess. Yang did not but he was comparatively well treated. He knew of other inmates who had been tortured into making a confession, although the law specifies that confessions extracted under torture cannot be submitted as evidence. He knew for a fact, he said, that in 1997–8 three detained suspects had been beaten to death in the detention centre of Chaoyang district, the diplomatic quarter and the very area in eastern Beijing where we were now sitting. Suspects have no legal right to remain silent in China, and the slogan 'Confess and seek leniency' is prominently displayed in interrogation rooms and courtrooms throughout the country.

'I refused to sign a confession because I had done nothing wrong in handling the case,' he said. 'But later on, they just wrote down whatever they thought would be good for them so they could wrap up the case and then they tried to force me to sign it.'

In 1997 China adopted a revised criminal procedures law which specifies that a suspect cannot be held incommunicado for more than seven days, but it was three months before Yang was allowed to see a lawyer.

'The police turned down all my demands, saying they were too busy or it was not convenient,' he said. And in the world outside, his wife and brother tried every avenue to find out what had happened to him, including contacting the National People's Congress. Just before his case came to trial, his own lawyer was allowed to see only one or two pages out of the hundreds of trial documents. There was little he could do for Yang. In theory, too, the proceedings were open to the public but when his family and supporters arrived they found that all but two of the one hundred seats available were occupied by the staff of the security forces. His family tried to get the case reported in the press but when they brought journalists to the court they were turned back and warned not to report anything.

Even now Yang was still trying to make sense of what had happened. He knew his client had received a seven-year sentence although he never met him again. Of the four witnesses he had found, three changed their testimony and the fourth disappeared.

'I learned later that three of the witnesses had been taken away by the state prosecutors. They were held in detention like me until they were persuaded to change their minds.'

What he found so difficult to accept, however, was the fact that the other side in the case had such powerful political connections that they could do what they liked with his life. Leaning forward in his chair and dropping his voice to a whisper, he said, 'You must not mention his real name or mine but I have photographs, proof, showing X sitting in front of a pile of money with the other man next to him.' The name he gave was that of a senior official in the Beijing municipal committee. It is this committee of senior Party officials which, sitting behind closed doors, decides on all legal cases well before a case reaches the courts. It was no surprise to me that the Party ignored legal procedures when sentencing political dissidents. That happened all the time. But it was shocking to discover that a senior Party member could wield such influence in a non-political affair of seemingly minor importance.

Yang now spoke with determination of how he was planning to take the Beijing procuracy to court to prove his innocence. As a convicted criminal, he had been expelled from the Party and could no longer practise his profession or even earn a living. Yet as he spoke, leaning forward, intense and bitter, my heart sank still further. He was about to join a long list of petitioners who spend their lives in a futile quest to extract justice or an admission of error from the Chinese state. The Party and its officials never admit to error. The Party is infallible.

In my time in China, I have come across dozens of such petitioners. For a number of years, on the fifth day of every month, a former PLA officer would ring up and politely ask for permission to send a long account of how he had been unfairly treated in 1973 during a purge of officers linked to Lin Biao, the former head of the PLA. Pages of densely written handwriting would then spill out of the fax machine. The fact that I never did anything about his case seemed not to disturb him unduly nor to deter him from repeating the exercise the following month.

One year another frequent visitor was a country girl from Henan who spent months traipsing from office to office seeking justice. Her father had been shot dead in their house by a police officer without cause. The police officer had subsequently got off with a reprimand. She wanted him tried and executed.

Another year, there were almost weekly calls and visits from Hu, a peasant boy from Anhui, who carried with him a bundle of smudged and faded documents. One night his elder sister had been arrested by local officials who suspected her, wrongly, of having become pregnant without permission. In detention, she was beaten, raped and left permanently brain-damaged. After fruitless efforts to bring those responsible to justice in Anhui, Hu's family had had to flee their village to escape further threats from the local cadres. Now Hu had come to Beijing with his sister and parents, and they lived on the streets while he tried every possible ministry, court and Party organ, and appealed to every lawyer, court official and delegate of the National People's Congress. He then worked his way through journalists at the *People's Daily* and the *Women's Daily*, officials of the All China Women's Federation and editors at Beijing Television. From time to time, he would call up from a phone box and report his progress, and we would try to come up with another name or phone number. Finally, one day he rang up with good news. A journalist from Chinese Central Television had agreed to go back to his village and investigate his case. Hu now had reason to hope.

I never heard what happened to Hu subsequently, but his thirst for justice, his belief that someone, somewhere in China's vast bureaucracy would one day intervene, was deeply moving. And he was not alone. Every year Chinese send millions of letters and petitions addressed to the bureaucracy. Some persist in the face of such official indifference and contempt that their attempts seem almost akin to madness. In Beijing the wretched claimants line up to hand over their letters in front of a small opening, barely big enough to thrust a hand through, which is occasionally unlocked in a high wall surrounding the Supreme Court, a towering block off Tiananmen Square. Dozens of others sit near a petition office in a rubbish-strewn alley at the back of Yongdingmen Station in a suburb of Beijing. These are mostly peasants from the provinces who wait innocently with their letters and crumpled documents. They are glad to talk to anyone who shows an interest but invariably an official soon emerges and brusquely detains the curious journalist, charging him or her with carrying out unauthorized interviews.

Yang was nothing like this flotsam and jetsam washed up from the countryside. His high social status and his professional qualifications should have protected him, and his case had struck fear in the hearts of other lawyers. 'If Yang can be imprisoned like this in Beijing, imagine what it is like in the rest of the country and how nervous everyone is about taking on a defence case,' one of them said to me, but he was reluctant to say more.[1]

In 1997, China adopted the Law on Lawyers which changed their status from 'state law workers' to that of practitioners providing legal services for society who are obliged to 'safeguard the legitimate interests of their clients'. The revision of the criminal procedures law a year earlier, which came into effect in 1997, also specifically entitled defence lawyers to visit and advise their clients before the police carried out their first interrogation.

Hitherto, it had been the firm duty of defence lawyers to help the state elicit a confession and carry out punishment of the accused.

The terms 'suspect' and criminal' were interchangeable. The new law moves closer to the assumption that suspects are innocent until proved guilty. When I mentioned Yang's case to the editor of the *Lawyer's Daily*, Sun Jibin, and questioned the effectiveness of the new laws, he shuffled slightly in his seat and eventually conceded that such cases do happen: 'But they are very rare. They only happened at first. Public security officials, prosecutors and court officials were at first not happy about lawyers helping their clients.'

At the Beijing Lawyers' Association, its director Gong Sha was more frank: 'It is true. Lawyers are arrested and charged quite often and it is difficult to do anything about it. In reality the police, the prosecutors and the courts have so much power.' Even so, Gong Sha could not quite bring himself to admit that Party officials in charge of these organs consider themselves to be above the law.

In 1990 China adopted an administrative litigation law under which citizens have the right to make complaints or charges against any state organ if it has violated the law. In reality no compensation could be obtained until 1995 when the state compensation law was enacted but this too lacks any procedures for enforcing compensation. So ineffectual are such laws at protecting the individual from both the policies and the administrative decisions of the Party apparatus that they often seem deliberately designed as window-dressing. Of the revised criminal procedures law, Amnesty International concluded: 'The amendments made are insufficient to ensure protection against human rights violations such as arbitrary detention, torture and ill-treatment, and the revised law still contains many loopholes allowing law enforcers to bypass the standard procedures and time limits stipulated by the law.'[2]

Individuals who have tried to fight the Party by resorting to the law have come to regret it. For example, after the abstract painter Yan Zhengxue was beaten up in 1996 by the Beijing police for arguing with a ticket inspector, he took them to court. He won his case but two weeks later the police came for him on the trumped-up charge of bicycle theft. He was sent to a labour camp for two years, though he was never tried or formally sentenced.[3]

Another court case, brought by 12,000 Shaanxi peasants against local officials who levied excessive taxes after a drought and floods, also ended badly. The peasants had banded together to hire a lawyer to fight local officials who had contravened the national laws restricting taxation to within 5 per cent of the peasants' incomes. Officials had confiscated the goods of peasants who refused to pay and beaten them up, and they paraded others through the streets. The peasants' lawyer, Ma Wenlin, was subsequently arrested, charged with 'disrupting social order' and sentenced to imprisonment in 1999.[4]

When the Party took up the slogan of 'the rule of law' (*yi fa zhi guo*) in the 1990s it was far from clear what was really meant by it. Did this mean the 'rule of law' in the Western sense, in other words laws which impose limits on government powers? Or was it a Legalist interpretation, indicating that the rulers were not constrained by laws but that their commands were now formally covered by a legal instrument? The two meanings are only distinguished in Chinese by slightly differing characters. Whatever the case, the slogan went down well with visiting foreign leaders and, despite lingering doubts, optimists argued that even the latter interpretation did at least represent a step forward in comparison with the Mao era when all legal forms disappeared. It is also undeniable that China must move towards a Western legal system, even if only to regulate its market economy, satisfy foreign investors and trade smoothly with the rest of the world.

This is not the first time that contact with the outside world has prompted a change in China's legal system. Growing contact with the West in the nineteenth century also stimulated change.

The penal code of the Qing dynasty still followed the pattern set by the Qin code of punishments two thousand years earlier. Indeed, some considered the Qing version even harsher. It listed 813 capital offences, including 'death by a thousand cuts' whereby the victim was slowly sliced into pieces. Political offences merited the most savage punishments. Loyal ministers were flogged in public if the sovereign was displeased with them, and the advisers who helped the unfortunate Emperor Guangxu to draw up his 'Hundred Day' reforms in 1898 were beheaded for their pains outside the city walls of Beijing.

In most cases under the Qing, the magistrate in charge of a district acted as investigator, prosecutor and judge. Suspects and witnesses were frequently tortured to extract confessions and then the magistrate would refer to the code and order the punishment. In most civil disputes, litigants preferred not to go to court but to resolve their differences according to local custom, perhaps with the help of a mediator.

As China opened to trade and investment, many foreigners were horrified by what they learned of Chinese justice and insisted upon the right of extraterritoriality within the treaty ports, that is the right to be tried according to their own laws. Gradually, their Chinese employees and Christian converts also claimed exemption and the tensions arising from this infringement of Chinese sovereignty helped fuel anti-foreigner protests such as the Boxer Rebellion of 1900.

Immediately after that rebellion, China embarked on reforms to bring its system closer to Western notions of justice, it being argued that this would help remove one justification for the continued existence of the treaty ports. In 1906, the Board of Justice became the Ministry of Law and by 1912, 345 courts had been established that applied a new set of legal codes. That year the new republic formally established the legal profession with the Provisional Regulations on Lawyers. For the first time in Chinese history, judges were also asked to act independently of the administrative bureaucracy and were barred from membership of any political party. Over the following decades an increasing number of judges and lawyers were trained, often being sent abroad to learn from other countries. Procedures such as the jury system were tried out and, despite the difficulties of financing it, the new legal system spread, although not as far as the local magistrate in his yamen.[5]

After 1949, the Communist Party quickly removed from office the 60,000 lawyers and judges who had practised under the previous regime, complaining that they were not severe enough. Many were subsequently imprisoned. At the same time it abolished all the laws promulgated by the Kuomintang government, declaring that 'the rotten capitalist legal system must be eradicated'. According to the Marxist view, 'the law is the tool of the ruling class' and the

Communists intended to use it as a weapon of dictatorship. However, whereas in the Soviet Union, the Communist government had published a criminal code within five years of coming to power and a civil code a year later, nothing of the kind would happen in China for another thirty years. All that appeared in 1951 were regulations on 'the suppression of counter-revolutionaries' comprising twenty-one articles that defined crime in political terms and that were so vague they could encompass anything. Article 16, for instance, provided for the punishment of any crimes not specified in the regulations. According to one expert, Harry Wu, these regulations were used to imprison 90 per cent of the inmates of the penal system, a vast network of camps known as the *lao gai*, short for reform through labour.

In the 1930s the Communists were the first to introduce into China the concentration camps that had already become a feature of the Soviet Union and Germany. However, it was Chiang Kai-shek's government which first established the crime of 'counter-revolution' when the KMT and the CCP split in 1927, using the Temporary Law on the Punishment of Crimes of Counter-Revolution against the Communists. It also began to reassert political control over the courts.

The Communists fled the cities and retreated into the mountains where they set up self-governing regions known as soviets. There, Mao put in place all the elements of dictatorship which were to become familiar after 1949.

In Mao's base on the borders of Hunan and Jiangxi, the Party issued a land reform law and proceeded to expropriate the land and possessions of richer peasants and landlords, many of whom were killed at mass rallies. The Party also established 'Elimination of Counter-revolutionaries' committees (*sufan weiyuanhui*) and a secret police force modelled on the original Cheka of Lenin. It soon instigated a series of purges. Party members had come under suspicion after the failure of the 1927 uprising, and Mao and his comrades themselves became caught up in the political struggles occurring within the Soviet Union. In 1927 Stalin had ousted Trostky who had hitherto overseen the Comintern's activities abroad. A year later Trotsky was forced into exile and Stalin organized a witch-hunt for his supporters and replaced the leaders of Communist parties around the world with those loyal to him. Within the Chinese Communist Party Stalin installed a disciple, Wang Ming.

The details of what then occurred amongst the Chinese leadership are murky but it is clear that in 1930 Mao started an internal witch-hunt against an Anti-Bolshevik Group and had thousands arrested and tortured into confessing membership of this fictitious organization. Among the victims was Hu Yaobang, who would become Party Secretary in the 1980s. After this so-called Futian Incident, in which at least 4,400 revolutionaries were executed, there appears to have been a rebellion within the leadership, and Zhou Enlai replaced Mao. In June 1932 Zhou established the first 'Labour Persuasion Camps'. These were subsequently renamed 'Labour Reformatories' to which 'hard labour teams' were sent. Zhou also set up a new organization, the National Political Security Bureau, to ferret out internal traitors, and a Judicial Department to deal with ordinary crimes. By 1934, Kang Sheng, who had been trained by the Cheka in the Soviet Union, was running a network of 'Investigation Committees' whose purpose was likewise to root out internal treachery.[6]

Keen to re-establish control over the Party in the mid-1930s, Mao was anxious to force out the Moscow-appointed faction and ensure that the internal Party police remained loyal to him and not Moscow. He controlled the Party organizations through an innocently named Social Affairs Department but to carry out the largest purge which culminated in the Yan'an Rectification movement of 1942, he set up a Central Study Committee of which he was chairman and Kang Sheng his deputy.[7] This purge bore all the hallmarks of later campaigns. Each Party organization had to come up with quotas of suspected enemy agents, and the records of over 160,000 Party members were examined. To extract confessions, lengthy self-criticisms, mass struggle sessions, torture, drugs and solitary confinement were all employed and many were executed on trumped-up charges or sentenced to hard labour.[8]

The Party applied the same methods to newly acquired territory. Class enemies were killed after being sentenced at rallies or by people's tribunals. Many others were sentenced without trial to corrective labour camps. Although the Party did issue provisional laws,

Peng Zhen, a Party leader closely associated with legal work first in the 1950s and then in the 1980s, later admitted that these had little meaning: 'Because there were no nation-wide people's political organizations during the revolutionary war period, the Communist Party decided everything and Party policies carried the weight of law . . . Generally, we just followed Party policies.'[9]

After 1949, the Party killed millions of rich peasants, landlords, counter-revolutionaries, bandits and others by resorting to people's tribunals. The tenor of these rallies was exemplified by a speech given by Peng Zhen when, as the first Mayor of Beijing, he attended a mass execution rally on 25 March 1951 in response to which the onlookers chanted 'Kill, kill': 'We are here representing the people. It is our duty to do the will of the people. We suppress the anti-revolutionaries. This act we perform according to the law. Those who have to be killed, we kill. In cases where we could kill or not, we do not kill. But when it has to be killing, we kill. Now you all want them to be suppressed. Tomorrow the Court will pronounce judgement and they will be executed.'[10]

Peng Zhen was also responsible for a refinement – the sentence of capital punishment with a two-year stay of execution if the condemned showed the correct attitude.

Another powerful figure in the early years of Communist rule was the Minister of Security, Luo Ruiqing. He controlled the secret police and, most importantly, the archives containing the individual dossiers compiled by the secret police on the entire population. He also oversaw the creation of a widespread network of informers and spies through the neighbourhood committees who kept a close watch on what everyone said and did. All citizens had to register and obtain a residence permit or *hukou* from the Public Security Bureau which drew up secret registers known as the 'priority population' list (*zhongdian renkou*). In June 1956 the Party set quotas for each area to collect the names of people requiring special scrutiny. They included: 'counter-revolutionary suspects: those suspected of various criminal offences, counter-revolutionary elements whose evil crimes have not yet been thoroughly investigated and uncovered: counter-revolutionary elements and hostile class elements who have not yet been fully reformed: and other persons already dealt with by the government who may well be, or are suspected of being, involved in criminal activities'.[11]

The *hukou* system, with its record of a person's class background and racial origin, enabled the authorities to single out anyone with the wrong political background, as well as their children and their relatives, in campaigns of persecution. For example, an edict issued during a national *hukou* work conference in 1956 required that 'during the two-year period 1956–7, approximately 50 per cent of the total number of persons to be placed under arrest or subject to control are to be drawn from among those persons named in the local "priority population" registers'.

In Mao's view '95 per cent of the people are good or relatively good, while only 5 per cent are reactionaries' and this was taken quite literally.[12] During the Anti-Rightist campaign the following year, which targeted intellectuals, each unit had to supply a 5 per cent quota of victims who were then arrested and punished as counter-revolutionaries.

In 1957, China introduced a further corrective, re-education through labour or *lao jiao*, which allowed Party organs to imprison people without any form of legal process. As justification it was explained that 'The policy of the Party is the soul of the law, and the law is the tool for implementing this policy.' After 1959, when the Ministry of Justice was formally abolished and China was in the midst of the Great Leap Forward famine, the prison population may have reached an all-time record according to one authority, Harry Wu.[13]

Once inside the *lao gai* system, even those prisoners considered to have been reformed had little chance of returning home. Under rules termed Forced Job Placement they were allowed to live outside a camp and even marry but they were also obliged to continue to provide forced labour. Many settled down permanently in exile as members of the production battalions of frontier provinces such as Xinjiang or Heilongjiang. A further peculiar characteristic of the Chinese *gulag* system was that prisoners were forced to take part in hours of ideological study sessions at the end of their work.[14]

Yet Mao was dissatisfied with the penal system which he felt had been taken over by his enemies in the Party. From the start of the

Cultural Revolution in 1966, he was determined to wreck it and his followers issued instructions to smash the *gongjianfa*, that is the police, the procuracy and the courts. Courtrooms and police stations were condemned as 'bastions of bourgeois justice' and in 1967, a *People's Daily* editorial appeared 'in praise of lawlessness'. It called for the complete destruction of the law so that 'the proletarian legal order can be established'. In another document, dating from 1968, Mao is quoted as saying that the Chinese should 'depend upon the rule of man, not the rule of law'.[15]

Among the first targets of the Cultural Revolution was Peng Zhen. Another was the former Minister of Security, Luo Ruiqing. He was thrown out of a window and his legs broken. Later he was paraded through the streets. His ministry, which held the files of Party members, was also attacked and, after a violent struggle, Red Guards seized control of the files which would be used to investigate and persecute other senior officials.

Mao again put Kang Sheng in charge of purging his enemies. He established a new Party organization called the Central Case Examination Group chaired by Premier Zhou Enlai, its purpose being to investigate various conspiracies to subvert the revolution by those who were spies and agents of foreign powers. It was also responsible for organizing the supposedly spontaneous actions of the Red Guards in beating, parading and humiliating Mao's victims. Some were imprisoned. Others were kept in makeshift cells called 'cowsheds' – Mao's appointed successor and the head of state, Liu Shaoqi, died in such a 'cowshed', the basement of an old bank in Kaifeng, a city in Henan.

Initially, most victims were placed under house arrest but after some committed suicide, important figures were taken into 'protective custody' where they were kept under constant observation, their every movement recorded in detail. Many were tortured and beaten in shifts, deprived of sleep, food and warmth, and given various drugs including hallucinogens. In all the Central Case Examination Group dealt with 2 million cadres, and recent research by the scholar Michael Schoenhals has shown that it had wider powers even than Stalin's secret police: 'As the distressing details of what it entailed begin to accumulate, it becomes clear that certainly by the 1960s and in the 1970s – and possibly all along – the repertoire of violent methods employed by the CCP in the search for "hidden enemies" included all those known from the history of the CPSU as well as some others.'[16]

Hu Yaobang was later to describe this security organ as 'a Gestapo, independent of the Central Committee' in a speech to the Central Party School in November 1978. There was no pretence at any legal form. Li Lisan, one-time Party leader in the late 1920s and a minister in Mao's government, was locked up in the room of an empty flat in Beijing. Although watched day and night, in June 1967 he supposedly committed suicide, but as with many cases the likelihood is that he was murdered. A verdict of suicide implied that the victim admitted his guilt. His Russian wife was kept in solitary confinement for eight years and then exiled to the countryside for a further three years without ever seeing a document to justify her sentence.[17] By contrast, those imprisoned by Stalin in Moscow in 1937 were at least accorded the semblance of a trial.

After 1979 Deng Xiaoping promised 'rule of law and radical changes' to the legal system but he insisted they must not transgress the vague boundaries of 'The Four Basic Principles'. Only those who upheld Marxism-Leninism-Mao Zedong Thought, the leadership of the Chinese Communist Party, the people's democratic dictatorship and the leading role of socialism could be considered to be acting within the law.

Peng Zhen, the veteran revolutionary and architect of the 1950s legal system, now rehabilitated, was put in charge of establishing a judiciary and appointed as head of the National People's Congress Legislative Commission and, more significantly, the Party's Political-Legal Committee. Despite his experiences during the Cultural Revolution he continued to act in the belief that Party policies remained 'the soul of the law'. One of his first acts was to adopt the first criminal code since 1949. It had 192 articles but he made clear that it was not intended to protect the individual against the power of the state or its representatives. On the contrary, the legal system would improve the exercise of an unqualified dictatorship: 'The people's security organs, the people's procuracy and the people's courts are the tools of the proletarian dictatorship for the protection of the people and for dealing severe blows to enemies.'[18]

This new criminal code retained the use of analogy which meant that even if an action was not listed in any law, it could still be treated as a crime if the Party decided to do so. The vague crime of counter-revolutionary activities was another part of the code. Three months after it came into force, the charge of counter-revolution was used against the dissident Wei Jingsheng who appeared in a televised court hearing and was given a fifteen-year prison sentence. He had put up posters on Democracy Wall in Beijing calling for democracy, had started a magazine and had made contact with foreign journalists.[19]

The Party also continued the practice of sentencing people to *lao jiao* without any judicial process. However, new regulations entitled 'Experimental Methods in Re-education Through Labour' were approved in 1982 that in theory limited *lao jiao* prison terms to less than four years, though the regulations were never published.

At the same time an effort was made to rebuild the neglected jails and prisons. Under Mao, it seems that the population of the prison system actually fell steeply during the Cultural Revolution, and the amount of land cultivated by its inmates dropped by 60 per cent.[20] A document published in 1980 complained that there were just 11,000 ill-educated and underpaid cadres running the camps. A further 50,000 were urgently needed: indeed the entire judicial, pro-curatorial and penal system required more than a million new staff. In 1982, the rules for prisoners were made public for the first time, and in 1994, a new law on prisons required the People's Procuracy to inspect prisons and determine whether their activities conform to the law.[21]

Early plans to train large numbers in the law were never carried out. In 1980, only 3,000 people in China could claim to have any legal qualifications and most of these were old men who had been per-secuted under Mao. Almost no books on law could be found and the Party complained of the difficulty of introducing even basic notions of legality. A 1984 report delivered to the National People's Congress admitted that 'to many people the notion of acting according to the law is new, unfamiliar, not something they are used to'.[22]

To remedy this deficiency, the state launched several mass propaganda movements to educate people in knowledge of the law. In 1985, officials talked of training two million lawyers, a million judges and a million defence lawyers but it was later decided that training 150,000 lawyers by the end of the century was all that was possible. Even this target was never reached, the number of lawyers remaining stuck at 100,000 in 2000.[23] Instead, the new legal apparatus was filled with demobilized PLA troops and officers who were sent to work at the new Ministry of Justice, which controls the courts and the prison system, to the Ministry of Public Security, which runs a police force of over one million men, and to a new organization, the People's Armed Police (PAP).

First introduced in 1983, the PAP is a paramilitary force. Initially it was manned by 600,000 troops drawn from different units – firefighters, border guards, coastguards and troops who had guarded key Party buildings. Their new job was to run the prisons, but also to guard gold mines, state forests and hydroelectric projects. After 1989, President Jiang Zemin poured money into the PAP to create rapid-response riot-control units. According to one scholar's estimate, about a million servicemen were transferred to the PAP between 1986 and 1992, and a further 400,000–450,000 between 1994 and 1996, bringing the total force to around 1.8 million by 1998.[24]

The security forces still appear to be badly paid and poorly educated. In 1988, the Minister for Public Security, Wang Fang, said 40 per cent had received only middle school education and a 'fairly large proportion' had received no police training at all. The Party then organized six-month crash training courses, not just for the semi-illiterate police but for judges and others working in the legal system.[25] In 1996, it was reported that only 22 per cent of the police had more than secondary school education. Low pay is blamed for the corruption of the police. Most earn less than 200 yuan a month and a lower court judge only receives 300–400 yuan a month.

The troops of the PAP are reported to be even worse off and dependent on handouts from local authorities. Their barracks, especially in outlying regions, are often run down and lacking electricity or running water. Most of the recruits have had only limited education, are given six months' training and serve a total of only three years. They are paid less than 100 yuan a month and serious doubts about their trustworthiness were raised in 1996 when a young guard robbed the home of Li Peiyao, a vice chairman of the National People's Congress, and then killed him when interrupted.[26]

Gradual steps to make the police more accountable have gone hand in hand with the corrosive effect of corruption. From 1987 police were required to wear identifying badges and a year later the public could for the first time call a police emergency number. Apart from attending training courses, police now have to pass examinations to be promoted in the new system of ranks established in 1992. The first policemen on the beat appeared on the streets of Shanghai in 1992 and at the same time the police also came under pressure to change their bullying behaviour. 'Policemen are asked to be polite and use such words as "please" when they deal with the public but some failed to do so and were even rude when communicating with the public,' reported the *China Daily*. Inspectors were sent to monitor the attitude of the police as their presence became more visible. By 1996 the authorities had increased the number of police patrolling Beijing's streets to 5,000.[27]

Police work is overwhelmingly concentrated on the cities, with over 40 per cent employed in just eleven cities, and the majority of crimes are recorded in urban districts. 'At present, police forces are far from sufficient in rural areas. About one-third of the townships have not set up their own police substations: and in a considerable number of already established substations, there are only one or two policemen,' complained the *Peasant's Daily* in 1991.

In the cities, in addition to the presence of the police, order continues to be maintained by the neighbourhood committees, first formed in 1951. In charge of between fifteen and forty households they report, as in the past, on all suspicious events, the comings and goings of their residents and visitors, and the political attitudes of residents to security protection committees. In the 1980s, Public Security Ministry cadres took charge of them and they were renamed public order committees. In 1987 there were 1.2 million such committees employing perhaps 12 million people.[28]

These organizations answer to local Party legal-political committees which have the power of detention. Similar committees also function in bigger work units, or *danwei*, but as employees in state-run organizations live in residential compounds operated by their work units, there is not necessarily any distinction between the two. The Public Security officials retain sweeping powers to place suspects in detention centres for up to three months under 'shelter and investigation' laws and in practice the police can keep someone in a detention centre indefinitely.

The legal-political committees probably have access to the personnel files which are maintained on every urban citizen. These *renshi dangan* files are started when children leave junior high school and are kept in neatly stacked brown envelopes that measure 8x11 inches.[29] In the early 1980s, an article in the *People's Daily* commented on the ubiquitous *renshi dangan*: 'Like a shadow, appearing and disappearing from time to time, every one of us is followed by a personal file . . . many people do not know what is in their personal files until the day they die.'[30]

Gradually, however, the importance of these files, especially for those no longer employed by the state, has diminished. In theory it is even possible for an individual to apply for permission to see their own file. Under Mao, such files were used to record ideological information but now they are used also for humdrum matters such as income tax, pensions, health and social security. Even so, those identified in their files as *zongdian renkou* – the 'priority population' group – are routinely rounded up during anti-crime campaigns such as the Strike Hard campaign of 1996. And even now this group still includes those suspected of having committed counter-revolutionary crimes or common crimes; those engaged in civil disputes; those sentenced to control through surveillance; and those on parole or who have earlier in their lives been released from labour camps.[31]

In 1998, China launched a new wave of reforms to make the legal system more creditable and accountable. The procuracy began to allow the public to attend some courts and it experimented with broadcasting trials. At the same time new rules were issued that required prosecutors to show suspects a card outlining their basic rights and informing them of the category of sentences, and their length, and whether or not an appeal could be made.

Xiao Yang, president of the Supreme Court, vowed that in future all judicial panels would be free of interference from above and he announced moves to establish a form of trial by jury in which a panel of experts rather than the masses would be invited to assist judges in cases that require special knowledge. Some proposed establishing a legal aid system and setting up hotlines which could offer legal advice to citizens but these have yet to be realized.[32]

Township courts, which handle half of all cases in the country, were also overhauled. They generally consist of no more than an extension of the local Party committee in which three officials act as both judge and jury. Xiao Yang insisted that this had to change and the courts be made more independent in order to stop corruption and promote respect for the law. He even suggested that local courts introduce trial by jury.[33]

So far these fresh efforts at judicial reform have brought about no substantial improvement because the political philosophy under-pinning state power has not changed. Admittedly, it is difficult to dis-cover much about such a secretive system, but it is hard to avoid the impression that all efforts to inculcate respect for the law have so far failed. Crime tends to be dealt with not as it occurs but rather in a series of political campaigns in which the Party orders officials to ignore the laws. Peng Zhen himself took the lead in 1983 when he ordered the judiciary to speed up convictions and executions in a huge crackdown on crime. The result was the execution of nearly 10,000 people, some of them within days of being arrested. And despite having introduced a criminal code in 1979 that ruled that the Supreme People's Court has to approve all executions, four years later he was absolving the courts from this obligation because it would cause delays.

In such campaigns, the police are generally set a quota of arrests and make a sweep of those listed as *zongdian renkou*. Suspects are then treated under special regulations that ignore the legal code. In the 1990 anti-crime campaign against the 'six evils', the police arrested 770,000 people but only 6,129 were given criminal convictions. Another 5,650 were given *lao jiao* prison sentences and the remaining

586,000 were punished under special public security regulations. Being formally arrested is usually tantamount to be being sentenced to a long prison term. In the first five months of the 1996 Strike Hard campaign, 245,000 people were formally arrested, of whom 219,000 were sentenced.[34]

Outside such campaigns, many people just disappear. The power of officials, no matter how low their status, to deprive people of their liberty seems unbounded. I have lost count of the number of times that I have, even as a foreign journalist, been detained or had my documents seized and not returned unless I signed a 'confession' admitting my mistakes. It can happen in the most ordinary way to anyone. One day my Chinese teacher arrived at my flat looking ashen-faced. His son, an undergraduate, had disappeared and had been missing for a week. The father had called police stations and hospitals and had tried to obtain help from the university, all to no avail. Then he asked a relative who worked in the Ministry of Public Services to make inquiries. The relative eventually found the son in a detention centre. It turned out that he had been riding his bicycle around the Haidian University quarter when he collided with another cyclist. A row ensued during which a plainclothes police officer had appeared out of nowhere and dragged him off. The young man was released.[35]

Many of those detained under the 'shelter and investigation' regulations are not freed so easily. A survey carried out in Hunan province in 1989 found that 30 per cent of detainees had been locked up in detention centres for over three months without being charged or their cases examined. Some had been detained for several years.[36]

There are certainly at least two thousand such detention centres in China and Harry Wu believes there may be twice that number. Reports by Amnesty International and Asiawatch garnered from first-hand testimonies describe how even in cities like Shanghai there are cells in which as many as forty prisoners may be crammed, and how their inmates are subjected to regular beatings and various kinds of torture and cruelty. Many other suspects are not even held in official detention centres but in what are known as 'black rooms'. According to an internal government report drawn up in 1992, these cells, often windowless, are used to punish uncooperative suspects without the bother of transferring them to a formal detention centre. A black room no larger than 11 square feet might house twenty-four people but if necessary as many as forty.[37] An estimated additional two million people are arrested each year off the streets under another form of arbitrary detention called 'custody and repatriation'. In these centres, children, vagrants and the insane are held indefinitely before being sent home or dispatched to a labour camp.[38]

Once inside the penal system, detainees have practically no rights, and the use of torture to extract confessions appears to be routine. An Amnesty International report released in 1987 concluded: 'We believe the law enforcement system and the justice system in China actually foster torture.' Without training in forensic science or any of the other tools of modern police work, the poorly educated police rely on torture and ill-treatment.[39]

In 1986 the government for the first time declared that a key task of the prosecutor was the 'eradiction of torture to extract confessions'. Newspaper reports appeared highlighting cases in which torture had been used. In one extreme example, a local Party secretary in Shaanxi province had ordered the torture of 17 villagers and illegally detained 72 others during an investigation into the theft of his bicycle bell.[40] In 1988, the authorities reported 4,700 cases involving police distortion, torture, frame-ups and illegal detention.

That same year China signed the United Nations Convention Against Torture and Other Cruel, Inhuman or Degrading Treatment or Punishment, but in practice little seems to have changed in the interim. In 1990, a deputy chief procurator, Liang Guoqing, admitted that in 2,900 cases, evidence of the perversion of justice by bribery, the extortion of confessions by torture and illegal detention had been found.[41] A year later, the *Yunnan Legal News* carried a report of how police regularly made suspects kneel on broken glass, jolted them with electric currents, and tied them up for long periods. 'Some law enforcement officers just don't care whether a criminal lives or dies,' it declared, adding that the police seemed to think that without a beating they would not obtain a confession. In another article, the *People's Public Security News* attributed this sort of behaviour to a 'small number' of public security officials subject to certain 'psychological factors'. Police officers resorted to torture because they were poorly educated, frustrated and angry or because they felt themselves above the law or protected by their superiors.[42]

An Asiawatch investigation into those arrested and imprisoned after pro-democracy protests in Hunan in 1989 painted a horrifying picture of the methods used in labour camps and prisons. 'Anthems of Defeat' devotes over twenty pages to detailing the punishments meted out either by the guards or by cell bosses on their orders. One prisoner mentioned in the report, a senior academic whom I met, had gone insane after being shackled to a board so that he was unable to move for three months. He was also regularly beaten and tortured. Other inmates were suspended by their wrists or forced to sit on stools without moving for days at a time. Many were tortured with high-voltage currents and kept in solitary confinement in window-less holes too small to stand up in.[43] So many similar reports have been published about the treatment of prisoners in Tibet and many other parts of China that one must conclude that the victims are not exaggerating.[44]

The use of torture to extract confessions has gone hand in hand with the increasing use of the death penalty. An Amnesty International report of 1999 concludes that 'Throughout the 1990s, more people have been executed or sentenced to death in China than in the rest of the world put together.' In particular, the report contains evidence of 6,100 death sentences and 4,367 executions during the 1996 Strike Hard campaign.[45] The number of criminals executed in China remains a state secret, but it seems likely that the real figure is far higher than that compiled by Amnesty International. The number of capital offences on the statute books is believed to have grown from 32 in 1980 to 65 by 1989. Since then non-violent and economic crimes such as speculation, bribery, the forging of value-added tax receipts and the infringement of trade-mark rights have been added to the list so that the current figure is probably around 90.

It is equally uncertain how many are serving prison sentences at any one time. Recorded crime has risen in recent years by at least 10 per cent annually and often at twice that rate. In 1994 the number of serious crimes rose 64 per cent on the previous year. The following year, despite the seizure of 260,000 guns, the number of armed crimes rose by 38 per cent. Overall, by the mid-1990s a million people a year were being charged with crime. The number of prison inmates is therefore almost certainly larger than the official figure of one million serving in *lao gai* camps and 200,000 in *lao jiao* camps. Experts outside China estimate that anything from 1.5 million to 4 million people are in prison at any one time, and Harry Wu believes that since 1949 in all some 50 million have been imprisoned.[46]

Chinese propaganda refers to the camps as a 'miracle on earth'. According to a report issued by the State Council in 1992, prisons used to be 'tools of the feudal bureaucratic comprador class who used them to persecute and slaughter revolutionaries and the oppressed people', but in today's China 'prisoners are regarded as human beings . . . their dignity is respected, their personal safety ensured and . . . they receive humane treatment . . . Many prisons and reform-through-labour institutions provide the prisoners with special teachers, painting rooms, and painting tools and materials, and offer calligraphy, painting and other art classes.'[47]

China does not permit any outside inspection of its penal system but the gap between reality and propaganda seems so vast that it suggests that the current leadership is not preparing to reform it. Most foreign governments committed to undertaking a dialogue with China on human rights now pin their hopes on the possibility that the market economy will force them to take cognizance of international practices. China wants to enter the World Trade Organization and is committed to complying with international rules on trade and investment. China also initialled the International Covenant on Civil and Political Rights in 1999 which, if it is adopted, may also require adapting domestic laws.

Outside pressure may become one instrument of change but there are also internal pressures. The failure to create a functioning legal system is hindering the development of a market economy. Chinese courts now handle three million or so civil cases a year but in 1997 there was a backlog of two million unresolved cases to which were added nearly a million additional cases the following year. By June 1999, China had 850,000 unenforced court verdicts, a third of the total, involving sums amounting to 259 billion yuan (US$31 billion). Many foreign companies have therefore been forced to rely on arbitration and special tribunals set up to deal with foreigners and which include foreign judges.

In many civil cases litigants have no faith in the justice dispensed and refuse to accept a judgement that goes against them. Local judges are all too easily bribed and court officials are sometimes killed if they try to take action, especially in another part of the country.[48] In 1999, the Procurator-General Han Zhubin declared: 'Some [prosecutors] violate legal procedures in holding suspects by force, some resort to torture to extort confessions. Others abuse their power for money, overstepping their authority to intervene personally in commercial disputes. There are also some who take advantage of their position to extort favours from units under investigation.'[49] Two years before, the *Worker's Daily* had described how in Hunan province, where verdicts in 100,000 civil and commercial disputes remained unenforced, frustrated litigants had taken the law into their own hands: 'People have persuaded their relatives or friends and gangster figures to enforce court verdicts by themselves. They kidnap hostages, detain motor vehicles, threaten, blackmail and injure debtors.'[50]

This anarchy has gone hand in hand with the advent of private debt collectors and armies of private security guards, many run by local police forces or the PAP, some by factories, tourist offices, banks or shops. In 1988 there were 685 private security companies employing 100,000 people. Ten years later security guards, often equipped with stun-guns and night-sticks, were visible all over China. Many Party organizations such as the procuracy and the judiciary also employ their own force of guards who may act outside the law. In one recently publicized case in Guangdong, a pregnant seamstress was shopping in a supermarket when she was seized by four guards who accused her of stealing a pack of ginseng worth 72 yuan. She was strip-searched and then held down while four of her fingers were chopped off. She escaped with her severed fingers, two of which were subsequently reattached in hospital.[51]

While hostage-taking has become a common means of settling debts, some debt collectors have resorted to guile. Yang Li, a professional debt-collector in Sichuan, collected debts by hiring 20 migrant workers to beg in a restaurant each day to force the owner to pay up.

In another case, he hired two women to put cushions under their dresses so that they appeared pregnant. The women then walked through the small town with the words 'collect debt' sewn on to the front of their dresses and entered the offices of the businessman who owed money, shaming him into honouring his debts.[52]

At the end of the 1990s, the Party launched a new initiative to improve the legal system and the image of the police. Some 7 million cases were reinvestigated, 827 unqualified prosecution officials were removed from office and the authorities admitted to 10,000 miscarriages of justice. China also began to send more judges abroad for training and invited British, American and German judges to China where they staged mock trials to demonstrate the workings of their legal systems.[53]

The fact remains, however, that genuine reform is unlikely to occur until there is a change in the status of the Party and its officials. As long as the law is not applied equally, as long as the 60 million Party members who run the administration and staff the judiciary and police apparatus feel themselves to be above the law, any legal system is bound to fail.

The actions of Party members are only supervised and investigated by Party organs such as the Central Disciplinary Inspection Committee which was set up after Mao's death when the Central Case Examination Group, the body which Hu Yaobang termed a Gestapo, was disbanded. Hu still recalled how he and his wife had almost been executed in the early 1930s during the Futian Incident and he and many others were determined to ensure that no such organization could ever again spread terror through the Party. The new supervisory organ was therefore granted only greatly reduced powers and a new Ministry of State Security was established with orders to confine itself to overseas intelligence-gathering.

In the 1980s, the liberal wing of the Party supported the development of a normal police and judicial force, and an increasing number of Party members investigated by the Central Disciplinary Inspection Committee were expelled from the Party and handed over to the procuracy for trial. However, the committee's main task was to identify those responsible for the worst abuses in the Cultural Revolution and investigate cases of wrongful persecution. The committee had offices in every major work unit and in 1988, as Zhao Ziyang pushed for a division of Party and government, a Ministry of Supervision was established to investigate the administrative doings of government officials. Zhao also acted to reduce the direct interference of the central Party's political-legal committee in the running of the police and the judiciary, and established a 'political legal group' to deliberate over broad policy issues.

When Jiang Zemin rose to power after 1989, he encountered the distrust of both the Beijing Party apparatus and the PLA generals with whom he had previously had little contact. In an attempt to build up his own power base he oversaw the dramatic expansion of the PAP and secretly poured funds into the Ministry of State Security. The former doubled in manpower but the Ministry of State Security grew from a few hundred thousand officials to at least two million. Thirteen departments were now responsible for national security both domestically and internationally.

Above all, Jiang wanted the ministry to spy on Party members, investigate their activities and maintain files on alleged cases of corruption. Such files might later prove useful should Jiang wish to remove enemies. The ministry is also said to run its own prison camps. It certainly has a large network of offices and facilities, and routinely taps phones and monitors the comings and goings of individuals in hotels and other public places. Some sources also claim it operates a network of informers throughout the Party machine which reports directly to Jiang. By contrast, the Central Disciplinary Inspection Committee, hitherto responsible for the investigation of Party members, has been subsumed within the Ministry of Supervision, and its main task now is simply to issue Party regulations and approve the punishment or expulsion of members.

In addition to its role as Jiang's power base, the Ministry of State Security has been made responsible for tackling corruption and it possesses unlimited powers of detention and interrogation outside the judicial system. Ministry officials routinely confine suspects in secret rooms in guest-houses or office blocks, and torture or blackmail them until they confess. Those undergoing what is known as *geli shencha* have no right to inform others or to ask for a defence lawyer. They simply disappear. The Party secretary of Beijing, Chen Xitong, was held incommunicado for three years before he was put on trial in 1998. Another senior official, the deputy mayor of Harbin, contacted Amnesty International in 1998 and told of how he had been held for two years and severely tortured until he confessed to accepting bribes. His family had been denied access to him, and his wife too had been held incommunicado for twenty months. Another 300 people connected with his case were also detained and probably coerced into making statements.[54]

The punishment of Party officials remains entirely arbitrary. While Chen Xitong was sentenced to sixteen years in prison for crimes involving 560,000 yuan, his successor, Jia Qinglin, a Jiang appointee, was allowed to retain his post after his wife was reportedly found to have profited from a smuggling operation worth an estimated US$10 billion while her husband was Party secretary of Fujian.

It seems improbable that China will move towards a depoliticized legal system as long as the Party treats even its own members without reference to any legal process or indeed a respect for basic human rights. And without any open system of elections, even within the Party, senior leaders such as Jiang Zemin have no legitimacy other than their ability to hold on to power. That fact alone probably explains Jiang's relentless expansion of the security apparatus. No one knows how big it is, but one Hong Kong magazine, *Contemporary*, reported in the wake of the 1989 massacre that in Beijing 61 per cent of all cadres were employed by one or other of the numerous Party, police and security organs. The majority of such cadres are concentrated in the politically important cities but, in the country as a whole, one in four officials may work for the security apparatus in one form or another. The total, including the PLA, could be anywhere between 9 and 21 million. The establishment of a working system of justice depends on the willingness of China's rulers to dismantle this oppressive machinery and relinquish their privileges, power and wealth. The saying that 'the rulers are the law' will hold good until there is political reform, which, as the next chapter explores, has not yet begun.

15

Between Heaven and Earth

As the last minutes of the millennium ticked away, the ranks of drummers, dancers and schoolchildren massed around the vast upturned semi-circular altar fell silent. Beneath a huge needle that pierced the heavens like a celestial sundial, a paunchy man in a sombre black coat stepped forward from a row of identically dressed men lined up in order of rank.

The choir of operatic voices exhorted the audience to 'Love the Motherland' as the cameras switched briefly to the face of a young Pioneer in the crowd, his expression one of ecstatic anticipation. Then, like a Greek athlete opening the ancient Olympic games, a young man dressed in white approached a giant incense-burner bearing a sacred torch, accompanied on either side by four maidens carrying vernal wreaths.

Before the rulers had arrived, a thousand children had recited 'An Ode to the Century', praising the Communist Party and eulogizing the Chinese race. Amidst the dragon dances, fifty men in coat-tails had waltzed their partners dressed in bright yellow gowns round the altar where the sacred flame would be lit. Children dressed in red from head to toe had raced around on roller-blades.

Now, in his sombre black coat, the supreme leader Jiang Zemin began to speak, raising his voice to signal when a phrase merited the approval of the handpicked crowd as he delivered a ten-minute lesson on history: 'Feudal society became capitalist and then in some countries a completely new socialist system emerged.' The cameras switched to show young and old waving their flags, beside themselves

341

with enthusiasm. 'Now the Chinese people have made great leaps towards modernization,' he went on, pausing again for more enthusiastic cheers before straining his voice to promise that 'the Chinese people will proceed unshakeably down the road towards Socialism with Chinese characteristics'.

Then, in an awkward show of bonhomie, the assembled rulers together chanted the last ten seconds to the year 2000 and Jiang pushed a button in the pedestal in front of him and looked up with a vague, benevolent smile as the flame was lit. He stayed for a few minutes longer, beaming and patting children on the head, before departing with the rest of the leadership in their limousines.

Jiang had demonstrated that he was heir to the mythical, semi-divine Yellow Emperor who in 2637 BC had fixed the time. Since then it had been the primary duty of each emperor, or Son of Heaven, to determine the beginning of the lunar calendar. Even at the start of the twentieth century, the Emperor would each year go to pray for heavenly assistance in the blue-domed Temple of Heaven in Beijing and make ritual sacrifices on the marble Altar of Heaven. Later the Emperor would carry out the first symbolic ploughing of the earth on the day which became known as the Spring Festival.

When the new year's calendar had been drawn up by the court's Board of Mathematicians, the precious documents would be carried in sedan chairs and greeted with prostrations by those who received them. The first calendars were distributed outside the main gate of the Forbidden City, which was thus called the Wu Men or Meridian Gate. Vassal states such as Korea or Vietnam regarded it as a high favour to be presented with a new calendar before the first day of the new year.

The calendar was as much a regulator of official life as it was of agriculture. Under the concept of 'Heaven's Mandate', it was believed that the people had the right to rebel if the current ruler was thought to lack the necessary virtue. If the Emperor upset the natural order then the whole universe would be thrown into chaos which might manifest itself as a comet or an eclipse. It was therefore in the Emperor's interest to ensure that his astronomers drew up an accurate calendar that would predict unusual movements in the heavens so that these might be interpreted as harmless. Otherwise such events might be taken as a sign that the Emperor had lost Heaven's Mandate. It was for this reason that the founder of each new dynasty drew up a fresh calendar, to show his understanding of the natural order, and his harmony with it. Only the Republican government established after the fall of the Qing dynasty broke with this tradition, adopting instead the Gregorian calendar.

The rituals surrounding the ceremony at which Jiang Zemin ushered in the twenty-first century were both risible and faintly sinister. Elements of the proceedings might have been inspired by Revolutionary France or Nazi Germany. Peculiar to China, however, was the symbolic acceptance of the Western calendar, despite its Christian connotations – an aspect of modernization that was accompanied by the expression of an aggrieved patriotism. For, above all, the ceremony illustrated how the Communist Party's leaders have cast themselves as the founders of a new dynasty with a divine mission to 'rejuvenate' the Chinese race and avenge its humiliations. Jiang Zemin presented himself as a sage emperor interpreting Heaven's Mandate, now conceived as the Mandate of History, and fulfilling the Party's manifest destiny to restore the empire to its former glory.

In his role as a new emperor, Jiang assumes an exclusive authority over the descendants of the Yellow Emperor wherever they may live. Consequently, it is impossible for him to tolerate the notion that any of his subjects can recognize the authority of any other body. The state is therefore automatically hostile towards the President of Taiwan, the Dalai Lama, the Pope, the United Nations, cult leaders such as Falun Gong's Li Hongzhi, indeed anyone with pretensions to command the loyalty of some of the Chinese. This results in the curious spectacle of the General Secretary of the Communist Party aspiring to be all things to all men – head of state, commander-in-chief of the armed forces, head of the Patriotic Catholic Church and head of the Tibetan Buddhists. This explains why Jiang has insisted that he, and not the Pope, must ordain new Roman Catholic bishops, that he, not the Dalai Lama, must have the final say over the arcane rituals that determine the selection of the reincarnation of new high lamas. Those who insist on defying this principle are severely punished. Lamas who during the selection of the twelfth Panchen Lama in 1996 were found to have shown allegiance to the Dalai Lama were sentenced to long terms in solitary confinement. Similarly harsh treatment has been meted out to Catholic clergy for no other reason than that loyalty to the Pope is regarded as high treason.

Likewise, only Jiang as head of the Communist Party, and not international organizations such as the United Nations, can define what constitutes the human rights of his subjects. Every effort is made to ensure that Chinese cannot meet or even petition foreign emissaries, whether they be Western leaders or the head of the United Nations Human Rights Commission. One petitioner who tried to hand a letter to Mary Robinson, the first UN Human Rights Commissioner to visit China, was dragged away screaming before her eyes in 1998.[1]

Chinese leaders routinely assert that China has a different definition of human rights, that they consist solely of the right to be adequately fed and housed. The state even sponsors research in an effort to prove that the Chinese belong to a separate species. Chinese palaeontologists believe that human beings evolved in China along a separate evolutionary path while the rest of humanity originated from a common ancestor in Africa.[2]

The legitimacy of the rulers is described in the traditional language used by religious sects. Chinese leaders speak as if they are passing on a doctrine from one generation to the next. Jiang Zemin calls himself 'The Third Generation' and describes Deng Xiaoping as 'The Second Generation', each carrying the torch of 'The First Generation', meaning Mao. In China, the founder of a Daoist or Buddhist sect would on his death-bed select as his successor a follower who he felt best understood his doctrine. The master of such a sect or the abbot of such a sect's monastery could often trace his predecessors back ten or even twenty generations, as do the Tibetan high lamas. Once appointed, the new leader in theory had absolute power to adapt the original doctrine but in practice with each generation it became increasingly difficult to do so. Similarly, the Communist Party holds up Mao Zedong Thought as its doctrine, a worthy heir to Marx, Lenin and Stalin. There is, however, no Deng

Xiaoping Thought, only Deng Xiaoping Theory, and as yet no Jiang Zemin Theory, although he is often portrayed in propaganda icons in the pose of a thinker.

When Deng came to power, it was as if a new dynasty had been born that had issued a new calendar. After the Third Plenum of the Eleventh Party Congress in 1979, all written or oral histories, all articles and statistics had to conform to the notion that everything started from this point, although in reality many policies originated before then. After Jiang became Deng's heir in 1989, the men who had led the Communist Party in the previous decade – Hua Guofeng, Hu Yaobang and Zhao Ziyang – were expunged from the record as if they were heretics. Mention of their contribution and of the existence of Zhao Ziyang, who is still alive, is taboo.

The fact that the Communist Party's doctrine now bears little resemblance to Mao Zedong Thought, that much of it seems to consist of illogical gibberish such as 'a democratic dictatorship' or 'a socialist market economy', does not necessarily matter. The state requires of its officials and its citizens a willingness to 'unify their thoughts' when asked to do so. Arguably, the less believable the idea, the better a test of loyalty it is.

The extraordinary durability of the Chinese state would not seem to depend on any fixed ideology. Quite why China should have survived into the twenty-first century against all expectations is not easy to explain but it is undeniable and a source of great pride to the Chinese themselves. A century ago, the British empire was at its height and the Manchu empire was fast disintegrating and was universally believed to be doomed. In the 1920s Mao himself agitated for independence for his native Hunan province, Yunnan declared itself a republic and provisional governments were established in Guangdong, Inner Mongolia, Manchuria, Xinjiang and elsewhere. Since then, however, the British empire has vanished from the map and all the other European powers have also left Asia – Germany, France, Russia, the Netherlands. Even the Portuguese, the first European explorers to arrive in the Far East, have gone, leaving Macao in the closing weeks of 1999. China is now the last empire left in the world, and it could be argued that it is actually expanding its territory. In the 1990s China famously reclaimed Hong Kong and Macao. What is less well known is that China has also annexed the South China Sea, establishing military bases on the Paracel and Spratly Islands and on some of the thousands of other uninhabited atolls that dot the sea. In doing so it has pushed its frontiers right up to the coastal waters of the Philippines, Malaysia and Indonesia, a thousand miles from the Chinese mainland. The Communist Party also considers that it has a mission to bring Taiwan and its 20 million people under its control and plans to do so, by force if necessary, within the next decade.

The Communist Party, so the official doctrine goes, has held China together in the face of the predations of the imperial powers and the Japanese invasion, and despite the collapse of its rival Communist power, the Soviet Union. And by portraying itself as heir to the imperial tradition, the Party leadership also demands the loyalty of all overseas Chinese citizens. They number perhaps 30 or 40 million and the majority of them are to be found in south-east Asia. The link is based on an exclusive definition of race. China has therefore only given asylum to refugees of Chinese origin, such as those who fled Indonesia after massacres in 1966 or who left Vietnam after pogroms in 1979. Other asylum-seekers from Vietnam and North Koreans who crossed into China to escape the famine in North Korea in the late 1990s have been forcibly returned. China acts as if it has no international obligations other than to ethnic Chinese.

Overseas Chinese often seem especially susceptible to the dream of restoring China's imperial greatness. After 1979, they became the largest investors in China, accounting for 80 per cent of recorded investment, and apart from a brief period in 1989 overseas tycoons have not financed anti-government organizations. Most overseas Chinese are grouped together in patriotic associations, some dating back to the days of Sun Yat-sen and his struggle to overthrow the Manchu Qing dynasty. After the KMT and the CCP split in 1927, both competed to win the loyalty of these overseas Chinese. Even now, virtually all overseas Chinese language publications are in the hands of those loyal to one or other party. They therefore share almost identical views, dating back to Sun Yat-sen and his contemporaries, about

Chinese history and the unity of the Chinese race. Hardly any seem to be able to conceive of the Chinese state as an aggressor, even an imperialist power, only as a victim of foreign forces. Since the days of the Emperor Qinshi Huangdi, the expansion of the Chinese state has always been described in terms of peaceful assimilation, unification and pacification, never invasion or conquest.

In its struggle to snuff out the independence of the KMT and Taiwan, the Communist Party also plays on the imperial notion that there will only be peace once the Chinese are 'one family under heaven'. Beijing portrays Taiwan's independence movement as a plot by the United States and its ally Japan to keep China weak and divided. Only when all acknowledge Jiang Zemin as the monarch of a unified state will China finally be at peace for the first time since the Opium Wars. This, the theme of Jiang Zemin's speech at the turn of the millennium and on every other public occasion, is not unlike the belief in medieval Europe that all members of society should belong to the one true Church. Even most overseas Chinese appear to subscribe to this belief, to the extent that it has paralysed those opposition groups operating abroad. Their only potent weapon consists of outflanking the Communist Party by accusing it of being too weak in asserting China's territorial claims in the face of foreigners. During the mid-1990s, democrats in Hong Kong whipped up public support by trying to land on the tiny and uninhabitable Diaoyu Islands, northeast of Taiwan, which have belonged to Japan for over a century. The aim was to embarrass Beijing which claims sovereignty over them but dares not assert it. And when in 1998, rioting Indonesians targeted the homes of wealthy Chinese and reportedly raped ethnic Chinese women, outraged 'patriotic' Chinese leapt into action to shame Beijing for having stood idly by. Reports of the routine violation of human rights on the mainland do not provoke anything like the same vociferous outpouring of rage.

During 1996, when the first open presidential elections ever to be held in Taiwan or in any Chinese territory took place, I met in Taipei a vehemently anti-Communist mainland writer whose works I knew. Pu Ning had spent over twenty years in labour camps and, now a brisk 70-year-old, was still investigating Communist atrocities, yet he seemed completely oblivious to the elections taking place. 'Oh, the elections, I haven't bothered much about them,' he said carelessly. Democracy so far from Beijing meant little to him and the general issue of human rights abuses outside the Chinese world even less. It is equally impossible for mainlanders to accept any notion that contact with the Western world has brought anything other than humiliation to China, although a very long list of benefits could be drawn up.

The brand of virulent nationalism that has been nurtured among many Chinese, and China's long history as the region's superpower, make Beijing deeply feared by its neighbours. The loyalty of the often wealthy overseas Chinese who dominate the economies of Indonesia, Malaysia and Thailand has regularly come under suspicion, particularly since such Chinese communities have often flaunted their separate identities. Governments representing the majority populations in Malaysia and Indonesia have therefore introduced discriminatory legislation which has in turn bred further divisions.

Until the Treaty of Nanjing was signed with Britain in 1842, China had never recognized any other state as its equal and regarded its neighbours as vassals. The legacy of this attitude lingered into the twentieth century. In the 1950s, the Prime Minister of the Thai kingdom, Pibul Songkram, chose a medieval method of establishing ties with the new rulers in Beijing, secretly sending young children of the Thai élite to be brought up in Zhou Enlai's household as quasi-hostages.[3] Equally medieval was Deng's justification for attacking Vietnam in 1979 in order to 'punish' it for its arrogance in invading Cambodia with the intention of overthrowing China's proxy rulers, the Khmer Rouge.

Whether China should be defined as a state, an empire, a self-perpetuating bureaucracy, a culture or a nation is an open question. Perhaps it is quite simply *sui generis*. Even so, the way of life that China's rulers have created for themselves since they won power in 1949 seems a peculiar retrogression. For they live as a separate caste, in a style as secluded as anything created by the Qing or earlier imperial dynasties.

From the very beginning, the Party introduced a system of carefully calibrated privileges that ensured that Mao and other leaders lived a life apart from their followers. Even during the Long March, Mao and his close companions travelled not on foot but on stretchers, and at Yan'an they were accorded special treatment. There their children too were placed in special schools and many were sent to be educated in the Soviet Union.

After 1949, these revolutionary families lived in guarded compounds reserved for senior leaders, and their children attended reserved kindergartens, schools and universities. They had access to special shops and ration tickets, to special books and internal information sources restricted to privileged circles according to their rank in the Party, and to much else forbidden to the rest of the population. Even during the Cultural Revolution, when the children of senior leaders were imprisoned, they were incarcerated together in a special prison camp, and most of the adults who were sent to the countryside did not end up in villages but laboured in camps called May 7th Cadre Schools. It is hardly surprising, therefore, to discover that virtually all of the Third Generation leaders have spent their entire lives completely cocooned within the Party. Even in retirement, Party members can be found in the same compounds, eating in Party canteens and attending special social clubs for retired cadres.

The best glimpse into this world is afforded when the Party leadership goes to the seaside for its annual summer holiday in the little fishing port of Beidaihe, 200 miles east of Beijing on the Gulf of Bohai. New air-conditioned trains carrying wives, children, grandchildren, nannies, secretaries, advisers, academic specialists, cooks, drivers and the entire palace guard arrive at a station cordoned off by armed and helmeted soldiers. More troops man checkpoints on the roads, and guards are posted around vast porticoed mansions, set deep within shady gardens, that resemble antebellum Louisiana houses. It is here that the leadership stays.

'Some of the houses are pre-Liberation but a lot of leaders have been building their own recently,' said a woman selling cold drinks at the edge of a six-mile stretch of closed-off beach. Along the road, black limousines and cars with darkened windows bearing the number plates of the armed police cruised past flanked by motorcycle patrols.

Here the rituals of a seaside holiday are observed with the same punctiliousness as marks the rites and etiquette of Beijing's bureaucratic life. Squads of the PAP march briskly past the sandy beaches where pasty-coloured cadres in swimming trunks and flip-flops assemble, each carrying an inflated rubber tube. Even here some officials wear identity cards pinned to their bathing trunks and a few of the very status-conscious cannot resist carrying their beepers and mobile phones with them.

Every place in the sun is determined according to Party hierarchy. The West Beach is reserved for Jiang Zemin, the Politburo Standing Committee and senior generals. The sea is closed off with nets and the sand marked off by plainclothes bodyguards dozing under umbrellas spaced at regular intervals. Each leader has his own bit of beach and beach house and so do the more important institutions – the Foreign Ministry, the *People's Daily*, research institutes of the Ministry of Aeronautics, the State Statistical Bureau and so on. At the far end is a large and gloomy mansion belonging to the State Council which local residents claim is used by the former Prime Minister Li Peng.

In the centre of the strip of coastline is a military hospital known only by its number, 281. This is where elderly generals convalesce amid the cool sea breezes. Just inside the entrance gate a large sign reads '*Ni hao, shou zhang*' ('Hello, senior leaders') but the armed soldier in front will not reveal the name of the institution – 'It's a secret,' he said nervously when I asked.

Beidaihe itself has few hotels. Visits are by invitation, and train tickets are monopolized by government units. The small area of beach allocated for public bathing is fenced off and is usually jam-packed, especially at weekends. A list of rules hangs on the perimeter fence. Those who enter are warned not to start fights, nor to urinate or defecate in the water. The fine for those caught doing the latter is set at between 10 and 20 yuan. Foreigners, of course, have their own separate beach, roped off and marked with warning signs stuck in the sand.

The holidaymakers, grouped by work unit, sit in open-air restaurants eating fresh crab, whelks, eels and scallops with gusto, but the atmosphere of organized collective fun suggests an extended summer camp for grown-ups. Beidaihe will never vie with Cannes and the Côte d'Azur. There are no glittering yachts in the harbour, no paparazzi spying out the rich and the famous emerging from casinos or bathing topless. Instead, a statue of Stalin's favourite writer, Maxim Gorky, stands wrapped in thought and in a thick winter coat, lending a chilly presence to the West Beach.

Beidaihe was first built for Western missionaries at the turn of the last century. They were followed by the diplomatic staff of the embassies in Beijing and by businessmen from nearby Tianjin. Families stayed for three months of the year although husbands were often forced to remain behind to work. Leaders of successive warlord governments and KMT ministries also built their resort homes here. The 281 hospital was first used by the KMT before being taken over by the general staff of the headquarters of the Japanese occupation forces.

After 1949, Marshal Zhu De took one of the villas for himself and soon the other nine Communist Marshals followed suit, including Lin Biao. Lin's fortress-like villa, which he designed and had built for himself, was opened to the public in the early 1980s. One can see his indoor swimming-pool, a wicker chair he left on a sun-terrace, and a room where he could watch films while lying in bed. There is also now an exhibition of fuzzy photographs of the charred corpses allegedly discovered at the crash site in Mongolia after he and his family tried to flee in an aeroplane in 1971 following a failed *coup d'état* against Mao.

Lin Biao's story seems designed to show that once admitted to this world, it is impossible to escape, no matter who you are. Party members are rarely expelled and all too few have defected from the higher ranks. Even after 1989 when some members did resign, they stuck to a Mafia-like code of *omertà*. One exception was Xu Jiatun, the former head of Xinhua, the Party's base in Hong Kong, who ended up in a Buddhist monastery in California; another was Yan Jiaqi, a senior scholar from the Academy of Social Sciences who also moved to the United States. Even so only one substantial portrait of life within the inner circle has ever emerged. *The Private Life of*

Chairman Mao was written by his erstwhile doctor, Li Zhisui, after he emigrated to America. In it, Li paints an extraordinary picture of personal debauchery and court intrigue that matches anything written about the Qin Emperor.

According to the Legalist Han Feizi, 'The wise sovereign governs like the Heavens and manipulates his subjects like a ghost.' An aura of mystery and secrecy is a necessary enhancement to the ruler's power and authority, and the ruler should distance himself from his subjects, operating behind a veil of secrecy and residing deep within the royal palace.[4] From Li Zhisui's description, it is clear that Mao's public and private life mirrored the notions put forward by the Legalists. Mao hardly ever mingled with his subjects, gave speeches or broadcast his orders. During the Cultural Revolution he made seven appearances on Tiananmen Square before the Red Guards but he spoke only once, uttering just two brief sentences.[5] Otherwise, he was invisible to his subjects, although his image was everywhere. 'The danger for the ruler is to trust men. To trust men is to be controlled by men,' Han Feizi had written. After the failure of the Great Leap Forward, Mao lived a life of total seclusion, suspicious of everyone, never attending official meetings and rarely dealing directly with the Party apparatus. In his final years, he stayed in his bedroom, in almost total isolation, attended only by a handful of young women.

When Deng Xiaoping came to power, the media deliberately portrayed him in a different light as a family man, celebrating Chinese New Year with his grandchildren or playing bridge with his friends, cracking jokes or watching football. In this, he personally embodied a shift in policy. Under Mao, the Party had intended to destroy the family as an institution and had banned playing-cards along with all other individual pursuits. While Mao boasted that he lived 'without regard for the law or Heaven', Deng tried to restore the pre-1958 institutions of the Party and promised a government that would 'rule by law'. Yet according to Zhao Ziyang's assistant, Bao Tong, it was Deng's word that remained pre-eminent: 'You know, we used to have Party meetings but there were not even votes cast for decisions made by the Politburo or the Standing Committee. Before Zhao Ziyang there was no voting at all. The one person said something and that was it.'[6] Indeed, one of the crimes later laid at Zhao's door was that in 1989 he had revealed a state secret to the visiting Soviet President Mikhail Gorbachev, namely that although Deng had stepped down from all his posts (except that of Chairman of the Chinese Bridge Association), he was still the supreme leader who decided everything.

As long as Deng lived, he remained the only leader who could be presented as an individual with his own personality and foibles. Ironically, when conservative leaders such as Yang Shangkun and Li Peng made a fresh attempt to push him aside after 1989, they failed, trapped by the very dictatorship that they had shed blood to preserve from democratic reforms. In 1992, they could not stop him from pushing through reformist policies and he remained China's ruler until he died in 1997 at the age of 93.

The night news of his death broke, I went to his house north of the Forbidden City. I was struck by its modesty. It was hidden behind high walls and guarded by a few plainclothes policemen but it was clearly no ostentatious palace. The houses in the alleyways around it were almost slums, without running water and with communal toilets. Across the road was a grubby bus station and a few dingy shops. Though he was a dictator, it was easy to believe that Deng genuinely hated the grotesque and vainglorious personality cult that Mao had fostered.

The status of Deng's successor, Jiang Zemin, is evoked by the phrase 'Third Generation with Jiang Zemin at its core'. He lacks the power to make policy or issue edicts spontaneously. He gives no interviews unless his answers, usually written down beforehand, are first vetted by the Standing Committee. And Jiang, as he mingles on a regular basis with other foreign leaders, seems more constrained by the international norms of behaviour than either Deng or Mao.

This attempt to conform to international norms, however, has resulted in some curious contradictions. On the one hand, Jiang regards himself as having semi-divine status. When a few dozen human rights protesters appeared in view at the start of his state visit to Switzerland in 1999, Jiang fell into a rage. 'You have lost a good friend,' he warned the Swiss President Ruth Dreifuss. 'I have never been treated like this before.' He broke off the arrival ceremony and in the Federal Parliament in Berne he asked his hosts, 'Don't you have the ability to run this country?'[7] On the other hand, he has taken pains to present himself as an ordinary human being, delighting in breaking into song at banquets, even on one occasion in the Philippines singing 'Love Me Tender'. On other occasions he has recited poetry, played musical instruments, danced or shown off his knowledge of English or Russian.

This buffoonish side to Jiang's character has not prevented the bureaucracy from attempting to bolster his aura of infallibility. Jiang is never publicly contradicted or challenged. Night after night on state television, the seven o'clock news shows Jiang issuing instructions at a meeting with his subordinates or holding forth in meetings with foreign leaders. Indeed nearly all news in the Chinese media, whether national or local, consists of a series of leaders' appearances at which they issue instructions to rows of obedient, seated officials. Only in the late 1980s was there a brief attempt at a change in style when Hu Yaobang urged senior officials to adopt a policy of 'mediation and discussion'. Zhao Ziyang took the idea further when, in 1988, he demanded that local leaders engage in a process of 'consultation and dialogue' with local citizens. For the first time, Zhao and others appeared in Western-style suits. Zhao even answered questions off the cuff at a reception with Western journalists. For a while Chinese politicians were expected to behave like those in Western countries and it was surprising how well some responded to the challenge of 'townhall democracy'. Driving home one day, I was astonished to hear the then Party secretary of Tianjin, Li Ruihuan, taking part in a radio phone-in show and speaking fluently and apparently unrehearsed.[8]

When Jiang Zemin returned to his old alma mater, Jiaotong University, to take part in a public dialogue and started off reading, as is customary, a prepared text, he was taken aback to find the boisterous students booing and shouting at him: 'Who elected you? Was it the people of Shanghai?' Incensed, Jiang demanded, 'What's your name? What class are you in?' The jeering increased and the students chanted Abraham Lincoln's words on government 'of the people, by the people, for the people'. Jiang angrily responded that they understood nothing of democracy or China's real situation and then he proceeded to recite the entire Gettysburg Address from memory.[9]

Ten years later, when Jiang gave an interview to the *Washington Post* before his first state visit to the United States in 1997, he said that elections are impossible in a country with a population of 1.2 billion, of whom 100 million are illiterate. Even in a city such as Shanghai, it would be impractical for people to elect their own representatives: 'The city of Shanghai has a population of 13 million, and it is impossible for me to be directly elected by the people of Shanghai. So I was elected to the National People's Congress of the city of Shanghai.'[10]

No reference is ever made in public to the elections that were held in China as early as 1909, and most mainland Chinese are unaware that for fifty years elections were a regular part of Chinese political life. At the end of the Qing dynasty every province had its own elected assembly, and in 1910 the government convened a National Assembly with 200 members. Two years later, a parliament was elected with a senate chosen by the provincial assemblies and a second chamber directly elected by voters. The franchise was limited, restricted to males and amounting to about 10 per cent of the population. A new parliament was elected in 1918 and the last elections were held in 1947–8 with universal suffrage, at least in those areas controlled by the KMT.[11]

Without the need for any regular contact with the 'masses', China's ruling élite not only lead lives entirely separate from their subjects but they also inhabit a political system that prevents any views from below ever reaching them. Dissidents are given lengthy prison sentences as a warning to all, and China is now one of the last countries in the world without a functioning parliament. The National People's Congress does exist but it has no building of its own, no permanent staff or offices, and it assembles for just ten days a year. During the rest of the year, only members of the Standing Committee, which is made up entirely of senior Party officials, meet. And in marked contrast to other countries, the Prime Minister gives only one press conference a year which is often restricted to three previously arranged questions.

Chinese leaders seem to inhabit a world of reflecting mirrors. When, as is the custom, they go on 'inspection tours' outside Beijing to try to find out what is going on, they learn nothing because their officials conspire against them. For instance, when in 1998 the Prime Minister Zhu Rongji went to Anhui province to inspect relief operations after summer floods, he visited a granary to see if there was a plentiful supply of grain and to judge whether prices would remain stable. On his return to Beijing a letter arrived, telling him he had been duped. He then sent one of his own officials to investigate. The official pretended to be a visiting grain buyer and discovered that the manager of the granary had borrowed grain from elsewhere before Zhu arrived to show that the state granary was functioning. After Zhu left the grain was returned, leaving the granary empty.[12] Similarly, when in 1997 his predecessor as Prime Minister, Li Peng, arrived in Wuxian to inspect the resettlement of locals who had to be moved to make way for the Three Gorges dam reservoir, he was taken to a meeting packed with Party officials instead of those who were to be resettled, and he was shown a Potemkin resettlement village built especially for his visit.[13]

Not only are such events common but the political system does not allow anyone to accept responsibility for what happens, no matter how small. This lack of personal responsibility can be taken to absurd lengths. When, in 1998, the Chinese national soccer team failed yet again to qualify for the World Cup, to universal public anger, the country's most senior sports official, Wang Junshen, refused to resign, saying he could not accept any blame because he had merely obeyed the Party's instructions. An exception occurred in 1988 when the then Minister of Railways, Ding Guang'en, accepted responsibility for a serious railway accident and resigned. Even so, his record did not prevent him from being put in charge of the Party's Propaganda Department after 1989.

In such a system, without popular elections, public accountability or any reliable way to assess an official's merit objectively, family connections are paramount. In different ways, both Mao and Deng endorsed nepotism. Mao's belief in class warfare rested on the premise that class status is hereditary. The children of landlords must be persecuted and the children of revolutionaries could be trusted: 'The wolf produces a wolf, the phoenix produces a phoenix.' By ending this permanent state of class warfare and by restoring the family, Deng opened the door to the more traditional practices of nepotism. His own family went into business, trading on his name and authority. One daughter, Deng Nan, became vice minister of the State Science and Technology Commission which supervises many military institutions, while her husband He Ping ran the PLA Equipment Department. Wu Jianchang, the husband of another daughter, Deng Lin, was chairman of the powerful China National Non-ferrous Metals Import and Export Corporation until it incurred heavy debts after speculating in commodities and foreign exchange. The younger son, Deng Zhifang, went into business on his own account, setting up the Grand Real Estate Company. In Hong Kong he teamed up with another 'princeling', Zhou Beifang, the son of the chairman of Beijing's Capital and Iron Steel Works. In February 1995, they were both detained and the latter was imprisoned (see Chapter 6).

At the height of the Dengs' economic fortunes, the Hong Kong magazine *Kaifang* claimed that the clan had total assets worth US$0.5 billion. Another Hong Kong publication, *Cheng Ming*, reckoned that 900 of the children of China's leading 1,700 families were managing directors of foreign trade companies and that another 3,100 were in high positions in either the military or the government; and if a Communist family was unable to acquire assets, it would install its offspring in a commanding position within the bureaucracy.[14]

China now seems to be run as a collection of family businesses. Many of the children of the élite joined the PLA during the height of its expansion in the early 1970s and from there they have branched out into running military-related businesses. For example, General Wang Zhen, one of the powerful figures in the 1980s who cracked down on liberal intellectuals, is the father of Wang Jun, one of the country's richest businessmen, first as head of the defence industry conglomerate Poly Technologies and later as director of CITIC, the state-run investment bank. Marshal Ye Jianying's son-in-law, Zou Jiahua, became minister of the ordnance industry, then vice minister for the Science and Technology Commission and a Politburo member. Marshal Nie Rongzhen, in charge of developing the PLA's rockets and nuclear weapons, ensured that his daughter Lieutenant-General Nie Li became deputy director of the

Commission for Science, Technology and Industry for National Defence (COSTIND) and that her husband, General Ding Henggao, became COSTIND's chief. The number of other, similar cases are legion.

In attempting to allay public anger at such blatant nepotism, in 1985 Hu Yaobang launched a crackdown on the 'princelings'. Relatives of Marshal Ye Jianying and children of leftists such as Hu Qiaomu and Peng Zhen were arrested for corruption. The daughter of Ye Fei, a former PLA Navy political commissar, was given a seventeen-year prison sentence for economic crimes, and the sons of three senior Party officials in Shanghai were executed after being found guilty of raping fifty-one women over a period of four years. Hu's attempt to deal with the princelings may have been one of the reasons why the hardliners, many of whose children were implicated, united against him in 1987.

Public calls for an end to nepotism persisted and in the 1989 democracy demonstrations, protesters demanded in addition that leaders should open their bank accounts for inspection. In a further effort to deal with the problem, at the first Politburo meeting which Jiang Zemin chaired after 4 June, he issued a seven-point circular banning children of senior cadres from 'engaging in business operations'. More regulations followed in 1992 and 1993, designed to bar all officials from employing relatives. Cadres were also ordered to report all sources of income to their respective personnel departments.

Such directives have proved futile. In the 1990s the son of Chen Yun, the veteran revolutionary and economic strategist who had once been a possible successor to Deng, was quickly promoted as vice governor of the central bank and then put in charge of the State Development Bank. Li Peng, prime minister for ten years, put his wife Zhu Lin in charge of China's first commercial nuclear reactor at Daya Bay, and his eldest son, Li Xiaopeng, became at the age of 34 vice president and then chairman of the China Huaneng Enterprise Group, a New York listed state company which is involved in raising funds abroad for China's power industry. Li Xiaopeng subsequently became heavily involved in raising money abroad for his father's greatest project, the Three Gorges dam. Jiang Zemin's own son, Jiang Mianheng, returned to Shanghai after graduating from Drexel

University in the United States and set up a number of tele-communications businesses including China Netcom Corporation which is building a fibre-optic network across China.[15]

Many princelings have been engaged by foreign companies. For example, British Petroleum paid the university fees for the son of the former head of China's Ministry of Petroleum who became a Sloan Fellow at MIT. The Prime Minister Zhu Rongji's son was engaged by Morgan, Stanley, Dean, Witter and Company to work in a joint-venture investment bank. A daughter of Liu Shaoqi, Liu Tingting, was employed by General Electric and then by Rockefeller and Company. After studies at Boston and Harvard Universities, she returned to set up her own consultancy, Asia Link Group, to advise multinationals on entry into the China market.

Ironically, many of the princelings are now well placed to intro-duce new technology, capital and business practices to China. For while at home in the 1980s and 1990s, the leadership launched cam-paigns against 'bourgeois liberalization' and attacked reformers for believing that 'the moon is rounder in the West', their children were studying in the West. Deng Xiaoping's son Deng Zifang studied physics at Rochester University in New York State. His wife accom-panied him and gave birth to a child while there, who thereby acquired US citizenship. Jiang Zemin found himself in the peculiar position of appealing to Hun Sun, a former classmate from a rich capitalist Shanghainese family whose possessions had been expropriated by the Communists and whose relatives had been per-secuted. Hun Sun had become a professor at Drexel University where Jiang now wanted him to find a place for his son.[16] In all over 300,000 Chinese studied abroad between 1979 and 1999, and in the 1990s, as many as 100,000 were studying in the United States at any one time.

These princelings' role as the new comprador class has infuriated government critics such as Professor Ding Zelin, whose own son was shot dead during the Tiananmen protests. In a 'Declaration on Civil Rights and Social Justice', issued on 22 September 1998, she railed against the injustice of allowing the children of Communist leaders to become the first to benefit from the *de facto* privatization of the economy: 'In the course of the fifty years that the CCP has been in power, it first expropriated the property of all citizens and then it encouraged some people to get rich. For the first thirty years, through exploitation and force, it turned almost all private property into state property: in the last twenty years, it has allowed what remained nominally the property of all the people and of the collective, including a considerable proportion of the newly accumulated state assets, to become in fact the private property of a few.'[17]

The privileged position of the children of the ruling élite has been one factor in the growth of widescale corruption and an accelerating flight of capital abroad that began after 1989. Some Chinese analysts have tried to calculate how much money is involved. The economist He Qinglian claims that up until 1992 cadres diverted on average 50 billion yuan (US$6 billion) a year into their own pockets, and she believes the sums became much greater after 1992, when financial reforms allowed SOEs to issue shares and bonds and to deal in property. In *Pitfalls of Modernization,* she describes in detail how officials running SOEs falsified accounts to disguise how they had diverted SOE bank loans or share capital into their own pockets.[18] The economist Yang Fan has argued in the Chinese-language journal *Strategy and Management* that since the reforms officials have appropriated 5 trillion yuan (US$602 billion) worth of state assets, initially by bribery or by profiting from the gap between low state fixed prices and higher market prices. Since 1992, the scope for corruption has expanded dramatically, as has its scale: 'Taking all the power-money exchange activities into account, no less than 3,000 billion yuan (US$361 billion) has fallen into private hands during the past twenty years.'[19]

Official reports by bodies such as the National Audit Office provide some concrete evidence. The Audit Office's report for 1998 put the loss of state property in that year at well over US$10 billion, equivalent to 2 per cent of China's annual GDP, in addition to the US$3 billion which the Audit Office had itself tracked down. The corruption seems to take place at all levels and in every organization although the heaviest burden falls on the weakest members of

Chinese society, the peasantry. For example, inspectors found that 69 per cent of the fees demanded by officials running irrigation schemes, some US$430 million, had been illegally diverted.[20]

The scale and extent of such corruption is staggering. Cadres in charge of the electric power industry are thought to have pocketed US$1.4 billion in illegal fees. Those charged with the resettlement of some of the 1.3 million people displaced by the Three Gorges dam were found to have embezzled US$28 million. In 1998 investigators discovered that US$7 billion earmarked for buying grain from the peasants had been misappropriated over a period of six years and that another US$9.6 billion had been spent on importing cars or speculating in stocks and futures or had been diverted into under-writing private businesses such as projects to build hotels, offices and residential buildings. Those involved in foreign trade had also defrauded the state, routinely falsifying documents to benefit from the US$28 billion dispensed annually as export subsidies or evading import duties by smuggling goods worth tens of billions of dollars a year. Chinese officials estimate that in 1997 alone, officials smuggled 100,000 luxury cars into the country.

Government-backed financial institutions such as the 200 international trust and investment corporations set up to raise foreign capital have been equally vulnerable. Not a trace has been found of the US$30 billion dispensed as official loans or of a further US$30 billion listed as unregistered debts. When investigators tried to discover what had happened to the money lent by the Guangdong government's international trust and investment corporation (GITIC), which collapsed in 1999 with debts of over US$4 billion, they found that the officials concerned had not even bothered to keep records of the loans they had handed out. In the same way, examination of the accounts kept by SOEs has repeatedly revealed that the vast majority have deliberately fabricated the figures reported for their loans, assets, profits and losses.[21]

Such figures point to a vast black economy and suggest that most published data about the Chinese economy must be treated with the deepest suspicion. Although China reports that it has been the world's second largest recipient of foreign investment during the 1990s, with US$45 billion invested in just one year, 1998, it has also seen enormous outflows of capital. A World Bank report, 'China weathering the storm and learning the lessons', has estimated that in 1997 the net capital outflow was US$44 billion and that in 1998 it might have amounted to US$72 billion.[22]

The virtual immunity from prosecution that Party members, and especially those related to senior officials, enjoy means that the Party cannot police itself. Although Jiang Zemin has warned that corruption is a virus that could destroy the Party, the results of efforts to stem the tide seem meagre. In its report of work carried out in 1998, the Central Disciplinary Inspection Committee, the Party organization charged with eradicating corruption, said that 3,970 Party members at the level of county magistrate or above had been penalized, in a year in which US$10 billion of state money had been embezzled. Of these only 304 could be said to be senior officials. Investigators had looked at 1.6 million cases, investigated 120,000 and recovered US$560 million. By contrast, during the period of political liberalization, the committee expelled 25,000 Party members in 1987 and 33,400 in 1989.[23]

Whether this kleptocracy will be willing to move towards a more accountable political system is a question often discussed in connection with the role which students returning from studying overseas will play in shaping China's future. When Qian Ning, the son of China's long-serving foreign minister Qian Qichen, returned home after six years in America, he published a book entitled *Studying in the United States: The Story of an Era* in which he too pondered on the impact this shared experience would have on his generation.

'They want China to be more modern and open-minded, they want change, but they are not coming back to overthrow the government,' he concluded when I met him in December 1996.[24]

He had returned to find himself at odds with his father who, like his contemporaries, had studied in Stalin's Soviet Union. He was now working as a consultant for a British accountancy firm, lobbying for a business licence, but he seemed more interested in literature and the works of Walt Whitman than in making money, and he looked a little lost in the new brash Beijing.

Qian Ning had also given thought to the fact that less than a third of Chinese students who go abroad to study ever return. He pointed out that a survey carried out among students in eighteen universities in the United States had found that about half were drawn from the families of intellectuals who had suffered under Mao, a quarter from rural China and the rest from the families of the élite. Those who did return were usually the latter, some of whom had been shocked to discover that in America their birth did not automatically entitle them to the privileges and status that were their due at home. Many observers in China assume that those who do return will be agents of change but Qian Ning is not so sure.

'Going abroad does change one deeply but this is a generation "born and raised under the red flag",' he said. Even when, in America, they would discuss politics, he found their thinking deeply coloured by their upbringing in revolutionary struggle and by their fierce sense of nationalism: 'Most of them believe in both the "unification of thoughts" and in democracy. None of them seems to see any contradiction in this. Besides, they know you cannot simply import American values into China.'

China's future is partly in the hands of a group who have a vested interest in maintaining the status quo. Few of them appear to have returned to rock the boat or to engage in any kind of opposition politics. In some ways this group seems to have more in common with the overseas Chinese. They have been to the same American universities as the children of those capitalists and KMT officials who fled to Hong Kong or Taiwan in 1949, and they now share the same lifestyle and aspirations. Many either own their own companies or are in joint ventures with these overseas Chinese capitalists. They travel abroad and often have much of their wealth safely secured offshore or they hold foreign passports. One can only speculate on what they will do with their wealth and power when the older generation leaves the scene but it is possible that they may lead China in the political direction pioneered by Taiwan or Hong Kong.

Many mainlanders visit Hong Kong and notice the contrast – the open atmosphere, free press, civic freedoms and trust in the legal system that make Hong Kong so different from the mainland – while Taiwan has become the first part of the Chinese world to hold truly free and open elections. In March 2000, the KMT's President was replaced by the former political dissident Chen Shui-bian. The Taiwanese, at least, have shown it is possible to escape from the prison of Chinese history.

EPILOGUE

Examining the Oracle Bones

E VEN IN LATE spring, no shoots of green yet grace the terraced loess hillsides around Yan'an, the capital of Mao's rebel Red Army in the 1930s. Everything is a shade of brown – the dusty fields, the silt-laden water, the houses carved out of hillsides, the donkeys ploughing the fields, the tanned skin of the peasants and the dirt roads that lead to their villages. The landscape, denuded of all trees, has an exhausted feel about it. The Chinese believe they sprang from this earth, and this is where the Revolution began. It seems a good place to end an account of the Chinese.

On my last trip before completing this book, I visited Zizhou county, about 200 miles north of Yan'an, where peasants had tried to engage a lawyer to defend themselves in the courts against the oppressive and brutal control of local Party officials. Not much had changed here in the seventy years since Mao's Long March and his 'liberation' of the peasants from their 'cruel landlords'. Now, the peasants were afraid not of landlords but of the Party officials who prey on them just as the landlords once did.

'Nothing has changed here since the Communists came. The Revolution only benefited corrupt leaders. See what conditions we live in,' complained Jing Xiuhu bitterly. A tall, sturdy peasant wearing a white cap over his stubbled head, he was one of the leaders representing several hundred thousand peasants who had been fighting to reduce taxes, taxes which in some years amounted to more than their annual net income.

He told a familiar story – of droughts and crops that fail, of poverty and the parents who cannot afford schooling for their children, of corrupt officials and police who beat the peasants and seize their goods if they do not pay their taxes. It was the lack of justice, however, in both the social and the legal sense that bothered him most. In 1997, villagers in a neighbouring district, Peijiawan, had won a lawsuit against local officials whom the court had then ordered to reduce taxes. It was the first time such a thing had ever happened in Shaanxi or anywhere else and the case received widespread publicity across the country. Here at last was proof that the Party was serious about the rule of law and intent on redressing the wrongs of the peasants.

In 1998 Jing and tens of thousands of others had banded together to engage a lawyer from Yan'an to take local officials to court over excessive taxes. The lawyer, Ma Wenlin, a schoolteacher who had been a fanatical Maoist in his youth, agreed to take on the case but no authority would give him a hearing. In the end Ma led a delegation to Beijing to press their case with the State Council. A meeting was arranged, but before it could take place the Beijing police arrested them. The peasants were sent back to Zizhou. The lawyer was detained and beaten, losing most of his teeth. A few months later he was tried by a kangaroo court. The witnesses were suborned, his defence lawyers silenced, the court packed with supporters of the officials. No one in the state media dared report the case. Ma was sentenced to imprisonment.

'We are afraid here, everyone is now afraid to talk,' said Jing. We were meeting in great secrecy and Jing said he was an exception. The rest had been cowed by the imprisonment and torture meted out to the ringleaders. They had talked about a rebellion but had lacked the necessary courage or leadership to take further action.'[1]

Some foreign and domestic observers have predicted that such an explosive mixture of corruption, poverty and unemployment in China must one day result in a rural revolt. Perhaps. The peasants of Zizhou are a testament to the deep anger and sense of frustration that exists in the countryside. But events there also demonstrate how difficult resistance is.

The Party, which in 1997 permitted the peasants of Peijiawan to pursue their case, quickly backtracked when it became apparent that the pursuit of such cases would undermine the power and therefore the loyalty of its cadres.

'When we went from office to office, they told us that the tax problem was the same all over the country. If they took on this case, the Party would have to do the same everywhere,' recalled Jing. 'Local leaders told us, "Jiang Zemin is corrupt too. All the leaders are corrupt, so who are you trying to fight?"'

In the 1920s and 1930s, Mao and other Chinese intellectuals had raised an army among the disaffected peasantry of northern Shaanxi and had fought their way to power. In doing so they were able to rely on the help of the Soviet Union and could exploit the lack of control at the centre that had resulted from the collapse of imperial China. The Japanese invasion also fatally weakened the KMT, and the world-wide depression that followed the 1929 crash threw millions out of work in China and destroyed their faith in world trade and the market economy. Such a combination of factors do not exist today.

Even if they did, many of the intellectuals who might lead a revolution seem determined to avoid the path of violence. The lessons of the Communist Revolution and the Cultural Revolution, the cycle of violence and dictatorship, have not been forgotten. Like Ma Wenlin, many feel that the Party élite would fight to keep their property and privileges, that civil war might be the result. Cautious movement towards a stable legal system, in which civil and property rights are guaranteed for all, seems preferable.

One thing has changed since the 1930s, however. With the advent of television, the peasants are no longer so easily duped by their political masters. Now they can find out for themselves what laws and regulations exist. In Zizhou, local officials have taken to censoring broadcasts which touch on government edicts on rural taxation, a measure of the threat posed by information technology. The communications revolution may only be beginning to change rural China, but change will occur.

There is another new factor in the equation. Unlike in the 1930s, when wealthy countries strangled world trade by erecting tariff barriers, China is now benefiting from open markets and the globalization of commerce. And while it is true that many parts of inland China are still barely touched by this, there is nevertheless optimism that the market economy will bring change.

Such optimism, however, must be offset against the fact that the central government and many local governments are deep in debt. The bureaucracy must be cut down and China desperately needs to create a fair and equitable tax system. Zizhou peasants claim their taxes are supporting three times the required number of officials, most of whom are the children of cadres. In addition, the state has still to restructure state-owned enterprises and to find a solution to acute unemployment amongst the peasants. It is also hard to see how China will pay for healthcare for its ageing urban population.

In all likelihood the state will be forced to issue an increasing number of treasury bonds and to borrow from abroad in some form or other. In a domestic crisis, Beijing may like Moscow be forced to go cap in hand to the International Monetary Fund. It is likely that such an approach would raise sufficient money to stave off the worst threats to social stability, for the rest of the world has too much at stake to risk destabilizing China.

When I spoke to the peasants of Zizhou, the villagers had just returned from a performance by a travelling opera troupe who had set up a temporary stage on the only patch of flat ground in the narrow valley. As we talked we could hear the high-pitched voices and the clash of cymbals as the troupe played out another tale of cruel tyrants, scheming officials, ill-treated wives and alluring concubines. The ritualized performance, and the peasants' delight in it, spoke of history's powerful and often merciless grip on the minds of so many in China.

The weight of over two thousand years of history is not easily thrown aside. In all likelihood a powerful centralized state bureaucracy will continue to govern China. A tiny élite will remain in charge of the destiny of the vast majority of submissive, relatively poor and ill-educated peasants. China will remain an essentially agrarian and autarkic economy in which living standards for all but the élite will improve only slowly. Vast disparities in wealth and status, which have always existed, will increase.

The greatest threat to China, it seems to me, is an environmental one. The drive from Beijing to Yan'an takes one across three provinces – Hebei, Shanxi and Shaanxi – with a combined population of at least 100 million. There every riverbed, be it large or small, is dry almost all the year round. Agriculture depends upon pumping water from underground aquifers, but the water-table is falling rapidly. In Shanxi, the ground water is so polluted that most visible surface water is black, green or yellow. The air too, acrid with pollution and so laden with particles that it often obscures the view ahead, is hard to breathe. And every hill has been completely stripped bare of trees or plants. The land has become a desert, devoid of wildlife and vegetation. All this has happened over the last hundred years but the pace of destruction has accelerated in the last fifty.

The same degradation is being repeated in Manchuria, in southern China, in the Yangtze basin, on the Tibetan plateau and in the valleys of Yunnan and Guangxi. It is hard to imagine how China's environment will cope with the additional demands made by another 300 million people, mostly peasants, who will be added to the population over the next fifty years.

More than any account of the horrendous human rights abuses that China has witnessed over the last fifty years, the state of the environment testifies to decades of bad government. Changing this is less a matter of ideology or politics than of changing the relationship between the state and its subjects. Since almost everything the state says is untrue, and most information is kept secret, there is no real trust or co-operation between its officials and the rest of the population. Even the weather reports are untrue. In 1999 it emerged that meteorologists had for fifty years been under orders never to report that the temperature had risen above 37° centigrade (98.6° Fahrenheit), although why no one would explain. Perhaps such an admission was seen as discrediting the Party.

It is astonishing what the state manages to keep secret. A few months later, it became evident that an earthquake in Yunnan province in 1970 that had killed at least 15,000 people had been concealed. When news reached the authorities at the time, the People's Liberation Army was dispatched to the area, and there it distributed not relief supplies but copies of *The Thoughts of Chairman Mao*.

The most basic facts about China remain elusive: the amount of available arable land, the earnings of peasants, even the size of the population. And since so much basic data is misreported from below, it is certain that those running the country are no better informed. The one-child policy is perhaps the best example of the state's inability to cope with the strain on China's natural resources posed by its rapidly growing population.

The policy was hurriedly conceived in 1979 by a handful of men without research or consultation and in the absence of current population statistics. The last census had taken place in 1964, in the wake of the famine that resulted from the Great Leap Forward and at a time when statistics were particularly prone to political manipulation. Its results were therefore far from reliable. The previous census had been taken twenty-six years before that, in 1938.

The one-child policy was adopted after Song Jian, a Soviet-trained nuclear scientist, had scribbled down some calculations on the back of an envelope while attending a population symposium. Using formulas employed to predict missile trajectories he projected China's population growth based on varying circumstances. Asked to calculate more detailed predictions he enlisted the help of four others, among them Yu Jingyuan, a mathematician and an expert in systems analysis: 'We collected data, established a model and then made forecasts for what the population would be, assuming people had one, two or three children. It was the first such forecast based on modern science,' Yu later claimed. Song Jian also travelled to Europe where he learned to use a computer programme to make further calculations. 'It was not a very sophisticated one compared to today's computers but the leadership paid great attention to it. And it was the very first time that anyone in China had used a computer to make such forecasts,' Yu commented.

Song Jian demonstrated that if a one-child policy were enforced immediately, then by the year 2000 China could keep its population to one billion. If the policy were rigorously implemented for longer then by 2050, the population would fall to 700 million, which he believed to be the optimum size. New advances in medical procedures, especially female sterilization, abortion and the insertion of IUDs, made such a goal technically feasible.

Deng Xiaoping personally approved the policy before it could be tested or studied by social scientists or any other experts. Although a key plank of China's reforms, it was never debated, enshrined in any law or approved by the National People's Congress, nor did it draw on any powers listed in the Constitution. Instead it was passed off as a temporary measure that has now lasted for over twenty years. The huge raft of implementing regulations, the harsh punishments meted out to those who disregard them and the 80,000 full-time family planning workers who enforce them were brought into being by Party diktat.

A one-child policy had in fact been introduced in urban areas such as Shanghai in the 1970s. There, where urban dwellers lived and worked in state units, officials were able to track each woman's menstrual cycle. In contrast, in 1979 the policy was chiefly directed at the countryside where, as the communes were disbanded and food production increased, the need for extra labour encouraged an increase in the rural population.

The policy was an example of pure Legalism, an exercise in reaffirming the need for individual interests to be subordinated to those of the state. Despite the new economic freedom granted the peasants, the policy allowed the state to monitor the most private and intimate aspects of an individual's life. Local officials could now control the reproduction rights of the peasants as if they were animals.

'People said the Party was trying to castrate us,' one peasant in Shanxi told me. The policy was brutally enforced. Quotas were set and the houses of those resisting the policy were burnt, the women themselves imprisoned and subjected to abortions even in the eighth month. In many places an abortion was performed as the baby was delivered. The peasantry put up a very strong resistance, often killing local Party officials and family planning workers in riots. Indeed, such was the level of violence, verging on rebellion in some parts of the country, that by 1984 the state was forced to retreat and began to soften the policy. In certain circumstances, for example where the first child was a girl or handicapped, peasants were now allowed to have a second child.

For all the ruthlessness of the campaign and the huge numbers of officials involved, the one-child policy was a failure. The original target set for the year 2000 was never realized. A new target of first 1.1 billion and then 'around 1.2 billion' was set. In the 1990s, the target was again raised, this time to 1.25 billion. It is now thought that by the end of 2000 the population will have reached 1.3 billion. But in truth no one really knows. Peasants mislead officials and officials misreport statistics. The extent to which this happens was illustrated in 1998 when PLA soldiers fighting the summer floods along the Yangtze rescued a young girl hanging from the branch of a tree above the raging floodwaters while a camera team was present. Pictures of the 6-year-old Jiang Shan tearfully asking about the fate of her four brothers and sisters were broadcast on national television. Her parents had five children. Many viewers were so indignant they wrote letters saying that she should never have been rescued because she should not have existed in the first place.

Jiang Shan came from Paizhou county in Hubei province where officials distributing emergency relief food were attacked by peasants who accused them of embezzling relief funds. Why else was there not enough to go round? The truth then emerged: there were about 10 per cent more people in the county than was recorded in the most recent census. Most families had three children and local officials had colluded in reporting false figures, which matched the official quota for births, to the central authorities. Local officials in Jiang Shan's county had also, it turned out, misreported not just the size of the population but also the amount of arable land and the number of livestock. It therefore follows that education and health standards must also be far lower than those reported. Many children, like Jiang Shan, are excluded from the system because children born outside the plan are barred from attending school. The high birth-rate in such areas is also linked to China's neglect of rural healthcare. In other countries, the birth rate has dropped when families have trusted the healthcare system.

The 1990 national census revealed that China had 20 more million people than had been assumed. By the end of the 1990s, experts thought some 30 million people had been lost in a statistical black hole. Critics of the Party's coercive birth-control policies believe widespread resistance has made the government miss its original target by 300 million. Its defenders maintain that without such severe measures, China would now be struggling to feed an extra 200 million or 300 million people.

Some little-publicized experiments suggest that policies which rely on co-operation rather than coercion might be more effective. In 1986 the government allowed two counties in Shanxi province to carry out experiments which allowed peasants to have two children provided their births were widely spaced. Professor Liang Zhongtang, who proposed and supervised the trial, said that after ten years the results showed what could have been done throughout China. The growth rate had fallen because there were fewer third children being born. In addition fewer abortions were carried out and there was less female infanticide, resulting in a normal ratio of girls to boys. With less coercion and better relations between the peasants and the authorities, the two-child policy was also easier to oversee. Local peasants said they were satisfied with two children, because they could expect at least one to survive to adulthood, and even if a family had two daughters, one could inherit the farm.

Population figures in Guangdong, where peasants were also exempted from the one-child policy on Deng's orders because he wished to encourage investment by overseas Chinese, many of whom originate from Guangdong, also support Professor Liang's thesis. There the birth rate fell almost as far as in neighbouring provinces where the one-child policy was strictly enforced. In fact some experts believe there would be no difference if neighbouring provinces provided data as reliable as that of Guangdong.

It is also debatable whether China has actually done any better than countries which have not resorted to coercion. Fertility rates in India have also dropped sharply, especially in areas where good healthcare is available. India's record is not considered particularly praiseworthy but the average fertility rate of 3.3 children is only a little higher than the real fertility rate in rural China. In addition India claims that its national family planning programme has avoided 230 million extra births and that its population will stabilize in 2040 just as is the case in China.

In addition to the failure of its aims, the one-child policy has carried a hidden cost. Good government depends on a level of honesty, trust and voluntary co-operation. The one-child policy has done nothing to foster such trust between the populace and the government, and much to undermine it still further.[2]

This deterioration in relations between the governed and those who govern has many ramifications. China is now a society in which everyone seems to be engaged in deceiving and cheating one another. In such circumstances, the transition to a market economy has not led to any fairness. Hard work and honesty are not rewarded; corruption is. The privatization process in a dictatorship such as China has brought about the criminalization of the state. Party members, who are beyond the law, have been free to engage in the theft of state assets on a grand scale. The cynicism and hypocrisy which this has fostered are destructive, particularly so in a society that has abandoned a once fanatically held ideology. A society in which no one is prepared to tell the truth, whether about historical events, small or large, or commercial transactions, individual or corporate, cannot prosper.

How then does China get from where it is now to where it should go? In ancient times, the Chinese foretold the future by reading oracle bones. Indeed the earliest Chinese writings ever discovered are the characters etched on the shoulderblade bone of a sheep. The bone, once etched, would be thrown on to a fire and a seer would then divine future events from the cracks that appeared on the surface. Today, China's future is foretold by examining the entrails of economic plans and statistical surveys. Given the nature of the data on which such plans are based, such a method seems no less fallible.

China's future depends on the extent to which a basis of trust between government and people can be established. China is trapped not only by its imperial legacy and the traditions of Legalism (or Confucianism, if you will) but also by the fateful choice made in the 1920s when the country had the opportunity to break free of the yoke of history, when Sun Yat-sen was struggling to build a party which could establish a new government in China after the fall of the Qing dynasty.

The CCP and the KMT, rulers of the Chinese for eighty years, are peas from the same pod, the fruit of Sun Yat-sen's fateful decision to ask the victorious Bolsheviks in Russia how to win power. It was Lenin's answer – a military-backed, one-party centralized dictatorship – that provided the model for the founders of both the KMT and the CCP. Lenin sent advisers to help Sun and to train soldiers at the Whampoa Military Academy under the control of Chiang Kai-shek. The CCP started its existence merely as the extreme left wing of the KMT, its members those intellectuals who wanted to discard the liberal democratic experiments launched in the previous two decades.

It is often forgotten that before the KMT and the CCP plunged the country into civil war, China was heading in a quite different direction. The holding of elections within China as early as 1909 and the establishment of independent universities, schools, courts, publishing houses, newspapers, business enterprises, hospitals and charities in the decades that followed have already been noted. Yet within a very short space of time both the CCP and the KMT had discovered the crime of 'counter-revolution' as a means to eradicate dissent. With the death of democracy began a brutal struggle between the two parties to establish a one-party state, each attempting to defeat the other. The struggle is still going on, with Beijing threatening to attack and subjugate Taiwan.

Even so, for a long period after 1949, the CCP was in no hurry to conquer Taiwan as long it was ruled by a party which was in so many ways a mirror image of itself. While this remained the case, the CCP did nothing, even during the massive arms build-up of the 1960s and 1970s. (The only serious military attack against Taiwan took place in 1958 when the island of Quemoy was bombarded, an assault that grew out of Mao's conviction that his Great Leap Forward had unleashed huge economic strength. Instead, China teetered on the verge of collapse, and the assault ceased.)

When, in 1987, the KMT lifted martial law in Taiwan and began to release its political prisoners, it was assumed on the mainland that these were no more than ploys designed to strengthen support for Taiwan in the United States. In fact, by doing so, the then President, Lee Teng-hui, transformed what had fifteen years before still been an ugly dictatorship run by a man, Chiang Ching-kuo, who had spent his youth in Stalin's Soviet Union.

China continued to do nothing until 1995. In that year Lee Teng-hui permitted the first openly fought election for the Legislative Assembly to take place, and a year later that for the presidency. Then, in March 2000, for the first time, a part of China seized the opportunity to free itself from its tragic history by electing a non-KMT president, Chen Shui-bian of the Democratic Progressive Party (DPP). The election marked the first peaceful transfer of power in Taiwan or anywhere else in China. Taiwan is now a fully fledged democracy.

In the weeks leading up to that election, China's Prime Minister, Zhu Rongji, warned the Taiwanese electorate that the PLA was ready to 'shed blood' if they made the wrong choice at the polls. The threats were dressed up as patriotism, a determination to prevent the United States supporting Taiwanese independence, but the real issue was democracy. Since China's current leadership are all in power because in 1989 they successfully suppressed the democracy movement inside and outside the CCP, they clearly cannot now stand idly by and watch a democracy flourish in Taiwan. These leaders have striven to block any political liberalization on the mainland and have crushed every attempt by dissidents to find some small space in which to manoeuvre. Even some tentative reforms made in the 1980s have been reversed. The system of people's congresses, for instance, is now more firmly under the grip of the Communist Party than ever before.

If a thriving and dynamic democracy is allowed to flourish anywhere in the Chinese world, then no one in Zhongnanhai can sleep easily. In the 1990s, the CCP under Jiang Zemin fought hard to prevent a fully fledged democracy from emerging in Hong Kong which might inspire a mainland democracy movement; and in the wake of Tiananmen, when many in Hong Kong, including leading tycoons, were tempted to fund an opposition movement, Deng Xiaoping opened up the mainland to fresh investment. Hong Kong's tycoons were quick to seize the opportunity, and the prospect of an overseas democracy movement faded.

A similar tactic has been tried with Taiwanese industrialists who, lured with special concessions, have been pouring money into the mainland. Their investments make them hostages to Beijing and they are now among the loudest voices being raised in favour of appeasing China. It remains to be seen how much influence the Taiwanese business lobby can exert. Compared with Hong Kong where a few giant conglomerates wield enormous influence, most Taiwanese companies are fairly small, family-run affairs.

Until the mid-1990s, the Communist Party avoided direct intervention in Taiwan's internal politics, and refrained from distributing donations to political parties as it tried to do in the United States. In turn, the Taiwanese élite avoided offering anything more than verbal support for mainland dissidents such as Wei Jingsheng. Now, President Chen Shui-bian or a successor may well decide that if Beijing does interfere, as it did before the presidential elections of 1996 and 2000, Taiwan may retaliate. The provision of funds, training and broadcasting facilities, and political asylum for mainlanders struggling to bring about change might seem attractive, especially if that is deemed essential for the preservation of Taiwan's newly won freedom.

For the first time, one of the two parties that have controlled China's destiny as a modern state has irrefutably abandoned the common heritage of dictatorship. One way or another this fact will determine China's future. The CCP may try to destroy democracy in Taiwan and extend its dictatorship across the Taiwan Strait. The failure of such an attempt might precipitate its own downfall. On the other hand, the mainland may slowly and haltingly move to reform itself along the path pioneered by the KMT. The next decade may prove to be a decisive turning-point in Chinese history.

APPENDIX I

Chronology

SPRING AND AUTUMN PERIOD 770–481 BC

WARRING STATES PERIOD 481–221 BC

QIN DYNASTY 221–206 BC

HAN DYNASTY 206 BC – AD 220

THREE KINGDOMS AD 220–265

PERIOD OF DISUNION AD 265–581

SUI DYNASTY AD 581–618

TANG DYNASTY AD 618–907

PERIOD OF DISUNION AD 907–960

SONG DYNASTY AD 960–1279

YUAN DYNASTY 1279–1368

MING DYNASTY 1368–1644

1583
The Jesuit missionary Matteo Ricci arrives in China

QING DYNASTY 1644–1911

1692
Jesuit missionaries welcomed by the Manchu court

1792–4
Lord Macartney's embassy to China

1839
Lin Zexu's destruction of 20,000 chests of opium leads to the deterioration of relations between Britain and China and the outbreak of the First Opium War

1842
The First Opium War concludes with the signing of the Treaty of Nanjing (Nanking) which provides for the opening of the first five treaty ports – in Shanghai, Ningbo, Xiamen (Amoy), Fuzhou (Foochow) and Guangzhou (Canton) – and the cession of the island of Hong Kong to Great Britain

1845
The Sino-American Treaty of Wangxia permits Americans to trade in the treaty ports and to purchase land for Protestant churches and missions. It also establishes the principle of extraterritoriality by which foreigners are tried only by their own consuls

1850–64
Taiping Rebellion, led by Hong Xiuquan

1856
Outbreak of the Second Opium War

1858
Signing of the Treaty of Tianjin (Tientsin) which allows for the opening of more cities to trade and foreign residence and the establishment of foreign ambassadors in Beijing

1860
The refusal of the Chinese to observe the terms of the Treaty of Tianjin results in renewed hostilities. An Anglo-French force occupies Beijing and destroys the Imperial Summer Palace

1860s–90s
The opening of a Foreign Office in Beijing in 1861 marks the beginning of a number of diplomatic and military modernization projects described collectively as the Self-Strengthening movement

1894–5
China's defeat in the Sino-Japanese War exposes the limitations of the Self-Strengthening movement. By the Treaty of Shimonoseki (1895) China is forced to cede the Liaodong peninsula and Taiwan to Japan in perpetuity and to permit Japanese to reside and trade in China. Young radicals, among them Sun Yat-sen, form Self-Strengthening and Revive China societies

1898

Foreign powers scramble for concessions in China. China is forced to grant a 25-year lease on Lushun (Port Arthur) and the Dalian (Dairen) peninsula. Germany acquires Jiaozhou (Kiaochow) Bay. France demands a lease on Guangzhou (Kwangchow) Bay and Britain obtains a lease on Weihaiwei for as long as the Russians remain in Lushun and on Hong Kong's New Territories for 99 years.

In an attempt to strengthen China the Guangxu emperor embarks on a programme of reform but the 'Hundred Days Reform' is ended by the Empress Dowager Cixi. The Emperor becomes a prisoner in his own palace

1900

The Boxer Rebellion leads to the siege of the legations in Beijing. The siege is lifted by an international force and the Dowager Empress and the court flee to Xi'an

1901

By the Boxer Protocol China is required to pay a large indemnity to the foreign powers

1905

Civil service examinations are abolished. In Tokyo Sun Yat-sen forms the Alliance Society, precursor of the Kuomintang or Nationalist Party

1908

The Empress Dowager dies and the 2-year-old Puyi is proclaimed emperor. China holds the first elections for regional assemblies the following year

1911

An uprising in Wuhan leads to the overthrow of the Qing dynasty. Nanjing is proclaimed the national capital

REPUBLIC OF CHINA 1912–1949

1912

On 1 January the Republic of China is declared with Sun Yat-sen as provincial president. Yuan Shikai, a Manchu general, then takes over. China's first constitution is proclaimed

1914

On the outbreak of the First World War China declares herself neutral

1915
Japan presents the Twenty-one Demands, calling for Japanese control of Shandong, Manchuria, Inner Mongolia, the south-east coast of China and the Yangtze valley, as well as the use of Japanese advisers in the Chinese administration

1916
Yuan Shikai declares himself emperor but dies soon after. Generals of provincial armies declare their independence as local warlords

1917
Sun Yat-sen's Kuomintang (KMT) Party sets up a military government in Guangzhou

1919
By the terms of the Treaty of Versailles, Japan's demands for control of all former German territories in China are accepted by the Western powers. On 4 May students in Beijing demonstrate in protest and organize a strike and boycott of Japanese goods. The cultural and intellectual revolution taking place during this period is subsequently commonly known as the May Fourth movement

1921
The northern warlords declare war on Sun Yat-sen's government in Guangzhou. The Chinese Communist Party is founded in Shanghai

1922
Sun Yat-sen launches the Northern Expedition against warlords

1925
Sun Yat-sen dies. A demonstration in Shanghai on 30 May is fired on on the order of a British police inspector: 9 students are killed. A general strike is called in Shanghai which leads to anti-British demonstrations elsewhere and a boycott of British goods

1926
Chiang Kai-shek assumes command of the KMT armies, relaunches the Northern Expedition and takes Hankou

1927
Chiang Kai-shek launches a purge of Communists. In Hunan Mao Zedong leads the Autumn Harvest Uprising. When the revolt fails he is forced to flee

1928
Japanese troops land in Shandong. Mao and Zhou Enlai establish a Soviet regime in Ruijin, Jiangxi

1930
Chiang Kai-shek launches the first of five campaigns of encirclement and extermination against the Communists. The first major internal purge of Chinese Communists takes place in what becomes known as the Futian Incident

1932
The Japanese attack Shanghai but then withdraw. Zhou Enlai establishes the first 'Labour Persuasion' camps in Communist-controlled territory

1934
KMT armies encircle the Communist Red Army in Jiangxi. In October, the Communists break out and begin the Long March to Yan'an in Shanxi province

1936
Chiang Kai-shek is kidnapped in Xi'an and forced to agree to a United Front with the Communists against Japan

1937
An incident at the Marco Polo bridge west of Beijing marks the beginning of the Japanese invasion of China

1938
Japan occupies most of eastern China. The KMT government moves its capital to Chongqing

1942
At Yan'an Mao purges his enemies in the Rectification movement. He also outlines Party policy on intellectuals at the Yan'an Forum

1943
Britain and America relinquish all extraterritorial privileges and concessions in China

1945
Japan surrenders. Civil war between the Communists and the KMT resumes

Chronology

THE PEOPLE'S REPUBLIC OF CHINA 1949–

1949
On 1 October Mao Zedong declares the People's Republic of China. Chiang Kai-shek and the KMT government flee to Taiwan

1949–51
Land reform, already undertaken earlier in Communist-controlled areas, is now enforced throughout China, leading to the persecution of millions of landlords and wealthy peasants

1950
China invades Tibet. Hostilities break out between North and South Korea. China sends 'volunteers' to assist the North

1953
The first five-year plan is launched

1955
Mao begins the collectivization of peasants' holdings into co-operatives

1956
Under the slogan 'Let a hundred flowers bloom and a hundred schools of thought contend' Mao launches the Hundred Flowers movement to encourage greater freedom of debate in political matters

1957
Those who have spoken out during the Hundred Flowers movement are condemned and imprisoned in the Anti-Rightist movement

1958
In an attempt to create a socialist Utopia Mao launches the Great Leap Forward. The peasants are stripped of their remaining possessions and forced to join communes

1959
In Tibet China suppresses a rebellion and the Dalai Lama and his supporters flee to India. By the autumn many parts of China are in the grip of a severe famine as a result of the policies of the Great Leap Forward. Between 1959 and 1961 over 30 million Chinese starve to death

1960
The Soviet Union withdraws all its experts from China and stops all aid

1966
In a bid to restore his authority after the failure of the Great Leap Forward Mao launches the Cultural Revolution

1969
Fighting breaks out along the Ussuri River between the USSR and China

1971
After a failed *coup d'état* against Mao, Lin Biao flees but dies in a plane crash

1972
The American President Richard Nixon visits China

1975
On Taiwan, Chiang Kai-shek dies

1976
The death of Zhou Enlai in January provokes demonstrations in Tiananmen Square in Beijing. Mao dies in September, having named Hua Guofeng as his successor. An attempted *coup* by the Gang of Four in October fails and its members are arrested and subsequently put on trial

1978
At the Third Plenum of the Eleventh Party Congress Deng Xiaoping becomes *de facto* successor to Mao and announces the Four Modernizations. Meanwhile posters begin to appear on what becomes known as Democracy Wall in Beijing in which issues of political significance are openly discussed and Mao is criticized. A young electrician, Wei Jingsheng, puts up a poster calling for a Fifth Modernization, democracy

1979
In January Deng visits the United States. In February China attacks Vietnam in punishment for its invasion of Cambodia but the Vietnamese successfully block the attack. China is forced to withdraw. In October Wei Jingsheng is put on trial and in December the Democracy Wall is closed down

1979–83
The communes are dissolved and free markets begin to spring up. Price controls on many goods are lifted. The one-child policy is introduced in the countryside

1982
Hu Yaobang becomes Party General Secretary

1983
Campaigns against crime and 'spiritual pollution' are launched

1986
Pro-democracy demonstrations by students occur in major cities

1987
Hu Yaobang is forced to step down and an Anti-Bourgeois Liberalization campaign is launched. Zhao Ziyang replaces Hu as Party General Secretary and Li Peng becomes Prime Minister

1987–9
Zhao pushes for political reform

1989
Hu Yaobang dies. In honour of his memory students hold demonstrations in Tiananmen Square and occupy the square for over a month. On 20 May martial law is declared in Beijing and on 3/4 June the army repossesses the square, killing hundreds. Zhao Ziyang is arrested and Jiang Zemin is declared Deng's successor. A clamp-down on political activity follows

1992
Deng embarks on a Southern Tour to relaunch his economic reforms

1995
Deng falls into a coma

1996
Taiwan holds its first open elections for the Presidency and the National Assembly. China fires missiles into the Taiwan Strait

1997
Deng Xiaoping dies. Hong Kong, hitherto under British rule, is returned to China

1998
Zhu Rongji becomes Prime Minister and seeks membership for China of the World Trade Organization

1999
Macao, the last territory on the mainland, occupied by the Portuguese for four hundred years, is returned to China

2000
The KMT Party loses a general election in Taiwan. Chen Shui-bian of the Democratic Progressive Party becomes President

APPENDIX II

Biographical Sketches

CHEN YUN (1905–95): a noted hardliner and rival to Deng Xiaoping, he was an advocate of central planning and was responsible for establishing a state monopoly of grain in the 1950s. Born in Jiangsu, he joined the Party in 1925 and led various peasant movements before, in 1933, joining the Jiangxi soviet. He took part in the Long March and became a supporter of Mao. After 1949, he held a series of economic policy posts but fell into disfavour with Mao and withdrew from view during the Great Leap Forward and the Cultural Revolution. In 1978, he became first secretary of the Central Disciplinary Inspection Committee and vice premier in charge of economic affairs, and in 1987 Chairman of the Central Advisory Committee of veterans. He called his ideal economic system the 'bird-cage economy', the bird being free-market forces and the cage being state planning. His son, Chen Yuan, is now a powerful official.

CHIANG KAI-SHEK (1887–1975): known as Jiang Jieshi on the mainland, he rose to prominence as the officer in charge of the military academy established at Whampoa in Guangzhou. He commanded the KMT army after the death of Sun Yat-sen in 1925 and led the Northern Expedition to break the power of the northern warlords. He then split with the KMT's Communist wing in 1927, ordering the massacre of Communists in Shanghai and establishing a government in Nanjing. In 1928 he put down a Communist uprising but his subsequent efforts to establish control over the country and carry out a programme of reform were hindered by the growing aggression of the Japanese. Kidnapped by the Communists in Xi'an in 1936, he was forced to enter into an alliance with them against the Japanese. When the Japanese launched an all-out war on China in 1937, Chiang moved his base to Chongqing. Throughout the Second World War he received substantial amounts of largely American aid but made little headway against the Japanese. The Allies treated him as the leader of a great power but after 1945 American efforts to broker a peace and create a democracy in China failed. Chiang lost the civil war and in 1949 retreated to Taiwan with part of his army and many followers. There he established a military dictatorship. After his death in 1975, he was succeeded by his son, Chiang Ching-kuo.

DENG XIAOPING (1904–97): born into a rich peasant household in Guang'an, Sichuan, he went to France under a work-study programme in 1920 and joined the CCP in Paris in 1925. Later he studied at the Sun Yat-sen University in the Soviet Union. On his return to China in 1926 he served as political commissar of a military school and then led a series of uprisings in Guangxi province in 1929–30. He joined the Jiangxi soviet, went on the Long March and then held a series of posts as political commissar in the Red Army. After 1949, he took charge of the south-west of China. In 1952 he moved to Beijing and rose through the ministerial ranks to become, in 1956, General Secretary of the CCP. As General Secretary he carried out the Anti-Rightist movement. During the Great Leap Forward famine, however, he advocated relatively free market policies that ran counter to Mao's views and he therefore became a target when the Cultural Revolution began. He was reinstated as Vice Premier in 1973 after a period of exile in the Jiangxi countryside, but then dismissed again. After the death of Mao and the arrest of the Gang of Four he was once more reinstated, and became the controlling force in China.

In 1979, he ushered in the economic reform programme termed the Four Modernizations, and instituted the open-door policy by which special economic zones, notably Shenzhen, were established. Deng generally sided with hardliners on political reform and was responsible for the dismissal of both Hu Yaobang and Zhao Ziyang and for the 1989 military crackdown after Tiananmen. At the end of 1991, he made another come-back and during his southern tour in 1992 he pushed through a new round of economic reforms. He fell into a terminal coma in 1995.

HU JINTAO (1942–   ): he graduated from Qinghua University having specialized in hydro-electrical engineering. He worked in Gansu during the Cultural Revolution and then at the Ministry of Water Resources and Electric Power. He has also worked as first secretary of the Communist Youth League and served as Party secretary of Guizhou and later Tibet, notably during the pro-independence Tibetan protests of 1987–9 which ended with the imposition of martial law in Lhasa. He is currently heir apparent to Jiang Zemin and Vice President of China.

HU QIAOMU (1912–92): long-time secretary of Mao and the scourge of liberal intellectuals, he drafted China's first constitution after 1949. After a period in disgrace during the Cultural Revolution he was rehabilitated in 1975, presided over the editing of Mao's works and became president of the Chinese Academy of Social Sciences in 1977 where he guided the drafting of official interpretations of the Mao era.

DENG LIQUN (1914–): like Hu Qiaomu, a leader of the hardline Marxist faction in the Party. A former secretary to Liu Shaoqi, in the 1980s he was head of the Party's Propaganda Department, masterminding campaigns against 'spiritual pollution' and 'bourgeois liberalism'. Since being ousted in 1987, he has continued to pen attacks against pro-market policies and has warned that political reform would bring about the downfall of the Communist Party.

HU YAOBANG (1915–89): his sudden death as the result of a heart attack, reportedly during a Politburo meeting, triggered the 1989 Tiananmen protests. Some believe he was the most liberal political reformer the CCP has ever had and he rehabilitated millions persecuted by Mao.

Born into a poor peasant family in Hunan province, Hu joined the Communist Youth League at the age of 14 as a 'red devil'. He survived the purges in the CCP's revolutionary base in Jiangxi, and on the Long March was wounded by shell fragments. During the civil war, he was a political commissar in the PLA and then worked in the Youth League. He supported Mao during the Great Leap Forward and was rewarded with senior posts in Hunan. He was persecuted during the Cultural Revolution but rehabilitated by Deng Xiaoping in 1975 when he was charged with recreating the Chinese Academy of Social Sciences and later the Central Party School. He joined the Politburo in 1979 and served as the Party's General Secretary for nearly eight years until he was ousted in 1987 after student pro-democracy protests. Throughout his years in power he battled with hardliners who accused him of fomenting 'bourgeois liberalism'.

HUA GUOFENG (1920–): born in Shaanxi, Hua joined the CCP in 1940 and became Party secretary of Xiangtan prefecture where Mao's home village is located. He backed Mao during the Great Leap Forward, denying that a famine was taking place. In 1970 he became Party secretary of Hunan. In

1976 he succeeded Mao, who had appointed him as his successor with a note saying 'With you in charge my heart is at ease'. However, he was gradually eclipsed by Deng Xiaoping and was ousted from the Politburo in 1982.

JIANG ZEMIN (1926–): born on 17 August 1926 into a prosperous household in the wealthy town of Yangzhou, Jiangsu, he was adopted by a Communist revolutionary martyr, Jiang Shangqing. He studied electrical engineering at Shanghai's Jiatong University and joined the CCP in 1946. In 1955 he was sent to train at the Stalin Automobile Works outside Moscow and later at a number of giant SOEs in Changchun, Shanghai and Wuhan. He became vice minister of the electronics industry, then Mayor of Shanghai and later that city's Party secretary. In June 1989, he was chosen as Deng's successor to replace Zhao Ziyang and is now President of China, General Secretary of the CCP and Chairman of the Central Military Commission. He is noted for his musical gifts and knowledge of several languages including English, Russian and Romanian. He is married to Wang Yeping and has two sons.

LI PENG (1928–): the son of Communist martyrs and the adopted son of Zhou Enlai, Li Peng was born in October 1928 and brought up in Yan'an. In 1948 he went to study in Moscow for seven years where he specialized in hydroelectrical engineering at the Moscow Power Institute. Most of his career was spent in the power industry and he is credited with promoting numerous hydroelectric projects, especially the Three Gorges dam on the Yangtze River. He became a vice premier in 1983 as a protégé of hardline state planners such as Chen Yun, and in 1985 was also put in charge of education. In 1987 he became Prime Minister, a post he was to hold for the next ten years despite his opposition to Deng Xiaoping's reform initiatives. Hated by the students during the 1989 rebellion, he was humiliated by them during a televised meeting with some of their representatives. He later became known as the 'Butcher of Beijing', having been the first to hail the PLA's assault on Beijing on 3/4 June. He has since retained his position as second-in-command in the Party hierarchy and is currently chairman of the National People's Congress.

LI RUIHUAN (1934–): born into a peasant family in Tianjin in 1934, he joined the CCP in 1969 after working on the construction of the Great Hall of the People. He was persecuted during the Cultural Revolution but afterwards served as Tianjin's Party secretary. Considered a liberal, he joined the

Politburo Standing Committee in 1989 and is currently chairman of the CPPCC.

LIN BIAO (1907–71): born in Hubei, Lin joined the CCP in 1925. He became Minister of Defence in 1959 and was designated as Mao's successor in 1969. However, in 1971, he died in a plane crash after fleeing China in the wake of a failed coup against Mao.

LIU SHAOQI (1898–1969): born just a few miles from Mao's village in Hunan, Liu joined the Party in 1921 and was trained in Moscow before returning to organize protests amongst coal miners. He worked in the Communist underground during the 1930s and promoted Mao's personality cult from the 1940s when he became second-in-command in the Party. In the late 1950s, he was made head of state and thus Mao's successor but he angered Mao when he relaxed rural policies in the wake of the Great Leap Forward famine. He was the chief target of the Cultural Revolution – 'the Number One Capitalist Roader' – and died in a makeshift prison from torture and ill-treatment. Liu was only rehabilitated in 1980.

MAO ZEDONG (1893–1976): the son of a well-to-do peasant family in Hunan, he was educated in Changsha and then dabbled in teaching, publishing and journalism. In 1918 he went to work as a librarian at the University of Beijing. Unlike many contemporaries, he did not take the opportunity to travel and study abroad. While in Beijing Mao embraced Marxism and he helped form the CCP in 1921. As a revolutionary dedicated to organizing the peasants into a political force, he took part in an uprising in 1928. After its failure he retreated to the Jiangxi soviet. When this was surrounded by Chiang Kai-shek's forces he and other survivors embarked on what become known as the Long March, during which he emerged as a leader. By the time Mao's much-reduced force reached Yan'an in the mid-1930s, he had been able to resist Stalin's efforts to impose his own Moscow-trained Chinese leadership and had built up his own personality cult and developed his own political philosophy, which became known as Mao Zedong Thought.

The alliance with the KMT during the anti-Japanese war, and the aid he received from Moscow, enabled him to build his military strength and expand his guerrilla network. The Party's survival under the most difficult circumstances and then his astonishing victories in the civil war gave him enormous prestige when he established the PRC in 1949.

Mao disliked the Soviet-style system established after 1949 and in an attempt to accelerate the march to a Communist Utopia in 1958 he launched the Great Leap Forward. The failure of the Great Leap was a personal humiliation. In an effort to restore his prestige and power and to eliminate opponents, in 1966 he launched the Cultural Revolution during which those Party members whom he suspected of disloyalty were persecuted.

By breaking off relations with the Soviet Union in 1959, Mao cut China off from most of the Communist bloc. Convinced that a nuclear war with the Soviet Union was imminent, he plunged China into a massive arms build-up which by the time of his death had bankrupted the economy.

PENG ZHEN (1902–97): he joined the CCP in 1923 and served with Liu Shaoqi in the Communist underground. He became Mayor of Beijing in 1951 and a key figure in the organization of the new legal and penal system. He disappeared after 1966, one of the first victims of the Cultural Revolution, but reappeared in 1979 when Deng put him in charge of the public security, judiciary and security apparatus. He drafted the first criminal code which was adopted in 1979 and was in charge of the massive anti-crime campaign of 1983 in which up to 10,000 were executed. He played a leading role in the ousting of Hu Yaobang in 1987 and in the order to send the PLA into Beijing in 1989.

SUN YAT-SEN (1866–1925): a Cantonese doctor of Western medicine who studied in Hong Kong and worked in Macao (and who is known as Sun Zhongshan on the mainland), he has been called the father of modern China. He became actively involved in politics in 1894 when he founded the Revive China Society. After an attempted uprising in Guangzhou in 1895 failed he went into exile abroad where he continued to develop his political philosophy and attempted to rally support for an anti-Manchu rebellion. He returned to China in 1911 and was elected president of the provisional government after the overthrow of the Qing dynasty. He resigned from that position in 1912 after facing opposition from more conservative reformers and, after an unsuccessful revolt in 1913, left the country once more. With assistance from the Soviet Union, he finally regained power in 1923 and was elected President of the Republic. He founded the KMT, the most important political party after 1911, and espoused the Three Principles of the People (Sanminzhuyi), that is nationalism, democracy and the people's livelihood.

WANG ZHEN (1908–93): a participant in the Long March and a former military political commissar, he played a prominent role in opposing bourgeois liberalism and persecuting liberals in the 1980s. Before 1949 he had been a political commissar in the Eighth Route Army and head of the Yan'an garrison. After 1949, he led the PLA in Xinjiang and established the paramilitary Xinjiang Construction and Production Corps. His two sons, Wang Jun and Wang Zhi, have held leading positions in state enterprises and banks.

YANG SHANGKUN (1907–98): born in Sichuan, he joined the Communist Youth League in 1925 and in 1927 began to attend the Sun Yat-sen University in Moscow where he remained until 1931. In 1933 he arrived in Jiangxi and then took part in the Long March and later worked with other war leaders, Zhu De and Peng Dehuai. A key figure in running both the Party's general office and its Central Military Commission during the 1940s and 1950s, he supported Mao but fell out of favour during the Cultural Revolution. He supported Deng in the coup against the Gang of Four and in 1982 was made secretary-general of the Central Military Commission where he wielded considerable power and opposed political reforms. He backed the declaration of martial law in 1989 and together with his brother, General Yang Baibing, made a bid for power. In 1992, however, Deng successfully ousted him and his followers.

ZHAO ZIYANG (1919–   ): born in Henan, he joined the Party in 1938. After 1949 he worked in Guangdong specializing in rural affairs. He was persecuted during the Cultural Revolution but was subsequently made Party secretary of Sichuan where he pioneered rural reforms including the dissolution of the communes. He was first appointed Prime Minister and then in 1987 replaced Hu Yaobang as General Secretary of the Party. He pushed for privatization, political reform and openness, and a separation of Party from government. Zhao challenged Deng's authority and supported the 1989 student protests until he was deposed and put under house arrest when martial law was declared. He was not expelled from the Party but has refused to make a self-criticism and has remained under detention in his house not far from Tiananmen Square ever since.

ZHOU ENLAI (1898–1976): Mao's right-hand man for most of his life, Zhou was born in Jiangsu, educated in Tianjin and went to France to study in the early 1920s where he joined the CCP. A brilliant figure who dazzled all who met him, he played a leading role in almost every major event in Party history but subordinated himself to Mao from the 1930s onwards. He was Prime Minister from 1949 until his death, and his adopted son Li Peng succeeded him in 1987. Zhou's record is portrayed in heroic terms although he carried out Mao's orders throughout the Great Leap Forward and the Cultural Revolution when he supervised the persecution of much of the Party élite. His death triggered huge anti-government protests in Tiananmen Square.

ZHU RONGJI (1928–): born into a wealthy family of Hunan landowners, Zhu joined the CCP in 1949 after graduating from Qinghua University in electrical engineering. He then worked for the State Planning Commission. He was a victim of the Anti-Rightist movement and from 1970 to 1975 worked at a May 7th Cadre School where he mucked out pigsties. After 1979, he rejoined the State Economic Commission and in 1987 was appointed Mayor of Shanghai. There he pushed for the development of Pudong and the rejuvenation of the city. In 1993 he joined the Politburo Standing Committee and in 1997 he was appointed Prime Minister. A blunt-speaking man, he has made a name for himself by reining in an over-heated economy in the mid-1990s and through his efforts to tackle corruption and reduce the size of the bureaucracy.

Notes

Introduction: Through the Open Door

1. Admiral Prueher speaking at a lunch at the American Chamber of Commerce, February 2000, see Jasper Becker, 'Washington Envoy hits first bump on road to smooth relationship with mainland', *South China Morning Post*, 8 February 2000; Jasper Becker, 'Getting the big picture on farming', *South China Morning Post*, 26 April 1998.
2. J.O.P. Bland, *China: The Pity of It*.
3. *South China Morning Post*, 26 July 1999.
4. Jasper Becker, 'Cantonese colonisers "may have been the first Chinese"', *South China Morning Post*, 4 July 1999. See Chapter 15, note 2.

Chapter 1: Eating Bitterness

1. This visit took place in April 1996. Its purpose was to look at the World Bank's South West Poverty Reduction Programme.
2. Jasper Becker, 'The Long March out of poverty', *Sunday Morning Post*, 28 April 1996.
3. This figure was released by the State Statistical Bureau in 1999. After 1949 the Communists followed Soviet practice and identified each individual according to his race or ethnicity. The majority population were defined as Han Chinese, a reference to the Han dynasty.
4. *State Statistical Yearbook*, 1996.
5. Vivien Pik-kwan Chan, 'Premier admits inability to lift 50 million out of poverty', *South China Morning Post*, 31 December 1997; and Daniel Kwan, 'Poverty "can never be fully wiped out"', *South China Morning Post*, 9 December 1999.

6. Michael Richardson, 'A revised look at China poverty. World Bank says it is worse than previously thought', *International Herald Tribune*, 26 September 1996.

7. See Press Trust of India, 'India's growth since 1980', 14 April 2000; 'Has liberalization helped the poor?' *The Economist*, 29 April 2000; 'Has economic liberalisation failed to reduce poverty?', *The Times of India*, 23 April 2000.

8. This draws on a 1996 statement by dissidents Liu Xiaobo and Wang Xizhe, published in *Mingbao*, 10 October 1996. They also cite official documents such as the declaration at the first Kuomintang National Congress in 1924 in which Sun Yat-sen acknowledged the right of self-determination by various nationalities. After 1930 the 'Constitutional Programme of the Chinese Soviet Republic' also declared that the Chinese Communist Party 'will consistently acknowledge that various weak minority nationalities have the right to break away from China to set up independent states'.

9. Sun Yat-sen, *The Three Principles of the People*.

10. Jasper Becker, 'The heart of Chinese sovereignty', *South China Morning Post*, 12 June 1999.

11. Catriona Bass, *Education in Tibet*.

12. Jasper Becker, 'Homage to missionary who freed the Miao', *South China Morning Post*, 23 November 1995.

13. Erik Eckholm, 'Birds or people? China argues the question', *International Herald Tribune*, 20 May 1999.

14. World Bank, 'Loess Plateau Watershed Rehabilitation Project: Credit and Project Summary', 1994; and World Bank, East Asia and Pacific Region, 'China-Qinba Mountains Poverty Reduction Report', 1997.

15. Jasper Becker, 'Saving Shanxi's sliding hillsides', *South China Morning Post*, 20 July 1998.

16. World Bank, 'China: Strategies for Reducing Poverty in the 1990s', October 1992.

17. World Bank, 'Loess Plateau Watershed Rehabilitation Project: Credit and Project Summary', 1994.

18. Reuters, 'Poorest of the poor pin hopes on massive population transfer', *South China Morning Post*, 11 August 1996; Xinhua, 'Migration lifts 130,000 people out of poverty in Guangdong', 19 July 1997; 'Poorest of poor villages should move, says official', *South China Morning Post*, 10 May 1997; and World Bank, 'Staff Appraisal Report, China South West Poverty Reduction Project', 18 May 1995.

19. World Bank Loan and Project Summary, 'Wanjiazhai Water Transfer Project', 1996.
20. Xinhua, 'Chinese taking a closer look at reasons for Yellow River's dryness', 16 April 1998.
21. Jasper Becker, 'The taming of the Yellow River', *South China Morning Post*, 16 November 1996.
22. Jasper Becker, 'Worn down by the source of life – decades of damming projects have uprooted millions of people', *South China Morning Post*, 3 May 1997. During Mao's rule China built 84,000 dams, including 2,700 large and medium-sized reservoirs. A Chinese government study released in 1984 found that a third of those displaced were living in abject poverty, and another third were living at mere subsistence level.
23. Lester Brown has written a study on Chinese water shortages which was published by the Worldwatch Institute, July/August 1988.
24. Wang Sangui of the China Poverty Research Foundation, Wu Guobao of the Rural Development Institute and Albert Park from the University of Michigan co-authored 'Regional Poverty Targeting in China'. The report was funded by two American charities, the Ford Foundation and the Luce Foundation, and appeared in May 1999.
25. See note 24 above.

Chapter 2: Local Despots and Peasant Rebels

1. Personal visit to Hunan, May 1999.
2. The riot was first reported by Reuters in Hong Kong on 31 January 1999, quoting the Hong Kong-based Information Centre of Human Rights and the Democratic Movement in China.
3. The Information Centre of Human Rights and the Democratic Movement in China reported that the nine peasants were given jail terms of two to six years for 'organizing the people to oppose government agencies'. Quoted by Reuters, 13 August 1999.
4. Elisabeth Rosenthal, 'Thousands of farmers clash with Chinese police', *New York Times Supplement/International Herald Tribune*, 16 January 1999; and Erik Eckholm, 'In China, protests by farmers provoke a violent response', *New York Times Supplement/International Herald Tribune*, 2 January 1999.
5. Jasper Becker, 'Hunan towns hit by wave of peasant protests', *South China Morning Post*, 25 April 1999; and Associated Press, 'Villagers who

attacked police station jailed for three years', *South China Morning Post*, 22 January 1999.

6. Jasper Becker, 'Dead man's tale reveals Party's famine disgrace', *South China Morning Post*, 9 April 1999, taken from *Nongmin Ribao*, 16 and 30 January 1999.

7. An article in the *China Daily*, 'Government tries to lift tax burden of farmers', 15 April 1995, later claimed that on average Chinese peasants contribute just 41 yuan in taxes and 16 days of corvée labour.

8. 'Leader's warning on farmer's plight', *South China Morning Post*, 22 March 1993. Peasants were angry because whilst they were paying taxes on their income city dwellers did not do so, this despite the fact that peasant incomes were reckoned to amount to only two-fifths of those of urban dwellers. In some instances farmers appeal against their taxes. The Sichuan courts dealt with 748 such cases in 1997. Occasionally the state sends inspectors to look at village accounts.

9. Lester Brown, *Who Will Feed China?*

10. Willy Wo-lap Lam, 'Party split on farming future', *South China Morning Post*, 7 September 1995. Du Runsheng had been forced into retirement after 1989 but re-emerged to claim that peasant land-use rights were often infringed and that the state forced them to sell their crops at low prices.

11. Associated Press, 'Village leaders deny farmers long leases', *South China Morning Post*, 25 May 1997.

12. Craig S. Smith, 'China admits to huge deficit in grain funds', *Asian Wall Street Journal*, 14 October 1998; and Vivien Pik-kwan Chan, 'Massive grain losses spark national audit', *South China Morning Post*, 9 June 1998

13. Mark O'Neill, 'Setting a trap for the "Grain Rats"', *South China Morning Post*, 21 December 1998. See also Craig S. Smith, 'China's grain policies sow the seeds for corruption', *Asian Wall Street Journal*, 27 January 1999.

14. Quoted by Reuters in *South China Morning Post*, 5 May 1999.

15. Xinhua, '18,000 cases of illegal government levies punished', 23 February 1999. The same report claimed that local governments have abolished 25,710 random fees involving some 98.5 billion yuan a year and that the central government has dealt with 18,000 cases, disciplining 1,272 officials.

16. Xinhua, 'First trial grain futures market successful', 10 March 1998.

17. Xinhua reports, for example, that there are now 100,000 Chinese earning a living as private traders and distributors of fruit and vegetables. See Yulanda Chung, 'Middlemen traders help boost distribution of food', *South China Morning Post*, 11 April 1998.

18. Sheel Kohli, 'World Bank funding targets grain demand', *South China Morning Post*, 20 June 1998. The World Bank expects Chinese grain demand to reach 700 million tonnes by 2020.

19. 'China Agriculture: Cultivated Land Area, Grain Projections and Implications' is a study using satellite photography carried out for the US National Intelligence Council and published in November 1997. It found that instead of 95 million hectares, the figure often used in China, there were 140 million hectares.

20. US Department of Agriculture, 'The future of China's grain market', 6 July 1997.

21. 'Female workers key to nation's growth', *South China Morning Post*, 24 June 1995, quotes a report that in 1995 100 million women contributed half the agricultural output and worked an average of 11.35 hours a day compared to 10 hours for males.

22. Jasper Becker, 'Freeing the grain market', *South China Morning Post*, 3 May 1998. China admits that 10 per cent of grain grown is lost but others believe the figure might be as much as 12 per cent or even 20 per cent. For an optimistic view see 'The Grain Issue in China' by the Information Office of the State Council, published in October 1996.

23. US Department of Agriculture, 'The future of China's grain market', 6 July 1997. China claims to feed 22 per cent of the world's population on 7 per cent of its arable land.

24. Jasper Becker, 'More delay for problem-struck US$980 million, China grain network', *South China Morning Post*, 29 April 1998.

Chapter 3: Getting Rich is Glorious

1. *People's Daily*, 13 June 1987.

2. James P. Sterba, 'China shows off change through tours for press', *Asian Wall Street Journal*, 28 May 1986.

3. Xinhua, 'Pioneer of China's enterprise reform never gives up', 30 December 1998; Edward Gargan, 'China's fallen hero: a hair shirt's not his style', *New York Times Supplement*, 16 February 1988; and Xinhua, 'Arrogant and high-handed factory director sacked', 16 January 1988.

4. Personal visit in 1987. See also James McGregor, 'Free enterprise blooms far from Beijing', *Asian Wall Street Journal*, 17 August 1992; and 'Boom time in capitalist Wenzhou', *The Economist*, 30 May 1998.

5. 'An investigation into the take-off of the Zhejiang economy', *Economic Information Daily*, 2 December 1997.

6. *Yazhou Zhoukan*, Hong Kong, No.2, 14 January 1996, pp.22–8. The article, by Deng Liqun, castigates China's 'new bourgeoisie'.

7. Jasper Becker, 'Opium city on a high', *South China Morning Post*, 7 June 1997.

8. Jasper Becker, 'Slump in countryside deepens as bubble bursts for rural enterprises', *South China Morning Post*, 27 August 1999.

9. Jasper Becker, 'Casting a safety net', *South China Morning Post*, 2 July 1995; and 'Surge of rural economy relies on township firms', *China Daily*, 12 October 1999.

10. The value of these unsold goods was put at US$64 billion, or a fifth of total industrial production in one year, and was worth several percentage points of GDP growth. 'China tackles wasted production in factory duplication', *Kyodo News*, 19 May 1997; Xinhua, 'China's shoe manufacturers facing serious challenges', 30 November 1998; and Tom Korski, 'China is proposing a sweeping plan to reform thousands of small state-owned factories', *South China Morning Post*, 28 April 1997.

11. Mark O'Neill, 'Farmers up in arms at debt-ridden Hunan's tax abuses', *South China Morning Post*, 4 July 1999. The same article quotes the *China Economic Times* as saying that 85 per cent of village and township governments are in debt to an overall total of 3.7 billion yuan.

12. Interview with the author, 1998.

13. Jasper Becker, 'Congress creates a party mood', *South China Morning Post*, 9 September 1997.

14. Cited in Jasper Becker, 'China counts the cost of a clean-up', *South China Morning Post*, 13 December 1996.

15. Jasper Becker, 'Cracking down on the chemical waste outlaws', *South China Morning Post*, 21 May 1999.

16. Jasper Becker, 'Coal mines to face safety measures blitz', *South China Morning Post*, 12 February 1997; and Mark O'Neill, 'Closures by small miners', *South China Morning Post*, 9 September 1998.

17. Jasper Becker, 'China counts the cost of a clean-up', *South China Morning Post*, 13 December 1996, quotes an interview with Yao Mei, an expert at the Institute of Rural Development, Chinese Academy of Social Sciences.

18. Jasper Becker, 'Slump in countryside deepens as bubble bursts for rural enterprises', *South China Morning Post*, 27 August 1999, quotes Chen Jianguang, chief economist in the Department of Township Enterprises at the Ministry of Agriculture.

Chapter 4: Behind the Walls

1. Jasper Becker, 'Banking on China's past', *South China Morning Post*, 13 June 1998.
2. Quoted in Jonathan D. Spence, *The Search for Modern China*, p.518.
3. Karl Marx and Friederich Engels, *The Communist Manifesto*, p.42.
4. Quoted in Jonathan D. Spence, *The Search for Modern China*, p.518.
5. *State Statistical Bureau Yearbook*, 1997.
6. Judith Banister, *China's Changing Population*, p.328.
7. See article by Harry Xiaoying Wu, 'Rural to urban migration in the People's Republic of China', *China Quarterly*, September 1994, p.669.
8. Judith Banister, *China's Changing Population*, p.327.
9. Judith Banister, *China's Changing Population*, p.334.
10. 'National conference of urban planners', SWC, 26 November 1980.
11. Fei Xiaotong *et al.*, *Small Towns in China: Functions, Problems and Prospects*, p.108.
12. He Bochuan, *China on the Edge*, p.110.
13. See note 12 above.
14. Agence France Press, 'Mega-cities needed to absorb peasants', in *South China Morning Post*, 23 October 1996. The nine mega-cities are: Beijing-Tianjin-Shijiazhuang; Shengyang-Dalian; Changchun-Harbin; Jinan-Qingdao; Nanjing-Yangzhou-Hefei; Wuhan-Changsha-Nanchang; Chongqing-Chengdu; Guangzhou-Shenzhen-Zhuhai; and Shanghai and its environs.
15. Ian Johnson, 'China fights to contain emergence of mega-cities', *Asian Wall Street Journal*, 11 December 1997.
16. Cathy Chen, 'Chinese flock to new cities as urban growth takes off', *Asian Wall Street Journal*, 5 January 1996.
17. *People's Daily*, 19 May 1997.
18. Xinhua, 'Zhejiang makes progress in urbanization', 22 March 1997.
19. Xinhua, 'Urbanization means change for East China's rural residents', 10 October 1997.
20. Jasper Becker, 'A journey through Jiang's Utopia', *South China Morning Post*, 26 January 1996.
21. *Jingji Cankao Bao (Economic Reference News)*, 10 November 1991.
22. 'Rise in floating migrants', *South China Morning Post*, 23 May 1992; 'Stop tide of jobless, urges official', *South China Morning Post*, 19 December 1992; and Steven Mufson, 'A Beijing "village" of migrant workers fights to stop bulldozers', *International Herald Tribune*, 29 November 1995.

23. Reuters, 'Forge-proof ID cards issued', in *South China Morning Post*, 29 December 1995; and 'Sterilisation law aimed at migrants seeking jobs', *South China Morning Post*, 4 July 1996.
24. Conghua Li, *China: The Consumer Revolution*, p.84.
25. Reuters, 'Beijing stems tide of floating population', 11 April 1998.
26. 'Urbanization lay-offs fuel city unrest fears', *South China Morning Post*, 7 July 1997.
27. Jasper Becker, 'The good news about being fired', *South China Morning Post*, 15 October 1997.
28. Other research suggests that the number of peasants who had actually left their native provinces to find temporary work was as low as 25 million, or 2.5 per cent of the total non-urban population.
29. Jasper Becker, 'The good news about being fired', *South China Morning Post*, 15 October 1997.
30. Reuters, 'Migrants resurrecting Shanghai, says professor', in *South China Morning Post*, 15 June 1996.
31. Jasper Becker, 'Getting the big picture on farming', *South China Morning Post*, 26 April 1998. Instead of losing 120,000 acres a year, China was losing over 490,000.
32. Ivan Tang, 'City growth eats into farmland', *South China Morning Post*, 30 March 1997.
33. From 0.19 of an acre in 1990 to 0.07 of an acre by the year 2030. Lester Brown, *Who Will Feed China?*
34. *People's Daily*, 18 May 1997. On 11 July 1997, Xinhua also reported that 163 million acres could be put to better use and another 49 million acres could be rehabilitated. Between 1986 and 1995 about 12 million acres of arable land was lost.
35. 'Hundreds protest over land loss', *South China Morning Post*, 28 January 1999.
36. Zhao Huanxin, 'Urbanization a top priority: nation to develop more cities', *China Daily*, 18 October 1999; and *People's Daily*, 18 October 1999.
37. *State Statistical Bureau Yearbook*, 1997, p.332, puts the non-agricultural population of cities in 1996 at 207.7 million. On p.348, it gives another figure – 219 million – for those people with access to tap water, another useful indicator of the true urban population. China lists only twelve cities with a population of over 2 million. More commonly used are the figures printed on p.69 of the *Yearbook* which for 1996 give the urban population as 359 million or 29.3 per cent of the total, which is also misleading.

Chapter 5: Inside the Zones

1. Deng Xiaoping, *Fundamental Issues in Present-day China*, p.44.
2. Jiang Zemin was vice-chairman of the State Commission for Import and Export Administration and was invited by the United Nations Industrial Development Organization to lead a study mission to ten countries.
3. The fourteen open coastal cities were, from north to south, Dalian, Qinhuangdao, Tianjin, Yantai, Qingdao, Lianyungang, Nantong, Shanghai, Ningbo, Wenzhou, Fuzhou, Guangzhou, Zhanjiang and Beihai. The fourteen coastal cities were never allowed the same scope as Shenzhen but they were able to negotiate foreign investment deals on their own below a certain ceiling. For Shanghai, it was US$30 million but in other cities just US$5 million.
4. 'State curb on zone building', *China Daily*, 22 April 1993; and 'Rampant founding of economic zones wastes good land', *China Daily*, 24 May 1993.
5. Ruan Ming, *Deng Xiaoping: Chronicle of an Empire*, p.138; and Uli Franz, *Deng Xiaoping*, p.291.
6. Ruan Ming, *Deng Xiaoping: Chronicle of an Empire*, p.141.
7. Quoted in Sheryl Wudunn, 'Bootleg tape of aide's jab is hit in China', *New York Times*, 31 May 1992.
8. Frances Wood, *No Dogs and Not Many Chinese*, p.59.
9. 'Shenzhen joint ventures boom', *South China Morning Post*, 30 December 1980.
10. Neil Pereira, 'Factories join the "exodus" to Shumchun [Shenzhen]', *South China Morning Post*, 16 November 1983.
11. *People's Daily*, 28 January 1988.
12. 'How frontier town grew into a key industrial city', *China Daily: Shenzhen Supplement*, 28 December 1992.
13. Dorinda Elliott, 'Empty riches', *Newsweek*, 26 February 1996.
14. Economist Intelligence Unit, 'Safety in numbers: Dongguan and its temptations', *Business China*, 3 August 1998.
15. 'Taiwanese companies in China', *The Economist*, 8 August 1998.
16. Vivian Chiu, 'Where dreams live and die', *Sunday Morning Post*, 29 March 1998.
17. Trish Saywell, 'Staying alert', *Far Eastern Economic Review*, 29 January 1998.
18. Chan Wai-fong, 'Safety rules "lag far behind" SEZ growth', *South China Morning Post*, 23 September 1994.

19. Anita Chan, 'Boot camp at the shoe factory', *Washington Post*, 17 November 1996.

20. Jasper Becker, 'Foreign bosses warned', *South China Morning Post*, 20 August 1995.

21. Jasper Becker, 'Mainland labour "abused"', *South China Morning Post*, 28 August 1997. For further examples of the abuse of workers, see Daniel Kwan, 'Workers still losing out on rights', *South China Morning Post*, 20 June 1995; 'Worker abuse, lack of safety rampant: survey', *South China Morning Post*, 29 November 1994; and Zhang Xia, 'Poll finds protection of women's rights still weak at foreign firms', *China Daily*, 6 July 1994.

22. Chan Wai-fong, 'Safety rules "lag far behind" SEZ growth', *South China Morning Post*, 23 September 1994.

23. Irene So and Agnes Cheung, 'Probe seeks factory owner', *South China Morning Post*, 3 January 1995.

24. Two examples were reported by the semi-official Chinese News Agency in 1997. On 25 September, *Zhongguo Xinwen She* reported the death of 32 people in a fire at a shoe factory in Jinjiang city, Fujian province. The workers' dormitory was above the factory and its exits were secured by iron bars. The factory had been burnt down four years before but in rebuilding it the Hong Kong owner had taken no notice of fire regulations. On 5 July *Zhongguo Xinwen She* reported the investigation of a Taiwanese shoe factory in Guangzhou where workers were punished for napping by being made to stand out in the sun for long periods. In addition it was reported that factory managers demanded a 500-yuan deposit from each worker at the time of recruitment. The net monthly wage paid to new recruits after deductions for meals was only 20 yuan, violating the 380-yuan monthly minimum wage. If workers wished to leave within the first month, they had to repay the company 10 yuan a day for meals, and an accommodation charge of 200 yuan. The factory also ignored the five-day week by requiring workers to work overtime without fair remuneration.

25. Ma Licheng and Ling Zhijun, *Crossed Swords*, p.293.

26. Kennis Chu and Gary Chan, 'Shenzhen shares frenzy', *Sunday Morning Post*, 9 August 1992.

27. Matthew Miller, 'Hainan battles homes surplus', *South China Morning Post*, 21 October 1999.

28. Jasper Becker, 'Tide has turned against Hainan', *South China Morning Post*, 19 April 1997; and Jasper Becker, 'Unfinished business', *South China Morning Post*, 10 May 1997.

29. Jasper Becker, 'Guangdong's stolen fortune', *South China Morning Post*, 26 June 1999.
30. Jasper Becker, 'Born to be king of Shantou', *South China Morning Post*, 19 June 1997.
31. Press conference held in September 1999 at the Shanghai *Fortune* Global Forum.
32. Daniel Kwan, 'Nobel winner in reform warning', *South China Morning Post*, 30 October 1993.

Chapter 6: The Iron Rice Bowl

1. Jasper Becker, 'Hardship in Shanghai as spindles stop', *South China Morning Post*, 21 December 1996.
2. Philip Segal, 'China layoffs putting millions on the street', *International Herald Tribune*, 3 June 1999; Mark O'Neill, 'Prospect in jobless prompts demand for spending', *South China Morning Post*, 4 September 1999; Bill Kazer, 'Five million mainlanders to lose jobs', *South China Morning Post*, 8 March 2000; and Daniel Kwan, 'Twelve million to lose jobs', *South China Morning Post*, 11 January 2000.
3. Jasper Becker, 'Mainland factories feel the pinch', *South China Morning Post*, 30 November 1996.
4. Elaine Chan, 'Bicycle makers hope for new dawn as sunset approaches', *South China Morning Post*, 10 October 1996.
5. Jasper Becker, 'Bankrupt pension system to undergo transformation', *South China Morning Post*, 31 July 1997; and World Bank, 'China Pension Reform', Report No.15121-CHA, 22 August 1996.
6. World Bank, 'Old Age Security, Pension Reform in China', China 2020, p.17.
7. World Bank, 'China Reform of State-owned Enterprises', Report No.14924-CHA, 21 June 1996.
8. Jasper Becker, 'Old industry dies hard', *South China Morning Post*, 9 August 1997.
9. Jasper Becker, '*Workers' Daily* says state-owned firms are money-wasting bottomless pits', *South China Morning Post*, 30 August 1997; Jasper Becker, 'Soaring debts slash the value of state firms', *South China Morning Post*, 30 July 1998; and Jasper Becker, 'Crisis of state firms pushed to the fore', *South China Morning Post*, 9 March 1997.
10. Jasper Becker, interview with Mu Suixin, Party secretary of Shenyang, March 1998.

11. Jasper Becker, 'The dark side of the dream', *South China Morning Post*, 12 October 1997.

12. Xinhua, 'Almost one billion US$ missing from pension funds', 25 July 1998. Many enterprise pension funds have been pilfered.

13. Jasper Becker, 'Unpaid miners blocking rail lines', *South China Morning Post*, 10 March 1998.

14. 'Wu Bangguo calls on coal industry to stop losses', *China Economic Times*, 27 July 1998.

15. Mark O'Neill, 'Output of coal falls with low demand', *South China Morning Post*, 22 August 1998.

16. China imported 12 million tonnes of steel in 1998. Xinhua, 'Steel makers buck adverse import trend', *China Daily*, 5 September 1999.

17. Lana Wong, 'Craze for red chips reaches fever pitch', *South China Morning Post*, 13 March 1998.

18. Jasper Becker, 'Steel merger and listing plans pave way for industrial reforms', *South China Morning Post*, 19 November 1997.

19. 'Wu Bangguo calls on coal industry to stop losses', *China Economic Times*, 27 July 1998.

20. Mark O'Neill, 'Liaoning using roadshow in bid to move 1,500 companies', *South China Morning Post*, 21 April 1998.

21. Mark O'Neill, 'Workers protest [over] sale of factory', *South China Morning Post*, 14 August 1998.

22. Jasper Becker, 'SAR "asset-stripping" slammed', *South China Morning Post*, 27 August 1997.

23. 'Dominance of SOEs highlighted', *China Daily*, 3 November 1999.

24. In 1998 the US investment bank Merrill Lynch thought 40 per cent of loans were non-performing. The rating agency Standard & Poor believed bad loans could amount to 60 per cent of GDP.

25. 'Beijing plans changes to state sector', *International Herald Tribune*, 28 September 1999; Winston Yau, 'Loss-makers in city leap', *South China Morning Post*, 12 June 1999; 'Chinese official says state firms still suffering despite reforms', *Asian Wall Street Journal*, 8 November 1999; Andy Xie, 'China's debt-driven growth runs out', *Asian Wall Street Journal*, 2 November 1999; and 'Reforming the SOEs', report by Dresdner Kleinwort Benson, 7 December 1999. This latter report estimated that US$500 billion are needed to recapitalize the SOEs and the process could take ten years. It points out that even in 1997, a peak year, China raised only around US$20 billion by issuing shares. The 'gearing' of SOEs, that is the ratio of assets to liabilities, reached an average of 80 per cent, the worst in Asia.

26. 'Firm action on steel', *China Daily Business Weekly*, 14 November 1999.
27. Wang Ying, 'Agreement to relieve Anshan Group's financial burden', *China Daily*, 17 November 1999.

Chapter 7: The Pig that Fears to Become Fat

1. Reuters, '"Toothless Tiger" telling it like it is', *South China Morning Post*, 12 March 1999.
2. Dow Jones Newswires, 'China's Jiang warns of privatization dangers', *Asian Wall Street Journal*, 2 July 1999.
3. Agence France Press, 'Private and state sectors placed on equal terms', *South China Morning Post*, 16 March 1999.
4. Jonathan Spence, *The Search for Modern China*, p.539.
5. Mark O'Neill, '"First peddler" hails era for entrepreneurs', *South China Morning Post*, 8 May 1999.
6. Wang Xiangwei, 'Private firms to get equal footing', *South China Morning Post*, 15 October 1998; and Ian Johnson, 'Beijing moves to help private enterprise', *Asian Wall Street Journal*, 1 February 1999.
7. Rose Tang, 'Hotpot king's humble recipe for success', *South China Morning Post*, 18 July 1999; and Mark O'Neill, 'Chongqing's hot-pot king courts banks, politicians', *South China Morning Post*, 3 February 1998.
8. Jasper Becker, 'How comrade Zhang Guoxi carved out an empire', *Business Week*, 19 September 1988.
9. Alexander Nicoll, 'Housewife who built empire from nothing', *Financial Times*, 9 June 1994.
10. Jasper Becker, 'Who wants to be a CCP millionaire? I do', *South China Morning Post*, 20 April 1991.
11. Julia Leung, 'Corruption may take its toll on China', *Asian Wall Street Journal*, 13 July 1989.
12. 'Officials' power abuse is major concern in poll', *China Daily*, 11 February 1989.
13. Jane MacCartney, Lai Pui-yee and David Chen, 'Deng cracks the whip on corruption', *South China Morning Post*, 9 October 1988.
14. Reuters, 'Fresh clampdown on corruption', *South China Morning Post*, 17 January 1989.
15. Edward Gargan, 'Corruption flourishes amid new Chinese vitality', *New York Times*, 11 July 1989.
16. Nicholas Kristof, 'China reviews enterprises amid tax allegations', *New York Times Supplement/International Herald Tribune*, 3 August 1989; and

Xinhua, 'Children of private entrepreneurs living "flashy" lives', 11 January 1992.

17. Willy Wo-lap Lam, 'Party ruling bars private businessmen', *South China Morning Post*, 2 October 1989.

18. S. Tomisaka, *Heirs of the Dragon*, p.52.

19. Pan Qing, 'China: profile – millionaire Yang professes investment enthusiasm', Xinhua, 25 August 1998.

20. Jurgen Kremb, 'Noch Wie in Eine Wilde Ehe! – Reportage uber China's ersten roten Milliardär Chen Yuguang' ('Like a wild marriage – Report on China's first red millionaire Chen Yuguang'), *Der Spiegel*, 4 October 1993.

21. Mark O'Neill, 'Connections keep modest entrepreneur in fast lane', *South China Morning Post*, 27 April 1988.

22. Mark O'Neill, 'Chinese see biggest business chance in history', Reuters, 14 November 1995.

23. Associated Press, 'China puts a top tycoon on trial', *International Herald Tribune*, 2 November 1999; Ian Johnson, 'China's Mou goes on trial on ill-fated satellite deal', *Asian Wall Street Journal*, 1 November 1999; and Mark O'Neill, 'Wheeler-dealer's day of reckoning', *South China Morning Post*, 29 October 1999.

24. Jasper Becker, 'Crisis feared in property sector', *South China Morning Post*, 3 December 1999.

25. Kathy Chen, 'China examines fund-raising by Wuxi firm', *Asian Wall Street Journal*, 18 April 1995.

26. Mark O'Neill, 'Futures scam victims pay big price for ignoring warnings', *South China Morning Post*, 17 August 1998.

27. Jasper Becker, 'Banking fall hits peasants', *South China Morning Post*, 20 November 1999.

28. Reuters, 'Tycoon Zhang sets personal aim of out-achieving Li Ka-shing', 4 December 1994.

29. Seth Faison, 'Caught in a web of corruption', *New York Times Supplement*, 7 March 1998.

30. Jasper Becker, 'Mainland's answer to Bill Gates', *South China Morning Post*, 5 May 1996.

31. Interview with the author, October 1999.

Chapter 8: The God of Wealth

1. Deng Xiaoping, *Fundamental Issues in Present-day China*, p.55.
2. Ma Licheng and Ling Zhijun, *Crossed Swords*, p.118.

3. 'Coca-Cola sales rise nearly 40 percent, taking a quarter of China market', *Asian Wall Street Journal*, 5 March 1996; and Nicholas Ionides, 'China learns to love Coke', *South China Morning Post*, 24 September 1998.

4. Matthew Miller, 'Maturity creates fresh challenge', *South China Morning Post*, 3 December 1998.

5. Adam S. Najberg, 'McDonald's chief in China can smell success brewing', *Asian Wall Street Journal*, 22 November 1995.

6. Sian Thomas, 'Coffee culture spreads inland as youth keep up with Western trends', *South China Morning Post*, 10 August 1998.

7. David Murphy, 'Fiesta falls flat for foreign breweries', *South China Morning Post*, 26 September 1999; and Reuters 'Oversupply brings beer bonanza hopes to head', *South China Morning Post*, 7 July 1999.

8. Austin Lobo, 'Icecream companies invest as sales grow', *South China Morning Post*, 13 June 1995.

9. Richard Tomlinson, 'Chinese develop chocolate cravings', *International Herald Tribune*, 11 October 1995; and Reuters, 'Foreigners bite off market chunk', *South China Morning Post*, 14 February 1999.

10. Xinhua, 'US potato chips squeezing into Chinese market', 4 January 1996; and Holly Hubbard Preston, 'Try the mousetrap angle? When it comes to cheese, China is a tough sell', *International Herald Tribune*, 7 May 1996.

11. Lana Wong, 'Beauty proves to be an irresistible lure', *South China Morning Post*, 3 December 1998.

12. Adam S. Najberg, 'McDonald's chief in China can smell success brewing', *Asian Wall Street Journal*, 22 November 1995.

13. Craig S. Smith, 'China struggles to defend its disappearing brands', *Asian Wall Street Journal*, 24 June 1996.

14. Mark O'Neill, 'End of "golden age" brings painful change', *South China Morning Post*, 12 March 1998.

15. 'Coca-Cola sales rise nearly 40 percent, taking a quarter of China market', *Asian Wall Street Journal*, 5 March 1996.

16. Xinhua, 'Foreign fast food not good for children's health, expert says', 29 April 1996.

17. Reuters, 'China crowing rights to KFC', *International Herald Tribune*, 3 October 1996.

18. Bruce Gilley, 'What's cooking?', *Far Eastern Economic Review*, 30 January 1997.

19. Matthew Miller, 'Kodak deal marks milestone', *South China Morning Post*, 25 March 1998.

20. Jasper Becker, 'Beijing briefing', *South China Morning Post*, 21 March 1998.
21. Jasper Becker, 'Volkswagen adds $12b to mainland investment', *South China Morning Post*, 8 November 1999.
22. In over twenty years Beijing has built just two subway lines, Shanghai and Guangzhou have each completed one and other major cities such as Tianjin have yet to start. Beijing also waited twenty years before investing in a fleet of comfortable public buses.
23. Karby Legget, 'Shanghai extends help to property sector', *Asian Wall Street Journal*, 20 October 1998; Jasper Becker, 'Crisis feared in property sector', *South China Morning Post*, 4 December 1997; and 'China Business Review', *South China Morning Post*, 8 October 1998.
24. Economist Intelligence Unit, 'China industry: business environment comes of age', 6 October 1999.
25. In an interview with Chen Jianguang, chief economist for township enterprises at the Ministry of Agriculture, he said official figures were unreliable. For example, research suggested that the number of heads of livestock owned was overreported by as much as 30 per cent.
26. William H. Overholt, *China: The Next Economic Superpower*, p.3.
27. Economist Intelligence Unit, 'China industry: business environment comes of age', 6 October 1999. This article points out that in 1981 China's GDP was 486 billion yuan, which was then equivalent to US$285 billion. By the end of 1997 its GDP was 7,345 billion yuan or the equivalent of US$885 billion.
28. The Ministry of Post and Telecommunications launched a new drive in 1992, setting a target of 36 million phones by 1995 and 78 million by 2000, bringing telephone density to 6 per 100 people. The target for the turn of the century was raised to 100 million lines, then to 114 million lines.
29. Jasper Becker, 'No wall can keep the Internet out', *South China Morning Post*, 3 October 1999.
30. Jasper Becker, 'Fairytale fans plan southern tour to Mickey', *South China Morning Post*, 3 December 1999.
31. *State Statistical Yearbook*, 1998.

Chapter 9: Guttering Candles

1. Jasper Becker, 'The peasant teachers', *South China Morning Post*, 30 October 1999.

2. In 1999 a film by the director Zhang Yimou, *Not One Less*, describing the life of a 12-year-old girl who becomes a substitute teacher in Hebei province, won a prize at the Venice Film Festival.
3. Zheng Yi, *Scarlet Memorial: Tales of Cannibalism in Modern China*, p.11: 'A local mob, stirred into a frenzy, bludgeoned to death eighty or ninety people on the spot with clubs and stones. Their victims included personnel from the county hospital: the executive and deputy executive directors of the hospital and directors of the various departments: interns, surgeons, gynaecologists, and pharmacists.'
4. UNESCO's World Education Indicators, 1998.
5. UNESCO puts the number at 478 per 100,000.
6. World Bank, *Report on Higher Education: Executive Briefing, 1996.*
7. For example, Cai Yuanpei, President of Yenching University, and first Minister of Education in the new republic, said in January 1917: 'We must reform the traditional Confucian way of education and develop a modern education system that cultivates a modern citizen's qualities and promotes modern science and technology.'
8. Mainland China now favours the term *putonghua*, meaning common language or words. The more general term *Han yu* or 'Han race language' is not officially used.
9. Bruce Gilley, *Tiger on the Brink*, p.27.
10. J.K. Galbraith, *A China Passage*, pp.52-3, 97-101, 134–5.
11. Xinhua, 'Comrade Fang Yi's report on China's Science and Education', 30 December 1977.
12. K.C. Tsang, 'Revolution in the classroom', *South China Morning Post*, 6 June 1985.
13. Nina McPherson, 'Bold reforms take blame for protests', *South China Morning Post*, 17 February 1987.
14. Mark O'Neill 'Low paid teacher's plea to escape poverty trap', *South China Morning Post*, 1 April 1988.
15. 'Teachers complain of too few titles', *China Daily*, 5 May 1988. The article reported that the restriction on the number of teachers who could acquire professional titles had caused bitter in-fighting. Higher academic titles were usually awarded to Party members as a reward for political loyalty.
16. 'Commission looks at speeding up education reform', *China Daily*, 4 February 1988; Agence France Press, 'Neglect of education at crisis level say experts', *South China Morning Post*, 22 April 1988; and *China Daily*, 12 March 1988.
17. National People's Congress press conference, 24 March 1989.

18. 'High schools draw sharp criticism for "élitist" status', *South China Morning Post*, 17 November 1986.
19. UNESCO World Education Indicators, 1998.
20. Agence France Press, 'Papers call for ethical education', *South China Morning Post*, 16 June 1997.
21. Kevin Murphy, 'China's cash crisis opens school door to private sector', *International Herald Tribune*, 10 May 1993; and UPI, 'Teachers rent pupils for funerals', *South China Morning Post*, 15 November 1995.
22. Xinhua, 'China's schoolyard business earns billions', 3 July 1996.
23. In the early years the Stone Corporation gave one million yuan and the US-based Banker's Trust promised one million yuan a year for five years. By 1998 cumulative donations reached 1.6 billion yuan (US$190 million).
24. In 1980 there were officially 250 million illiterates. The 1982 census recorded 519 million categorized as illiterate or semi-literate. A target of reducing the number of illiterates from 182 million in 1990 to 145 million by 1996 to just 12 per cent of the population, was then set. The target for the turn of the century was set at 5–7 per cent of the population. However, at the end of 1999, China reported there were 153 million illiterate and semi-literate people over the age of 15 (and 127 million under the age of 15) and that illiteracy among young and middle-aged adults had declined from 10.4 per cent to less than 5.5 per cent. By 1997 the percentage of women who could not read had increased by 4.5 per cent, reaching 71 per cent. Zhang Feng, 'Nation takes on illiteracy', *China Daily*, 13 December 1999; and Agence France Press, 'More than 300 million still illiterate', 12 December 1999.
25. 'Migrant schools: basic education not universal', *Chinabrief*, Vol. II, No. 3, August–November 1999
26. See Catriona Bass, *Education in Tibet*.
27. There are about 30,000 foreign English teachers working in China each year. And each year some 60,000 Chinese students graduate in English language teaching and another 50,000 in English language and literature. Many students are keen to pass the TOEFL (Test of English as a Foreign Language) and some 44,000 take the test each year as a passport to studying abroad.
28. The first private school, the Hanzheng Street Entrepreneurs Private School, opened in Wuhan and was funded by private businessmen.
29. Jasper Becker, 'Reader's gift saves only son from leukaemia', *South China Morning Post*, 3 September 1995; Xinhua, 'No more expensive

schools to be approved in Guangdong', 21 February 1995; and Daniel Kwan, 'Elite schools warned on fees', *South China Morning Post*, 3 March 1995.

30. Xinhua reported in 1999 that Guangdong is losing 1 billion yuan a year in pre-university education income because at least 5,000 children, and perhaps more, are being sent abroad to study. Guangdong's banks are even offering loans to help parents afford the costs. 'Province loses as students go abroad', *South China Morning Post*, 19 July 1999.

31. Jasper Becker, 'Home truths about one-child policy', *South China Morning Post*, 31 March 1999; and Jasper Becker, 'The young introduced to the ancient', *South China Morning Post*, 28 March 1999.

32. On 22 September 1995 Xinhua reported that 1,100 methods of unauthorized collecting had been revealed in twenty provinces.

33. The state promised to step up spending on housing so that by the turn of the century 60 per cent would live in decent homes. Spending on teachers' housing was supposed to double after 1994 and total 34 billion yuan by 2000. In 1997 the Minister of Education Zhu Kaixuan promised that every teacher would be offered state housing by 1999 and that, by the turn of the century, all urban teachers would enjoy improved living conditions.

34. Some 82,000 were reported to be in this position. Senior high school teachers were the worst off with 180,000 without housing and half of the rest living in housing which failed to meet minimum standards.

35. Li Lanqing was quoted by the BBC on 14 November 1994. One survey of 200,000 children found that between the ages of 7 and 8 a fifth were short-sighted. By the age of 15, the proportion had risen to 60 per cent and by the age of 18 to 75 per cent. *The Shanghai Youth Daily*, 15 November 1995, reported that up to 20 per cent of students suffer from some sort of psychological disorder and that suicide rates are high.

36. Jasper Becker, 'Lessons from a shrinking city', *South China Morning Post*, 11 March 1999.

37. Jasper Becker, 'Education braces for new leap forward', *South China Morning Post*, 25 March 1999.

38. 'Scholars' contributions vital' and 'Centre will tap skills of talented seniors', *China Daily*, 5 February 1999.

39. Agence France Press, 'Student outcry at university merger', *South China Morning Post*, 12 December 1999.

40. 'State to recruit more postgraduates', *China Daily*, 28 October 1998.

41. *Beijing Review*, 31 August 1998. When the Central China University of

Science and Engineering held a Chinese test for 3,500 new students in 1996 it discovered that even some of the doctoral students failed.

42. Jason Dean, 'Course in China seeks to foster creative process', *Asian Wall Street Journal*, 30 November 1999; and Economist Intelligence Unit, *China Industry: Telecoms and MBAs*, 3 August 1999.

43. Wang Ying, 'Students offered new loans', *China Daily*, 5 December 1999. This points out that students have to offer collateral in order to obtain the loans and that only fifty had so far been successful in doing so.

Chapter 10: Barefoot Doctors and Witch-doctors

1. Jasper Becker, 'Fight for a healthy state of mind' and 'Return of the shamans' *South China Morning Post*, 19 October 1999.

2. Charlotte Cailliez, 'Collapse of the rural health system', *China Perspectives*, No.18, July/August 1998.

3. Willy De Geyndt, Xiyan Zhao and Shunli Liu, 'From barefoot doctor to village doctor in rural China', *World Bank Technical Paper*, 1992, No.187.

4. Xinhua, 'Doctors face licence tests for first time', *China Daily*, 1 November 1999. In a report on the introduction of the licensing system for doctors in 1999, Xinhua commented that: 'Statistics show that China has more than 1.5 million doctors and some 460,000 medical assistants. However, the number of new physicians in recent years has far exceeded the number of graduates from medical college, which suggests that many unqualified people are practising medicine.' Willy De Geyndt, Xiyan Zhao and Shunli Liu, 'From barefoot doctor to village doctor in rural China', *World Bank Technical Paper*, 1992, No.187.

5. The number of outpatient visits to township health centres fell by a quarter between 1986 and 1993. One study found that a third of those referred did not turn up because the cost was ruinous. A study by the Shanghai Medical University found a sharp decline in immunization since 1993 after local authorities decided to save money by charging for each injection.

6. World Bank, 'China: long term issues and options in health transition', March 1992.

7. UPI, 'Medicine misuse kills thousands', *South China Morning Post*, 23 May 1995; and Rahul Jacob, 'Medical emergency', *Time*, 15 April 1996.

8. Xinhua, 'Guangxi develops folk medicine', 18 June 1996.

9. This was reported to me by a reliable informant.

10. Frank Dikotter, *The Discourse of Race in Modern China*, p.163, quoting L. Weiger, *Moralisme official des écoles*, 1920.

11. Tan Sitong, *Collected Writings,* p.336.

12. Agence France Press, 'Fitness drive to "lift nation"', *South China Morning Post*, 29 June 1995.

13. Jasper Becker, '400 million lack safe water', *South China Morning Post*, 29 July 1997, taken from a UNICEF report, *Progress of Nations*. The mortality rate among those under the age of 5 deteriorated between 1985 and 1990 from 44 deaths per thousand to 44.5 deaths per thousand – significant in a period when living and nutrition standards were rising so sharply. See also World Bank, 'China: long term issues and options for health transition', March 1992.

14. M. Giovanni Merli, 'Under-reporting of births and infant deaths in rural China: evidence from field research in a county of northern China', *China Quarterly*, No.155, September 1998.

15. Judith Banister, *China's Changing Population*, pp.179–82.

16. 'Where have all the little girls gone? In rural China no one knows', *International Herald Tribune*, 18 June 1991; and Agence France Press, 'Abortion rate is one in three', *South China Morning Post*, 23 November 1985.

17. 'China's birth rate declined in 1987', *China Daily*, 16 May 1988.

18. Lena H. Sun, 'Chinese push down birthrate', *International Herald Tribune*, 23 April 1993.

19. '6.3 brides for seven brothers', *The Economist*, 19 December 1998.

20. The data suggests that 8.7 million are missing for the period 1979–85, or 5 per cent of those born, and the situation worsened considerably in the 1990s.

21. *The Economist/South China Morning Post*, 13 January 1999.

22. Nicholas D. Kristof, 'In China's crackdown on population growth force is a big weapon', *International Herald Tribune*, 28 April 1993; and 'Death penalty for bribe-takers', *South China Morning Post*, 2 October 1993. In one reported case two hospital officials were sentenced to death for helping women escape sterilization and six others were jailed for taking bribes (Associated Press, 'Birth permits sold in get-rich scheme', *South China Morning Post*, 27 January 1999). There have been reports of officials imprisoning peasants who refuse to pay a fine for forty days in a crowded room without a toilet. Some corrupt officials have also apparently levied fines but refused to give receipts so that the victims can be fined again.

23. By the year 2010, 11 per cent of the population will be over 65. By the year 2020, there will be 428 million people aged between 20 and 39 but 392 million aged between 40 and 59.

24. Chris Yeung, 'Planners look to offspring of literate', *South China Morning Post*, 12 April 1993. The children of parents who have had only one child are now allowed to have two children which means that by 2005 nearly every urban couple will probably be eligible to have two children.

25. 'Genetics plea in fight against birth defects', *South China Morning Post*, 20 March 1996; and Associated Press, 'Dietary push to cut rate of birth defects', *South China Morning Post*, 23 July 1997.

26. Vivien Pik-kwan Chan, 'Medicine measures after pupils fall ill', *South China Morning Post*, 5 April 1998. There have also been numerous cases in which people have been poisoned after consuming fake iodine pills. In one case up to 17,000 pupils reportedly fell ill at one time (Agence France Press, 'Iodine pills ban after 17,000 pupils fall ill', *South China Morning Post*, 7 May 1998).

27. China 2020, 'Financing health care: issues and options for China', World Bank, September 1997; and '310,000 Chinese babies die from malnutrition', *South China Morning Post*, 7 February 1997.

28. Frank Dikotter, *Imperfect Conceptions*, p.144.

29. 'Genetics plea in fight against birth defects', *South China Morning Post*, 20 March 1996.

30. Frank Dikotter, *Imperfect Conceptions*, p.144.

31. 'Death by default: a policy of fatal neglect in China's state orphanages'. The report accused an orphanage in Shanghai of starving handicapped children, a policy known as 'summary resolution'.

32. Liu Aihong, 'Mental health patients: can we do something?', *Outlook Weekly Magazine*, 20 December 1999.

33. Agence France Press, 'Reforms "hurt women more"', *South China Morning Post*, 29 January 1999; and Lijia MacLeod, 'The dying fields', *Far Eastern Economic Review*, 23 April 1998. The figures come from a study conducted by the World Bank, the World Health Organization and Harvard University. Thom Beal, 'Warning issued on future of mentally ill', *South China Morning Post*, 21 December 1995.

34. Daniel Kwan, 'Medical reform fails to help poor villagers', *South China Morning Post*, 23 April 1998.

35. China 2020, 'Financing health care: issues and options for China', World Bank, September 1997.

36. Jasper Becker, 'Smoking will kill a third of young men', *South China*

Morning Post, 19 November 1998. Ten per cent of government revenue comes from taxes levied on the tobacco industry. China may be forced to raise taxes to pay for the health costs of caring for smokers.

37. Erik Eckholm, 'China bans sale of blood, but few people donate it', *International Herald Tribune*, 2 October 1998.

38. China has more than 4,000 enterprises making Chinese and Western medicines, many of them small factories which often operate at a loss. Cut-throat price-cutting, for instance, forced two-thirds of China's Vitamin C producers out of business by 1996 (Lana Wong, 'Price war forces two-thirds of vitamin C producers to close', *South China Morning Post*, 16 September 1996). China plans to set up ten large pharmaceutical groups over the next five years in an attempt to address the problem.

39. American Chamber of Commerce in China, White Paper on American Business in China, March 2000. These figures appear to cover drugs made in China by Western firms, and those imported.

40. 'Medicine price regulation to help health care reform', *China Daily*, 8 December 1999; Daniel Kwan, 'Moving towards a possible cure for health system's ills', *South China Morning Post*, 15 January 1995; and Elizabeth Rosenthal, 'What ails China? Drug prices', *International Herald Tribune*, 20 November 1998.

41. Sales of non-prescription drugs are expected to be worth US$3 billion by the year 2003.

Chapter 11: The Stinking Ninth

1. *Grass Soup* and *My Bodhi Tree*.

2. Jasper Becker, 'Thoughts of a dissident writer', *South China Morning Post*, 25 April 1996.

3. A view also expressed by Wang Furen in the journal *Fangfa*, No.1, 1999.

4. *The Songs of the South: An Anthology of Ancient Chinese Poems by Qu Yuan and Other Poets*, trans. David Hawkes (Penguin Books, Harmondsworth, 1995).

5. Dai Huang, *Nine Deaths, One Life: My Progress as a Rightist*.

6. Dai Huang, *Hu Yaobang and the Righting of Wrong Cases*.

7. Ma Licheng and Ling Zhijun, *Crossed Swords*.

8. Wang Shiwei, *Wild Lilies*.

9. Mao Zedong, 'Talks at the Yan'an Forum on Literature and Arts' in *Collected Works*.

10. Lao Gui, *Blood Red Sunset*.

11. *Xinhua Ribao*, 21 March 1941.

12. Ruan Ming, *Deng Xiaoping: Chronicle of an Empire*, p.101.

13. Seth Faison, 'Joint bid to back Chinese artists', *South China Morning Post*, 27 February 1988.

14. *China Daily*, 25 February 1988.

15. Yan Jiaqi and Gao Gao, *Turbulent Decade: A History of the Cultural Revolution*.

16. 'Revolution may be marked', *South China Morning Post*, 29 April 1986. Ba Jin, then Chairman of the Chinese Writers' Association, said: 'We should earnestly learn lessons from this experience. To build Cultural Revolution museums in China would have the same educational effect [as the museum at Auschwitz]. The great Cultural Revolution brought untold suffering to the Chinese nation and should never be repeated.' See also 'Cultural Revolution museums urged', *China Daily*, 30 April 1986.

17. *People's Daily*, 15 August 1985.

18. 'China writer slams culture', *Hong Kong Standard*, 11 March 1987; and interview with the author.

19. Mao Zedong, *Selected Works*.

20. Mao Zedong, *Selected Works*.

21. W.K. Liao , *Complete Works of Han Feizi*, Ch. 8.

22. Marlow Hood, 'Zhao claims stability will follow campaign', *South China Morning Post*, 19 February 1987.

23. *Beijing Review*, No.3, 12 January 1987.

24. Associated Press, 'China re-activates May 4th Movement', *South China Morning Post*, 4 May 1987; and Xinhua, 'What did *River Elegy* advertise?', 19 July 1989.

25. Jasper Becker, 'Hu's errors listed in leaked documents', *Guardian*, 2 March 1987.

26. Lu Xun, 'Lao tiao-tzu i-ching ch'ang wan' ('The old tune has been sung long enough'), a speech delivered in Hong Kong on 18 February 1927, quoted in Chow Tse-tsung, *The May 4th Movement: Intellectual Revolution in Modern China*.

27. Louise Bransom, 'Beijing glasnost brings home reality to Chinese', *Sunday Times*, 21 March 1988.

28. Nina McPherson, 'Teacher faces Beijing's wrath', *South China Morning Post*, 12 January 1987.

29. A *People's Daily* editor was arrested in 1991 when the paper ran a patriotic ode ostensibly written by an overseas student. Hidden in the eight-line poem, if read diagonally from right to left, was an acrostic: 'Step down Prime Minister Li Peng, assuage popular anger'.

30. Jasper Becker, 'Confucius pays a price', *South China Morning Post*, 30 May 1995, quoting Xinhua.
31. Xinhua, 'China orders new controls on book market', 16 June 1999.
32. *Ming Bao*, 10 October 1996.

Chapter 12: Secret Empire

1. Jasper Becker, 'Mao's defence legacy a commercial liability' and 'Tank producer rolls again with US cash', *South China Morning Post*, 21 November 1998.
2. John Frankenstein and Bates Gill, 'Current and future challenges facing Chinese defence industries', *China Quarterly*, June 1996, No.146, p.403.
3. Claire Hollingworth, *Mao and the Men Against Him*, p.91.
4. Li Zhisui, *The Private Life of Chairman Mao*, p.125.
5. Nie Liesheng, 'Military plants turn to civilian production', *China Daily*, 7 January 1988.
6. John Frankenstein and Bates Gill, 'Current and future challenges facing Chinese defence industries', *China Quarterly*, June 1996, No.146, p.403.
7. Information Office of the State Council, July 1998.
8. James C.F. Wang, *Contemporary Chinese Politics*, quotes the *Beijing Review* of 1 August 1982, p.195.
9. James C.F. Wang, *Contemporary Chinese Politics*, p.176; and Ellis Joffe, 'Party–army relationships in China: retrospect and prospect', *China Quarterly*, June 1996, No.146, p.299.
10. Mark O'Neill, 'Staking out a home in a divided land', *South China Morning Post*, 30 May 1998.
11. Deng Xiaoping, *Selected Works*, Vol.III, p.334.
12. Yitzhak Shichor, 'Demobilisation: the dialectics of PLA troop reduction', *China Quarterly*, June 1996, No.146, p.146.
13. Associated Press, 'China's civil servants will wear Cardin designs', *Asian Wall Street Journal*, 20 March 1996.
14. Dorinda Elliott, 'Xian aircraft's long march forward', *Newsweek*, 11 July 1988.
15. Xinhua, 20 January 1996.
16. David Shambaugh, 'China's military in transition: politics, professionalism, procurement and power projection', *China Quarterly*, June 1996, No.146, p.265.
17. Wang Shaoguang, 'Research note estimating China's defence expendi-

ture: some evidence from Chinese sources', *China Quarterly*, No.147, September 1996, p.888.

18. Reuters, 'PLA seeks foreign funding boost', *South China Morning Post*, 19 August 1997.

19. Richard Bernstein and Ross H. Munro, *The Coming Conflict with China*, p.11.

20. John Frankenstein and Bates Gill, 'Current and future challenges facing Chinese defence industries', *China Quarterly*, June 1996, No.146, p.394.

21. On 8 July, 700 workers blocked the streets and the next morning tens of thousands of citizens took up the protest, erecting road blocks and smashing bus windows. Troops of the PAP were called in and unofficial reports say that over 100 were injured and 80 arrested: Nisid Hajari, 'Taking to the streets', *Time*, 4 August 1997. Similar protests involving 20,000 workers took place in Nanchong where employees from the city's largest silk factory took their manager hostage and paraded him through the streets. They had not received wages for six months. Disgruntled workers from other factories quickly joined the protest and more than 20,000 besieged the city hall for 30 hours: Matt Forney, 'We want to eat', *Far Eastern Economic Review*, 26 June 1997.

22. Interview with John Frankenstein, October 1998, following publication of a study on China's defence industry conversion for the European Commission ('Defence Industry Trends: A Background Paper for Policy Directorate 1'), quoted in Jasper Becker, 'Mao's defence legacy a commercial liability', *South China Morning Post*, 21 November 1998.

23. Willy Wo-lap Lam, 'PLA gets pay-off for business loss', *South China Morning Post*, 3 August 1998; and Willy Wo-lap Lam, 'PLA chief accepts US$47b payout', *South China Morning Post*, 9 October 1998.

24. Xinhua, 'Military paper praises missile brigade', 10 April 1996.

25. Oliver Chou, 'Cash-strapped PLA officers run up debts', *South China Morning Post*, 30 March 1999. The *Liberation Army Daily* commented: 'The debts run up by officers in their desire to match the income of others around them has provoked negative thinking and revealed the constant impact of the market economy on our troops.'

26. Reuters, 'Top PLA pair executed as spies', *South China Morning Post*, 14 September 1999. Retired Major-General Liu Liankun (58) and Colonel Shao Zhengzhong (56) were court-martialled in the biggest spy case since 1949: Reuters, 'PLA pay frozen amid anger at spying case', *South*

China Morning Post, 15 September 1999; Willy Wo-lap Lam, 'Jiang steps in to halt leaking of secrets', *South China Morning Post*, 18 September 1999; and Oliver Chou, 'Spy probe targets PLA senior ranks', *South China Morning Post*, 14 September 1999.

27. Richard Halloran, 'China has ambitious military plans but it will take time', *International Herald Tribune*, 29 January 1997.

28. Willy Wo-lap Lam, *China after Deng Xiaoping*, p.224

29. Oliver Chou, 'Gulf War a turning point in beefing up air power', *South China Morning Post*, 23 November 1999. The *Liberation Army Daily* has reported that between 1994 and 1999 the PLAAF also built 37 new military airports and 100 command posts, operational stations and aviation control centres, renovated 100 weapons and logistics warehouses, built three new military railways and acquired a large quantity of advanced missiles, anti-air artillery and radar. Xinhua has quoted Lieutenant-General Liu Shunyao as saying that the airforce is switching from a purely defensive strategy to one in which it can both defend and attack: Daniel Kwan, 'Air force flying into attack role', *South China Morning Post*, 8 November 1999. China has built its own fighter bomber, the Flying Leopard, which was flown during the October 1999 military parade, but it is not being bought by the military. Instead it has ordered up to 60 SU-30 MKK fighter jets from Russia in a deal negotiated in 1999.

30. Willy Wo-lap Lam, 'Nato's war speeds PLA's pace of change', *South China Morning Post*, 12 May 1999.

31. Xinhua, 'Chinese president approves new army system to win high-tech wars', 1 January 2000.

32. Bruce Gilley, 'Chinese book outlines how it spies on US', *Far Eastern Economic Review*, 15 December 1999.

33. Oliver Chou, 'Neutron bomb puts Beijing in weapons' élite', *South China Morning Post*, 16 July 1999; and Reuters, '$74b boost to nuclear second-strike power', *South China Morning Post*, 25 October 1999.

Chapter 13: Tremble and Obey

1. Jasper Becker, 'China's battle to cut back on the cadres', *South China Morning Post*, 26 October 1998. Hou also explained that China is introducing civil service examinations with written and verbal tests. The examinations are supposedly set by each ministry so there are no common entry requirements nor any independent examination board. All candidates are pre-selected by the Party. Annual performance

reviews have also been instituted. Cadres are assessed on both their personal performance and on achievements in reaching certain policy objectives such as enforcing birth-control targets or reducing pollution. New regulations also specify the grounds for dismissal such as the refusal to accept assignment to a new job, failure to complete education courses or a lapse in discipline including being absent from work for more than thirty days a year.

2. Fu Zhengyuan, 'China's Legalists; the earliest totalitarians and their art of ruling', p.12, taken from *Records of the Historian*, ch.130.

3. His ideas were written down by later scholars in *Guan Zi* (*Works of Master Guan*).

4. The works of Han Fei, the most extensive body of Legalist teachings, were subsequently adopted by the Han dynasty. Han Fei served the founder of the Qin dynasty.

5. A former chancellor of the Qin state, he introduced the legal code drawn up by an earlier Legalist, Li Kui.

6. James C.F. Wang, *Contemporary Chinese Politics: An Introduction*, p.122, claims that 20 million were re-educated during this period.

7. Jasper Becker, 'China's battle to cut back on the cadres', *South China Morning Post*, 26 October 1998.

8. Jasper Becker, 'How Karl Marx survived it all', *South China Morning Post*, 1 October 1999.

9. Interview with Sun Yueyu of the Jiangsu Institute of Administration.

10. David Chen, 'Manoeuvring round a resignation', *South China Morning Post*, 19 January 1987.

11. Jasper Becker, interview with Bao Tong, *South China Morning Post*, 3 June 1998.

12. David Chen, 'Revamp will strengthen Zhao's hold', *South China Morning Post*, 20 November 1987.

13. Jasper Becker, 'Shuffling the cards', *South China Morning Post*, 26 October 1996.

14. Willy Wo-lap Lam, *China after Deng Xiaoping*, p.249.

15. Sheryl WuDunn, 'Beijing to shake up Party membership', *New York Times Supplement*, 20 February 1990.

16. Willy Wo-lap Lam, *China after Deng Xiaoping*, p. 283.

17. 'Cadres told to go back to school', *South China Morning Post*, 16 March 1990; and Associated Press, 'Figures for Party expulsions revealed', *South China Morning Post*, 28 March 1990.

18. John Kohut, 'If you have to celebrate, have a tea party, cadres told', *South China Morning Post*, 18 December 1991; UPI, 'Cadres ignore drive

against luxury cars', *South China Morning Post*, 17 June 1994; and 'No luxury cars for top officials', *South China Morning Post*, 29 June 1994.

19. Jasper Becker, 'Fear invades the halls of bureaucracy', *South China Morning Post*, 8 March 1998. I am particularly indebted to Dr Jean-Pierre Cabestan's book *L'Administration Chinoise après Mao: Les Réformes de l'ère Deng Xiaoping et leurs limites* for many of the details and ideas in this chapter.

20. 'Anger at $336b state employee food bill', *South China Morning Post*, 3 April 1998.

21. Mark O'Neill and Willy Wo-lap Lam, 'Technocrats selected for Zhu's cabinet', *South China Morning Post*, 19 March 1998.

22. Jasper Becker, 'Rural reflection of China's ills', *South China Morning Post*, 23 January 1999.

23. Jasper Becker, '2.2m will lose jobs in official shake-up', *South China Morning Post*, 23 August 1999; and 'Sixty percent of government and Party institutions redundant at county level', *Newspaper and Journal Digest*, 24 June 1999.

24. Xinhua, '18,000 cases of illegal government levies punished', 22 February 1998.

25. Daniel Kwan, 'Cadres tighten control of villages', *South China Morning Post*, 22 June 1999.

26. Jasper Becker, 'Image change for family planners', *South China Morning Post*, 7 January 2000, based on an interview with Professor Ma Xu of the Research Institute of the Family Planning Commission.

27. There were 500,000 tax collectors in 1993 and the number has since increased by 15,000 a year.

28. Zhang Dingmin, 'Income tax challenge grows', *China Daily*, 6 December 1999. Personal income tax revenues were worth 34 billion yuan (US$4.1 billion) in 1998.

29. John Stuart Mill, *On Liberty and Utilitarianism,* p.82.

Chapter 14: The Rule of Law

1. Jasper Becker, 'Lawyers behind bars', *South China Morning Post*, 29 January 2000.

2. Amnesty International, 'Law Reform and Human Rights', ASA, 17 January 1997.

3. George Wehrfritz, 'Rulers are the law', *Newsweek,* 29 September 1997.

4. Ian Johnson, 'Class action suits in China', *Asian Wall Street Journal*, 25 March 1999; Agence France Press, 'Lawyer jailed for five years', *South*

China Morning Post, 19 January 2000; and Jane's Information Group, 'An odd sort of Chinese justice', 27 January 2000.

5. Xu Xiaoqun, 'The fate of judicial independence in republican China, 1912–37', *China Quarterly*, No.149, March 1987.

6. Harry Wu, *Laogai: The Chinese Gulag.*

7. David S.G. Goodman, 'JinJiLuYu in the Sino-Japanese War: The Border Region and the Border Region Government', *China Quarterly*, No.140, December 1984.

8. Kang Sheng reportedly gave a speech in December 1942 in which he explained that 'A rectification campaign inevitably leads to the checking of cadres and that checking is inevitably followed by the elimination of counter-revolutionaries . . These three things are inevitably linked and that is an iron-clad law.' See also Fu Zhengyuan, *Autocratic Traditions and Chinese Politics*, pp.272–4, and Laszlo Ladany, *The Communist Party of China and Marxism, 1921–1985: A Self-Portrait*, p.55.

9. Peng Zhen, 'The importance of improving China's legislation', speech delivered in 1984, quoted by Michael Dutton in *The Police, Public Order and the State.*

10. Quoted in Laszlo Ladany, *Law and Legality in China*, p.63.

11. 'Whose security? "State security" in China's new criminal code', *Human Rightswatch Asia*, Vol.9, No.4, April 1997. It quotes *Hukou Guanli Xue (The Science of Residence-Registration Management)*, published by Zhongguo Jiancha Chubanshe (China Procuracy Press), April 1992.

12. 'Whose security? "State security" in China's new criminal code', *Human Rightswatch Asia*, Vol.9, No.4, April 1997, p.30, which quotes *Hukuo Guanli Xue (The Science of Residence-Registration Management)*, Ch. 13.

13. Harry Wu, *Laogai: The Chinese Gulag*, p.21.

14. The Huai River water conservancy and hydroelectric scheme employed a million prisoners over a period of ten years. Laszlo Ladany, *Law and Legality in China*, p.124.

15. Michael Dutton, *The Police, Public Order and the State*, pp.189–213.

16. Michael Schoenhals, 'The Central Case Examination Group, 1966–1979', *China Quarterly*, No.145, March 1996.

17. 'Big brother is watching', *Far Eastern Economic Review*, 3 November 1988; and Patrick Lescot, *L'Empire rouge Moscou-Pekin, 1919–1989*, p.21.

18. Quoted in Laszlo Ladany, *Law and Legality in China*, p.82.

19. In fact Wei was sentenced under the old 1951 Regulations on the Punishment of Counter-Revolution. However, even if he had been

tried under the new law, it would not have resulted in a more lenient sentence. An identical fifteen-year sentence was handed down to a fellow activist, Xu Wenli, two years later.

20. Harry Wu, *Laogai: The Chinese Gulag*, p.60.

21. 'Zhonggong Zhongyang Wenjian', Central Party Document No.67, quoted in James D. Seymour and Richard Anderson, *New Ghosts, Old Ghosts*.

22. Laszlo Ladany, *Law and Legality in China*, p.95.

23. Laszlo Ladany, *Law and Legality in China*, p.102.

24. Yitzhak Shichor, 'Demobilisation: the dialectics of PLA troop reduction', *China Quarterly*, No.146, June 1996. The police force was put at one million in 1995 and the target is a force of two million. All these numbers are kept secret so it is difficult to make convincing estimates of the total size of the security apparatus at the end of the century. It might include 3 million PLA, 2 million PAP, 2 million police under the Public Security Ministry, 2 million employed by the State Security Ministry and 12 million employed to some degree in various street committees and public order committees, giving a total of 21 million. Yitzhak Shichor suggests that China's various public security forces total 5–10 million.

25. Jasper Becker, 'Elite units train in West to fight terrorist threat', *Guardian*, 9 October 1988.

26. Tai Ming Cheung, 'Guarding China's domestic frontline: The People's Armed Police and China's stability', *China Quarterly*, No.146, June 1996. Following the failure of the police to control the demonstrators in Tiananmen Square in 1989, the PAP was expanded and provided with helicopters, armoured cars and artillery as well as vehicles with loudspeakers and water-cannon. Some units are now equipped with body armour, batons, helmets and shields, and practise dealing with urban riots.

27. Hong Xia, 'Policemen warned of incorrect behaviour', *China Daily*, 1 October 1992; and Reuters, 'Beijing to boost police patrols', *South China Morning Post*, 22 April 1996.

28. BBC, Short Wave Broadcasts, summary, 1 November 1991. By reputation, many of the civilian members of these committees are bossy old women, empowered to snoop around at will and enter people's houses as they choose. Many are also responsible for administering other laws and regulations on everything from birth-control policies to public sanitation. Such people are paid a wage and increasingly now have to take responsibility for dealing with social security questions as

urban dwellers lose their jobs or struggle to obtain their pensions and to find the money to pay medical fees.

29. Lena H. Sun, 'China's secret dossiers to keep people in place', *Hong Kong Standard*, 19 March 1992.

30. Lena H. Sun, 'China's secret dossiers to keep people in place', *Hong Kong Standard*, 19 March 1992.

31. Michael Dutton, 'Missing the target: policing strategies in the period of economic reform', *Crime and Delinquency*, Vol.39, No.3, July 1993.

32. Daniel Kwan, 'Trials to be opened up across the country', *South China Morning Post*, 3 December 1998; and Xinhua, 'Comprehensive reform of judicial system planned', 4 December 1998.

33. Xinhua, 'Government to shake up township courts for rural stability', 29 November 1998; and Reuters, 'China unveils sweeping legal reforms', 2 December 1998. The first national conference on courts was held in 1998.

34. Michael Dutton, 'Missing the target: policing strategies in the period of economic reform', *Crime and Delinquency*, Vol.39, No.3, July 1993.

35. A similar story was reported by the Chinese press in 1995 concerning a sports coach called Guo Jiming who worked at a school in Jinan province. When Guo came across a dispute outside the school gate, he tried to mediate but the local police arrived, grabbed him and began to beat him without first asking questions. He was handcuffed, driven in an unmarked van to a police station, tied to a bench and then beaten again by a group of policemen. When they got tired, they rested and then began once more. Eventually the school authorities intervened and rescued him, but not before he was severely injured and had lost the hearing in one ear. He subsequently lodged a complaint against the police.

36. Li Kungrui, Xu Deyong, Zhou Jingnan and Mao Tongkun, 'Some initial thoughts on a number of problems relating to the legislation covering investigations carried out while in detention', in *Gong'An Yanjiu (Police Research)*, quoted in Michael Dutton, 'Missing the target: policing strategies in the period of economic reform', *Crime and Delinquency*, Vol.39, No.3, July 1993.

37. Nicholas D. Kristof, 'Secret China report cites police torture', *New York Times Supplement*, 27 May 1991.

38. Human Rights in China, 'A report on administrative detention under "custody and repatriation"', September 1999.

39. Amnesty International, 'China: torture and ill treatment of prisoners', 1987.

40. Patrick Lescot, 'Police urged to abandon torture', *South China Morning Post*, 29 October 1986.
41. BBC, Short Wave Broadcasts, 'Security office on "rather grim" public order situation', 7 January 1992.
42. Reuters, 'Policemen take torture for granted', *South China Morning Post*, 19 November 1991.
43. Human Rights Watch, 'Anthems of Defeat: Crackdown in Hunan Province, 1989–92', 1992.
44. In 1999 the case of Yao Xiaohong, a judge in Shanxi province who killed a number of people in detention, routinely hanging them from trees or the banister of a staircase in the court, was publicized: 'Court boss beats detainees to death', *South China Morning Post*, 19 July 1999. The report was based on an article in the *China Youth Daily*.
45. Amnesty International, 'PRC: The death penalty in 1998', December 1999.
46. The *Legal Daily* has reported that between 1957 and 1997, more than 2.5 million underwent *lao jiao* in camps. It has also reported that there are currently 280 *liao jiao* camps with a population of 230,000: Reuters, 'Labour camps defended', 4 August 1997. Two American academics, James D. Seymour and Richard Anderson, estimate that China has 1,250 prison camps, fewer than half the number in the late 1950s. After looking closely at the current populations of camps in Xinjiang and Qinghai, provinces which in Mao's era had a concentration of penal camps, they estimate the national prison population could be between 1.5 and 2 million.

   Harry Wu estimates that of the 50 million sentenced to *lao gai* camps since 1949, between 16 and 20 million never left the system, including 8 to 10 million held under the terms of temporary job placement. He has identified nearly 1,100 camps and thinks that there could be four times as many, housing at least 4 million in the mid-1980s and 6 to 8 million ten years later. Wu believes that since 1949 some 20 to 25 million people have disappeared in the prison camps. See James D. Seymour and Richard Anderson, *New Ghosts, Old Ghosts*; and Harry Wu, *Laogai: The Chinese Gulag*. See also Information Office of the State Council, 'Criminal Reform in China', August 1992.
47. Information Office of the State Council, 'Criminal Reform in China', August 1992.
48. He Sheng, 'Courts face hurdles in backlog', *China Daily*, 30 November 1998.

49. Daniel Kwan, '"Rampant corruption" among prosecutors', *South China Morning Post*, 10 March 1999.
50. Jasper Becker, 'Litigants hire thugs to beat up debtors', *South China Morning Post*, 22 December 1997; and Frank Ching, 'Rough justice', *Far Eastern Economic Review*, 20 August 1998.
51. Matthew Miller, 'Damages paid to assaulted shopper', *South China Morning Post*, 15 January 2000. The story was also reported in the *Guangzhou Daily*.
52. Mark O'Neill, 'Debt collectors by any other name muscle in on growth business', *South China Morning Post*, 6 December 1999.
53. Vivien Pik-Kwan Chan, 'Cross-country sweep to clean up judiciary', *South China Morning Post*, 16 January 1999; 'Faults found with 9,400 court cases, legislators told', *South China Morning Post*, 15 September 1998; and Xinhua, 'Judiciary reports seven million cases re-examined in clean-up', 12 February 1999.
54. Reuters, 'China Communist Party expels rights row official', 8 July 1998.

Chapter 15: Between Heaven and Earth

1. Jasper Becker, 'Robinson on the sidelines', *South China Morning Post*, 17 September 1998. Chu Hailan, the wife of an imprisoned labour activist Liu Nianchun, was dragged away by police as she was waiting to meet Robinson in the lobby of the Hilton Hotel in Beijing. Chu later said she had subsequently been beaten and detained for more than seven hours.
2. Jasper Becker, 'Cantonese colonizers "may have been the first Chinese"', and 'The walk out of Africa that upsets Beijing', *South China Morning Post*, 4 July 1999. The bones of Peking Man were hailed as a missing link in human evolution when they were discovered at Zhoukoudian outside Beijing in the 1930s. It is also claimed that the first traces of man-made fire, dating back 700,000 years, have been discovered there. More recently, the age of Peking Man has been reduced to 580,000 years. Chinese scientists such as Professor Wu Xinzhi of the Institute of Vertebrate Palaeontology and Palaeo-anthropology are now dedicated to showing that in China early man is as old as, if not older than, early man anywhere else. Wu claims that China has found more than sixty sites containing hominoid fossils that date back 1.7 million years and that the remains bear distinct features that differ from those of Africans or Caucasians. Sun Qigang, at the Museum of

Chinese History, further claims that these remains support the theory that the Chinese originated in China.

However, research by Professor Jin Li at the Human Genetics Centre of the University of Texas in Houston and other geneticists in China has shown through gene-mapping techniques that the Chinese, like other East Asians, are descended from a common African ancestor who lived 200,000 years ago and moved into Asia 100,000 years ago.

3. The story is recounted in *The Dragon's Pearl: Growing up Among China's Élite* by Sirin Phathanthai with James Peck.
4. Fu Zhengyuan, *China's Legalists: The Earliest Totalitarians and Their Art of Ruling*, p.82.
5. At the seventh mass rally in November 1966, he said: 'Long live comrades! You must let politics take comand, go with the masses, and be with the masses. You must conduct the Great Proletarian Cultural Revolution even better': see Jonathan Spence, *Mao Zedong*, p.168.
6. Interview with Bao Tong, June 1998.
7. Kyodo News, 26 March 1999.
8. Edward A. Gargan, 'Zhao starts to spell out policies by advocating town-hall democracy', *New York Times/Intenational Herald Tribune*, 22 March 1998. Zhao said that conflicts between different interest groups were inevitable. 'Therefore at present and for some considerable time to come, consultations and dialogues should be held to ensure the smooth implementation of the various measures taken in reforms, to mitigate social contradictions and consolidate social stability and unity . . . In the future, draft laws involving major reforms, as well as plans for major reforms such as the price readjustment and labour and wage reform, should solicit the opinions of people from all walks of life before and after they are decided upon.'
9. Bruce Gilley, *Tiger on the Brink*, pp.84–92.
10. Steven Mufson and Robert G. Kaiser, 'Chinese leader urges US to seek "common ground"', *Washington Post*, 19 October 1997.
11. Andrew Nathan, *China's Transition*, p.64.
12. Mark O'Neill, 'Premier nurtures seeds of grain sector reform', *South China Morning Post*, 27 May 1998.
13. Personal visit in April 1999. See also Wu Ming, 'Major problems found in Three Gorges dam resettlement', a report by two pressure groups, International Rivers Network and Human Rights in China, March 1998.
14. Associated Press, 'Chinese "princes and princesses" jockey for power',

18 March 1986; 'Deng family splendour dimmed by corruption case', *Kaifang*, 3 September 1998, pp.32–4.

15. Matt Forney, 'Chinese leader's son builds an empire', *Asian Wall Street Journal*, 3 November 1999.

16. 'Who gets to study abroad', *South China Morning Post*, 3 November 1986; Louise do Rosario, 'A new Chinese class', *Far Eastern Economic Review*, 18 September 1986; and Sarah Burgess, 'Sinotrash: China's new brat pack', *New Republic*, 7 November 1988.

17. See also a second declaration issued in the same names: 'Declaration on Civil Rights and Freedom', 22 September 1998, signed by Ding Zilin, Lin Mu, Jiang Qisheng, Jiang Peikun and Wei Xiaotao.

18. He Qinglian, *Pitfalls of Modernization*, p.106; and Jasper Becker, 'Open to criticism', *South China Morning Post*, 27 November 1998.

19. 'The crisis of the Chinese economy and anti-crisis policies', *Zhanlu yu Guanli* (*Strategy and Management*), Vol.5, September 1998.

20. Sun Yong, 'Black hole', *Economic Daily*, 8 January 1999; and 'Big Chinese firms cited for corruption in audit', *Asian Wall Street Journal*, 11 January 1999.

21. Mark O'Neill, 'No price too high to maintain control of grain supply', *South China Morning Post*, 21 December 1998; Mark O'Neill, 'Setting a trap for the grain rats', *South China Morning Post*, 21 December 1998; and William Kazer, 'China move on GITIC hints at skeletons in closet', Reuters, 12 January 1999, quoting the 30 November edition of *Outlook*, an official weekly magazine.

22. World Bank, 'China: weathering the storm and learning the lessons', Country Economic Memorandum, 25 May 1999, p.43.

23. Xinhua, 'Central Disciplinary Inspection Committee issues statistics', 13 January 1999. Figures issued in 1991 showed that from 1982 to 1990, the Central Disciplinary Inspection Committee looked at 1.54 million cases and punished 0.3 per cent of all Party members each year, or 150,000. In 1989 and 1990, the committee placed on file 400,000 cases: Xinhua, 'Central Disciplinary Inspection Committee meets', 4 June 1991.

24. Jasper Becker, 'The American Way', *South China Morning Post*, 1 January 1997. The book was published in China in 1996.

Epilogue: Examining the Oracle Bones

1. Personal visit to Shaanxi, March 2000. Jasper Becker, 'The Party and the peasant uprising', *South China Morning Post*, 5 April 2000.

2. Jasper Becker, 'Home truths about one-child policy', *South China Morning Post*, 31 March 1999; Jasper Becker, 'A new balance born of moderation', *South China Morning Post*, 31 March 1999; Jasper Becker, 'Mainland barriers to family planning', *Sunday Morning Post*, 7 November 1999; Jasper Becker, 'A failure to control the population', *South China Morning Post*, 19 April 1999.

Bibliography

Banister, Judith, *China's Changing Population*, Stanford University Press, Berkeley, 1987

Bass, Catriona, *Education in Tibet: Policy and Practice since 1950*, Tibet Information Network and Zed Books, London, 1998

Bernstein, Richard, and Munro, Ross H., *The Coming Conflict with China*, Alfred A. Knopf, New York, 1997

Black, Georges, and Munro, Robin, *Black Hands of Beijing: Lives of Defiance in China's Democracy Movement*, John Wiley, New York, 1993

Bland, J.O.P., *China: The Pity of It*, William Heinemann, London, 1932

Bo Yang, *The Ugly Chinaman and the Crisis of Chinese Culture*, trans. and ed. Don J. Cohn and Jing Qing, Allen & Unwin, Sydney, 1992 (first published in Chinese in 1983)

Brown, Lester R., *Who Will Feed China? Wake Up Call for a Small Planet. Worldwatch Environmental Alert*, W. W. Norton, New York, 1995

Cabestan, Jean-Pierre, *L'Adminstration Chinoise après Mao: Les Réformes de l'ère Deng Xiaoping et leurs limites*, Editions du Centre National de la Recherche Scientifique, Paris, 1992

Chow Tse-Tung, *The May 4th Movement: Intellectual Revolution in Modern China*, Harvard University Press, Cambridge, Mass., 1960

Criminal Reform in China, Information Office of the State Council, Beijing, 1992

Dai Huang, *Nine Deaths, One Life: My Progress as a Rightist (Jiu Si Yi Sheng Wode 'Youpai' Licheng)*, Zhongyang Bianyi Chubanshe, Beijing, 1998

——*Hu Yaobang and the Righting of Wrong Cases (Hu Yaobang yu Pingfan Yuanjia Zuoan)*, Xinhua Chubanshe, Beijing, 1998

Dai Qing, *Wang Shiwei and 'Wild Lilies': Rectification and Purges in the Chinese Communist Party 1942–1944*, M.E. Sharpe, New York, 1994

Deng Xiaoping, *Fundamental Issues in Present-day China*, Foreign Languages Press, Beijing, 1989

——*Selected Works*, Vol.III, Renmin Chubanshe, Beijing, 1993

Denis, Fred Simon, and Goldman, Merle (eds.), *Science and Technology in Post-Mao China*, Harvard University Press, Cambridge, Mass., 1989

Dikotter, Frank, *The Discourse of Race in Modern China*, Hong Kong University Press, Hong Kong, 1992

——*Imperfect Conceptions: Medical Knowledge, Birth Defects and Eugenics in China*, Hurst & Co., London, 1998

Dutton, Michael, *The Police, Public Order and the State*, Macmillan Press, London, 1988

Fei Xiaotong *et al.*, *Small Towns in China: Functions, Problems and Prospects*, New World Press, Beijing, 1986

Franz, Uli, *Deng Xiaoping*, trans. Tom Artin, Harcourt Brace Jovanovich, Boston, 1988

Fu Zhengyuan, *Autocratic Traditions and Chinese Politics*, Cambridge University Press, Cambridge, 1993

——*China's Legalists: The Earliest Totalitarians and Their Art of Ruling*, M.E. Sharpe, New York, 1996

Galbraith, John Kenneth, *A China Passage*, Paragon House, New York, 1973

Gilley, Bruce, *Tiger on the Brink: Jiang Zemin and China's New Elite*, University of California Press, Berkeley, 1998

He Bochuan, *China on the Edge: The Crisis of Ecology and Development*, China Books and Periodicals, 1991

He Qinglian, *Pitfalls of Modernization (Xiandai Huade Xianjiang)*, Jinri Zhongguo Chubanshe, Beijing, 1998

Hollingworth, Claire, *Mao and the Men Against Him*, Jonathan Cape, London, 1983

Hu Sheng, *A Concise History of the Communist Party of China*, Foreign Languages Press, Beijing, 1994

Human Rightswatch, 'Anthems of Defeat: Crackdown in Hunan Province 1989–92', New York, 1992

Jenner, W.J.F., *The Tyranny of History: The Roots of China's Crisis*, Allen Lane, London, 1992

Kemenade, Willem van, *China, Hong Kong, Taiwan, Inc: The Dynamics of a New Empire*, Little, Brown, London, 1998

Ladany, Laszlo, *Law and Legality in China: The Testament of a China-watcher*, Hurst, London, 1992

——*The Communist Party of China and Marxism, 1921–1985: A Self-Portrait*, Hurst, London, 1988

Lam, Willy Wo-lap, *China after Deng Xiaoping: The Power Struggle in Beijing since Tiananmen*, PA Professional Consultants Ltd. HK, Hong Kong, 1995

——*The Era of Zhao Ziyang: Power Struggle in China, 1986–88*, A.B. Books & Stationery (International) Ltd, Hong Kong, 1989

——*Towards a Chinese-style Socialism: An Assessment of Deng Xiaoping's Reforms*, Oceanic Cultural Service, Hong Kong, 1987

Lao Gui, *Blood Red Sunset: A Memoir of the Chinese Cultural Revolution*, trans. Howard Goldblatt, Penguin Books, Harmondsworth, 1996

Lescot, Patrick, *L'Empire rouge Moscou–Pekin, 1919–1989*, Editions Belfond, Paris, 1999

Li Conghua, *China: The Consumer Revolution*, Deloitte & Touche Consulting Group, published by John Wiley, Singapore, 1998

Li Zhisui, *The Private Life of Chairman Mao: The Inside Story of the Man Who Made Modern China*, Chatto & Windus, London, 1994

Liao, W.K., *Complete Works of Han Feizi*, Probstain Oriental Series, vols. 25 and 26, Probsthain, London, 1939

Link, Perry, *Evening Chats in Beijing: Probing China's Predicament*, W.W. Norton, New York, 1992

Ma Licheng and Ling Zhijun, *Crossed Swords* (*Jiao Feng*), Jinri Zhongguo Chubanshe, Beijing, 1998

Mao Zedong, *Selected Works of Mao Tse-tung*, Foreign Languages Press, Beijing, 1965

Marx, Karl, and Engels, Friederich, *The Communist Manifesto*, 1848

Nathan, Andrew, *China's Transition*, Columbia University Press, New York, 1993

Overholt, William H., *China: The Next Economic Superpower*, Weidenfeld & Nicolson, London, 1993

Paludan, Ann, *Chronicle of the Chinese Emperors: The Reign-by-reign Record of the Rulers of Imperial China*, Thames & Hudson, London, 1998

Phathanthai, Sirin, with Peck, James, *The Dragon's Pearl: Growing up among China's Élite*, Simon & Schuster, New York, 1994

Qian Ning, *Studying in the United States: The Story of an Era*, Jiangsu Literary and Art Publishing House, Beijing, and Tiendi Publishing Co. Ltd, Hong Kong, 1996

Ruan Ming, *Deng Xiaoping: Chronicle of an Empire*, Westview Press, Boulder, 1992

Schwartz, Benjamin, *The World of Thought in Ancient China*, Harvard University Press, Cambridge, Mass., 1985

Seymour, James D., and Anderson, Richard, *New Ghosts, Old Ghosts*, M.E. Sharpe, New York, 1998

The Songs of the South: An Anthology of Ancient Chinese Poems by Qu Yuan and Other Poets, trans. David Hawkes, Penguin Books, Harmondsworth, 1995

Spence, Jonathan D., *Mao Zedong*, Penguin Books, Harmondsworth, 1999

——*The Search for Modern China*, Hutchinson, London, 1990

Statistical Yearbook of China, 1996, 1997, State Statistical Bureau, Beijing

Sun Yat-sen, *The Three Principles of the People (San Min Chu I)*, trans. Frank W. Price, Commercial Press, Shanghai, 1927

Tan Sitong, *Collected Writings (Tan Sitong Qianji)*, Zhonghua Shuju, Beijing, 1981

Tomisaka, S. *Heirs of the Dragon: China's New Entrepreneurs in the Aftermath of Tiananmen Square*, Cadence Books, 1996

Wang, James C.F., *Contemporary Chinese Politics: An Introduction*, Prentice-Hall, New Jersey, 1995

Wood, Frances, *No Dogs and Not Many Chinese: Treaty Port Life in China, 1843–1943*, John Murray, London, 1998

Wu, Harry, *Laogai: The Chinese Gulag*, Westview Press, Boulder, 1992

——*Bitter Winds: A Memoir of My Years in China's Gulag*, John Wiley, New York, 1994

Wu Jie, *On Deng Xiaoping's Thought*, Foreign Languages Press, Beijing, 1996

Yan Jiaqi and Gao Gao, *Turbulent Decade: A History of the Cultural Revolution*, University of Hawaii Press, 1996 (first published in Chinese in 1986)

Zhang Xianliang, *Grass Soup*, trans. Martha Avery, Secker & Warburg, London, 1994

——*My Bodhi Tree*, trans. Martha Avery, Secker & Warburg, London, 1996

Zheng Yi, *Scarlet Memorial: Tales of Cannibalism in Modern China*, Westview Press, Boulder, 1996

Zhou, Kate Xiao, *How the Farmers Changed China*, Westview Press, Boulder, 1996

Index

Index

China Democratic Party, 265
China Economic Times, 60
China Education Daily Survey, 170
China Genetics Institute, 239
China Human Rights League, 260
China International Trust and
Investment Corporation (CITIC),
137, 270
China Kang Hua Development
Corporation, 168
China Merchants' Steam Navigation
Company, 116–17
China on the Edge (He Bochuan), 97–8,
106
China Reform Daily, 129
China Youth Daily, 84
Chinese Academy of Social Sciences,
222
Chinese characters: education and,
206–7; laser printing, 178, 179; and
literacy, 216; retention, 208–9, 216;
universality, 206–7, 208
Chinese Committee for Racial
Hygiene, 234
Chinese Communist Party (CCP),
14–15, 66; and altruism, 303–4; and
assimilation, 28–30, 33; and
collective enterprises, 81–4;
concentration camps, 322; and
consumerism, 184–5; and criticism,
251–3; and democracy, 253–4, 305,
306, 376–7; de-urbanization, 93;
doctrine, 344–5; and education,
201–5, 207, 208, 209, 210–15, 302;
entrepreneurs, membership, 165–6,
167; expulsions, 351; and family,
181; foundation, 92, 375; and gift-
giving, 167–8; health campaigns,
234; and human rights, 344;
immunity from prosecution, 362;
imperial tradition, 91, 346, 347;
infallible, 317; information control,
198–9, 209; and injustice, 314–18;

and intellectuals, 245, 246–7, 265–7;
internal conflict, 16, 17, 260; KMT,
split with (1927), 346; land reform,
322; and law, 320, 323–4, 327, 374;
leadership, 348–51; and legal system,
338; liberalization, 256, 260, 307–8,
359; literacy, 302; and livestock, 160;
membership, 8, 297, 298, 301;
mistakes, 251; name, 157; and
nepotism, 359–60; and non-
governmental organizations, 299;
organization, 298–9; and overseas
Chinese, 346; PLA power, 307; PLA
role, 297; and planning, 139, 143;
and police, 338; post-Deng, 307–8;
post-Mao, 301–2; and poverty, 24–6;
and press, 256; private enterprise
denounced, 156–8, 169–70, 177–8,
359–60; private enterprise
encouraged, 158–9, 160–1, 163–4,
165, 171, 174, 176, 359–60; purges,
322, 323–6; reform, inevitable, 266;
relaxation of supervision, 307–8;
reorganization (1982), 305;
resignations, 351; and rich peasants,
65–72; rural, 311; secrecy, 2, 186–7;
secret police, 322, 323, 324; social
engineering, 4, 90; and SOEs, 139,
143, 147, 148–9, 151–2, 154; status,
338; successful propaganda, 253;
and Taiwan, 375–7; and tax cases,
366–7; and Westernization, 260–1;
witch hunt (1989), 306–7; and
witch-doctors, 231–3
Chinese language, 10
Chinese medicine, 232
Chinese people, 10, 233–4, 240
Chinese People's Political Consultative
Committee, 299
Chongqing (Chungking) (Sichuan), 14,
103, 115, 162–3, 176, 195, 207, 219
Chongqing Cygnet Diet Culture
Company, 162–3

Manchuria, 28; Chinese expelled from, 11; control, 118; defence industry, 271; Japanese occupy, 14; republic, 345; water supply, 369
Mandarin Chinese, 207
manufacturing: and agriculture, 91; domestic, 194; military, 269–70, 279–81, 283–4, 286–7; *see also* multinationals
Manzhouli (Nei Mongol Zizhugu), 174
Mao Dun, 199
Mao Fang, 105
Mao Peiyan, 104–5, 220
Mao Zedong, 390–1; agriculture, collectivization, 51–2; Anti-Rightist campaign, 248, 250, 258; anti-urban bias, 93, 95; birthplace, 42, 44–6; and capitalism, 158; and class enemies, 162; and communes, 299–300; criticism, 251–3, 257; and defence, 271–3; and democracy, 254; demolishes Beijing's ramparts, 87; destroys government apparatus, 300; education policy, 207–10, 212; and eugenics, 235–6; and fairy stories, 199–200; and family, 352; and famine, 52–3; and First Emperor, 258–9; as First Generation, 344; founds People's Republic, 15–16; and healthcare, 225–7; and Hong Kong, 118–19; Hundred Flowers campaign, 258; and imperial system, 50, 91; instructions (1942), 252; and intellectuals, 206, 246, 300; as leader, 17; and Liu Shaoqi, 48, 49; mistakes, 9, 251; and nepotism, 356–7; and Party structures, 299; and peasantry, 367; and penal system, 325–6; and 'people's war', 274, 277; personality cult, 353; physical training, 234; and PLA, 275; political philosophy, 47; and population control, 235–6;

private life, 351–2; and private property, 156, 157–8; privileges, 349; purges, 300–1, 323–6; satirized, 262; social engineering, 4; and Soviet Union, 93, 271, 323; and Third Front, 271–2; and traditional culture, 17, 90; wages, 309; in Yan'an, 15; *see also* individual campaigns
Mao Zedong Thought, 344, 345
market economy, 304; agriculture in, 58; benefits, 367–8; and penal system, 336–7; socialist, 293; markets, free, 54
Mars Corporation, 190
martial law (1989), 306–7
Martin, Ron, 285–6
Marx, Karl, 157
Marxism, 252, 261, 303, 321–2
Marxism-Leninism, 9, 48
Maternal and Infant Health Law (1995), 239–40
May Fourth movement (1919), 13, 206, 213, 220, 245–6, 260, 261, 262
May 7th Cadre Schools, 94, 300, 349
Médecins sans Frontières (MSF), 225, 226, 227, 228, 229, 230, 244
media: PLA run, 275
medical treatment: *see* healthcare
Meiji Restoration (1868), 117
mental illness: as stigma, 240
mental retardation, 22, 34, 238, 239
Meo people, 26
Mercedes-Benz, 280
Merli, Giovanni, 235
Metro company, 192
Mianyang (Sichuan), 285
Miao people, 10, 26, 225; alphabet, 216; literacy, 30–2
Middle Kingdom, 5
migrant workers: control of, 101–3; unemployment and, 104

Shougang steel company, 149–51; and
  pollution, 151; share trading, 171
Shuangyashan (Heilongjiang), 147
Shunde prefecture, 81
Shunyi, Guizhou, 45
Sichuan province, 6, 23, 27, 63,
  222–3
Simao (Yunnan), 115
sinification policy, 10
Sino-British Treaty (1943), 118
skills: lost, 86
Small, Frank & Associates, 191
small towns strategy, 95–101, 106
Smith, Adam, 61, 63
smoking, 242
smuggling: from Hong Kong, 73, 78
  as industry, 129–31
snail fever, 234, 235
social security: lack, 237
Sofres Media Establishment, 189
soft drinks industry, 185–6, 193
Sogo company, 192
soil erosion, 34, 36–7, 39–40
Somalia: aid to, 274
Song Jian, 370
Song Ping, 60
Soros, George, 256
*Sources and Methods of Obtaining National
  Defence Science and Technology
  Intelligence,* 289
South China Morning Post, 4, 126, 151
South China Sea: annexed, 346
South Korea, 79, 106, 188
South Korean companies: and
  working conditions, 124–5
southern China, 26, 170
south-west China, 23, 37–8
South-West University of Politics and
  Law, 223
Soviet Union: aid, 367; and CCP, 14,
  15, 16; criminal code, 322;
  education, 349, 362; food shortage,
  94; intellectuals and, 246; internal

disputes, 322–3; nuclear threat, 93,
  268, 270–1, 279; and Outer
  Mongolia, 28; relations with, 273–4;
  secret police, 296–7; technology
  transfer (1950s), 268–9; thaw with
  USA, 271
soviets, 322
space industry, 280, 290
Spark Plan, 285
Special Economic Zones (SEZs), 70,
  109–13; bubble economy, 126–7;
  corrupt joint ventures, 121;
  corruption, 132; and democracy,
  113; housing oversupply, 196;
  investment in, 120; labour costs,
  121; and mind emancipation, 112;
  prosperity, 120; subsidization, 126;
  Taiwanese investors, 122–3, 124; tax
  incentives, 120; women workers,
  123, 124, 125; working conditions,
  123–6
spies, 289
Sports Commission, 310
Spring Festival, 43, 342
Spring Love Operation, 215
Stalin, Joseph, 15, 248; factories,
  relocation, 271; intellectuals and,
  246; and Trotsky, 322–3
state: domestic debt, 155; durability,
  4–5, 345–6; expansion, 346–7;
  revenue, 154; as sole moral arbiter,
  263–5; unification, 347
State Assets Law, 153
State Development Planning
  Commission, 98, 107–8
State Land Administration Bureau,
  106, 107
state ownership: loss, 360–2;
  privatization, 148, 156, 157;
  separation from management, 148
State Planning Commission, 309,
  310
State Security Ministry, 338, 339